The Life of William Robertson

This book is dedicated to Paige, John, and Alec,
who should always be first.

The Life of William Robertson

Minister, Historian, and Principal

Jeffrey R. Smitten

EDINBURGH
University Press

Edinburgh University Press is one of the leading university presses in the UK. We publish academic books and journals in our selected subject areas across the humanities and social sciences, combining cutting-edge scholarship with high editorial and production values to produce academic works of lasting importance. For more information visit our website: edinburghuniversitypress.com

© Jeffrey R. Smitten, 2017, 2018

Edinburgh University Press Ltd
The Tun – Holyrood Road
12(2f) Jackson's Entry
Edinburgh EH8 8PJ

First published in hardback by Edinburgh University Press 2017

Typeset in 11/13 Ehrhardt by
Servis Filmsetting Ltd, Stockport, Cheshire
and printed and bound in Great Britain by
CPI Group (UK) Ltd, Croydon CR0 4YY

A CIP record for this book is available from the British Library

ISBN 978 0 7486 4610 4 (hardback)
ISBN 978 1 7444 3228 3 (paperback)
ISBN 978 0 7486 4611 1 (webready PDF)
ISBN 978 1 4744 0485 3 (epub)

Contents

Preface

There has been no book-length biography of William Robertson since Dugald Stewart published his *Account of the Life and Writings of William Robertson* in 1801. First delivered as a paper presented to the Royal Academy of Edinburgh in 1795, Stewart's *Account* has been and remains a valuable resource. He prints, either whole or in part, about one-fourth of Robertson's known correspondence, and he offers a detailed narrative of Robertson's mature career. Robertson's deathbed request that Stewart write the book was clearly a good choice. But much more material is available today than was at Stewart's disposal. Robertson's known correspondence has increased from Stewart's citation of approximately 200 to almost 800 items, with more certainly to be found. We have excellent accounts of how he engaged Enlightenment ideas in history, politics, and religion. This book draws on the work of some of these recent scholars, who have done much to define the temper of Enlightenment in Scotland: Thomas Ahnert, David Allan, Stewart J. Brown, Alexander Du Toit, Colin Kidd, Karen O'Brien, Nicholas Phillipson, J. G. A. Pocock, Richard B. Sher, Jonathan Yeager, and William J. Zachs, among others.

This biography attempts to make three contributions to our knowledge of Robertson's life and writings. It provides fuller, more nuanced context to his motives and to events in his life than is currently available. A second contribution is a fuller sense of the personality and character of Robertson. Although Alexander Carlyle left a fascinating, first-hand account of his knowledge of Robertson, Carlyle often had his own axe to grind. The narrative here draws as much as possible from Robertson's correspondence in order to see events from his point of view and in his voice. Yet Robertson was complex, difficult to know, a great talker who was reticent about his inner life. At the opposite extreme from someone like James Boswell, Robertson left no journals, diaries, memoirs, or personal notebooks (except financial accounts). Even his youthful commonplace books have been lost. But with the large increase in his known correspondence, there is at least a fuller picture of him than we have had, if not an intimate one. Finally, this book pays greater attention than do previous accounts to Robertson's religious outlook. Nicholas Phillipson has rightly said that

Robertson's mind is a closed book, and his statement is especially true of his religious views and intentions. I have foregrounded the religious implications in his work because Robertson's biography makes that demand: he was born into a ministerial family; he was educated in divinity; he spent fifteen years as minister of the parish of Gladsmuir; and, although not a devoted parish minister, during his busy years as principal and historian, he remained sincerely committed to the Church of Scotland. His purpose throughout his life was to give it strength, independence, and relevance in a civil society, making him part of a movement spread across Europe that embraced Enlightenment ideas, not to attack religion, but to reinvigorate and redefine it.[1] There is currently growing interest in what is termed the "Christian Enlightenment," and it is a helpful framework in which to understand Robertson's intentions. Although the documentation of Robertson's religious beliefs remains difficult, this book tries to offer a more detailed picture than we have had of religion in his career.

The writing of any scholarly work incurs debts to friends and colleagues, and this biography is no exception. My greatest debts are to Richard B. Sher and William J. Zachs, for whose generosity over many years, whose knowledge of the Scottish Enlightenment, and whose assistance in more ways than I can count, I am deeply grateful. Many others also deserve my sincere thanks for help along the way: John Allen, Kate Anderson, Iain Gordon Brown, Stewart J. Brown, Jorge Cañizares-Esguerra, Mark Damen, Alexander Du Toit, Roger Emerson, Joshua Ehrlich, John Evans, the late Jane Bush Fagg, László Kontler, the late Leah Leneman, Stephen Massil, Dorothy Medlin, James Moore, Alexander Murdoch, David Raynor, Marion Richardson, Robert Sparling, M. A. Stewart, Marie-Paule Stone, Jeannie Thomas, the late Donald J. Withrington, David Womersley, and Jonathan Yeager. My wife, Paige, not only endured the project but kindly helped me proofread the manuscript.

I have drawn upon the generous assistance of many libraries, collections, and institutions, and I gratefully acknowledge their permission to make scholarly quotations from their materials: Bayerische Staatsbibliothek; Bedfordshire Record Office; Biblioteka Jagiellonska, Krakow; Bibliothèque de Lille; Bibliothèque publique et universitaire, Genève; Blairadam Muniments; Bodleian Library, Oxford University; British Library; Brown University Library; Clements Library, University of Michigan; Duke University Library; Dunedin Public Library; Edinburgh City Archives; Edinburgh University Library; Folger Library; Houghton Library, Harvard University; Huntington Library; Massachusetts Historical Library; Midlothian District Council; Mitchell Library, University of Glasgow; National Archives of Scotland; National

Library of Scotland; National Library of Wales; New College Library, University of Edinburgh; Pierpont Morgan Library; Princeton University Library; Public Record Office, London; Sheffield City Libraries; State Historical Museum (Moscow); University College London Library; Yale University Library. I would also like to thank Interlibrary Services at Utah State University for their unfailing attention.

I would like to acknowledge the generous support of research related to this project from the National Endowment for the Humanities; the Office of the Provost at Texas Tech University; and the Department of English, the Office of the Dean of Humanities and Social Sciences, and the Office of the Provost at Utah State University. At Edinburgh University Press, I would like to thank Carol Macdonald, Ersev Ersoy, and Peter Williams for their patience, advice, and efficiency.

Some portions of my earlier essay "William Robertson: The Minister as Historian," in *A Companion to Enlightenment Historiography*, ed. Sophie Bourgault and Robert Sparling (Leiden: Brill, 2013), pp. 101–31 appear in reworked form in Chapters 4, 5, 6, and 7. Likewise, segments of "The Scottish Enlightenment in Action: The Correspondence of William Robertson and J.-B.-A. Suard," in *British–French Exchanges in the Eighteenth Century*, ed. Kathleen Hardesty Doig and Dorothy Medlin (Cambridge: Cambridge Scholars Press, 2007), pp. 83–98 are reworked for Chapters 5 and 6. I am grateful for permission to reuse this material. I have also reused some of the editorial commentary in my edition of Robertson's *Miscellaneous Works*.

Note

1. Helena Rosenblatt, "The Christian Enlightenment," in *Cambridge History of Christianity, Volume VII: Enlightenment, Reawakening and Revolution 1660–1815*, ed. Stewart J. Brown and Timothy Tackett (Cambridge: Cambridge University Press, 2006), p. 283. See also Jonathan Sheehan, "Enlightenment, Religion, and the Enigma of Secularization: A Review Essay," *American Historical Review*, 108 (2003), pp. 1061–80.

Abbreviations

BL	British Library
ECA	Edinburgh City Archives
EUL	Edinburgh University Library
NAS	National Archives of Scotland
NLS	National Library of Scotland
Works of Robertson	*The Works of William Robertson*, gen. ed. Richard B. Sher, 12 vols. London: Routledge/Thoemmes Press, 1996.*

* This edition includes *Miscellaneous Works and Commentaries*, ed. Jeffrey Smitten, cited as *Miscellaneous Works*. All citations to Robertson's works are to the numbered volumes within the specific work, not to the volume number in the edition as a whole.

Bibliographical Note

For a printed bibliography of secondary material on Robertson, see Jeffrey Smitten, "Bibliography of Writings about William Robertson, 1755–1996," in *William Robertson and the Expansion of Empire*, ed. Stewart J. Brown. Cambridge: Cambridge University Press, 1997, pp. 231–67. An updated version of the bibliography may be found at http://tinyurl.com/RobertsonBib.

CHAPTER 1

Early Years, 1721–1735

On Sunday, 14 September 1721, the Reverend William Robertson, minister of Borthwick, administered the sacrament of baptism, as he had done many Sundays before. The small parish church, an old "popish building in the form of a cross"[1] built in a plain Norman style dating to the middle of the twelfth century, was dilapidated, as were many of the churches of early eighteenth-century Scotland.[2] Yet despite the modest setting, this was an important occasion for the minister, for the child to be baptized was his first child, a son born six days earlier.[3] He was also to be named William, and he would become one of the best known figures in eighteenth-century Scotland. With the minister as witnesses of the baptism were four of the most prominent heritors of the church from around the parish of Borthwick: from the south John Mitchelson of Middleton; the west James Dalrymple of Harviston; the north Walter Welsh; and, most prominent of all, Robert Dundas, Lord Arniston, the parish patron whose estate lay in the far western corner of the parish.[4] Lord Arniston's attendance was a particular honor because at this time his health was failing, and he was suffering severely from gout.[5]

The minister was not new to the Borthwick community, having been ordained to the parish in 1714.[6] Born in 1686 in Fife, where his father, William Robertson of Gladney, was a factor on the Wemyss estate, he had been granted a license to preach by the presbytery of Kirkcaldy in 1711. First ordained to Founder's Hall in London (later to be called the Scots Church at London Wall), he served as an assistant to the prominent minister Robert Fleming.[7] A close ally of William Carstares, Fleming was learned, tolerant, and versed in anti-Calvinist Arminian thinking. He was also coping with depression during 1712–14, requiring him to make a trip to the Netherlands to aid his recovery. Thus, although it is uncertain just how much contact Robertson actually had with him, the experience seemed to have left a mark on his thinking, giving a tolerant cast to his ministerial teachings. Born in 1686, the Reverend Robertson was one of those clergymen who bridged "the formidable gap between the rigid Calvinism of the post-Revolution period and the polite Presbyterianism of the Moderate era."[8] His political outlook was apparent in his Borthwick appointment because Lord Arniston, a sound Whig,[9] named him as the most proper candidate, though he shied away from making the presentation himself and asked the presbytery to issue the call to Robertson, which it did with no dissenting votes.[10] No record remains of Robertson's preaching in Borthwick (his Edinburgh sermons will be discussed later), though Robert Wodrow made comments around 1730 that suggest his wariness of Robertson's apparently tolerant leanings. In Wodrow's mind, Robertson was associated with the suspicious "young men, who bear the name of 'Bright Youths,' and 'Oratoriall Preachers,'"[11] and he comments briefly on one of Robertson's sermons, "The Unity of Spirit in the Bond of Peace," which dealt with the prosecution of John Simson, a professor at Glasgow University. The presbytery of Glasgow had accused Simson of Arianism, and the prosecution went to the church's General Assembly. A compromise was reached in 1729–30 to suspend but not depose Simson, and Robertson apparently had entered the battle as a peacemaker. According to Wodrow, Robertson "had some things, but pretty cautious, upon doctrine, and pointing a little favourably to Mr. Simson's prosecution; that retractions should not be uncharitably judged of, and the like; and pressed peace very much." One can see shadowed forth here the same cautious attitude toward church doctrinal disputes that his son would develop as part of his stance as leader of the Moderate Party.

But the minister did not come from a ministerial family, and he appears to be the only son who followed a clerical path. His father, William Robertson of Gladney, was very much of this world: a dynamic, canny entrepreneur, one historian calling him "a remarkable man, and a pioneer in the industry of post-union Scotland."[12] Born in 1656, the second son of William Robertson of Muirtown, Gladney was working as a bailie or principal factor on the estate of Margaret, Countess of Wemyss, in 1685. At the same time, he purchased a small estate at Gladney near Cupar in Fife, perhaps as part of his marriage settlement with the daughter of a doctor, Margaret Mitchell.[13] His community standing was significant because he was named justice of the peace for Fife in 1690 and, by 1696 he was prosperous enough to invest £1,000 in the disastrous Darien venture. Undaunted by his losses, probably because he still held several tacks in salt and coal mining, Gladney was in a financial position to push ahead to his most famous scheme, the joint creation in 1714 of a successful brick and tile works in Linktown with the architect William Adam.[14] The connection of the Adam and Robertson families was formalized in 1716 with the marriage of William Adam to Gladney's daughter Mary, a connection that united two families crucial to the cultural establishment of Scotland in the latter half of the eighteenth century. Between 1717 and 1728 William Adam and Mary Robertson lived in Gladney House, Abbotshall, which Adam built, and Gladney, at least in part, helped to underwrite.[15] Upon Gladney's death in 1728, his share of the holdings passed to the Reverend Robertson's older brother David, and the minister's family remained in circumstances "far from affluent."[16]

In addition to Gladney's entrepreneurial energy, the Robertsons could also claim ties to Highland nobility. Beyond Robertson of Gladney the family genealogy reaches back through five generations to John, who was the son of Alexander, 5th Baron of Strowan or Struan.[17] The family ultimately even had royal connections because John's wife, Margaret Crichton, was the granddaughter of Margaret Stewart, the daughter of James II. Ironically, given the Whig stance of the future historian's side of the family, Jacobite sentiments could be found,[18] most famously, perhaps, in Alexander Robertson's participation in the three Jacobite risings and his publication of *The History and Martial Atchievements, of the Robertson's of Strowan*, which included his *Poems*. His "Epitaph on Himself" gives an indication of the bitter spirit the future historian of Mary, Queen of Scots, would have to confront:

> Tenacious of his Faith, to aid the Cause
> Of Heav'n's Anointed, and his Country's Laws,
> Thrice he engage'd; and thrice, with *Stuart's* Race,
> He fail'd; but ne'er comply'd with foul Disgrace,
> Tho' some, despising Heav'n's most sacred Tyes,
> Perjur'd for Int'rest, acquiesc'd to Lies,
> *Clan-Donnoch's* Chief maintain'd his Reputation,
> And scorn'd to flourish in an Usurpation.[19]

During the first half of the sixteenth century, Alexander's son John became overseer of the Moray estate of Robert Reid, abbot of Kinloss, and for several generations the Robertsons were based in Muirton, Invernesshire, until Gladney moved south to Fife to pursue wealth through commerce. In another ironic twist after the historian's death, his youngest son David married Margaretta Macdonald and retired to Kinlochmoidart and its association with Prince Charles.

The historian's mother, Eleanor Pitcairn, has not been so well traced. Lord Brougham contrasts Eleanor with the "sweetness" of her husband's "placid temper": she was "a woman of great ability and force of character; but like many of that cast, women especially, she was more stern, even severe, than amiable."[20] Her firmness, Brougham speculates, contributed to the historian's "inclination towards the Stoical system of morals" as well as a "certain degree of Stoical feeling."[21] She was from an apparently comfortable family, the daughter of David Pitcairn, a Writer to the Signet in Edinburgh who occupied Dreghorn Castle, Colinton, until his death in 1709.[22] The family sold the house in 1717, and Eleanor married her husband three years later, perhaps under some economic duress. Her brother Thomas entered the ministry about the time of her marriage and would eventually become minister of St. Cuthbert's in Edinburgh. A friend of George Whitefield, Thomas seemed to have evangelical leanings, but he also courageously prayed for the king in the face of the Jacobites' capture of the city following the battle of Prestonpans.[23] Eleanor's mother was Mary Anderson, whose brother was James Anderson, a notable Scottish historian who has been shown to have influenced Robertson's thinking in his *History of Scotland* regarding Queen Mary as well as on issues of Scottish independency.[24] Anderson may have been known to Robertson's father, too, given the latter's interest in Scottish history. Finally, and perhaps most importantly, Eleanor's sister Mary would, in 1707, marry James Nisbet, who would eventually become minister of the Old Kirk in Edinburgh, and their daughter Mary would become the historian's wife in 1751.[25]

We know little about the childhood milieu into which young Robertson was born in 1721, and what little we have requires context to be understood. Alexander Carlyle reports that the young Robertson "was bred in all the Strictness of an Ecclesiastical Family at That Period, having been Denied the Amusements of the Theatre and other Publick places, which favor'd his Recluse and Studious Bent."[26] Brougham, although he never knew the historian's father, likewise claims that he was outwardly a severe, traditional Presbyterian, holding "opinions more strict on some subjects than the relaxed rigour of the Presbyterian rule prescribed half a century later" but neither sour nor stern when *en famille*, "how severe and unbending soever may have been his moral feelings."[27] John Erskine, who knew the historian at Edinburgh University and could have known the elder Robertson, noted that his "courteous and engaging manner, and his frankness and ease in conversation, rendered him highly agreeable and useful, both to his own family, and to the young people who visited them."[28] It may be possible to flesh out these bare statements by examining the records of the Reverend Robertson's ministry to see what tone might have been set there and, by implication, in the household atmosphere. We can also discover in these records suggestions of the model of ministerial practice that the historian would inherit from his father since he "was early destined for the church."[29]

Looking at the remaining kirk session records of Borthwick parish, we can see that there is some truth to Carlyle's claim of strictness. Particularly important in this regard are the discipline cases recorded in the parish minutes. During the seventeenth and early eighteenth centuries, the parish kirk session functioned essentially as the local judicatory body. Calvin saw church discipline as "the ligaments by which the members of the body are joined together and kept each in its proper place."[30] It was essential to keep the members in their proper place because the membership was the body of the elect, and no congregation could remain such a body unless it maintained careful group discipline. As Rosalind Mitchison and Leah Leneman explain:

> The system of regular discipline enforced by the church courts in Scotland in the early modern period was therefore an essential part of the affirmation by the community of its membership in the elect. If they did not enforce Christian discipline, their very salvation was in doubt.[31]

It was the weight of this responsibility that gave rise to some of the excessive and primitive punishments infamous from earlier centuries. By the first half of the eighteenth century, however, sexual offense cases along with Sabbath violations were almost the only offenses still being recorded, and church discipline as a whole showed major signs of relaxation by the 1780s.[32] We can therefore expect that ministers, such as the Reverend Robertson, would still endorse the rationale behind church discipline in the early decades of the century.

The records of Robertson senior's ministry in Borthwick and in Edinburgh are incomplete. The Borthwick kirk session records stop in 1714 with the death of the previous incumbent, Dr. Henry Traill, and do not resume until 1728, then running to 5 December 1731 where the manuscript appears torn away and does not resume again until 1769. Despite the mere fragments that we have, we may be able to form an impression of the elder Robertson's work and attitudes. First, the great majority of discipline cases in the records we have are sexual offenses, but others include a "dead child found in the parish near Middletoun," a case of slander, and one involving a "scandalous paper."[33] The parish did not seem interested in pursuing these non-sexual offenses very rigorously. Alexander Wood promised to read no more scandalous papers after church, and the session acknowledged that slander is difficult to establish and that in future accusers must make the case. The investigation of the dead child had to be delayed "till Providence should see meet to bring it to further light." The sexual offense cases were more invasive: the offenses are investigated and guilt established, and punishments retain something of an earlier rigor. For example, in August and September of 1731 Agnes Borrowmans was reported by kirk elder Robert Wilson to be pregnant. She appears before the session and denies the fact, but women "trying her breasts[,] milk was found in them upon which she declared that she was with Child & that to one James Bailley Weaver in Esperstoun."[34] On 15 August the two are cited to appear before the session. Bailly is required to appear before the session on the 22nd and is rebuked, and on the 29th he appeared before the congregation and was rebuked and absolved. On 10 and 17 October Borrowmans undergoes the same punishment. Although the punishments here do not have the severity of the form described in standard handbooks, such as Walter Steuart of Pardovan's *Collections and Observations*,[35] including public appearances in sackcloth, they still retain rigor and have not yet reached the midcentury point when G. D. Henderson describes them as "rare."[36]

The Reverend Robertson's administration of the oath of purgation, a solemn swearing in the name of God of one's innocence of a charge, is also strictly but carefully done. The Dalkeith presbytery minutes contain a complex case of fornication illustrating the care and persistence of the Borthwick minister who managed the investigation. The case of Andrew Dickson and Janet Douglas occupied the Borthwick session and the Haddington presbytery at least from 2 July 1717 to 2 September 1718. In addition, because the charge originated in Inveresk, the case also drew in the Inveresk session and the Musselburgh presbytery as well. Douglas had accused Dickson of fathering her child, which he strongly denied. After appearing together three times before the session, Dickson asked to take the oath to purge himself of the scandal, and the session ordered him to do so. Steuart of Pardovan points out that in taking the oath

> all tenderness and caution is to be used, nor is the session to press any man thereto, but they are to deal with him and his conscience, as in the sight of God, and if he offer to give his oath, the judicature are to accept it or not as they shall see cause, and then proceed to remove the scandal, with the advice of the presbytery, as may be most to edification.[37]

This appears to be the process that the Borthwick session followed, treating the oath with the utmost seriousness and care. Between 3 December 1717 and 1 April 1718, Dickson was further questioned, presbytery advice obtained, and the oath administered with the assistance of two neighboring clergy. Then Douglas was referred to the Musselburgh presbytery for further examination and further attempts to have her give what they would consider an ingenuous confession.[38] Finally, the Dalkeith presbytery simply recommended that the Inveresk session do what was best for edification, probably by having Douglas lay the narrative before the congregation and pressing her to take the oath as well. This complicated and protracted case shows that sexual offenses were not treated perfunctorily and were prosecuted diligently under the elder Robertson's ministry. Yet the prosecution was conducted carefully and in accordance with the most recent formulation of the church judicial procedures.

But in the minister's few sermons that remain, a pragmatic spirit tempers discipline. He left six sermons in manuscript,[39] one of which (the fourth in the collection) was published in 1737 as *Ministers Ought to Please God, Rather Than Men*. The sermons were all given in Edinburgh after his translation from Borthwick to Old Greyfriars and delivered between 10 October 1736 and 23 October 1737. It is uncertain whether or not they were also delivered earlier in Borthwick, and it is possible, though unlikely, that the minister had adopted a more tolerant stance once he had moved to the city. In manuscript, the sermons are not finished drafts but detailed notes in a very small hand, perhaps suggesting that Robertson, like John Tillotson, preached *memoriter*. He would prepare himself in advance and use his notes in case his memory failed. That fact alone would put him with the "bright Youths" and "Oratoricall Preachers" that aroused Wodrow's suspicions.[40] Robertson clearly did not preach these sermons extempore, as did the evangelicals, nor was he reading a complete manuscript, though one could be drawn up from the notes. They represent only a narrow slice of his pulpit oratory during his clerical career, but Brougham declared his one published sermon to be "able, judicious, correctly composed, both for accuracy of diction and severity of taste, and contains passages of great beauty and effect."[41]

The published sermon demonstrates a particular style of thought that Robertson believes ministers should model. Its occasion was the opening of the Synod of Lothian and Tweeddale for 1737, and it offers a balanced, practical discussion of ministers' attitudes toward their duties and an exhortation for performing those duties with a sincerely committed heart. With secession having surfaced in 1733 along with the shock waves still emanating from the Simson controversy and Ebeneezer Erskine's deposition lying just ahead in 1739–40, Robertson in 1737 can be understood to take a peacemaker's role again, seeking to find a common ground amid potential theological difference in the membership of the synod. Indeed, his sermon carefully balances reason and passion. On one hand, in the performance of their duty, ministers owe something to men: "'Tis plain, we cannot live peaceably and amicably with others, unless we take Care to suit ourselves to their Temper and Inclination, and to do such Things as are agreeable and well-pleasing to them."[42] On the other, it is equally true that ministers "must not, for the Sake of pleasing Men, do any Thing that may be offensive and displeasing to God."[43] Ministers can resolve the tension if they think in a balanced way about their duty as preachers:

> For *what God has joined* together, *must not be* separated or *put asunder*. True Christian Morality is the same Thing with Gospel-holiness; and to engage Men to this, is the great Design of all preaching, and of the whole Gospel-Dispensation . . . [W]hen we are inculcating upon our Hearts the Practice of moral Duties, let us be careful to take the Christian Scheme along with us, and to make use, not only of such Arguments as arise from the Nature and Reason of Things, but likewise of those Motives which the Gospel itself proposes to us; and particularly, such as the Consideration of the Death and Sufferings of our Saviour and the Redemption he has thereby purchased, suggests to us.[44]

Reason leads us part of the way but only faith joined to reason will complete our journey to salvation.

Robertson's other sermons bear out this balanced approach, putting the minister squarely in the line of development leading to the moral culture of the Scottish Enlightenment. The clergy of the Church of Scotland who would eventually be designated Moderates embraced moral teaching but believed it was incomplete without the all-important truth of the Gospel.[45] This is the minister's guiding principle, as it would be for his son. For example, the first sermon in the collection on Ephesians 5: 11 is a caution against immoral behavior and the pleasures of sense. But Robertson is careful to take a balanced view of social behavior:

> If you would have no fell:p [with works of darkness] ʸn let me ext: you to avoid as much as poss: ʸe comp: & qvers:n of wick: men. Not ʸt I would you turn Monks or Hermits, to aban: hum Society, to retire into desarts, & dwell in dens & caves.[46]

Likewise, sermon two on 1 Corinthians 1: 23 acknowledges the light of nature in religious belief but argues that it cannot be the center of the Christian religion. Only the preaching of Christ crucified will bring us to true knowledge of salvation. The third sermon on Psalm 81: 10 turns on the contrast of corporeal and spiritual so that although some may be pleased with the light of the sun, true believers will only be satisfied with the light of God's countenance. The fifth sermon on Hebrews 13: 16, a charity sermon preached at Heriot's Hospital, begins with a discussion of duty and motives to duty based on naturalistic reasoning and concludes with an argument from Scripture showing how pleased God is with charity. The one apparent exception to this pattern is sermon six on John 20: 17, which is a lengthy theological meditation on the meaning of Christ's ascension into heaven.

One of the most often cited features of young Robertson's strict religious background is Carlyle's claim that his father exacted a promise from the young man never to enter a theater. For Carlyle, notorious as the supporter of John Home's *Douglas* in 1757, such an oath was a symbol of old Presbyterian ways. But perhaps in light of the minister's sermons, we may gain a more nuanced understanding of what was at stake in the oath and in the temper of the Robertson household. The historian's own understanding about what he had sworn to was specific:

> In a debate concerning the playhouse in the synod in May 1757, Dr Robertson surprised both sides by saying, that for his part he has never been within the walls of a playhouse, nor had ever been in the company of a player, male or female. When asked afrerwards to explain it, he said: "My father who was not indulgent to me on other matters made me, at an early period of life, promise most solemnly not to go to the playhouse. It gives me pleasure to think I have kept that promise sacred. At the same time, I do not condemn members that go occasionally, without giving scandal to their people."[47]

One should distinguish, as Robertson does, the traditional promise not to attend the theater (restriction of action) from the qualification that Robertson adds in the quoted version (judgment about the act). The traditional Presbyterian view held theaters to be idle amusements that contributed to the corruption of the community's morality (especially that of young people), undermined religious practices, and drew Christians away from the serious work they should devote to the community's affairs, ideas that would still be maintained vigorously even during the *Douglas* controversy of the later 1750s in which the historian himself would be engulfed. The prohibition on theaters grows out of an austere view of the world expressed, for example, by George Anderson, a minister with strong views on public morality. In one sermon, he charges that Christianity "teaches our sinful and ruinous State by Nature, and calls upon us to look upon ourselves as Criminals in the Sight of God." Consequently, such a penitent's

> Business is serious and grave, his Vocation laborious, and such as requires Diligence, Activity, Patience and Self-denial. It is therefore impossible for a Man, as a Sinner, and as a Christian, to discharge his Duty, if the whole or the main of his Life is spent in Pleasure, Ease and Idleness; if his Thoughts from Morning to Night, and his Dreams from Night to Morning, run upon nothing but the vain and idle Amusements of this World, and that, tho' those Amusements in themselves, were as innocent as lifting up or laying down the Hand.[48]

For Anderson, the act of going to the theater is inseparable from its condemnation. But the younger Robertson's distinction of act and judgment raises the question of just what such a "promise" actually meant to the elder Robertson, and why he would want such a promise from his son in the first place. These questions are significant not only because Robertson separates his judgment from his act but also because he disregarded the promise on his London excursions, leaving the implication, for someone like Carlyle, that the elder Robertson was simply old-fashioned and quaintly strict, and Robertson, the Moderate leader during much of the period, was hypocritically ignoring it when he was out of Scotland.[49]

It is perhaps a little bit surprising that someone like the elder Robertson would ask for such a promise. As we have seen, the minister was identified with the modern improvers of preaching and was also sufficiently versed in Latin to cite Horace, Quintilian, Sallust, and a civil law maxim in his published sermon. In his library of Arminian divines (with whom he did not necessarily agree, of course), he might have found works endorsing the value of drama for education, such as Samuel Werenfels' "Oratio de Comoedius."[50] Werenfels argues for the benefit of stage interludes (not professional theater) in the education of youth on the grounds of their portrayal of the human heart and their opportunity of improving style, allowing young people to learn about life. The elder Robertson even sent his son to the Dalkeith Grammar School, which put on plays annually. In 1734, for example, they presented "before a large assemblage the tragedy of 'Julius Caesar' and the comedy of 'Aesop' – the cast performing 'with a judgment and address inimitable beyond their years.'"[51] It would not appear to be a sense of the theater as a *necessarily* hellish, sinful place that motivated his request for the promise from his son.

To understand his motives, we should look again to his discussion of the ministerial role described in his published sermon. The year he delivered his sermon at the Synod of Lothian and Tweeddale, 1737, comes in the midst of a decade or so of widespread concern about the theater in Edinburgh. The elder Robertson's sermon does not directly address theater attendance, but when seen in the context of concern about the theater among Edinburgh clerics it helps explain why this issue was important to him. The theater in Edinburgh became an ideological battle-ground, particularly in the 1720s, when Anthony Aston rented Skinners' Hall and challenged the magistrates on the right of actors to put on plays in 1727.[52] The magistrates quickly saw the threat to their authority and joined forces with the Edinburgh presbytery, which "did prepare a Paper, which was read from the several Pulpits within their Bounds, warning their People against the dangerous Infection of the Theatre then erected there."[53] In 1736–7, the poet Allan Ramsay, a "hate figure among the clergy,"[54] attempted to establish a theater in Carrubber's Close, but his efforts were thwarted by the passage of the Licensing Act in London in 1737. Ramsay continued to defy the law by putting on concerts with plays as afterpieces and circulating playbooks so that, in Wodrow's conservative view, "'vice and obscenity [were] dreadfully propagated.'"[55] The outbreak of the Porteous Riots in September 1736, though not connected to the theater, simply added more nervous tension to the situation, making the magistrates leery of any public gathering, especially when challenging legal authority. By 1739, the town council was opposing the bill of John, Lord Glenorchy, to legalize playhouses, arguing that the bill was costly and would only lead to the corruption of youth, something particularly deplorable in a university town.

It is not known for certain when Robertson asked his son for the promise, but a plausible guess would be during this tense period of the 1730s when the young Robertson was enrolled in Edinburgh University where he would be making his final choice of vocation. *Ministers Ought to Please God* argues that clergy are expected to perform as models of Christian behavior for parishioners. Not that they should *never* please men, but, when there is a choice of pleasing God or men, ministers must have a clear sense of obligation to the Gospel. In contrast to a minister like Anderson, the elder Robertson counsels deliberate, judicious choices in light of proper Christian behavior. Playhouses pose an immediate risk to a minister: they are illegal, a threat to public order, and a distraction to the main purpose of a minister. It is far better for a minister to leave aside skeptical views stemming from liberty of thought and follow the admonitions of the presbytery, thereby displaying the behavior sought from the parishioners. Robertson believes ministers must exert extra self-discipline in order to protect their flock: "We may indeed, and in some Cases, ought to abridge our Christian Liberty, and to abstain from those Things that are indifferent in their own Nature, and may be either lawfully used or forborn; when we know that our doing such Things, will be grievous to some of our weaker Brethren."[56] A minister's failure to be an example to others undermines his primary mission with his own hand. Later, when the younger Robertson declared in the debates on John Home's *Douglas* in 1757 that he intended to abide by his promise to his father even though "'I perceive nothing sinful or inconsistent with the spirit of Christianity in writing a tragedy which gives no encouragement to baseness or vice,'"[57] even though he had read the part of Randolph among his friends,[58] even though a year later he would openly attend the theater in London, and even though he would become a friend of David Garrick and visit Mrs. Siddons,[59] he was not being simply hypocritical or self-important; he was invoking the pragmatic spirit of the promise his father requested. In such a matter, if conditions warrant and if there is no explicit command against it, the minister has some discretion. From these hints, we can perhaps conclude that the Robertson household was more reasonable and flexible than old-fashioned, rigid, or austere; but it was a household that took the profession of ministry seriously and placed great importance on respectable Christian appearance as part of that profession.

What lay outside this ministerial household in the village of Borthwick in the 1720s that might draw young William's attention? In the *Statistical Account of Scotland*, the Rev. John Clunie reported the parish population in Alexander Webster's 1755 survey was 910, though in the 1720s it may have been slightly larger since most rural parishes lost population during the latter half of the century.[60] The people were "chiefly employed in husbandry," there being "no manfactures or commerce of any consequence."[61] Clunie complained that the parish of Borthwick with respect to cultivation had for a long time been thought backward, though he noted a trend of recent improvements.[62] The church is said to have been in a decaying state since the early seventeenth century because the parishioners were unwilling to tax themselves, and it ultimately burned down in 1780 through improper handling of the two fireplaces, "thus bringing to a close the two centuries of neglect and carelessness."[63] The manse may have been in a similar decayed state because Clunie speaks of part of it being "very old" but, thanks to renovations begun in the late 1780s, is "now a good lodgeable house."[64] The minister's stipend was comparable to most and better than some at £100 3s. 10d. all in money and nothing in kind.[65] Adjacent to the manse was the parish's most notable antiquity, Borthwick Castle, one of the finest examples of a form of Borders military architecture known as a peel tower. Described as an "amazing mass of building,"[66] it is an imposing block with 100-foot blank walls, punctuated only by a few small windows, built on high ground so that three sides drop steeply into the river beds of the Gore Water and the Middleton North Burn. Its formidable sight could easily trigger the historical imagination of a young boy – or for that matter even an older cleric – especially if romantic stories of Mary, Queen of Scots, and the Earl of Bothwell are included.

The minister of Borthwick appears to have accumulated just such materials concerning the reign of Mary, and these were shared with his son, who transformed them into his first book. According to Alexander Bower:

> I have been assured on the authority of the late Rev. Mr. Macaulay of Queensferry, that Dr. Robertson's father had been engaged for a considerable number of years in investigating the same subject [the reign of Mary]. Though he appears never to have arranged any materials for publication, yet this circumstance could not fail of exciting Dr. Robertson's curiosity to inquire more carefully than he had yet done, into

that part of the History of Scotland which had occupied so much of the attention of a father for whose memory he entertained so sincere a regard.[67]

No manuscript evidence survives to support such a claim, though an inventory of Robertson's papers done by the historian's eldest son in 1793 recorded "Twelve books of Notes, & Excerpts chiefly my Grandfathers."[68] These could have contained the material Bower cites, presumably left to Robertson on or before his father's death in 1745. Carlyle claimed to have seen a manuscript, presumably (but not necessarily) the historian's, in 1744 when Robertson showed him the beginning of his history, opening with the portrait of Cardinal Beaton, which eventually became the second chapter of the published version.[69] It is even possible that father and son had a shared interest in the history's central figure, Mary, Queen of Scots, because stories of her circulated in the Borthwick area and in the Gladsmuir/Haddington area where the historian began his ministry.[70] The role of Borthwick parish in Mary's history is small though notable. She paid two visits to the castle, one in 1562 and the other in 1567, the latter being more dramatic. On 6 June 1567 Bothwell took Mary from Holyrood to Borthwick Castle to escape the growing threat of the confederate lords in Edinburgh.[71] The lords followed and surrounded the castle, but Bothwell managed to escape to Dunbar, leaving Mary to hold the castle. She refused surrender. After shouting insults "too evil and unseemly to be told," the lords returned to Edinburgh, and Mary escaped to Dunbar "in men's clothes, booted and spurred."[72] When she and Bothwell finally separated again at Dunbar, he to sea and death abroad, she to humiliation, imprisonment, and execution in England, it was the last time they would see each other. After Bothwell's departure, the lords and Mary confronted each other at Carberry Hill, near Musselburgh, but Mary realized her troops were not ready to fight, and she surrendered and was taken to Edinburgh.

Robertson must have enjoyed his younger years in Borthwick because Clunie recalled Robertson "ever cherished an attachment to the place of his nativity, and to the latest period of life, talked of the scenes of his youth with a pleasing and interesting warmth."[73] In a parish of just eleven square miles and fewer than one thousand inhabitants, those scenes would have had a distinctly rural flavor. Perhaps, like Henry Cockburn in the 1780s, young Robertson enjoyed the Gala Water, a few miles to the south of Borthwick. Cockburn loved its pastoral valley:

It is bleak and wet no doubt; but so is most of the pastoral scenery of Scotland, the whole of which requires the attraction of a bright day. But with such a day, the sparkling stream of the Gala, the range of its wild unenclosed hills, and its impressive solitude, to say nothing of its coming in for a share of the historical interest which belongs to the whole of our southern border, gives it powerful charms.[74]

A couple of miles to the east, there were the grounds of Arniston, where Robertson's uncle William Adam was beginning to plan the redesign of the house. The grounds featured the famous ash tree, which Lord Arniston displayed proudly. At its fullest growth, in 1792, it measured thirty feet in circumference with the trunk separating into eight or nine large limbs. Lord Arniston's grandson claimed that "three or four persons could have stood without inconvenience in the centre where the limbs diverged." Coincidentally, the tree came down in a storm during the winter of 1793, shortly before Robertson died.[75]

His appreciation of rural life was not confined to Borthwick. Even in his later years, Robertson still enjoyed riding through the countryside in a carriage, surveying the progress of crops, which, on one occasion in England, were so abundant, he commented approvingly, "we have not seen better wheat, nor so good oats & turnips . . . [and he noted with enthusiasm] we met with the first harvest on the borders of Shrop-shire."[76] He failed in his attempt in 1769 to buy his own country house at Leuchold, near Dalmeny Park, using the proceeds from the sale of *Charles V*.[77] But he subsequently managed to rely on friends and family for regular periods of rural retirement. He was fond of leaving the closeness and smell of Edinburgh for the more open land of Lavrock Bank; Merchiston, where the Adam family owned a house; and Grange House, owned by the Dick family. After the marriage of his daughter Mary to Patrick Brydone, Lennel House in Coldstream became a favorite resort, where he attributed his good health to "the virtues of the air I breathed, & the satisfaction I enjoyed on the banks of the Tweed."[78] In 1783, Robertson made a "Highland jaunt,"[79] according to his son William, and during the 1780s he visited the health resort at Buxton in Derbyshire on a number of occasions, enjoying not only its associations with Mary, Queen of Scots, but also its open country, very suitable for hunting:

> A capital pack of harriers are kept by subscription, where all the Gentlemen resorting to *Buxton*, may have the pleasure of hunting from *Michaelmas* to *Lady-day*; and the country being high and open, forms a pleasing contrast to those who are accustomed to low and flat situations, to which his Grace the *Duke of Devonshire* is considerably adding, by planting the hills round *Buxton*, with trees.[80]

Childhood in Borthwick was also enlivened by the rapidly growing Robertson household. Between 1721 and 1739, the Robertsons gave birth

to nine children, only one of whom, Robert, died before reaching adult-
hood. Six of the children were born in Borthwick and three in Edinburgh
after the family's move there in 1733. Apart from his brother Patrick
(1729–90) and his short-lived brother Robert (1722–3), the historian's
siblings were all younger sisters: Mary (1723–1803), Margaret (1725–81),
Elizabeth (b. 1727), Helen or Helenora (1734–1816), Jean (1738–89), and
Eupham (1739–1807). The family seemed to be amicable, though perhaps
not very close, judging from the absence of family correspondence. The
lack of correspondence could also indicate frequency of face-to-face
contact that removed the need for letters as well as implying issues of
literacy. Although the women's known marriages were with a clergyman,
an accountant, a baxter (baker), and a ferrier – and Patrick's was with the
daughter of a surgeon – there may have grown up social distance between
Robertson and his siblings, as his fame as historian and Enlightenment
leader developed. Carlyle reports a comment by Patrick that suggests at
least his awareness of his brother's self-importance. Invited to dine with
Patrick, Carlyle was surprised not to find Robertson there as he usually was.
To Carlyle's inquiry, Patrick replied, "'I have not invited him to-day, . . .
for I have a very good company, and he'll let nobody speak but himself.'"[81]
When their parents died a week apart in November 1745, Robertson
became the head of a household whose ages ranged from twenty-four
down to six. But it is not clear how many of these children were then residing in Edinburgh and how many, if any, were with him in Gladsmuir. The
four oldest could have already been on their own, with Patrick apprenticed
to his trade as a jeweler, and Margaret, Mary, and Elizabeth in trade and to
be married in 1750, 1751, and 1754 respectively. Nonetheless, Robertson
worked to secure the family support and to create a stabilizing influence
by applying to the Kirk's newly established Widow's Fund and securing
the support of the Adam family.[82] In later years, traces of evidence show
the family in Edinburgh remained in contact: for instance, Patrick assisted
Robertson on occasion as a member of the Edinburgh Town Council;[83]
Elizabeth's husband, Archibald Hope, was a witness along with Robertson
to the birth of Mary's grandson, Henry Brougham;[84] and Robertson
sought positions for Margaret's children in India.[85]

However strong his attachment to home and countryside, it was no
match for his attachment to books. We have noted Carlyle's reference to
Robertson's "Recluse and Studious Bent," and Dugald Stewart speaks
of Robertson's "early and enthusiastic love of study" and of "the patient
culture" that he employed to develop it.[86] It was probably these qualities that prompted his father to destine him for a clerical career, though
Carlyle observed that young Robertson was not at all precocious.[87] John

Erskine believed the elder Robertson put education ahead of all else: "though in circumstances far from affluent, he [Robertson's father] grudged no proper expense in the education of his children."[88] Exactly what that statement meant for Robertson's siblings is uncertain because none of them attained his level of education. His only adult brother, Patrick, apprenticed to a goldsmith as an adolescent, was quite literate as indicated by his Town Council posts. Several of Robertson's sisters were engaged in commerce and must have had at least basic education. Robertson's wife, Mary, perhaps represented his sisters' level of education: her few surviving letters show her to be literate but very far below the level attained by her husband.[89]

Robertson first attended "a small school in his father's parish" to learn the rudiments of his education.[90] Most of his training would consist of reading and writing English along with the study of Latin grammar and some arithmetic. Most of the English reading would have been based on the Bible.[91] Robert Dundas, Lord Arniston, was the patron and principal heritor, though the kirk session, led by the elder Robertson, would have responsibility for day-to-day administration. Clunie mentions two schools in the parish: one in the town of Borthwick itself, and another for workers on the Vogrie estate maintained by the Dewar family located about two miles north of the Borthwick school.[92] Robertson likely attended the first. The average age for a child entering a parish school was 5½ years,[93] although Robertson himself may have been as old as seven as judged by the date he entered Edinburgh University. It is uncertain how satisfactory the parish school education was because one common complaint among parishes was the exploitation of schoolmasters.[94] Clunie was particularly blunt on this point: "This [parish school], though by no means one of the worst livings of the kind, never can be an object to a man who has got any thing like a liberal education."[95] The Borthwick schoolmaster's basic salary in 1791 was £5 3s. 5½d. (compared with a national average of £10[96]) but was supplemented because in rural parishes like Borthwick the schoolmaster also acted as session-clerk and precentor, collector and distributor of poor rates, collector of statute-money, and registrar of births, marriages, and funerals. Thus, his total salary in 1791 was £17 3s. 5½d., with a small house and garden.[97] Moreover, the position may have been more attractive in the earlier part of the century because Clunie observes that while the wages of the schoolmaster's employers had doubled or tripled over the century, those of the schoolmaster had remained unchanged. One hopes, at any rate, that the Borthwick parish minister, who was crucially responsible for the maintenance and support of the school, was able to ameliorate the schoolmaster's situation.

Perhaps in 1730, when Robertson was age nine, the usual age for entrance into grammar school,[98] the elder Robertson enrolled his son in the grammar school at Dalkeith, a distance of six miles north from Borthwick largely along the Gore Water. Although children sometimes walked long distances to school during this period,[99] it seems more likely Robertson was boarded "with a number of other lads under the schoolmaster."[100] One inducement for the minister to enroll his son at Dalkeith may have been familial. Among his son's contemporaries there was John Adam, the eldest son of his uncle William Adam and also born in 1721. In light of the close connection between the Robertsons and the Adams, the presence of the two boys in the school may not have been coincidental. Another inducement was the reputation of the school. According to Stewart, Robertson "received the first rudiments of his education at the school of Dalkeith, which, from the high reputation of Mr. Leslie as a teacher, was from that time resorted to from all parts of Scotland."[101] The attraction may not have been the schoolmaster alone because Leslie did not arrive at the Dalkeith Grammar School as a master until 1731, making Robertson's exposure to him a relatively short two years.[102] For the six years between the death of the former master, Alexander Dykes (serving from 1707 to 1725), and Leslie's arrival in 1731, there was apparently no headmaster. Leslie later became rector and died in 1739. Nonetheless, the Dalkeith school did maintain a high reputation in the country,[103] and, according to Bower, Robertson's education there left a lasting mark: "At this seminary young Robertson was thoroughly grounded in the principles of the Latin language, and formed a taste for classical learning, which never forsook him."[104] The typical grammar school stay was four or five years, though a six-year curriculum was possible.[105] The curriculum ranged between various Latin grammar texts and readings from authors including Ovid, Erasmus, Virgil, Terence, Buchanan, Horace, and Sallust. Leslie was also fond of having students perform plays. He is probably the "Mr Leslie" referred to in the Burgh Records of Haddington for whom the rector of the grammar school in Haddington (where Leslie had been teaching before his move to Dalkeith) ordered a stage to be erected on 5 August 1729 so Leslie's students could act a comedy.[106] His interest in the instructional power of drama continued after his move to Dalkeith.

In 1733-4, the Robertson family experienced a major change. Robertson's father was first called to Lady Yester's Church in Edinburgh, where he was admitted 22 November 1733, and then ordered to Old Greyfriars on 10 October 1736 (though the Edinburgh presbytery did not finally approve the move until 8 July 1737). The elder Robertson was approved by the Dalkeith presbytery for transportation on 16 October

1733, and presbytery efforts to refill the vacancy at Borthwick were begun in the first half of December. By February 1734 the family's move was probably completed because Robertson's sister Helen was born on 5 February in Edinburgh, and the minister himself was admitted as a burgess and guild brother to Edinburgh's only guild – the merchants' – on 27 February.[107] It is unclear if Robertson was with the family in February 1734. The Edinburgh University matriculation roll indicates Robertson began there in February 1735. Since the year 1734–5 would have been the fifth in his curriculum at Dalkeith if Robertson entered in 1730, and if he were boarding, which seems most likely, he could easily have stayed to finish his course of study at Dalkeith while the family completed their move to Edinburgh during 1733–4. Alternatively, Robertson might have joined the family and enrolled at the University of Edinburgh as early as November 1734 because students signed the matriculation roll relatively late in the term,[108] and Robertson signed for John Ker's humanities class on 21 February 1735.[109] But whether he entered in November 1734 or February 1735 makes little difference in the end because in either case Robertson was slightly younger than the average student entering of fourteen.[110]

Although the Robertsons were no doubt familiar with Edinburgh, it was nonetheless a major change from Borthwick and Dalkeith. A city of approximately 40,500 in 1735, Edinburgh was on the edge of the Enlightenment period that would transform the city physically, socially, and intellectually, and the young William Robertson would be part of this transformation. He told Gilbert Elliot in 1755, the city was the "place where all my relations live, & my habits of friendship have been formed."[111] The inhabitants of Edinburgh densely populated the narrow volcanic ridge that runs from Edinburgh Castle on the west end to Holyrood Palace on the east, the two landmarks connected by the High Street now known as the Royal Mile. Off the High Street ran the characteristic fish-bone pattern of wynds running north and south down toward the Nor' Loch and the Grassmarket and Cowgate to the south. Urging the construction of the New Town to the north, Gilbert Eliot of 1752 complained that the wynds were narrow, steep, and dirty and "the houses stand more crouded than in any other town in Europe, and are built to a height that is almost incredible."[112] It is not known where the Robertsons lived upon their move to Edinburgh, but a reasonable guess is the area around the head of the Cowgate and the West Bow, one of the major centers of the city. In 1752, the minister's successor, James Stevenson, lived in Friershaw's Land in the Grassmarket, suggesting this area was a likely location for those at Old Greyfriars.[113] This guess is also based on the fact that the

Robertsons in subsequent years seemed to gravitate to this area, which was very convenient not only to Old Greyfriars Church but also to the university. The registration of the marriage of Margaret Robertson and Alexander Bruce in 1750 listed her residence as the North West parish, the old name for the Tolbooth, which included the north side of the West Bow.[114] In 1752, she and her husband were living in Fairholm's Land in the West Bow.[115] In 1752, Patrick Robertson, established as a jeweler, was living in or near the Luckenbooths on High Street near St. Giles, about 800 yards away from the Bruces in Fairholm's Land.[116] Patrick's sister Mary, after the death of her clergyman husband, James Syme, in 1752, lived at the head of the Cowgate, located just a couple hundred yards down from Fairholm's Land and looking up Candlemaker's Row toward Greyfriars Kirk.[117] The historian himself would later locate at the head of the Cowgate, when he moved to Edinburgh from Gladsmuir in 1758.[118]

The institutions father and son were to join – the church and the university – were in varying states of evolution. After his initial appointment at Lady Yester's Church, located between the college buildings and the high school to the east of the head of the Cowgate, the minister was translated to Old Greyfriars Kirk, where he spent the remainder of his career. It was an important church in the religious history of the city and the scene of major events in Presbyterian faith in the seventeenth century. In 1718, gunpowder, which had been stored in the steeple, exploded, destroying two of the west bays as well as the steeple. The Town Council decided not only to repair the church but also to build a new church against the west wall to accommodate the parish's growing congregation, creating New Greyfriars (the West Church) and Old Greyfriars (the East Church). The Old Greyfriars parish was not among the wealthiest of the city. Edinburgh's wealth throughout the first half of the century was concentrated more in the south central districts of the city rather than the south west,[119] but given Edinburgh housing patterns, where rich and poor often lived in close proximity, wealth would not necessarily imply physical exclusivity. The college in which the young Robertson enrolled was a short distance due east from the kirk, but its buildings were in dilapidated condition. The historian himself described them in 1768:

A stranger, when conducted to view the University of Edinburgh, might, on seeing such courts and buildings, naturally enough imagine them to be alms-houses for the reception of the poor; but would never imagine that he was entering within the precincts of a noted and flourishing seat of learning.[120]

He may have been drawing upon his own youthful first impressions: "when ideas of poverty, meanness, dirtiness, and darkness, are connected in youth with a literary education, such a debasing association is not likely to favour the proper fruits of education in future life."[121] Improvement of the university's physical plant was to become a career-long goal for the future principal.

The Robertsons got an early indication of the volatility of city life. About two years after they were settled, the Porteous Riots, "one of the most dramatic incidents in the national history,"[122] erupted in April 1736 on what may have been, at least figuratively, the Robertson family's doorstep. On 9 January 1736, Andrew Wilson, William Hall, and George Robertson robbed James Stark, a collector of excise taxes, in Pittenweem. The three were sentenced to death, though Hall's was commuted to transportation for life. On 11 April, Robertson made a daring escape from the Toolbooth Church, where Alexander Carlyle happened to be in the congregation: the fugitive, "springing up, got over the pew into the passage that led in to the door in the Parliament Close, and no person offering to lay hands on him, made his escape in a moment."[123] As he crossed the church, he "passed close by the pew where I was," Carlyle added. Given the unpopularity of the excise and a long tradition of popular protest, the Edinburgh mob was not unsympathetic to the robbers, and it was not surprising that Robertson escaped. The city magistrates were uneasy and decided to supplement the city guards with several companies of soldiers when Wilson was to be executed on 14 April. The captain of the city guards, John Porteous, irritated at what he felt was unnecessary and demeaning support – and inflamed with wine – led his prisoner down the West Bow, leading from the Lawnmarket to the place of execution in the Grassmarket, growling, "'What! Was not he and his Guard fit to hang a rascal without help!'"[124] Carlyle's tutor, Patrick Baillie, had taken windows for his pupils to watch the proceedings on the north side of the Grassmarket some seventy or eighty yards west of the place of execution. (Was young Robertson, just four months older than Carlyle, also watching with equal excitement somewhere in the vicinity?) After Wilson was hanged, the mob began to pelt his body with dirt and rocks (as usual). When they surged forward, Porteous ordered the city guard to open fire, and panic ensued. In Carlyle's words, "We had seen many people, women and men, fall on the street, and at first thought it was only through fear, and by their crowding on one another to escape. But when the crowd dispersed, we saw them lying dead or wounded."[125] Six were killed and many wounded. For Carlyle, shocked by having witnessed one execution already in his life,[126] this must have been a terrifying incident, especially since one young man whom they had displaced from the windows from which they were watching was shot through the head during the melee.

Such a scene must have been equally shocking for young Robertson and his family – if they were there.

Porteous was arrested and brought to trial. On 20 July 1736 he was found guilty, but, thanks to a petition mounted by some of his friends, Porteous received from Queen Caroline a reprieve until October. This action only hardened sentiment, which now had taken on populist overtones, and by September Edinburgh was rife with rumors that Porteous would be killed. Carlyle even suggested there was almost public hysteria: "So prepossessed were the minds of every person that something extraordinary would take place that day [7 September 1736], that I, at Prestonpans, nine miles east from Edinburgh, dreamt that I saw Captain Porteous hanged in the Grassmarket."[127] As feared, on the night of 7 September, a mob estimated at four to five thousand of uncertain origin but appearing to many observers to be well coordinated, broke into the Tolbooth, dragged Porteous forth, and, torches in hand, surged down the West Bow to the Grassmarket, intending to hang him in the same place where he had committed his murders. The execution itself was brutal:

> [Porteous] desired some time to prepare for death, but was answered, They would allow him no more than those had who were shot. They then pulled him up in the dress in which they found him, viz. a night gown and cap. His hands not being tied, he fixed them between his neck and the rope, whereupon one with a battle-ax struck at his hands. They then let him down, and he having on two shirts, they wrapt one of them about his face and tied his arms with his nightgown, and then pulled him up again, where he hung till day-light next morning . . .[128]

"'Now,' said one of [the mob], 'the Queen can wipe her backside with her reprieve.'"[129] When the city magistrates sent people to take down the body and carry it to Old Greyfriars Church, "in the Yard of which it was buried that day following,"[130] the fate of Porteous came a step closer to the Robertson family. One wonders what went through the mind of the soon-to-be minister of Old Greyfriars when he confronted the fact of Porteous' mangled body in his church yard? The *Caledonian Mercury* declared the riot the "most outrageous and violent insult to the laws and constitution of the nation . . . that perhaps ever happened in any civilized country."[131] The minister may well have felt the evil of human nature had welled up uncontrollably because just a month later, on 10 October, the day of his admission to Old Greyfriars, he preached there on 1 Cor. 1: 23.[132] In it Robertson proclaims that we know by the light of nature God is the cause of all things and the supreme ruler of the universe, but the light of nature cannot teach us the acceptable way of worshipping God, it cannot discover the mediating role of Christ with sinners, and it informs us that humans, weak, degenerate, corrupt, cannot trust their own powers. The light of nature cannot discover the path to salvation, and only the preaching of Christ crucified, which transcends nature, can reveal it. In the face of the degeneracy and corruption of human nature, one must hold fast to the permanent truth of the Gospel.

But the role of faith for the minister and his family was soon put to a further test in the riot's aftermath. On 13 June 1737, some nine months after the riot, Parliament passed a bill charging all magistrates and other civil officers and citizens in Scotland to come forward with any information they may have regarding the persons responsible for the violent incidents of 7 September. Carlyle's father, a minister at Prestonpans, was also caught up in this act of governmental revenge.[133] Ministers were required to read the proclamation from the pulpit on the first Sunday of every month in the midst of the service between the lecture and the sermon. For the Scottish clergy, already wracked by one secession and about to face another and with ongoing struggles between liberal and conservative views of doctrine, this was a serious blow because it pitted the more "high flying" against the more "moderate." The former wished to refuse to read the act because it inserted the secular (honoring a villain by seeking punishment for his death) before the sacred (honoring the sacrifice of Christ) on the Sabbath.[134] The latter were more comfortable, perhaps, with Erastian thinking, and they could also understand Carlyle's conclusion that the Act was designed to flush out fanatics among the clergy. But regardless of a minister's views, Carlyle knew first hand there was anguish:

> The distress and perplexity which this Act occasioned in many families of the clergy, was of itself a cruel punishment for a crime in which they had no hand. The anxious days and sleepless nights which it occasioned to such ministers as had families, and at the same time scruples about the lawfulness of reading the Act, were such as no one could imagine who had not witnessed the scene.[135]

Carlyle points to his grandfather, who decidedly embraced the Act and read it, and to his father, who had scruples. But his father, after weighing the "consideration of eight or nine children,"[136] ultimately chose to read the Act. The Reverend William Robertson, given his Hanoverian allegiances and his five children at this time, on the one hand, and his belief that ministers ought to please God rather than man on the other, probably experienced painful scruples just as did Carlyle's father. In the end, however, he probably read the Act.

Whether or not young William Robertson witnessed some or all of the Porteous upheaval, mob violence and its aftermath made its way into the Robertson household and left its mark on the historian. Of course, mob violence was nothing new in Edinburgh, and the Porteous riots followed the typical patterns of protest from the past. But the attention of government in the case of Porteous was distinctive and was a sign of a new attitude toward public order.[137] For the future historian William Robertson, the volatility and anger of the mob stayed in his mind. It must have come back, for example, as an unsettling memory in 1778–9 with the "No Popery" riots in Edinburgh, particularly in view of the several death threats he and his family received.[138] Echoes of the mob's disregard for public order also lingered in his writing. After Mary's surrender at Carberry Hill in 1567, she was conducted to Edinburgh by the confederate lords.

> The streets were covered with multitudes, whom zeal or curiosity had drawn together, to behold such an unusual scene. The queen, worn out with fatigue, covered with dust, and bedewed with tears, was exposed as a spectacle to her own subjects, and led to the provost's house . . . But the people beheld the deplorable situation of their sovereign with insensibility; and so strong was their persuasion of her guilt, and so great the violence of their indignation, that the sufferings of their queen did not, in any degree, mitigate their resentment, or procure her that sympathy which is seldom denied to unfortunate princes.[139]

Likewise, in the wake of the David Black incident of 1596, King James was threatened by an Edinburgh mob incensed at his rejection of their petition on behalf of the clergy who had criticized the king's ministers.

> When they reported that the king had refused to listen to their petitions, the church was filled in a moment with noise, threatenings, execrations, and all the outrage and confusion of a popular tumult. Some called for their arms, some to bring out the wicked Haman; others cried, The sword of the Lord and of Gideon; and, rushing out with the most furious impetuosity, surrounded the Tolbooth, threatening the king himself, and demanding some of his counselors, whom they named, that they might tear them in pieces.[140]

How much Robertson's distaste for popular protest stemmed from his early personal experience or was simply part of the general change in public attitude that followed the Porteous riots cannot be known. But the evil of public disorder would become a theme in Robertson's work, shaped by the philosophy and theology he would discover at the University of Edinburgh.

Notes

1. John Clunie, "Parish of Borthwick," in *The Statistical Account of Scotland*, ed. Sir John Sinclair, 20 vols. (1791–9; rpt. Wakefield: EP Publishing,

1973–83), II, 73 n. For details about the church, see T. A. Bickerton, "Borthwick Church," *Transactions of the Edinburgh Architectural Association*, 7 (1912), p. 86; and David Macgibbon and Thomas Ross, *The Ecclesiastical Architecture of Scotland*, 3 vols (Edinburgh, 1896–7), III, 214–18.

2. *The Arniston Memoirs*, ed. George W. T. Omond (Edinburgh, 1887), p. 7

3. The dates are Old Style. In New Style, Robertson's birth would be 19 September and his baptism 25 September.

4. Information courtesy of Marion Richardson, Midlothian District Council.

5. *Arniston Memoirs*, ed. Ormond, p. 57.

6. Hew Scott, *Fasti Ecclesiae Scoticanae: The Succession of Ministers in the Church of Scotland from the Reformation*, 11 vols to date (Edinburgh: Oliver & Boyd, 1915–), I, 40.

7. George G. Cameron, *The Scots Kirk in London* (Oxford: Becket Publications, 1979), pp. 23, 240; Walter Wilson, *History and Antiquities of Dissenting Churches and Meeting Houses in London, Westminster, and Southwark*, 4 vols (London, 1808), II, 468–87.

8. Richard B. Sher, *Church and University in the Scottish Enlightenment: The Moderate Literati of Edinburgh* (Princeton: Princeton University Press, 1985), p. 152.

9. *Arniston Memoirs*, 52; see also Michael Fry, *The Dundas Despotism* (Edinburgh: Edinburgh University Press, 1992), p. 5.

10. NAS MS, CH2/424/10, p. 192.

11. Robert Wodrow, *Analecta; or Materials for a History of Remarkable Providences*, 4 vols (Edinburgh, 1843), IV, 238.

12. James T. Davidson, *The Linktown of Abbotshall: A Study in Social and Economic History* (Kircaldy: Fifeshire Advertiser, 1951), p. 89.

13. John Gifford, *William Adam 1689–1748: A Life and Times of Scotland's Universal Architect* (Edinburgh: Mainstream, 1989), p. 75.

14. William R. M. Kay, "What's His Line: Would the Real William Adam Please Stand Up? Some Recent Research Discoveries," *Architectural Heritage I: The Journal of the Architectural Heritage Society of Scotland* (Edinburgh: University Press, 1990), p. 50.

15. Davidson, *Linktown*, pp. 80–1; David Macgibbon and Thomas Ross, *The Castellated and Domestic Architecture of Scotland*, 5 vols (Edinburgh, 1892), V, 286–9.

16. John Erskine, "The Agency of God in Human Greatness," in *Miscellaneous Works*, p. 263.

17. The basic outline of the Robertson family genealogy is provided in Sir Robert Douglas, *The Baronage of Scotland* (Edinburgh, 1798), pp. 405–10, 413–14. The Highland associations and implications of the Robertson genealogy are discussed by Owen Dudley Edwards, "Robertsonian Romanticism and Realism," in *William Robertson and the Expansion of Empire*, ed. Stewart J. Brown (Cambridge: Cambridge University Press, 1997), pp. 97–9.

18. Possible Jacobite loyalties have been said to appear in the elder Robertson's

interest in the visual arts. Lord Brougham possessed "a miniature in Indian ink of James, Earl of Seafield, one of the forfeited Lords" ("Robertson," in *Miscellaneous Works*, p. 256). The most likely candidate for the portrait, James Ogilvy, 4th Earl of Findlater and 1st Earl of Seafield, was one of the architects of the Treaty of Union. Although he did become disaffected with the treaty, he never openly committed to the Jacobite cause and never forfeited his estate. There were members of the Ogilvy family who were sympathetic to the Jacobite cause in both 1715 and 1745, but these were earls of Airlie, not Seafield. One wonders if Brougham actually had a drawing done by William Robertson (fl. 1727–83), a portrait painter active in Edinburgh, who was in fact patronized by families with Jacobite sympathies (James Holloway, *Patrons and Painters: Art in Scotland 1650–1760* (Edinburgh: Scottish National Portrait Gallery, 1989), p. 147). That attribution does not solve the uncertainty about the identity of the sitter, but it does help resolve the anomaly as to why a Hanoverian minister allied closely with the Dundas family would leave behind a portrait of a supposedly forfeited lord.

19. (Edinburgh, 1775), pp. 152–3.
20. "Robertson," in *Miscellaneous Works*, pp. 257–8.
21. Ibid., p. 258.
22. David Shankie, *The Parish of Colinton: From an Early Period to the Present Day* (Edinburgh: J. Wilson, 1902), pp. 92–3.
23. Scott, *Fasti*, I, 97.
24. Alexander DuToit, "'Unionist Nationalism' in the Eighteenth Century: William Robertson and James Anderson (1662–1728)," *Scottish Historical Review*, 85 (2006), pp. 305–14.
25. Scott, *Fasti*, I, 71–2.
26. "A Comparison of Two Eminent Characters Attempted after the Manner of Plutarch," in *Alexander Carlyle: Anecdotes and Characters of the Times*, ed. James Kinsley (London: Oxford University Press, 1973), p. 277.
27. "Robertson," in *Miscellaneous Works*, pp. 257–8.
28. "Agency," in ibid., p. 264.
29. EUL MS 3,979, f. 22.
30. Quoted in G. D. Henderson, *The Scottish Ruling Elder* (London: James Clarke, 1935), p. 101.
31. *Girls in Trouble: Sexuality and Social Control in Rural Scotland 1660–1780* (Edinburgh: Scottish Cultural Press, 1998), p. 6.
32. Henderson, *Ruling Elder*, p. 137; Mitchison and Leneman, *Girls in Trouble*, p. 17.
33. NAS MS CH2/38/1, s. v. 2 August 1730, 24 May 1729, and 19 January 1729.
34. NAS MS CH2/38/1, s. v. 1 August 1731.
35. See, for example, the edition of Edinburgh, 1780, p. 183.
36. *Ruling Elder*, pp. 137–8.

37. *Collections and Observations Concerning the Worship, Discipline, and Government of the Church of Scotland* (Edinburgh, 1770), p. 250.
38. NAS CH2/424/10, p. 431.
39. EUL MS ROB 4.
40. Ann Matheson, *Theories of Rhetoric in the 18th-Century Scottish Sermon* (Lewiston, NY: Edwin Mellen Press, 1995), pp. 23–34.
41. "Robertson," in *Miscellaneous Works*, p. 257. Brougham also praises three scriptural paraphrases (XXV, XLII, and XLIII) Robertson published in *Translations and Paraphrases of Several Passages of Scripture* (Edinburgh, 1745). This collection was done by Edinburgh ministers who, as they explained in the preface, "chiefly aimed at having the Sense of Scripture express'd in easy Verse; such as might be fitted to raise Devotion, might be intelligible to all, and might rise above Contempt from Persons of better Taste." Like many of the contributions, Robertson's are adaptations of hymns by Isaac Watts and demonstrate the fundamental importance of simple faith in the Gospel message.
42. *Ministers Ought to Please God, Rather than Men* (Edinburgh, 1737), p. 9.
43. Ibid., p. 17.
44. Ibid., p. 24.
45. Thomas Ahnert, *The Moral Culture of the Scottish Enlightenment 1690–1805* (New Haven, CT: Yale University Press, 2014), pp. 12–13 and *passim*. Anhert uses the term "religious Enlightenment" to refer to this combination of moral teaching and the Gospel message.
46. EUL MS ROB 4, p. 11. In fuller transcription: "If you would have no fellowship [with works of darkness] then let me exhort you to avoid as much as possible the company and conversation of wicked men. Not that I would you turn Monks or Hermits, to abandon human society, to retire into deserts and dwell in dens and caves."
47. John Ramsay of Ochertyre, "Literary and Biographical Anecdotes," NLS MS 1,636, f. 219. This seems to be the earliest version of this popular story. George Gleig in "Some Acount of the Life and Writings of William Robertson," in *Works of William Robertson*, 12 vols (London, 1819), I, xxxv, prints a rather heightened version of the speech. See also Carlyle, "Comparison," p. 277; Stewart, "Account of the Life and Writings of William Robertson," in *Miscellaneous Works*, p. 111; Brougham, "Robertson," in ibid., p. 257; and Stewart J. Brown, "William Robertson," in *William Robertson*, p. 18.
48. *The Use and Abuse of Diversions* (Edinburgh, 1733), pp. 15–16.
49. Robertson wrote a long letter reporting first hand on the performance of Home's *Agis* (Robertson to Margaret Hepburn, 22 February 1758, NLS MS 16,707, ff. 92–5). Brougham must assume the promise applies only to Scotland because he says Robertson "strictly adhered through life to the promise," even though he reprints the letter indicating attendance at *Agis* ("Robertson," in *Miscellaneous Works*, p. 257).

50. In *Opuscula theologia, philosophica et philologica*, 2 vols (Basil, 1718), II, 793–806. Translated as *The Usefulness of Dramatic Interludes in the Education of Youth: An Oration* (London, 1744).

51. James Grant, *History of the Burgh and Parish Schools of Scotland* (London, 1876), p. 414.

52. R. A. Houston, *Social Change in the Age of Enlightenment: Edinburgh, 1660–1760* (Oxford: Oxford University Press, 1994), pp. 205–7.

53. Quoted from the 1757 Admonition in Alice Edna Gipson, *John Home: A Study of His Life and Work* (Caldwell: Caxton Printers, 1917), p. 72.

54. Houston, *Social Change*, p. 207.

55. Quoted in ibid., p. 208.

56. *Ministers Ought to Please God*, p. 16.

57. Quoted in Gleig, "Account," I, xxxv.

58. The event was verified by Alexander Carlyle in a letter. See *The Life and Times of Henry, Lord Brougham*, 3 vols (London, 1871), I, 540–2.

59. Alexander Carlyle comments that Robertson and Hugh Blair regretted not having gone "openly" to the theater to see Mrs. Siddons in 1784, "which would have put an end to all future animadversions on the subject. This conduct of theirs was keeping the reserve of their own imaginary importance to the last; and their regretting it was very just, for by that time they got no credit for their abstinence, and the struggle between the liberal and the restrained and affected manners of the clergy had been long at an end, by my having finally stood my ground, and been so well supported by so great a majority in the Church" (*Autobiography of Dr. Alexander Carlyle*, ed. J. H. Burton (London: Foulis, 1910), p. 339). What Carlyle interprets as "imaginary importance," Robertson might understand as performing his ministerial role.

60. "Parish of Borthwick," p. 76.

61. Ibid., p. 71.

62. Ibid., p. 70.

63. *Arniston Memoirs*, ed. Ormond, p. 8.

64. "Parish of Borthwick," p. 73. For a somewhat idealized picture of the church and the manse together with Borthwick Castle as they were in the mid-nineteenth century, see Robert W. Fraser, *The Kirk and the Manse* (Edinburgh, 1866).

65. Clunie, "Parish of Borthwick," p. 73.

66. Ibid., p. 79.

67. *History of the University of Edinburgh*, 3 vols (Edinburgh, 1817–30), III, 76–7.

68. NLS MS 3,980, f. 129.

69. Carlyle to Dugald Stewart, n. d., NLS MS 23,920 [scroll copy], ff. 81–5.

70. See James Miller, *The Lamp of Lothian; or, the History of Haddington*, new edn (Haddington: W. Sinclair, 1900).

71. Robertson describes the event and its consequences in *History of Scotland*, in *Works of Robertson*, I, 441–6.

72. *Ordnance Gazetteer of Scotland: A Survey of Scottish Topography*, ed. Francis H. Groome, 6 vols (Edinburgh, n.d.), I, 178.
73. "Parish of Borthwick," p. 83.
74. *Memorials of His Time* (1856; rpt. Edinburgh: James Thin, 1988), p. 16.
75. *Arniston Memoirs*, ed. Ormond, pp. 46–7.
76. Robertson to Mary Brydone, 26 August 1790, NAS MS WRH TD 77/142/4/300/25.
77. Robertson to William Mure, 14 December 1769, in *Selections from the Family Papers Preserved at Caldwell*, 3 vols (Glasgow, 1854), II, pt 2, 160–1.
78. Robertson and Mary Robertson to Patrick and Mary Brydone, 4 November 1789, NAS MS WRH TD 77/142/4/300/19.
79. William Robertson to Robertson, 23 August 1783, NLS MS 3,943, f. 156.
80. Antonia Fraser, *Mary Queen of Scots* (New York: Delacorte Press, 1969), pp. 437–9; William Bott, *A Description of Buxton and the Adjacent Country* (Manchester, 1790), p. 13.
81. *Autobiography*, p. 300.
82. NAS MS CH2/121/16, pp. 152–3.
83. Patrick as a goldsmith was elected several times to represent the trade on the Edinburgh Town Council, including his election in September 1763 during the complicated struggle over the appointment of John Drysdale when additional backing for Robertson and the Moderates would have been welcome. See Richard B. Sher, "Moderates, Managers and Popular Politics in Mid-Eighteenth Edinburgh: The Drysdale 'Bustle' of the 1760s," in *New Perspectives on the Politics and Culture of Early Modern Scotland*, ed. John Dwyer et al. (Edinburgh: John Donald, n. d.), pp. 179–209.
84. Robert Chambers, *Traditions of Edinburgh* (1824; rpt. Edinburgh: James Thin, 1980), p. 81 n.
85. Robertson to Robert Orme, 24 January 1769, Princeton University Library MS Wild Autograph Collection, vol. 39, leaf 126A; Robertson to unidentified correspondent, 22 October 1781, Pierpont Morgan Library MS.
86. "Account," in *Miscellaneous Works*, p. 104.
87. Carlyle comments: "In their Boyish Days, Blair was the Most Distinguish'd of the two, For in Robertson there appear'd not then, any Symptoms of his Future Fame" ("Comparison," p. 277).
88. "Agency," in *Miscellaneous Works*, p. 263.
89. See, for example, Robertson and Mary Robertson to William Robertson, 7 June 1789, NLS MS 3,944, ff. 12—3; and the same to Patrick and Mary Brydone, 4 November 1789, NAS WRH TD 77/142/4/300/19.
90. Bower, *History*, III, 25.
91. Alexander Law, *Education in Edinburgh in the Eighteenth Century* (London: University of London Press, 1965), p. 33.
92. "Parish of Borthwick," pp. 73–4.
93. T. C. Smout, *A History of the Scottish People, 1560–1830* (1969; rpt. London: Fontana Press, 1989), p. 430; Charles Camic, *Experience and Enlightenment:*

Socialization for Cultural Change in Eighteenth-Century Scotland (Chicago: University of Chicago Press, 1983), p. 160).

94. Maisie Steven, *Parish Life in Eighteenth-Century Scotland: A Review of the Old Statistical Account* (Aberdeen: Scottish Cultural Press, 1995), ch. 9; Henry Gray Graham, *Social Life of Scotland in the Eighteenth Century*, 4th edn (1937; rpt. London: Adam & Charles Black, 1950), ch. 11.

95. "Parish of Borthwick," p. 74; Steven, *Parish Life*, p. 54.

96. Marion Lochhead, *The Scots Household in the Eighteenth Century: A Century of Scottish Domestic and Social Life* (Edinburgh: Moray Press, 1948), p. 231.

97. "Parish of Borthwick," p. 74.

98. Law, *Education in Edinburgh*, p. 58; Camic, *Experience and Enlightenment*, p. 138, says the age is seven.

99. Marjorie Plant, *Domestic Life of Scotland in the Eighteenth Century* (Edinburgh: Edinburgh University Press, 1952), p. 8.

100. Camic, *Experience and Enlightenment*, p. 138, citing Bower, *History*, III, 25, and Alexander Allardyce, "Introduction," in *Scotland and Scotsmen in the Eighteenth Century*, ed. Allardyce, 2 vols (Edinburgh, 1888), I, x.

101. "Account," in *Miscellaneous Works*, p. 103. Leslie was the father of John Leslie, professor of Greek at King's College, Aberdeen (Bower, *History*, III, 25), with whom the historian corresponded (see Robertson to Leslie, 4 May 1770, in *Scottish Historical Review* 13 (1916), pp. 40–1) and who was one of the signatories on the historian's honorary degree conferred by King's College in 1764.

102. *New Statistical Account of Scotland*, 15 vols (Edinburgh, 1845), I, 525.

103. NLS MS 3,979, f. 22; Law, *Education in Edinburgh*, p. 59.

104. *History*, III, 25.

105. Law, *Education*, p. 58; Graham, *Social Life*, p. 443, n.2.

106. James Grant, *History of the Burgh Schools of Scotland* (London, 1876), p. 413.

107. *Scots Origins* at http://www.origins.net (Old Parish Register Index, extract no. 2424597); *Roll of Edinburgh Burgesses and Guild-Brethren, 1406–1700*, ed. Charles B. Boog Watson (Edinburgh: Scottish Record Society, 1929), p. 174.

108. M. A. Stewart "Hume's Intellectual Development, 1711–1752," in *Impressions of Hume*, ed. M. Frasca-Spada and P. J. E. Kail (Oxford: Clarendon Press, 2005), p. 17.

109. "Matriculation Roll of the University of Edinburgh Arts, Law, Divinity," transcribed by Alexander Morgan, 4 vols, typescript (Edinburgh: Edinburgh University Library, 1933–4), s.v., 1735. Carlyle confirms the possibility of Robertson's beginning in November 1734 because he remarks that Robertson entered College "one session before me" (*Autobiography*, p. 53); Carlyle entered on 1 November 1735, enrolling in Ker's humanity class (ibid., p. 34). But Dugald Stewart maintains that Robertson joined the family in 1733 upon their moving to Edinburgh and enrolled in the

university "towards the end of the same year" ("Account," in *Miscellaneous Works*, p. 103). John Erskine ("Agency," in *Miscellaneous Works*, p. 262) says that he and Robertson became acquainted in Ker's humanity class in 1737, not 1734–5. Henry Moncreiff Wellwood discusses the problem without reaching a conclusion (*Account of the Life and Writings of John Life of Erskine* (1818; rpt. Bristol: Thoemmes Press, 1997), pp. 14–17). Stewart's date of 1733 is discounted by the evidence of the matriculation roll. The discrepancy among the dates recorded in the matriculation roll and in Carlyle's and Erskine's accounts may be explained by the fact that Ker offered two "colleges." At both Glasgow and Edinburgh, humanity professors offered both an ordinary class and a private class for more advanced work (M. L. Clarke, *Classical Education in Britain 1500–1800* (Cambridge: Cambridge University Press, 1959), p. 143). The first was public and general, focused on the basic elements of Latin grammar and rhetoric; the second private, focused on a selection of major Latin authors. In 1741 at Edinburgh, the former ran from 1 October to the end of July, while the latter ran from 1 November to 1 June (Alexander Grant, *The Story of the University of Edinburgh during Its First Three Hundred Years*, 2 vols (London, 1884), I, 266). It may be that Robertson took one "college" in 1734–5 and another in 1737. There is a William Robertson enrolled for Ker's class in February 1737, and we know he was enrolled in Stevenson's that same spring.

110. Smout, *History*, p. 449.
111. Robertson to Elliot, 15 October 1755, NLS MS 16,693, ff. 95–6.
112. *Proposals for Carrying on Certain Public Works* (Edinburgh, 1752), p. 7.
113. *A Directory of Edinburgh in 1752*, comp. J. Gilhooley (Edinburgh: Edinburgh University Press, 1988), p. 48.
114. *The Register of Marriages for the Parish of Edinburgh, 1701–1750*, ed. Henry Paton (Edinburgh: Scottish Record Society, 1908), p. 71.
115. *Directory*, comp. Gilhooley, p. 58.
116. Ibid., p. 76.
117. Chambers, *Traditions*, p. 80.
118. William Strahan to Robertson, 22 February 1759, MS 3,942, ff. 23–4, addressed "To The Reverend Dr. Robertson One of the Ministers of Edinr. At his House near the Head of Cowgate."
119. Houston, *Social Change*, p. 130.
120. "Memorial Relating to the University of Edinburgh, 1768," in *Miscellaneous Works*, p. 132.
121. Ibid., pp. 131–2.
122. P. Hume Brown, quoted in *Trial of Captain Porteous*, ed. William Roughead (Glasgow: William Hodge, 1909), p. 1. My narrative of events is indebted to Roughead.
123. *Autobiography*, p. 39.
124. Ibid., p. 41.
125. Ibid., pp. 42–3.

126. Ibid., p. 41.
127. Ibid.
128. *Account of the Cruel Massacre Committed by John Porteous* (n. p., 1789), p. 5–6.
129. Quoted in Robert McNeil, *The Porteous Riot* (n. p., n. d.), p. 19.
130. *Trial*, ed. Roughead, p. 242.
131. Quoted in ibid., p. 238.
132. EUL MS ROB, pp. 25–40.
133. *Autobiography*, p. 45.
134. See J. Madden, *A Memorial for the People of Scotland, or Some Brief Animadversions on the Infamous Act of the British Parliament* (Dublin, 1737).
135. *Autobiography*, p. 46.
136. Ibid., p. 47.
137. Houston, *Social Change*, p. 318.
138. See Chapter 6 below for further discussion.
139. *History of Scotland*, in *Works of Robertson*, I, 445–6.
140. Ibid., II, 240.

CHAPTER 2

Education of a Minister, 1734–1744

When young William Robertson entered the University of Edinburgh in 1734–5, he became part of a university, which, like the city, was in the midst of transformation. The intellectual environment both in and around the university was lively as the thought of Francis Hutcheson, John Locke, and the Earl of Shaftesbury collided with traditional Calvinist forms and beliefs. Such intellectual debate was facilitated by the abolition of the regent system by William Carstares in 1708. Under this older system, each instructor taught a cohort of students all subjects as they moved through in a fixed curriculum. Drawing on his experience with Dutch universities, Carstares instituted reforms in the arts curriculum to begin appointment of specialized professors responsible for teaching a specific discipline, and by the 1730s the new system was solidly in place, and its effects were notable.[1] The professors of arts acquired a new energy and distinction based on their expertise, making them the "midwife" to the Scottish Enlightenment's republic of letters.[2] For the students, the benefits were mixed. They were no longer kept within a fixed curriculum, and they had a greater range of choices among classes. But they were no longer under pressure to complete a curriculum or to graduate. William Robertson is a case in point: he enrolled for classes in the academic years 1734–5, 1735–6, 1736–7, 1738–9, and 1739–40,[3] but he never felt it necessary to take a degree, or to spread himself – at least formally – across the whole of the offered curriculum. He took the basic arts courses in Latin, Greek, and logic (including rhetoric and literary criticism) that were expected of students preparing for the ministry. In addition, he studied history and theology, although his son William told Dugald Stewart that history did not seem to be one of his father's favorite studies.[4] Nor does he appear to have branched out into mathematics, moral philosophy, or natural philosophy, subjects that were not required for the church. But we do learn the historian's "favourite Studies Seem in the early period of his life to have been Philosophy and particularly the Stoic Philos: of which he was a great Admirer."[5]

The picture of his interests would be clearer if the commonplace books that Robertson kept during this period had survived. Stewart described them as central symbols of Robertson's character because they "bear marks of a persevering assiduity, unexampled perhaps at so tender an age; and the motto prefixed to all of them, '*Vita sine literis mors est*,' attests how soon those views and sentiments were formed, which to his latest hour, continued to guide and to dignify his ambition."[6] Although Stewart said they covered just the years 1735–7, William Robertson indicated there were others for "[17]38 &c."[7] Moreover, the inventory of papers done at Robertson's death mentions "A parcel of my Father's juvenile Common place Books" but leaves us to wonder how large a parcel it was.[8] The last recorded appearance of the commonplace books was in 1827, when they were in the hands of Lord Brougham, who had borrowed them from Lord Robertson as he was thinking about writing his memoir of Robertson.[9] But if we do not know first-hand what Robertson took away from his classes (with the exception of one surviving essay), the teachers he encountered indicate the diverse intellectual cross-currents he found as a student.

Robertson is twice registered for John Ker's humanity class, once in 1734–5 and again in 1736–7, and these enrollments were for Ker's public class and his more advanced private class.[10] In the public class, starting with Caesar, Ker moved to prose selections from Sallust, Cicero, and Livy and then to poetry with selections from Virgil, Horace, and Juvenal, all accompanied by texts in grammar, rhetoric, and geography. The private class focused on texts by Plautus or Terence, Horace, Cicero, Tacitus, and perhaps Suetonius or Pliny.[11] One feature of the class Robertson may have found especially useful was the composition and delivery of Latin orations, a task that he would perform for several years as university principal.[12] Ker himself, who moved to Edinburgh from his post as professor of Greek at the University of Aberdeen just as Robertson entered in 1734, was an accomplished Latin poet and a Jacobite, having written, among other poems, two fine elegies for one of Scotland's more notable Jacobites, Archibald Pitcairne. Although no examples of Robertson's work in Latin poetry remain, Ker seems to have earned his students' respect and affection. Carlyle believed he was "a master of his business"; John Erskine acknowledged that "great was [his] success, in exciting and directing their study of the Latin classics"; and, as a result, Robertson "acquired a rich fund of instruction and entertainment."[13] One personal mark of his immersion in Latin poetry was a fondness for Virgil throughout his life.[14]

In his second year, 1735–6, Robertson was enrolled in Colin Drummond's Greek class. Nearly at the end of his career, Drummond was old and sick, employing frequent substitutes to cover his classes.[15] Besides often relying on substitutes, Drummond may also have been distracted with financial problems.[16] Drummond had previously been a regent and, when the system disappeared, held the chair of Logic and Metaphysics, where he had taught David Hume as a student. Hume was disgusted by the course, in which religious values were prominent, and it gave him "an edifice to destroy, not a path to follow."[17] In 1730 he transferred to the chair of Greek, thus making way for John Stevenson, whom he soon found to be a troublesome rival. But Drummond's tenure in the Greek chair was not a success, and in 1734, in the face of diminishing numbers of students enrolling for his class, he drew on a recommendation from a parliamentary visitation made in 1699 to file a petition with the Edinburgh Town Council requesting that Greek be a mandatory class for all students. His complaint was aimed at teachers like his colleague John Stevenson, the current holder of the Logic and Rhetoric chair who taught Longinus and Aristotle and thus in Drummond's eyes had invaded the right of the Greek chair.[18] But the Council declined to approve the petition. In 1735 Drummond apparently tried a different tack and sought (unsuccessfully) to secure a transfer from the Greek chair to the chair of Moral Philosophy. Although Robertson probably found Drummond's religious values more of a pathway than Hume did, Drummond's Greek class was doubtless pedestrian. Yet Robertson felt skilled enough to attempt a translation of Marcus Aurelius beginning in January 1742, in the interim between university studies and entering the ministry, and Brougham judged him to be a "perfect master" of the language.[19]

In his third year, 1736–7, Robertson enrolled in Ker's private class as well as the class of Drummond's rival, John Stevenson. Stevenson's course in logic and rhetoric was the most celebrated class in the university,[20] and Carlyle captured the sense of excitement the students felt:

> Whether or not it was owing to the time of life at which we entered this class, being all about fifteen years of age or upwards, when the mind begins to open, or to the excellence of the lectures and the nature of some of the subjects, we could not then say, but all of us received greater benefit from that class than from any other.[21]

Taking the class some twenty years after Carlyle did, Thomas Somerville still praised Stevenson in almost exactly the same terms: "I derived more substantial benefit from these exercises and lectures than from all the public classes which I attended in the University."[22] During Robertson's first year as principal (1762–3), he delivered a Latin address to Stevenson's class that echoed his enthusiasm of earlier years: "Here I first approached the source of philosophy; here I derived knowledge of many subjects, which remain even now preserved in my deepest thoughts, which I often recall with greatest pleasure and no less usefulness."[23] Yet Stevenson was a modest presence in the classroom, Peter Jones calling him a lightweight,[24] and his obituary in the *Edinburgh Magazine and Review* noting: "His lectures were solid rather than brilliant, formal rather than penetrating. But, if he wanted the boldness of invention and genius, he possessed amply the advantages which flow from study and knowledge."[25]

What, then, accounts for the lasting impact he had on these students? In Jones's view, Stevenson made his students members of the wider intellectual world, partly through his own charm and humanity and partly by challenging them with contemporary debates. But comments like Robertson's also stress something more basic. What Stevenson offered his students was what today we might call critical thinking. As stimulating as his readings of Longinus and the *Ars Poetica* were for his students, one key innovation in his class was the introduction of Lockean philosophy. The description of his class in the *Scots Magazine* emphasizes its philosophic content:

> He gives lectures upon *Heineccii Elementa Philosophiae rationalis*, and the abridgement of Mr. Locke's *Essay on Human Understanding*: in which he explains all the different forms of Reasoning, the nature of Certainty both Mathematical and moral, with the different degrees of Probability; and shews how the understanding is to be conducted in our enquiries after Truth of all kinds.[26]

Stevenson dealt with "big ideas," and that is why Robertson spoke to Stevenson's class of reaching the sources of philosophy and why the class had such a lasting impact on him. It also explains the content of the only surviving academic writing from Robertson's university years, an essay he wrote for Stevenson covering the topics listed in the description. The essay is preserved in a collection written by Stevenson's students for presentation to the class between 1737 and 1750. The authors represent a good cross-section of the future educated elite in Scotland, and they illustrate the topics he treated – not only philosophical subjects but also taste, literary criticism, and education. It develops a pattern of thought that he would carry with him into all his historical and religious thinking.

Titled "De probabilitate historica, sive evidentia moralis," the essay treats probable reasoning, condensing Book IV, Chapters 13–20, of Locke's *Essay concerning Human Understanding*. Robertson's method of thought not just in this student essay but throughout his career may be described as an incorporation of Locke into his Presbyterian beliefs. Robertson focuses on evidence of which we have "no absolute certainty," distinguishing the varying degrees of belief that we can place in such ideas.[27] That topic alone is significant because one of the key issues between conservative and more liberal Calvinists in Edinburgh in the 1730s was precisely how much faith can be put in merely probable ideas.[28] To what extent, in other words, can we rely on the light of nature as opposed to the light of faith? In his essay, Robertson does not address revealed truth directly, though he does allow that

> the greatest and most useful part of our learning and knowledge, the truth about what has been done, and whatever can be comprehended under the name of history, even including faith in our most holy Christian religion, depends on and is sustained by testimony of this sort, as on a foundation (of a building).[29]

The image of the foundation of a building ("fundamento nititur & sustentatur"[30]) implies that probable reasoning offers support to both religion and history provided it is conducted with rigorous care, pays attention to the weight of evidence, and abides by the canons of logic.

Following this starting point, he distinguishes six forms of evidence in historical probability, concluding: "Evidence of this kind, therefore, does not seize nor compel our assent as mathematical evidence normally does, but most certainly it wins it."[31] But Robertson then turns to confront an important religious question. Why does human nature have the capacity to give rational assent to probable evidence? "[W]e must admit," he argues, "this faculty has been given to us for this reason, that we use it in investigating the truth, and once it has been found, in embracing it."[32] We can trust probable reasoning because it confirms the truth of God's goodness: "It would afflict the infinite perfections of God with most grievous insult, if we were to suspect him of having created an animal so crude, so shameless, so misshapen, that obscurity motivated its faculties, and uncertainty by itself could determine its course of action."[33] "God the Best and Greatest" has created congruence between the light of nature and the light of faith, in which they are complementary, not competitive, and provide each other mutual support. As he declared in a sermon of 1760, "we do not live in a world of anarchy & confusion," and "we have by ye light of reason and more so by revelation, knowledge of what is fit & certainty of God protecting us."[34]

In 1737–8, Robertson did not enroll in the university perhaps because he was severely ill. Certainly, the winter of this year was conducive to illness. According to one contemporary, in the period of December through February, "there was the most severe frost in this country that perhaps was ever felt."[35] Carlyle alludes to Robertson's bad health when he mentions becoming acquainted with Robertson during the fall and winter of 1737–8 even though he was never in the same class with him. To emphasize the disparity in their curricular patterns, he adds vaguely that "One of the years, too, he was seized with a fever, which was dangerous, and confined him for the greater part of the winter."[36] Because there is no record of enrollment for Robertson, the year 1737–8 looks to be a good candidate for this missing year. Possibly Robertson started the year with a class in October or November but then became ill and dropped out before signing the matriculation roll in late winter. The nature of the illness itself is uncertain. One possibility, especially given Robertson's age (16), is rheumatic fever, which is common among early adolescents and could certainly have the chronic effects Carlyle mentions. Severe recurrent pneumonia could be another diagnosis, and it is certainly the case that Robertson suffered over his lifetime a number of debilitating breakdowns accompanied by heavy chest and head congestion. The periods of deafness attending these breakdowns seriously troubled him, and their frequency and intensity increased with age. Although Robertson may have suffered deafness from other, perhaps congenital, causes as well, the congestion made it even more acute.[37] Lord Cockburn described him in his later years as wearing a small hearing trumpet fastened to his coat, and "when his eye told him that there was something interesting, it was delightful to observe the animation with which he instantly applied his trumpet, when having caught the scent, he followed it up, and was leader of the pack."[38] But behind this charming picture, we see also that deafness seriously troubled a great talker like Robertson, who complained that it isolated him and who vividly described his symptoms: "Yesterday for this first time this ten weeks I heard the ticking of my watch with my left ear, so that now I hope to get the better of this fit of deafness."[39] One response to the isolation of deafness for a great talker is to dominate conversations, a fault often ascribed to Robertson.[40]

Robertson's health improved during the following year, and records indicate that, together with his close friend John Home, he enrolled in Charles Mackie's universal history class in 1738–9, running from November to the end of May.[41] Henderson tells us that Mackie followed Orazio Torsellino's *Epitome historiarum, ab urbe condito, usque ad annum 1595*, and in his lectures, he

> explains the great revolutions that have happened in the world. After the declension of the Roman empire in the West, he gives us an account of the migrations and settlement of the several nations which overspread that empire, and of the different forms of government by them introduced; upon the ruins of which the present constitutions of most countries in Europe are founded. He likewise shews the rise and progress of the Papal tyranny, &c.[42]

The course left an impression on him because this description clearly suggests Robertson's future work in the introductory volume of *Charles V.*

Torsellino's work is very basic, consisting of brief year-by-year summaries of universal history from Genesis to 1598 with a continuation to 1642. Judging from surviving documents, Mackie used Torsellino as a skeleton, fleshing out his bare summaries by elaborating on events and by including a broad cultural perspective, treating the arts and social history. From his sermon on *The Situation of the World at the Time of Christ's Nativity* (1755) to the *Historical Disquisition on the Knowledge the Ancient Had of India* (1791), Robertson would see history unfolding from a broad perspective, passing from biblical and Roman history, through the emergence of modern Europe and colonial expansion westward in the sixteenth and seventeenth centuries and eastward to trade with India.

But in Mackie as a teacher Robertson found a congenial spirit as well as a historical plan and inspiration that he could develop. Mackie was related to William Carstares, and he had responsibility for Carstares' papers, which he preserved "with a religious care" until he passed them on, shortly before his death in 1770, to his executor, Robertson's close friend Joseph Maccormick, who introduced his edition of them with a short biography.[43] According to Maccormick, Mackie "had lived much in Mr. Carstares's family in the early part of his life, and, by that means, had access to be acquainted with many circumstances in his private deportment and character, unknown to the world."[44] Those circumstances included Maccormick's assertion that Carstares' values stemmed from Holland: his "principles, both in religion and politics, were mightily confirmed by his residence in that country, and by his personal attachment to a Prince who was the avowed patron of all the friends of liberty."[45] Carstares would have been right at home in the Robertson family theological library with its Arminian tendencies; and it is scarcely a surprise that Mackie himself was a Mason, a Whig, and a member of the Revolution Club,[46] which Robertson himself would join in 1748 and having, in the words of his diploma of membership, "Declared the Gratfull Sense he has of the Deliverance of the Kingdoms of Great Britain & Ireland from Popery & Slavery by King William and Queen Mary."[47]

But the affinity of Robertson and Mackie runs even deeper. Both Carstares and Mackie built their historical positions on skepticism. Carstares' advocacy of toleration was based at least in part on his belief that "difference in opinion was the natural effect of the weakness and corruption of the human mind,"[48] a principle consistent with the mitigated skepticism found in Arminian thought. Likewise, one of the central themes in Mackie's surviving lecture notes is the possibility of error in history and the necessity of separating reliable from unreliable sources.[49] Typical is his paper on "The Sources of Vulgar Errors in History and

How to Detect and Verify Them," read to the Philosophical Society on 4 March 1741. It catalogues seven causes of error, with Mackie maintaining as his guiding principle: "When events are related several different ways, 'tis a certain rule in history that we ought to suspect falsity . . . Truth is single, & cannot be related several different ways."[50] Such an acute awareness of error leads to the tolerance, caution, and peacemaking in debatable issues, a stance we found in the elder Robertson's sermon as well as implicit in his son's "Probabilitate historica."

After completing Mackie's class in the spring of 1739, Robertson moved to the Divinity Hall during his next two years at the university to conclude his ministerial training. It was not necessary to complete a university degree, but prospective ministers were required to enroll in the theology class. Three courses were offered, all overseen by the General Assembly: Hebrew, church history, and theology, though only one of them, theology, was required. Carlyle reports that the instruction in theology was limited and dull. John Gowdie, whom Carlyle described as "dull, and Dutch, and prolix," inched his way through Benedict Pictet's *Theologia christiana* (1696), lecturing on just half of it over a period of seven years.[51] A determined but plodding moderate in his thinking, Gowdie opposed the evangelicals during the Marrow controversy, was a defender of John Simson, and was moderator of the General Assembly in 1733, casting the deciding vote to depose Ebenezer Erskine.[52] For such efforts, Gowdie came under the patronage of the Argathelian interests and was rewarded with the principalship of the university in 1754, ultimately to be succeeded as principal by his student Robertson in 1762, who was left with the task of reinvigorating the university after Gowdie's ineffectual tenure.

But if Gowdie was dull, prolix, and ineffectual, he was also learned and sincere, and Robertson may have gained something from him. Although Gowdie was moderator when the Edinburgh presbytery initially refused to sustain the call of William Wishart to Edinburgh in 1736, his surviving sermons, for example, show a simple, unadorned, albeit conservative version of moderate ideas and one that Robertson, though he would add considerable nuance, could have accepted. Among the general tenets the two men would share are such standard points as Gowdie's embrace of the Reformation as a second revelation; his firm belief in the importance of church unity in the face of Catholic threats and internal dissension; his endorsement of the necessity of good works and rejection of reliance on deathbed conversions as opposed to a lifetime of deeds; his distrust of party spirit in the church; and his advocacy of "affectionate *pathos*" in delivering sermons because "Our discourses must not come from us like a violent torrent, that carries down all before it; but like a thick gentle shower, that sinks into the earth, and softens it."[53] Perhaps the most striking connection appears when we place Gowdie's thinking beside the *Reasons of Dissent* that Robertson and his colleagues would write in 1752 and would become the "cornerstone of Moderate thinking about church and society."[54] Gowdie comments on the importance of maintaining order within the church structure and doctrine so as not to stir anxiety in the populace:

> To appeal to the People in these Matters, is to appeal, for the most Part, to an incompetent Judge; a Judge that cannot weigh the Reasons on each Side; that ordinarily hears only the Arguments of one Side; that is, for the most Part, determined by Affection rather than Judgment, and an implicite Faith rather than a well informed Understanding.[55]

Sentiments like these ally him with the Whig-Presbyterian conservatism that *Reasons of Dissent* strongly articulates. At the same time, Gowdie appears to have been open to currents of thought inspired by Arminianism. While Robertson was in the Divinity Hall, one of the exercises prescribed him was a history of those theological doctrines condemned by the Synod of Dort.[56] The small library Robertson's father had compiled whose impact on Robertson led to his "early and high esteem" for the thought of the Continental Arminians doubtless played an important role in his writing the exercise. The finished product, *De historia Arminianorum usque ad finem Synodi Dodracenae*, would become the chronological discourse he delivered during his trials before the presbytery of Dalkeith a few years later. Of course, these views hardly make Gowdie the father of the Moderates, but he did, despite the weaknesses that Carlyle characterized, perhaps help shape Robertson's Moderatism alongside more notable figures like Mackie and Stevenson.

These are the figures whose classes Robertson is known to have attended, but two other Edinburgh teachers deserve attention because their impact was widespread across the university. The first is Colin Maclaurin, the most important Scottish mathematician and natural philosopher of the period and the best interpreter of Newton in the Enlightenment. Arriving in Edinburgh in 1725 from Marischal College, Aberdeen, Maclaurin had established his courses as key to the dissemination of Newtonian ideas. Thomas Seccombe claimed that Robertson attended his lectures, but his only source is Dugald Stewart's vague allusion: "The bent of his [Robertson's] genius did not incline him to mathematical or physical pursuits, notwithstanding the strong recommendations he derived from the popular talents of Mr. Maclaurin; but he could not fail to receive advantage from the eloquence with which that illustrious man knew how to adorn the most abstracted subjects."[57] But even if Robertson did not attend lectures, he would still be well aware of the implications of Newtonianism. As we saw in the essay he wrote for Stevenson, the world is open to rational investigation, and on that basis Newtonianism readily became a strong defense for Christianity. In a letter of 1714, Maclaurin justified his efforts to establish gravitation as a universal law on the grounds that "'tis a sort of impiety to have no regard to the course of nature and frame of nature as indeed it is a piece of real worship to contemplate the great beautiful drama of nature, the admirable law by which the world's great Lord rules this his workmanship.'"[58] The application of such thinking to history and the course of Revelation would become the subject of his first published sermon, *The Situation of the World*.[59] We are equipped by virtue of faith to understand the unfolding drama of Revelation in history, just as we are equipped by mathematical reasoning in the discoveries of Newton to understand the complementary drama of nature.

One other prominent figure may have helped to synthesize religion and scientific thinking in Robertson's mind: William Wishart, whom M. A. Stewart describes as "one of the most significant and progressive figures at Edinburgh University and in the Scottish church in the generation between William Carstairs and William Robertson."[60] He was nominated to be principal late in 1736 but was not appointed to his ministerial charge in New Greyfriars until February 1739. The delay was caused by the Edinburgh presbytery's objections to two of his early sermons that claimed "there is . . . a disposition of Benevolence, or social affection in Human Nature, independent of all deliberate views of self-interest," an idea drawn from Francis Hutcheson, whom Wishart styled "my worthy and ingenious friend."[61] For stricter Calvinists, Hutcheson-inspired ideas not only seemed to contradict God's eternal decree of the corruption of human nature as stated in the *Confession of Faith* but also were in violation of the *Confession*'s provisions for liberty of conscience, with one pamphlet going so far as to compare Wishart's influence to that of freethinkers such as Matthew Tindal, Anthony Collins, William Wollaston, and Bernard Mandeville.[62] Despite his controversial appointment, Wishart quickly settled into his role and brought new vigor and energy to the university's leadership. Although as principal, Wishart did no formal teaching, he engaged both students and professors by reviving the practice of delivering, as principal and as professor of divinity, public orations upon literary, philosophical, or theological subjects.[63] For Robertson's colleague John Erskine, who shared much with Robertson and his circle of Moderates despite his evangelical leanings, Wishart was a dedicated academic, playing close attention to individual student progress and achievement.[64]

He earned Erskine's praise in particular for "depth of knowledge, origi-
nality of genius, and the art of gaining attention to the most common and
necessary subjects, by new reflections, illustrations and arrangements."[65]
It is unlikely that Robertson would fail to be impressed by such a figure,
and in fact his subsequent writings echo some of Wishart's ideas.

One of Wishart's leading ideas chimed well with Robertson's early
thinking about history and Newtonian philosophy: the importance of
incremental progress in moral and spiritual development. At the heart of
Wishart's view of the Christian life is a conception of gradual improvement that parallels Newton's. In an essay published in 1753, though probably written earlier, Wishart argues that:

> The *perfection* of any creature is the foundation of its *happiness*; and the *utmost*
> happiness any creature is capable of, is only to be obtained in the state of its *utmost*
> perfection: and as the true perfection of *such* creatures as *we* are, consists in rational
> and virtuous improvements, it is only so far as we advance in these that we can enjoy
> our true happiness; and in all nature, the most perfect state of any creature does
> not take place *all at once*, but arises from *small beginnings*, by a *gradual* and beautiful
> progress.[66]

Robertson repeats this moral theme throughout his sermons, as captured
in the notes taken by David Dalrymple, in statements such as

> the life of holiness is progressive & if we do not gain, we must lose ground [4 March
> 1759]

> in the next life will be the fulfilling of those begun graces [i.e. graces begun on earth]
> [18 March 1759]

> Their works follow them. Their good dispositions are perfected in another state [15
> August 1762]

> yᵗ religion was progressive: as in a journey, at every height a new prospect arises [and]
> the encouragement for us in this progressive state [dated only as 2 September].[67]

It is a small step from Wishart's emphasis on the moral progress of the
individual to Robertson's argument in the *Situation of the World* that
the larger plan of Providence for entire peoples also unfolds by gradual
development. Sacred and civil history, together with the personal moral
world, were capable of progressive motion toward a final fulfillment, and
Wishart's gradualist thinking likely had a share in shaping Robertson's
belief in continuing progress toward an ever-fuller divine revelation.

Ideas were, of course, disseminated very effectively outside the classroom and lecture halls among students themselves, just as they continue to be today. In his discussion of John Gowdie's boring theology class, Carlyle cynically suggested that dull teachers like Gowdie could not form a school, and students were therefore left to themselves to create more interesting intellectual experiences and more liberal opinions.[68] He points to the circle of students that he shared with Robertson comprising the younger generation of Moderates: Hugh Blair, George and Hew Bannatyne, John Jardine, John Blair, John Home, George Logan, and William Wilkie. All of these would pursue clerical careers, though John Blair would join the Church of England. Although Carlyle seems to imply this was a more or less organized group, he merely says that he became acquainted with them in this context. Stewart also names several of these same individuals and adds William McGhie and William Cleghorn, commenting that they formed a "society, where their object was to cultivate the study of elocution, and to prepare themselves, by the habits of extemporary discussion and debate, for conducting the business of popular assemblies."[69] Davis D. McElroy adds Alexander Wedderburn to the group and asserts that "All of these men, in fact, were members of the *same* debating club."[70] These descriptions may perhaps all be of the famous Hen Club, which, according to Henry Moncrieff Wellwood, included "gentlemen who had attended the Humanity Class at Edinburgh in 1737, 1738, and 1739," and he adds John Erskine to this group for good measure.[71] Wellwood tells us the Hen Club endured for fifty years, and Carlyle reports a meeting of the club in 1793 where all the participants were over seventy.[72] Hugh Blair endorsed debating clubs because they accustomed students "to know their own powers, and to acquire a command of themselves in speaking; and what is, perhaps, the greatest advantage of all, they give them a facility and fluency of expression, and assist them in procuring that *Copia verborum*, which can be acquired by no other means but frequent exercise in speaking."[73] Likewise, during his principalship, Robertson constantly encouraged the formation of such societies because of their great benefit to the students.[74]

But the debating societies had their critics. One complained that "I do not see that our knowledge is by any means increased, on account of the multitude of our disputes. On the contrary, I think these disputes stand very much in the way of learning, and are at present almost an insuperable obstacle."[75] Wellwood describes a crucial incident involving Robertson and Erskine that illustrates the dangers and the consequences of student clubs. George Whitefield, the dissenting Anglican minister, visited Scotland in the summer of 1741 and 1742, and his visits launched the revival at Cambuslang with its powerful evangelical outpouring. According to Wellwood, the society to which Erskine and Robertson belonged took up the topic of Whitefield's "character and usefulness," with Robertson and Erskine on opposite sides. The debate "was agitated with so much zeal and asperity, that it occasioned the dissolution of their society, and is said to have, for some time, interrupted even their intercourse in private life."[76] We do not know what exactly the subject was of the debate, but whatever it was it was significant. Erskine was profoundly affected by the Cambuslang revival, so much so that it determined his future course in the ministry. He became assured of his vocation, switching his studies from law to divinity, and he expressed his thoughts in his first pamphlet, *The Signs of the Times Consider'd*, published in 1742.[77] Robertson was as skeptical of the revival as Erskine was moved by it, and he, too, felt he must take a stand by beginning, in the midst of the evangelical turmoil, what he must have intended to be a publishable translation of the *Meditations* of Marcus Aurelius. Although he did not complete or publish the translation, what we have reveals much about how he read the signs of the times, and his reading sheds light on the nature of the dispute.

Robertson began working on his translation on 21 January 1742, according to the date affixed to Book I, coinciding with the first stirrings of the Cambuslang Revival. He completed the first seven books before breaking off sometime around mid-April or the beginning of May after translating the second article of Book VIII.[78] The likely reason was that on 13 May he found himself pre-empted by the first advertisement for the translation by Francis Hutcheson and James Moor in Edinburgh's *Caledonian Mercury*. Robertson may have been disappointed because, along with Montesquieu, he must have believed Marcus "made men feel the sweetness of virtue and the dignity of their being."[79] Perhaps first planted by his mother, Robertson's interest in Marcus would have been piqued in Stevenson's university class because one segment of the course covered the lives of philosophers, he may have worked with Marcus' Greek in Drummond's class, and he may have gained an appreciation of Marcus' contemporary importance in religious controversy from Wishart.[80] When Robertson attended his first General Assembly meeting as the minister of Gladsmuir in 1746,[81] Wishart gave the opening sermon, and Robertson would have responded warmly to Wishart's allusion to Marcus:

> That *Society* is natural to Men, and necessary to their Improvement and Perfection; both the natural Abilities, and the natural Weaknesses of Mankind concur to shew.
>
> The Powers we are furnished with; the Affections of our Hearts; the Circumstances of mutual Dependence, in which we are placed; and the Opportunities afforded us, of giving mutual Assistance; do *all* speak us formed by the great Parent of Mankind, not to stand, each of us, by himself, or improve alone: but to be *all* Members of one

Body; every Part of which is preserved, and its Welfare promoted by mutual Aids: To be Citizens of the World, as one common City, under Divine Government.[82]

The message of social virtue contained within Marcus' Stoicism was very much in the air: it had been vividly presented in "The Stoic," an essay in the second volume of Hume's *Essays: Moral and Political*, which appeared in January just as Robertson was beginning his translation;[83] and it was the central theme in the Hutcheson/Moor translation. It seems also to have been one of the sparks that kindled Robertson's desire to write the translation in opposition to the evangelism of Whitefield and his followers.

Although we do not know the exact topic over which the debating society dissolved, the historical context in which their religious differences were aired is clear. In February 1741, William McCullogh, the minister at Cambuslang, having been inspired by the Great Awakening in America, began preaching on the subject of spiritual regeneration. At the same time, between July and October 1741, Whitefield made an extensive speaking tour through Scotland at the invitation of Ralph and Ebenezer Erskine, stirring a wider evangelical following. By early 1742, McCullough's following began to increase so that in April he wrote to Whitefield for assistance. The Cambuslang Wark reached its climax in the summer of 1742 with extraordinary emotional and physical displays among the spiritually awakened, including, in Erskine's description, "Crying, Faintings, Tremblings, and other such like bodily Agitations."[84] These manifestations are to be expected "along with the Down-pouring of the Spirit" because the events at Cambuslang were certain signs of future regeneration. They foretell the coming of "the glorious Days of the Church before the End of Time," which will be remarkable for the "Multitude of these who shall be convinced of their lost and undone State by Nature, and made willing to embrace an offered Saviour."[85] Not only are congregations reborn but also collegiate and church structures will have to give way:

Has not God endued many of our own Ministers with uncommon Zeal for promoting the Interests of his Kingdom, and given them *the Tongue of the Learned to speak a Word in Season to weary Souls*? And have not even some, whose Gifts were reckoned mean and contemptible of late found an uncommon measure of Divine Assistance in their publick Ministrations, and *seen the Pleasure of the Lord prospering in their Hands*?[86]

Although Erskine sought to moderate enthusiasm and avoid narrow sectarian viewpoints, his endorsement of the revival was something that young clerical students could well dispute.[87]

How, then, is Robertson's translation of the *Meditations* a reply to

Erskine's thinking? Robertson stakes out his position in terms of both ideology and style. Lying behind Robertson's interest in Stoicism was not only his education but also the issue addressed in his father's published sermon and, less directly, in Robertson's student essay: how much should be granted to the concerns of this world, and how much to the next? Reason tells us this world is knowable, and knowledge is a sign of God's benevolent superintendence; but salvation demands we reject this world and devote all our energies to our coming eternal life. The issue was sparked by Hutcheson's ideas, as we saw in the case of William Wishart's battle for ministerial appointment, but the issue very soon was widely discussed.[88] For Robertson, Marcus provided an eloquent defense of reason in the face of what he and his colleagues saw as exclusive, irrational claims of faith emerging from the revival. But the issue was not simply the opposition of the light of reason to the light of faith. A place had to be found to accommodate both.

To gain a sense of how Robertson might have seen events in opposition to Erskine, we can turn to George Wishart, the younger brother of William Wishart, minister at the Tron Church, though both were ministers of the elder Robertson's generation who helped to lay the groundwork for the Moderate party.[89] In a sermon of 4 January 1742, George Wishart alludes obliquely to the revivals of the previous summer and fall, describing

> that false religious Zeal which belongs to Enthusiasm and Superstition; when People have not been at Pains to exercise their Reason and Judgment in religious Matters, but have given themselves up to the Dictates of wild Fancy and Imagination, and are governed by mere Passion in these Matters; from this springs Rage and Fury in behalf of what is fancied sacred and divine.[90]

In November 1742, Wishart sharpened his critique. Fresh on the heels of Erskine's *Signs of the Times*, he published in Edinburgh a letter written by the anti-evangelical Charles Chauncy in Boston concerning the revivals in America that were coincidental with those in Scotland. In the revivalist churches, Chauncy saw the living embodiment of Wishart's general concerns. The revival had brought indecency and disorder into the American church: "In the same House, and at the same time, some would be *praying*, some *exhorting*, some *singing*, some *clapping their Hands*, some *laughing*, some *crying*, some *shrieking and roaring* out."[91] Visions and trances became common in which the converted imagined themselves "transported from Earth to Heaven, where they saw and heard most glorious Things; conversed with *Christ* and *holy Angels*; had opened to them the *Book of Life*, and were permitted to read the Names of Persons there, and the like."[92] The sermons delivered in these churches were equally grotesque and devoid of meaning: "The *Speaker* delivers himself, with the *greatest Vehemence* both of *Voice* and *Gesture*, and in the most *frightful Language* his Genius will allow of."[93] The result was a complete collapse of the church's mission to improve moral and spiritual goodness:

> The Goodness that has been so much talked of [in the revival], 'tis plain to me, is nothing more, in general, than a *Commotion in the Passions* . . . They place their Religion so much in the *Heat* and *Fervour* of their *Passions*, that they too much neglect their *Reason* and *Judgment*: And instead of being more kind and gentle, more full of Mercy and good Fruits, they are more bitter, fierce and implacable.[94]

In the eyes of a young, intellectual divinity student, the *Meditations* could be a cure for such behavior because Marcus rigorously addresses the role of reason and the social virtues.[95] The threat the revivals pose is exclusive reliance on passion and imagination with the result that the converted will turn their back on all their social obligations in order to dwell in the celestial kingdom. Like Bunyan's Christian in *Pilgrim's Progress*, they will run from wife, family, and society with fingers in their ears, crying "Life, life, eternal life." At first glance, Marcus may seem to urge this same rejection of the world in favor of the soul's transcendence. Marcus admonishes himself: "don't allow thy soul to continue any longer in a state of slavery; nor to be governed by opinions repugnant to its nature, or moved like a puppet by powers foreign to itself. Don't suffer it to repine at the lot which Fate has assigned it, or to dread what it may hereafter carve out for it."[96] Instead, the soul is like a sphere, neither extending beyond itself to things external, nor drawn inward upon itself. It should shine with a steady light discovering truths in the outer world and within itself.[97] For, the soul "alone enjoys the power of changing & moving itself."[98] A man with true grandeur of soul transcends the passions and tumult of the mortal world: "Will ever he who is endowed with a sublime & magnificent understanding, & has beheld all time, & contemplated every object, discover any thing grand or noble in this mortal life? It is impossible."[99]

But if the understanding is transcendent, it is nonetheless tethered to the social nexus of the mortal world:

> If the Understanding faculty is common to us, reason by which we are rational creatures is also common; if that, then likewise that reason which prescribes what is or what is not to be done is common to us; if so, then we have one common law, & must be fellow-citizens, & if fellow citizens we must be members of the same political society, & consequently the World is like to a great City.[100]

Human beings are therefore by nature well adapted to play a beneficial role within the "great City": "The principal thing . . . in the human constitution is to study to advance the publick good."[101] How is the public good to be advanced? For someone whose understanding is the leading principle it means being a good citizen of the "great City" taking care "to worship & bless the Gods; to do good unto men, to bear with their faults, & abstain from doing them injuries, & not look upon things external to thy body or soul, as belonging to them, or lying within their power."[102] It means promoting and trusting in the well-ordered institutions of the City and not giving way to the fears and fantasies of the private imagination. But that does not require ignoring the transcendence of the soul or one's role in the "great City."

The translation not only afforded Robertson an opportunity to begin to define his ideological stance, but it also provided occasion to develop an appropriate prose style. Robertson believed translation was important as a means of mastering English composition. Robertson believed that translation obliges us "to weigh the shades of difference between words and phrases, and to find the expression, whether by the selection of terms or the turning of the idiom, which is required for meaning."[103] Thus, part of Robertson's goal in the translation is in fact developing a style, and Erskine provides a clue about its source. In his discussion of Robertson's interest in Arminian thought, he adds a footnote: "He particularly admired Werenfelsius de Logomachiis eruditorum, et de meteoris orationis. He thought the false sublime, exposed in the last, might have been amply exemplified in passages from Lord Shaftesbury."[104] Samuel Werenfels, ultimately Rector of the University of Basle, was well known on the Continent and in Britain during the eighteenth century as a scholar and theologian with a special interest in religious controversy. The work to which Erskine refers was translated anonymously in 1711 as *A Discourse of Logomachys, or Controversy about Words . . . to Which Is Added a Dissertation concerning Meteors of Stile or False Sublimity*. Erskine is the only one who has mentioned the importance of Werenfels to Robertson, but the precision of the comment suggests the Rector figures very tangibly in Robertson's thinking.

Werenfels' *Meteors of Stile* is primarily concerned with issues of diction, though these issues are discussed within the larger context of the transactional nature of language. Werenfels defines meteors of style as "Phrases, which seem to be sublime, but are indeed trifling and vicious."[105] They are worthy analysis because they cause a breakdown in communication between speaker and audience, and it is the speaker's task to choose the words that will produce the exact effect desired in the audience. If the speaker misjudges, choosing a word either too high or too low for the subject matter, the communication process breaks down.

Things must always be estimated at their true public value and described in words that accurately reflect that value so that the resulting style may then be characterized by politeness. This is the literary goal to which the Moderates would aspire. As Robertson, Adam Smith, and Hugh Blair agree, a writer like Shaftesbury is an example of the false sublime because he relies on pompous diction. As Blair put it, "he is never satisfied with expressing any thing clearly and simply; he must always give it the dress of state and majesty."[106]

Brougham said that Robertson himself admired the narrative styles of Jonathan Swift and Daniel Defoe,[107] and we can test his claim if we set a portion of Robertson's translation against his three English competitors. The two standard translations that preceded Robertson's were those of Meric Casaubon (1634) and Jeremy Collier (1701). His immediate competitor was the Moor/Hutcheson version, which had driven him from the field. For Moor and Hutcheson, and likely for Robertson, Casaubon "can scarce be agreeable to any reader; because of the intricate and antiquated stile," while Collier "seems not to preserve sufficiently the grand simplicity of the original."[108] Here are four translations from the end of Book II of the *Meditations*:[109]

CASAUBON: The time of a man's life is as a point; the substance of it ever flowing, the sense obscure: and the whole composition of the body, tending to corruption. His soul is restless, fortune uncertain, and fame doubtful; to be brief, as a stream so are all things belonging to the body; as a dream, or as a smoke, so are all that belong unto the soul. Our life is a warfare, and a mere pilgrimage. Fame after life is no better than oblivion. What is it then that will adhere and follow? One only thing, Philosophy.

COLLIER: The Extent of Human Life is but a point; *Matter* is in perpetual Flux: The Faculties of Sence, and Perception, are Weak, and Unpenetrating: The Body slenderly put together, and but a Remove from Putrefaction: The Soul a rambling sort of a Thing. Fortune and Futurity, are not to be guess'd at: And Fame does not always stand upon Desert, and Judgment. In a Word; That which belongs to the Body streams off like a River; And what the Soul has is but Dreams and Bubble: Life, to take it rightly, is no other than a Campaign, or Course of Travels; and Posthumous Fame has little more in't than Silence, and Obscurity. What is it then that will stick by a Man and prove significant? Why, Nothing but Wisdom, and Philosophy.

MOOR/HUTCHESON: The duration of human life is a point; its substance perpetually flowing; the senses obscure; and the compound body tending to putrefaction: The soul is restless, fortune uncertain, and fame injudicious. To sum up all, the body, and all things related to it, are like a river; what belongs to the animal life, is a dream, and smoak; life a warfare, and a journey in a strange land; surviving fame is but oblivion. What is it then, which can conduct us honourably out of life, and accompany us in our future progress? philosophy alone.

ROBERTSON: The time of the life of man is a point; the matter of which he is made up is in a perpetual flux; his sensations are obscure & doubtfull; the constitution of his whole body tends toward corruption; his soul a fleeting breath; his fortune dark & impenetrable; & his reputation uncertain. To say all in a word; All the concerns of the body flow down like a river; & those of the Soul are like to a dream or vapour; life is a state of warfare, & a pilgrimage in a foreign country; & fame after death, is but oblivion. What is it then that is able to carry & bear up a man thro' all this? It is Philosophy alone.

Two features of Robertson's version stand out and point in the direction of his mature prose style. Robertson's diction is polite because it is drawn from words in general educated usage, neither too low nor technical, on the one hand, nor elevated and emotive, on the other. In opting for this polite middle ground, he departs from the concreteness and vigor of Swift and Defoe. He avoids "low," informal, or technical-sounding terms such as "stick by," "Bubble," "smoke," "compound body," or "animal life." He uses the more biblical "fleeting breath" instead of Collier's more literal but awkward "rambling sort of a Thing," or Casaubon's and Hutcheson/ Moor's "restless" for Marcus' unusual and, in Robertson's view, perhaps, less dignified image of the soul as a spinning top. Robertson's translation is also marked by his doubling of terms when the original Greek does not call for it: "obscure & doubtfull," "dark & impenetrable," and "carry & bear up." None of the others insist on these doublets, and they call attention to what one critic has called his contiguous style, which insists on parallel syntactic relationships.[110] Matching these doublets is the insistent parallelism of the seven clauses in the opening sentence. Again, none of the others match this degree of insistence, the effect of which is to create a highly controlled structure. The same pattern organizes the second sentence with the first two clauses paralleling the similes and the three following clauses built around linking verbs with subject–verb–object syntax. A key theme throughout the *Meditations* is order and control, whether in the individual, the state, or the universe, and we have seen how Robertson's embrace of this theme figures in his religious differences with the revivalists like Erskine. With his prose style, Robertson sought to reinforce his religious views aesthetically: by employing a polite diction and a rigorously balanced phrasing and syntax, he aims to vindicate the claims of reason, progress, and civic virtue without relinquishing faith.

After abandoning his translation project, Robertson may have been a bit at sea because in the spring of 1742 he was 21 with no immediate prospects. One possibility could have been to become a tutor to a gentleman's son, but, like Carlyle, John Home, and George Logan, Robertson rejected that option. They scorned the position because, as Carlyle said, "we

thought we had observed that all tutors had contracted a certain obsequi-
ousness or *bassesse*, which alarmed us for ourselves."[111] Carlyle admits that
subsequent experience changed his view, but the importance of "a manly
independency" was consistent with what he and Robertson had learned
from Marcus Aurelius. But with the death on 21 April 1743 of his cousin
Andrew,[112] minister in the parish of Gladsmuir, a new scene opened.
The parish of Gladsmuir was modest with about 1,400 parishioners and
revenue of £900 Scots (£75 sterling). But the kirk was adjacent to the
Edinburgh–Berwick post road and only twelve miles from Edinburgh (a
relatively easy few hours ride on horseback), close to his family and college
friends, and thus an excellent career stepping stone. In eighteenth-century
Scotland, appointment as a minister in the Church of Scotland was both
religious and political.[113] The church itself conducted trials in which the
candidate had to demonstrate satisfactory knowledge of theology, oratorical ability, and mastery of Hebrew, Greek, and Latin as well as show
sound moral character and judgment. At the same time, the candidate
needed the backing of the patrons of the parish as well as representatives
of the political establishment. The role of parishioners themselves was
uncertain. The patronage law of 1712 gave the right of appointment to
the parish patrons, but many parishioners resented the loss of the tradition that had developed over the latter half of the seventeenth century in
which the appointment was subject to the approval of the parish. There
had sprung up protests against the patronage law, the most notable being
Ebenezer Erskine's secession from the church in 1733. By 1743, the issue
had become increasingly vexed because the patronage law was neither
enforced nor discarded as cases of protest grew, and in a few years the law
of patronage would be the first major challenge Robertson and the emerging Moderate party would face in church policy.

In Robertson's appointment, there were no protests because "there
are a few wild people in the [Gladsmuir] Parish yet they are not much
to be minded & resort to their own Ministers when they come about."[114]
Robertson had several solid backers within the Haddington presbytery
and the government, though he was not without some opposition. The
long, intricate process leading to ordination got underway swiftly. On 23
April, just two days after Andrew Robertson's death, the secretary of state
for Scotland, John Hay, 4th Marquess of Tweeddale, received a letter
from his Edinburgh agent, Thomas Hay, alerting him to the vacancy and
mapping out the complicated claims over who has standing as a heritor
and who has the right of presentation. The claims in the Gladsmuir case
were complex because the parish was formed in 1692 from portions of
the surrounding parishes of Tranent, Haddington, and Aberlady, each of

which had their own heritors. In his letter, Thomas Hay was uncertain just how the appointment would be made, but the strongest presence in the negotiations would turn out to be Robert Dundas, Lord Arniston, the son of the elder Robertson's patron. As Hay recounts, Dundas favored Robertson because of loyalty to his father: "Lord Arniston told me he had little or no relation to Mr Robertson but that his father had been his Minister at Borthwick."[115] On 27 April the process began when John Hepburn, who was the second or collegiate charge with Robertson's father at Old Greyfriars, proposed to the presbytery of Edinburgh (where the candidate resided) that Robertson be entered upon trials, and "the young man being very well known to the Brethren as a Person of a good Behaviour and of pregnant parts," the presbytery agreed.[116] Following the act of the General Assembly regarding the licensing of probationers just passed in the 1742 meeting, the presbytery also took the first step in Robertson's entering the ministry by agreeing to meet on 30 April to examine him in a "private and previous trial"[117] where they would examine his readiness in a number of areas ranging from preparation in ancient languages to knowledge of church history and government to his maturity in dealing with difficult or hostile parishioners. The presbytery reported itself "extremely well pleased with him" but because of the press of business passed the trials to the presbytery of Dalkeith. Thus, on 4 May, Thomas Turnbull, the elder Robertson's successor at Borthwick in the presbytery of Dalkeith, reported to the Synod of Lothian and Tweeddale that they would examine him in trials for a license to preach, the second and public step toward securing ordination as a minister.[118] Robertson was approved again and now asked to prepare a homily on Galatians 3: 26 ("For ye are all the children of God by faith in Jesus Christ") and an exegesis on the necessity of divine revelation to be delivered on 4 June. The young divinity student was now officially launched into his probationary trials.

As Robertson prepared his theological materials, political negotiations about the presentation were still in progress behind the scenes. Tweeddale wished to fill the Gladsmuir church with John Bertram, his chaplain, who was approved for trials before the presbytery of Dunbar the same day Robertson was for his with Dalkeith.[119] There was also the possibility that Archibald Lundie, minister of Saltoun in the presbytery of Haddington, would make an effort on behalf of one of his sons. Hay reported to Tweeddale that Dundas would have been happy with Bertram but that he was yielding to Lord Arniston's wishes and that Lundie could split support for either Robertson or Bertram. According to Hay, Dundas believed "there would be an opposition in the Parish both to him [Bertram] & Mr Robertson by which means Mr Lundies party might defeat both."[120]

But Lundie did not pursue the appointment, and Tweeddale decided not to push Bertram's candidacy.[121]

If Robertson knew of these dealings, he did not have much time to worry over them. He had to spend the month of June passing the trials necessary to secure a license to preach in the presbytery of Dalkeith.[122] Fortunately for him, his training in the Divinity Hall probably incorporated most of the tasks that would be put to him by the Dalkeith presbytery.[123] The Latin exegesis on supernatural revelation and the English homily on Galatians 3: 26 having been approved, the presbytery now prescribed for 21 June a lecture on Acts 7, relating the stoning of Stephen, and an "exercise and addition" on Hebrews 8: 2 ("A minister of the sanctuary, and of the tabernacle, which the Lord pitched, and not man"), a topic recalling that of his father's published sermon. Both of these tasks involved biblical interpretation, the former being a regular feature of the church service alongside the sermon, the latter requiring the candidate to put forward an interpretation that is then "added to" by two or three other speakers. Upon his successfully passing these assignments, Robertson was given more for 28 June: delivery of a popular sermon on Romans 8: 28; presentation of a chronological discourse, *De historia Arminianorum usque ad finem Synodi Dodracenae*, the thesis of which he was expected to defend; and an interpretation of Psalm 119 in Hebrew along with a portion of the Greek New Testament to be chosen at random. These topics were aimed at sensitive theological questions,[124] and Robertson surely had to couch his sentiments in the balanced manner his background provided. With passage of these trials, the presbytery of Dalkeith gave him a license to preach, and he was now deemed a probationer.

On 4 July, the heritors and elders of the Gladsmuir parish issued a request to the Haddington presbytery that Robertson be invited to preach there, and he was charged by the Dalkeith presbytery to do so the first and last Sundays of August.[125] Because the Gladsmuir kirk session did not meet from the beginning of July until the beginning of December, we do not know from the kirk session records how Robertson was received, but it must have been favorably enough to continue the process. At this point, the presbytery of Haddington took over the proceedings because Gladsmuir was within their boundaries. In October, they first had to resolve the problem of there being two presentations, both on Robertson's behalf, one by the Earl of Hopetoun, the other by the king.[126] Once the presentations were agreed upon, they dispatched George Murray, minister of North Berwick, to preach at Gladsmuir on 1 November and at that time to ask the parish to approve a call for Robertson to be minister, which they did, with the presbytery requesting that he do it "so oft thereafter as he can conveniently supply that Congregation."[127] The presbytery also launched a new series of trials that essentially reprised the ones Robertson had undergone before Dalkeith, his first effort being once more an exegesis on the necessity of supernatural revelation. In the new year, there followed a lecture on Acts 17 (7 February 1744); an exercise and addition on Ephesians 5: 27 (28 February); and, as the culmination, a popular sermon on Hebrews 2: 3, an interpretation of Psalm 119 plus a random portion of Greek New Testament, and a defense of his Arminian thesis in which he was questioned by three prominent ministers from the presbytery, Edward Stedman, George Murray, and Archibald Blair (27 March).[128] The defense may not have been pleasant for Robertson. In his canvass of the presbytery preparatory to his campaign for the Musselborough parish, Carlyle talked with each of the three ministers but found only Stedman, minister of Haddington, "a man of first-rate sense and ability." The other two were dull and heavy: Murray, who asked for the call from Gladsmuir, was "a dry, withered stick . . . torpid in mind and body," while Blair, of Garvald and Bara, "seemed as torpid as George Murray."[129] But, despite the unpromising interview, the presbytery approved Robertson's performance, and asked him to read and sign the formula for those entering the ministry in which he swore to adhere to the doctrine in the *Confession of Faith* and to uphold the government and ordinances of the presbyterian Church.[130] With that act, he was ready for ordination, which took place on 17 April with Steadman preaching first, most likely on "the qualifications of ministers, and the reciprocal duties betwixt them and their people," and then asking Robertson to face the congregation and answer a series of eight questions concerning his faith and diligence.[131] Seated with the congregation was his pleased father, who had conveyed his thanks in a letter to Lord Arniston for his "civility & kindness" in making the appointment.[132] On 22 April, the youthful Robertson moderated his first kirk session meeting, and his church career, which would have such an impact on the institution of which he was now a part, was begun.

Notes

1. D. B. Horn, *Short History of the University of Edinburgh 1556–1889* (Edinburgh: Edinburgh University Press, 1969), pp. 40–1; Grant, *Story*, I, 259–63.
2. Peter Jones, "The Scottish Professoriate and the Polite Academy, 1720–46," in *Wealth and Virtue: The Shaping of Political Economy in the Scottish Enlightenment*, ed. Istvan Hont and Michael Ignatieff (Cambridge: Cambridge University Press, 1983), p. 91.

3. The "academic year" at the University of Edinburgh depended upon the offered class. Typically, they would begin in October or November and run until sometime between March and as late as July or August.

4. NLS MS 3,979, f. 22.

5. Ibid.

6. "Account," in *Miscellaneous Works*, p. 104.

7. NLS MS 3,979, f. 22.

8. NLS MS 3,980, f. 131.

9. Brougham to Lord Robertson, [July or August?] 1827, NLS MS 3,950, ff. 85–6.

10. Alexander Carlyle followed the same pattern, enrolling in the public class in 1735–6 and the private class the next year (*Autobiography*, pp. 35, 47). John Erskine did so as well. He claims to have met Robertson in the 1736–7 private class, though he may have actually done so in the earlier public class of 1734–5 (Jonathan M. Yeager, *Enlightened Evangelicalism: The Life and Thought of John Erskine* (Oxford: Oxford University Press, 2011), p. 28).

11. Robert Henderson, "A Short Account of the University of Edinburgh, the Present Professors in It, and the Several Parts of Learning Taught by Them," *Scots Magazine*, 3 (1741), pp. 373–4.

12. Grant, *Story*, II, 269.

13. Carlyle, *Autobiography*, p. 35; Erskine, "Agency of God," in *Miscellaneous Works*, p. 265.

14. For example, William Adam said, "My earliest particular recollection of him [Robertson] was his examining me in Virgil, on the story of Nisus and Euryalus" (*Sequel to the Gift of a Grandfather* (n.p., 1839), p. 45). Robertson's fondness annoyed James Boswell. In 1773, when Robertson greeted Samuel Johnson and Boswell upon their return from the Hebrides, "he advanced to Dr. Johnson, repeating a line of Virgil . . . Every body had accosted us with some studied compliment on our return" (*Life of Johnson*, ed. George Birkbeck Hill, rev. L. F. Powell, 5 vols (1934; rpt. Oxford: Clarendon Press, 1979), V, 392).

15. Carlyle, *Autobiography*, p. 48.

16. Grant, *Story*, II, 323.

17. James A. Harris, *Hume: An Intellectual Biography* (Cambridge: Cambridge University Press, 2015), p. 39.

18. L. W. Sharp, "Charles Mackie, the First Professor of History at the University of Edinburgh," *Scottish Historical Review*, 41 (1962), p. 41.

19. "Robertson," in *Miscellaneous Works*, p. 260.

20. Bower, *History*, II, 280–1.

21. *Autobiography*, p. 48.

22. *My Own Life and Times 1741–1814* (1861; rpt. Bristol: Thoemmes, 1996), pp. 13–14.

23. Quoted in Andrew Dalzel, "Account of the Late Duke Gordon, M.A.,

Including Anecdotes of the University of Edinburgh," *Scots Magazine*, 64 (1802), p. 22.

24. "Scottish Professoriate," pp. 92–3.

25. 4 (1775), p. 560.

26. Henderson, "Short Account," p. 373. The texts in question are J. G. Heineccius, *Elementa philosophiae rationalis et moralis* (1729) and Locke, *Essay concerning Human Understanding*, abr. John Wynne (1700).

27. "Student Essay on Historical Probability, 1737," in *Miscellaneous Works*, p. 8.

28. These issues are argued in, for example, Robert Wallace, *The Regard Due to Divine Revelation, and to Pretences to It, Considered* (London, 1733), and James Bannatine, *Mistakes about Religion amongst Causes for Our Defection from the Spirit of the Gospel* (Edinburgh, 1737).

29. "Historical Probability," trans. Mark Damen, in *Miscellaneous Works*, p. 8.

30. Ibid., p. 2.

31. Ibid., p. 11.

32. Ibid., p. 12.

33. Ibid., p. 13.

34. NLS MS 25,411, f. 63. This manuscript consists of notes of Robertson's sermons taken by David Dalrymple, Lord Hailes, primarily during the 1750s and 1760s. The exact words are, therefore, not necessarily Robertson's own.

35. Sir John Clerk, *Memoirs*, ed. John M. Gray (Edinburgh, 1892), p. 149.

36. *Autobiography*, p. 53.

37. William Robertson also suffered deafness, causing him to retire from the bench in 1826 (John Kay, *Edinburgh Portraits*, 2 vols (London, 1885), II, 384).

38. Cockburn, *Memorials*, p. 48.

39. Robertson to Gibbon, 30 July 1788, BL Add. MS 34,886, f. 166; Mary Robertson and William Robertson to William Robertson, 26 May [1789], NLS MS 3,944, f. 8.

40. Carlyle speaks of "Robertsons Great Love of Dissertation," which made him "tedious" in company ("Comparison," p. 278).

41. See Mackie's commonplace book (EUL MS Dc. 5. 242, f. 217). In addition to his work in Mackie's class, Robertson was engaged in another project during 1738. EUL New College MS CHU 22 is a small quarto of fifty-three leaves dated 28 November 1738 that is attributed to Robertson. It is an alphabetical list of all the parishes in Scotland together with their patrons from before 1688, so dated because the list includes the Scottish bishops. The purpose of such a list is unclear.

42. "Account," p. 372.

43. *State-Papers and Letters Addressed to William Carstares*, ed. Joseph Maccormick (Edinburgh, 1774), p. vii.

44. Ibid., p. iii.

45. Ibid., p. 7.

46. Sharp, "Mackie," p. 45.

47. EUL MS PC 53.2.

48. *State-Papers*, ed. Maccormick, p. 73.

49. Sharp, "Charles Mackie," pp. 33–4.

50. EUL MS La. II.37, f. 9.

51. *Autobiography*, p. 63.

52. Bower, *History*, II, 283–5.

53. Gowdie, *The Salvation of Souls the Desire and Endeavour of Every Faithful Minister* (Edinburgh, 1736), p. 33.

54. Sher, *Church and University*, p. 54. The *Salvation of Souls* is in part the substance of the sermon he delivered at the admission of George Logan to the ministry in 1732, and Logan, who was enrolled in Gowdie's class along with Robertson and Carlyle, would be one of the signers of the *Reasons of Dissent*.

55. *Sermon Preached at the Opening of the General Assembly . . . 2d of May 1734* (Edinburgh, 1734), p. 13.

56. Bower, *History*, III, 31.

57. Seccombe, *Dictionary of National Biography*, s.v. "William Robertson"; Stewart, "Account," in *Miscellaneous Works*, p. 105. The courses offered by Maclaurin do not on their face seem like the subjects someone whose bent is not mathematical or physical would enjoy. See Paul Wood, "Science in the Scottish Enlightenment," in *Cambridge Companion to the Scottish Enlightenment*, ed. Alexander Broadie (Cambridge: Cambridge University Press, 2003), p. 101.

58. Quoted in Wood, "Science," p. 104.

59. A strong claim for the influence of Maclaurin and Newtonianism on Robertson has been made by Joshua Ehrlich, "William Robertson and Scientific Theism," *Modern Intellectual History*, 10 (2013), pp. 529–42.

60. Stewart, *Oxford Dictionary of National Biography*, s. v. "William Wishart."

61. Wishart, *Charity the End of the Commandment; or, Universal Love the Design of Christianity* (Edinburgh, 1731), pp. 7–8.

62. George Lindsay, *Some Observations on These Two Sermons of Doctor Wishart's which Have Given Offence to the Presbytery of Edinburgh* (Edinburgh, 1737). See also *Confession of Faith*, chs 3, 6, and 20; and *The Presbytery of Edinburgh's Reply to the Case of the Magistrates and Town-Council of Edinburgh, in the Affair of Mr. William Wishart* (Edinburgh, 1737), p. 106.

63. Bower, *History*, II, 210.

64. "Agency of God," in *Miscellaneous Works*, p. 267.

65. Ibid., p. 270.

66. *An Essay on the Indispensible Necessity of a Holy and Good Life to the Happiness of Heaven* (London, 1753), pp. 15–16.

67. NLS MS 25,411, ff. 55, 57, 92, and 145 respectively.

68. *Autobiography*, p. 63.

69. "Account," in *Miscellaneous Works*, p. 107.

70. *Scotland's Age of Improvement: A Survey of Eighteenth-Century Literary Clubs and Societies* (n. p.: Washington State University Press, 1969), p. 106.
71. *Account of Erskine*, p. 16.
72. Carlyle to Earl of Buccleugh, 1 March 1793, Clements Library, University of Michigan, MS GD 224/295/2/31.
73. Quoted in McElroy, *Scotland's Age of Improvement*, p. 105.
74. Bower, *History*, III, 29–30.
75. Quoted in McElroy, *Scotland's Age of Improvement*, p. 106.
76. *Account of Erskine*, p. 100. See also Yeager, *Enlightened Evangelicalism*, pp. 32–9, for a fuller account of Erskine's views. Robertson later told Johnson that "Whitefield had strong natural eloquence, which, if cultivated, would have done great things" (Boswell, *Life*, V, 35–6). The comment indicates Robertson's preference for a middle ground in matters of faith between reason and passion to the exclusion of neither.
77. Yeager, *Enlightened Evangelicalism*, p. 32.
78. NLS MS 3,955. The start of Book II is dated 29 January, eight days after he had started Book I. None of the other books are dated. Thus, assuming each book took about ten days to complete, he may have been working on the project until about mid-April or early May.
79. Quoted in Peter Gay, *The Enlightenment: An Interpretation*, 2 vols (New York: Knopf, 1966–9), I, 120–1.
80. John Pringle's class on moral philosophy also covered Marcus Aurelius, and Pringle's influence cannot be dismissed, though Robertson, according to matriculation records, did not officially enroll in his class (Sher, *Church and University*, p. 29).
81. *The Principal Acts of the General Assembly of the Church of Scotland* (Edinburgh, 1746), p. 22.
82. *Publick Virtue Recommended* (Edinburgh, 1746), pp. 3–4. See Robertson's version of the city image in NLS MS 3,955, IV, iv. The folios in MS 3,955 have been numbered, but for convenient reference it will be cited by book and subsection.
83. E. C. Mossner, *The Life of David Hume*, 2nd edn (Oxford: Clarendon Press, 1980), p. 141.
84. *The Signs of the Times Consider'd* (Edinburgh, 1742), p. 28.
85. Ibid., pp. 29, 9, and 10 respectively.
86. Ibid., p. 10.
87. Ned C. Landsman, "Presbyterians and Provincial Society: The Evangelical Enlightenment in the West of Scotland, 1740–1775," in *Sociability and Society in Eighteenth-Century Scotland*, ed. John Dwyer and Richard B. Sher (Edinburgh: Mercat Press, 1993), pp. 194–209. The grounds of concern for those, like Robertson, Carlyle, and Blair, belonging to the "religious Enlightenment" is described by Ahnert, *Moral Culture*, pp. 10–11.
88. See, for example, Bannatine, *Mistakes about Religion*, and James Nisbet, *The Perpetuity of the Christian Religion* (Edinburgh, 1737). Both works weigh

the opposing arguments, and both see the necessity of somehow combining the social virtues and the urgency of salvation, with salvation carrying the greater but not exclusive weight. Bannatine and Nisbet (the future fathers-in-law of Hugh Blair and of Robertson, respectively) anticipate the Moderate theological position, particularly in their trying to bring reason and faith together.

89. Sher, *Church and University*, pp. 152–3.
90. *The Case of Offenses against Christianity Considered* (Edinburgh, 1742), p. 40.
91. *A Letter from a Gentleman in Boston, to George Wishart* (Edinburgh, 1742), p. 14.
92. Ibid., p. 13.
93. Ibid., p. 12.
94. Ibid., pp. 21–2.
95. Sher, *Church and University*, pp. 31–2.
96. NLS MS 3,955, Book II, ii.
97. *Marcus Aurelius Antoninus the Emperor to Himself*, in *Marcus Aurelius*, ed. and trans. C. R. Haines, rev. edn (Cambridge, MA: Harvard University Press, 1930), Book XI, xii.
98. NLS MS 3,955, Book V, xix.
99. Ibid., Book VII, xxxv.
100. Ibid., Book IV, iv.
101. Ibid., Book VII, lv.
102. Ibid., Book V, xxxiii.
103. Brougham, "Robertson," in *Miscellaneous Works*, p. 260.
104. "Agency of God," p. 264.
105. *A Dissertation concerning Meteors of Stile, or False Sublimity* (1711; rpt. Los Angeles: William Andrews Clark Memorial Library, 1980), p. 187.
106. Blair, *Lectures on Rhetoric and Belles Lettres*, 4th edn, 3 vols (London, 1790), I, 243; Smith, *Lectures on Rhetoric and Belles Lettres*, ed. J. C. Bryce (1983; rpt. Indianapolis: Liberty Press, 1985), p. 59.
107. "Robertson," p. 304.
108. *The Meditations of the Emperor Marcus Aurelius Antoninus*, trans. Francis Hutcheson and James Moor, ed. James Moore and Michael Silverthorne (Indianapolis: Liberty Fund, 2008), p. 3.
109. The comparison texts are drawn from *Marcus Aurelius Antoninus the Roman Emperor His Meditations concerning Himself*, trans. Meric Casaubon (London, 1673), p. 51; *The Emperor Marcus Antoninus His Conversation with Himself*, trans. Jeremy Collier (London, 1701), p. 26; *Meditations*, trans. Hutcheson and Moor, p. 38; and NLS MS 3,955, Book II, xvii.
110. Thomas Reuben Brooks, "Transformations of Word and Man: The Prose Style of William Robertson" (PhD diss., University of Indiana, 1968), ch. 4. My discussion in this paragraph is indebted to Brooks.
111. Carlyle, *Autobiograhy*, p. 70.
112. Andrew Robertson was the son of Robertson's uncle David Robertson. Some

genealogical details are provided in Stephen W. Massil, "Andrew Robertson of Gladsmuir; in America 1756–1782, and His American Family," *Scottish Genealogist* 59, No. 4 (December 2012), pp. 159–70. The inventory of papers done at Robertson's death listed a parcel of manuscript sermons by Andrew Robertson that were apparently in the family's possession (NLS MS 3,980, f. 129).

113. The following discussion is indebted to Sher, *Church and University*, pp. 46–50.

114. Thomas Hay to 4th Marquess of Tweeddale, 23 April 1743, NLS MS 7,054, ff. 148–9. I am grateful to Roger Emerson for bringing the letters between Hay and Tweeddale to my attention.

115. Ibid.

116. NAS MS CH2/121/15, p. 129.

117. Nathaniel Morren, *Annals of the General Assembly of the Church of Scotland from 1739 to 1766*, 2 vols (Edinburgh, 1838–40), I, 34.

118. One reason Turnbull would report to the Synod may have been to secure approval for Robertson's young age, twenty-two at the time, which was less than the required twenty-five to enter the ministry (Steuart of Pardovan, *Collections and Observations*, p. 12).

119. NAS MS CH2/252/11, p. 261.

120. Hay to Tweeddale, 21 May 1743, NLS MS 7,055, f. 44.

121. Hay to Tweeddale, 26 May 1743, NLS MS 7,055, f. 127.

122. The following discussion is indebted to Bower, *History*, III, 33–6.

123. There are no specific records of what Robertson may have covered in Gowdie's Divinity Hall course. But years later, William Mair noted six things students ought to cover in the Hall: (1) Latin exegesis on a controverted issue in divinity; (2) an English homily; (3) a critical exercise on an Old Testament passage; (4) a comparable exercise on a New Testament passage; (5) a lecture on a Scripture passage; and (6) a popular sermon (*Digest of Church Laws*, 2nd edn (Edinburgh, 1895), p. 193).

124. Bower, *History*, III, 36.

125. NAS MS CH2/185/12, p. 212.

126. NAS CH2/185/12, pp. 217–18. The presbytery of Haddington decided that the Earl of Hopetoun had the right of presentation but agreed that both presentations would be read, the earl's coming first.

127. Ibid., p. 223.

128. Ibid., pp. 226–33.

129. Carlyle, *Autobiography*, p. 104.

130. NAS MS CH2/185/12, pp. 232–3.

131. The formula for ordination day as outlined by Steuart of Pardovan, *Collections and Observations*, pp. 8–9.

132. Robertson, Sr, to Arniston, 14 April 1744, NAS MS RH4/15/3.

CHAPTER 3

Parish Ministry, 1744–1750

The parish of Gladsmuir derived its name from gleds or kites, birds of prey, which, in the heat of clerical debate, became disparaging symbols for Robertson himself.[1] The Edinburgh–Berwick post road (now the A1) passes along a stony ridge running east to west across the middle of the parish. From the kirk situated by the post road, one could see down the gentle slope to the Firth of Forth on the north and down the equally gentle slope to the Tyne River valley to the south. The chief natural resource was coal, which had been mined in the western portion of the parish for centuries. Those not employed in the mines were engaged in agriculture. Near the kirk, a brickwork operated that may have brought his grandfather to Robertson's mind. There were no towns in the parish and besides Gladsmuir just a handful of villages: Longniddry, Penston, Samuelston, and Macmerry. The kirk itself dated just from 1695, though it now forms only picturesque ruins. But it was an interesting structure, featuring crow-step gables, an elegant bellcote, and two galleries inside the church. Built in 1725, the manse was the second for the parish. It was now near the church (the former manse was a half mile away in Penston) and by virtue of its recent construction was probably still in good condition, although the minister's glebe was six and one half acres of "indifferent land."[2] In about 1750, the minister's income was £69 (£53 in victual and £16 in cash) plus the value of the glebe and pasture, making a total of £75, modest when compared with Hugh Blair's £103 and Carlyle's £86.[3]

The parish population was mixed. On the one hand, there were distinguished figures like William Law of Elvingston. He was a very active heritor, and Robertson often acted in concert with him. His father had been professor of moral philosophy at Edinburgh, and he himself had a distinguished career in law, serving as sheriff of Haddingtonshire for fifty years and holding a prominent place in the Scottish bar. He was also an important agricultural improver, becoming one of the first to practice harrowing wheat in the spring months. Robertson probably found Law a congenial spirit because, apart from his accomplishments, he was also a staunch Hanoverian and supporter of the church establishment. On the other hand, there were less congenial features of the parish that Robertson probably found either galling, comic, or both. The area had a long tradition of belief in witchcraft, and one of Robertson's predecessors as minister, John Bell, had even published a pamphlet on the subject, offering a detailed analysis of the signs by which witches can be known.[4] In the later seventeenth century, Samuelston was said to be particularly infested with witches, and halfway between Penston and the Gladsmuir manse there was said to be a "Witches Tree," which was a common gathering place for them.[5] By 1744, when Robertson was ordained, the witchcraft tradition was certainly waning; but in 1755 Robertson encountered a case of demonic possession in the nearby parish of Morham, and from his tone one might guess it was not the first time. He wrote to David Dalrymple:

> The story of the possession about which you express your concern made a good deal of noise in our country, but gained credit only with the lowest of the people. I am sorry that the weakness & credulity of the Minister obliges me to reckon him among that number. The Girl was subject to hysteric fits, & her parents were artfull enough by the help of some manoeuvre of theirs to make it pass upon the neighbours for supernatural. However some folks of better sense having visited the Girl, plainly discovered the imposture, & have put an end in a great measure to the gain they made of it. Mr Purdie [the minister] I am told is still a believer, & continues his exorcisms. His behaviour has been so imprudent, & brings such a reflection upon our order, & might have done so much harm among the people, that both for our own sake & theirs, I believe we shall take some method of expressing our dissatisfaction with Mr Purdie against our first presbytery.[6]

Robertson's discomfort is evident in his concern about how the incident reflects on the clergy, suggesting his seriousness about their public role, and the discovery of fraud in the case simply confirms his scorn.[7]

One can also detect in this passage signs of the minister's sense of intellectual and social distance between himself and the ordinary people of his parish. There is a pervasive sense of hierarchy: some of those ordinary people are "low," there are others of "better sense," and the clergy ought to act to protect the credulous by disciplining Purdie.[8] It is in such a moment that we catch a whiff of Robertson's strong personal ambition to reshape his world. It is worth noting here, at the start of his career, just how strong this drive would become because there was a disparity between it and his limited rural locale. In the Life of Johnson, Boswell records a conversation held in the spring of 1778 between Robertson and Johnson concerning the character of Robert Clive, first Baron Plassey, who led British conquests in India. Robertson was profoundly impressed by the power of Clive's personality, especially his ability to take command and engage in decisive action. Clive was, according to Robertson,

one of the strongest-minded men that ever lived: [. . .] he would sit in company quite sluggish, while there was nothing to call forth his intellectual vigour; but the moment that any important subject was started, for instance, how this country is to be defended against a French invasion, he would rouse himself, and shew his extraordinary talents with the most powerful ability and animation.[9]

It was commonly thought that Clive had met his death in 1774 by deliberately stabbing a penknife into his throat. But Robertson explained this view by arguing that Clive "'cut his throat because he was weary of still life; little things not being sufficient to move his great mind.'"[10] Johnson contemptuously dismissed Robertson's claim, and after Robertson had left the room, he observed that "'Robertson was in a mighty romantick humour.'"[11]

Boswell and Johnson were not the only ones surprised by this "romantick" streak of ambition in Robertson. Stewart also noted it:

His talents fitted him in an eminent degree for the business of the world; and the station in which Providence placed him opened to him a field, which, however unequal to his ambition or to his genius, afforded him the means of evincing what he might have accomplished, if his sphere of exertion had been more extensive and brilliant.[12]

Not content simply as a parish minister, cloistered scholar, or academic administrator, Robertson saw himself as a social leader committed to fostering the ideals of the Enlightenment within Scottish religious and social institutions. His histories, church policies, and university leadership were means toward this end. Though Robertson did not command troops and empires, his pulpit oratory, books, and academic influence could bring change in his society – not revolution, but greater order, reason, and stability. But, in the meantime, the Gladsmuir parish would prove to be what Robertson called "still life."

Sermons were the most public signs of the new minister's religious stance. By most accounts, Robertson was an effective parish preacher, but we have no records of Robertson's pulpit oratory until 1754, a decade into his ministry. Bower maintains he was highly regarded in the parish:

Dr. Robertson was careful to be well prepared when he appeared in the pulpit, and I have been assured by one who was his parishioner about that time, that from the very first he was an exceedingly popular preacher, and that during the fourteen years of his residence at Gladsmuir his popularity was daily increasing.[13]

The members of the Haddington presbytery shared this opinion, and Stewart claims that he lost "before his removal from Gladsmuir [in 1758], a volume of Sermons which he had composed with care."[14] But no other evidence survives testifying to the existence of this volume except for a reference in the inventory of papers done at his death to "A parcel of old notes of Sermons."[15] The notes and the volume of completed sermons raise the question of just how Robertson preached.

An anecdote that first appeared in 1836 offers a comic perspective on the issue. The author tells us Robertson "always kept pretty close to his paper" when preaching, but on one Sunday during his Gladsmuir years his man, carrying the Bible to the church, noticed a fine hare and thought he would "'hae' a rap at her" – using the minister's Bible. As the book flew through the air, the manuscript, which the minister had placed in the bible and "on which were written the heads, exhortations, reflections, &c. of the forenoon discourse," flew out and was lost in the breeze. When Robertson arrived at the church, he was confounded. After worrying throughout the service, he desperately roused his memory, and when his moment came, he ascended the pulpit and went "at once into the heart of his subject, and to the hearts of his hearers. A better sermon he had never preached within the walls of any church; and it was universally noticed by his numerous congregation, that he had never preached with more spirit and feeling than on that day."[16] We notice that the manuscript paper that flies away does not contain a full sermon but notes for the sermon, suggesting that Robertson did not simply read a full text. Nor did he usually preach extempore, though the point of the article is that he would do better if he had. Notes also seem consistent with the parcel of "old notes of Sermons" mentioned in the inventory as well as with his father's practice. Robertson would have his ideas mapped out in advance; but since he was working from notes, he could also develop those ideas according to the moment, injecting spontaneity into his discourse. Erskine says that several years before Robertson's death he seldom wrote out his sermons "or exactly committed his older sermons to memory."[17] In 1766, when Elizabeth Montagu praised Robertson's "extempore manner of preaching,"[18] it was likely that Robertson was not actually preaching completely extempore in the manner of an evangelical but working from memorized notes that allowed him extemporaneous insertions. Likewise, when an observer noted in 1791 that "'He wrote his sermon on one side of the paper, in separate leaves, pushing gently the page he had read to the left side of the pulpit Bible,'"[19] it is probably an exception to his usual practice. We have a largely complete manuscript of his sermon on the Glorious Revolution, and there must have been one for the publication of *Situation of the World* in 1755. But these were special occasions, not ordinary sermons. Although reliance on the read sermon was a growing trend among Moderate preachers after 1750,[20] rhetoricians like Hugh Blair condemned the practice on the grounds that "No discourse, which is designed to be persuasive, can have the same force when read, as when spoken." The fully memorized sermon is ideal, but notes are acceptable "to preserve, in a great measure, the freedom and ease of one who speaks."[21] Robertson seems to have sided with Blair and relied primarily, but never exclusively, on notes rather than full texts.[22]

Accent was also an important part of pulpit style. In 1789, Samuel Rogers heard Robertson preach in the morning and Blair in the afternoon. He preferred Robertson "both for matter and manner of delivery. Blair's was good, but less impressive; and his broad Scotch accent offended my ears greatly."[23] Although his two written sermons are in correct English, Robertson spoke from the pulpit – and in daily life – in what Henry Cockburn called "good honest natural Scotch."[24] Robertson's possible attendance at Adam Smith's lectures in Edinburgh in 1748 as well as Thomas Sheridan's in 1761 may have somewhat Anglicized his delivery.[25] Thomas Ritchie said that Roberson was so carried away with English "that he *sported* on all occasions, his progress in speaking English, and to the day of his death, persevered in the practice of enunciating his words with the most pointed correctness."[26] As happens in Scotland today, Robertson likely used several speech registers, the choice depending on the company and context in which he found himself. Preaching to parishioners, his pronunciation and accent may have been "strongly marked with the peculiarities of his country" because he wished to give his discourse the force of spoken, not written, language.[27] But for a very formal occasion, such as the centennial of the Glorious Revolution or preaching in England, he may have leaned as much as he could toward English pronunciation.

The content of Robertson's sermons fit their polite style. Besides the two largely complete examples of his sermons, there are notes of sixty-one other sermons and thirty-seven lectures that Robertson delivered in Edinburgh between 1754 and 1764. The notes were taken by David Dalrymple, who attended the churches of a number of prominent Edinburgh ministers, and from these we can form at least an impression of the content of Robertson's regular Sunday sermons. Only one of Robertson's sermons, a Fast Day sermon delivered at the Tron Church in 1754, predates his formal admission to Lady Yester's Chapel (15 June 1758) and Old Greyfriars (26 November 1761), and we do not know if any of these sermons might have been delivered in Gladsmuir. But the consistency of the themes running through Dalrymple's notes suggests there probably was not a great difference between those of the 1740s and those of the 1750s and 1760s. In Presbyterian practice, a sermon would be accompanied by a lecture in both the morning and the afternoon services. Robertson typically gave one of the services to a colleague, a practice followed by the other Edinburgh preachers.

In keeping with church tradition, Robertson's sermons on a given text might stretch over three to five Sundays forming his "ordinary" for those weeks. His most common texts in the records we have were from Proverbs followed by 1 Corinthians, Galatians, Luke, Matthew, and Acts. His lectures also developed his topics at length according to church custom. Between 25 June 1758 and 6 April 1760, while Robertson was at Lady Yester's, Dalrymple recorded lectures on Luke nineteen times (as well as six sermons on texts from Luke). He did not attend every Sunday during this period, but presumably Robertson lectured on the Gospel from beginning to end. Luke's distinctive message is universal salvation for all of humankind, and it places particular emphasis on a loving God and the value of human understanding. Although probably coincidental, such a message, bypassing matters of election in favor of inclusiveness and invoking sympathetic understanding, accords well with Robertson's Moderate stance. Ten other lectures (plus five sermons) are devoted to Acts, a gospel also attributed to St. Luke. Of the thirty-seven lectures and fifty-eight sermons by Robertson that Dalrymple heard between June 1758 and June 1764, 78 percent of the lectures and almost 20 percent of the sermons were drawn from texts by St. Luke with his distinctive humanistic message.

Robertson's tone and approach seem to resemble those of his father, and at one point he even seems to echo his father's published sermon. In his sermon on 2 March 1760, Robertson preached that "Civility when confined to things indifferent is praiseworthy & necessary, but when our Conscience & our God are concerned Civility is sinfull."[28] The earliest sermon Dalrymple records was delivered on a Fast Day, 31 October 1754, at the Tron Church. The text is Psalm 19: 13: "Keep back thy servant also from presumptuous sins; let them not have dominion over me: then shall I be upright, and I shall be innocent from the great transgression." The entry in Dalrymple's notes is worth quoting because it is as close as we can come to a sample of Robertson's regular early preaching.

He [Robertson] observed that sin might be considered three ways. 1st in itself. 2ly. by Comparison with other sins. 3ly By the circumstances of Aggravation that in this last light the Psalmist considers it in the text. He shewed what were the Chief aggravations of sin. 1. when it is committed against knowledge. 2. when the sinner resists conviction. 3. when he perseveres in evil. 4. when he sins impiously & ingratefully, notwithstanding of God's threats & his goodness, of the promises & terrors of the

Gospell. 5. when sin is committed after serious & repeated promises of amendment. He said that many other aggravations there were of sin, that these were the Chief: he pathetically addressed himself to his hearers & told them that he hoped every one's heart had been comparing his sins with the degrees & aggravations above described & that therefore no application was necessary from the pulpit. Our hearts were to make the application.[29]

If we compare this sermon with one on the same text delivered by the orthodox Robert Walker, who was translated to the first charge at St. Giles in 1754, we can see Robertson's approach.[30] Although both men categorize kinds of sin and focus on the individual ways in which sin can be aggravated, Robertson and Walker differ on the emphasis granted to original sin. Walker concludes his sermon by exhorting his parishioners to call on God's help: "Let us therefore, under a deep sense of our depravity and weakness, humbly and importunately cry to God, that he may deliver us from the oppression of our tyrannical lusts; and these cries of the oppressed shall enter into the ears of the 'Lord of sabaoth.'"[31] Human beings, caught in the toils of original sin, must realize their helpless state and constantly implore God for divine assistance. At the Tron Church, by contrast, Robertson "pathetically addressed" his audience, asking them to reflect upon their state as sinners and then to trust their own hearts to lead them to reformation. Human nature can be trusted because, as Robertson argued in his student essay, it is an insult to God to think He would have created human beings incapable of knowing their proper courses of action.[32]

An even more striking example of his religious stance appears in November 1758, the second earliest year in Dalrymple's record, when Robertson preached on Hebrews 4: 16 ("Let us therefore come boldly unto the throne of grace, that we may obtain mercy, and find grace to help in time of need"). According to Dalrymple, Robertson

shewed 1. what was implyed by ye Throne of God. God is represented in scripture as a monarch powerfull to punish, y^t we may be deterred from evil, or gracious to pardon, y^t we may be encouraged to come before him: in ye last sense is *throne* here understood. II. What we are to ask at this throne. 1. pardoning mercy for sins past. 2. grace to keep us from ye commission of more since. III. how we are to approach, *boldly*, not presumptuously nor with indecent familiarity for ye distance between God & Man is great, between God & sinners, infinite: But with humble confidence & assurance of faith. IV. the reason given in ye text, because of X^{ts} character, which implys. 1. y^t he has reconciled us to God. 2. y^t he makes continual intercession for us. 3. that he is sensible of the infirmities [one word illegible] our frame & remembers we are dust. Inference 1. Gratitude to God & X^t. 2. that we approach him in ye ordinances wherein he manifests himself particularly to us.[33]

Robertson's tone is positive, stressing God's readiness to pardon, not judge. We are to approach the throne with "humble confidence," a near oxymoron that suggests the meeting of two well-bred gentlemen, one of much higher rank than the other, but each having a clear sense of his own worth and status. We can have "humble confidence" because Christ has reconciled us to God, continually intercedes for us, and knows our weaknesses so that we may be assured of our faith and pardon.

By contrast, Walker's sermon on this same text sees the sinner's plight very differently:

> Are you solicitous about *grace* for future emergencies? Let me ask you, I pray, have you got all the *grace* you need for present duty? – If you think you have, I can, without further inquiry, assure you that you are mistaken. – At this very moment you need grace to cure your anxiety and distrust, to check your impatience and presumptuous curiosity. Cast your care upon God for every needful support, when you shall be called to suffer and die, and come to his throne for grace that may enable you to live to some good and useful purpose in the mean time. Seek grace to mortify your remaining corruptions, to strengthen your faith, and to inflame your love.[34]

For the orthodox Walker, the sinner's struggle never ends. No sinner can rest assured or possess "humble confidence" that grace is sufficient in the time of need; instead, it must be sought continually because the time of need is the sinner's time on earth. When we sue for grace, moreover, we do so not as gentlemen, but with "a child-like freedom, to pour out our hearts before him."[35]

As a Presbyterian minister, one of Robertson's key themes is providence, a topic at the center of Calvinist thought.[36] But Robertson qualifies and modifies this theme by counterpointing it with the theme of incremental moral progress, which carries implications for human agency. For example, in a sermon of November 1759 on Psalm 64: 8–9, Robertson states the orthodox position of "acknowledgement of his [God's] hand in every thing that happens. [W]hile the thoughtless observer of events imputes our success to fortune & the haughty soldier to his own prowess, let our language be, it is the finger of ye Lord," and we must "trust in him for future deliverance."[37] This position is clearly consistent with the *Confession of Faith*, which maintains that

> God, the great Creator of all things, doth uphold, direct, dispose, and govern, all creatures, actions and things, from the greatest even to the least, by his most wise and holy providence, according to his infallible foreknowledge, and the free and immutable counsel of his own will, to the praise and glory of his wisdom, power, justice, goodness, and mercy.[38]

But Robertson also counterbalances his references to the orthodox view of providence with allusions to Hutcheson's somewhat more controversial sense of moral progress (perhaps also filtered through William Wishart), which was becoming a hallmark of Moderate thinking. Here human agency comes into play, as he showed in a series of three sermons given in March and April 1760 on Matthew 10: 22 ("And ye shall be hated of all men for my name's sake: but he that endureth to the end shall be saved"):

30 MARCH. 1. By practice the power of goodness becomes daily more strong & the allurements of vice less powerfull. 2. All graces are connected, the excelling in one naturally leads one to excel in another. Thus the love of God is connected with the love of man, & Benevolence again with piety . . .

6 APRIL. 4. That as we continue in well-doing our joy will be increased, & the work will become more easy. If we endure, our loves of another world will grow stronger & stronger. 6. Our graces will increase, & the spirit of God will support our weakness more & more.

13 APRIL. II. That we must persevere unto the end, this implys vigor & patience . . . 3. Our behaviour here is so connected with our reward hereafter that perseverance in virtue is necessary. Here we are to form habits for eternity . . .[39]

There is nothing here about immediate, irresistible grace, and there is no room for miraculous deathbed conversions, not to mention strict election. Robertson's focus is on the labor of incremental moral progress, something that is realizable within human terms, does not demand divine intervention, and calls for moral teaching. Like the Gospel message itself, providentialism is by no means denied, but it is complemented by human moral culture.

As Robertson well knew from his father's career, preaching was far from the only duty of the parish minister. Most biographers have offered hagiographic accounts of his parish ministry. Stewart praised his "punctuality" in the performance of his duties, which earned him the "veneration and attachment" of his parishioners.[40] George Gleig claimed to have obtained information from Robertson's sister Helenora that allowed him to describe Robertson's domestic day while in Gladsmuir. He would rise early in the morning and devote time before breakfast to reading and study; the rest of the day was given over to "the duties of his office; which he was so far from neglecting that he increased them."[41] Bower also delivers a glowing report:

His attention to his parochial duty was laborious and exemplary – he punctually tended to what, in the language of the Church, is called "The ministerial visitation of families," that is, he regularly visited the inhabitants of his parish at their own houses in the capacity of their minister. During the summer months he catechized the youth for some time previous to the ordinary hour of the commencement of the morning service. He visited the sick, administered comfort to the afflicted, and such was the superiority of his judgment and readiness to serve them, that in every emergency they applied to him for advice.[42]

Brougham agrees that Robertson spent his time in "constant study" and that he was diligent in visiting the sick and the poor and in catechizing the young, though Brougham also scoffs at the claim that he spent his whole time after breakfast in parish duties, for "it would have been utterly impossible to find subjects for his visits in that small country parish, not containing two hundred families."[43] But the parish register tells a different story. Although Robertson may have performed his "minimum duties"[44] as minister, the register reveals a great deal of negligence in his handling of such important tasks as the upkeep of the parish baptismal records and the kirk session minutes, the maintenance of the parochial school, and his representation of the parish in the presbytery of Haddington. He may well have preached, catechized, visited the sick and the poor, and worked to maintain poor support, and, even though he may have been reprimanded by the presbytery, he seems to have dealt humanely with the sexual lapses brought to the kirk session.[45] But if the general neglect of the other aspects of parish infrastructure is any indication, these tasks were performed alongside neglect serious enough to have forced Robertson's (not unwilling) departure for Edinburgh.

The first thing one notices about the kirk session minutes during Robertson's tenure is that they break off on 15 October 1746 and, except for a few sporadic entries beginning in 1750 concerned with levies for the poor, do not resume their regular form until April 1759 when the new minister, Francis Cowan, took charge of the parish. The problem lay with the hiring of William Pentland as schoolmaster and session clerk. The entry for 15 October 1746 notes that the previous schoolmaster and clerk, William Douglas, had been indisposed for some time and had recently died, and Pentland was instructed to complete the minutes from the slips that Douglas and his substitutes had left behind. Judging from the handwriting, Pentland apparently entered the minutes from 15 April 1742 up to his appointment on 15 October, but as the session later complained, Pentland soon became distracted with his farms, neglected the school, and abandoned the kirk session minutes together with the baptismal register. It was hardly surprising his farms were a distraction since his salary was only about £9 Scots with the addition of a few pence for his clerkship. Matters became so bad with the school that Pentland was forced to resign in 1759 and the session asked the presbytery to inspect the school and help them bring it back to life after nearly a decade of neglect. They also put out an extraordinary call to Gladsmuir parishioners to provide information for the baptismal register on any births since 1746 so that it could be brought up to date. Although Pentland was clearly derelict, ultimate responsibility for not keeping the parish in good order was Robertson's. That Pentland could continue to draw his salary and ignore his duties for so long is bad enough, but Robertson also had the temerity in 1762 to request to be reimbursed for £3 sterling for an advance he made to help pay for the poor.[46]

Some of this laxness spilled over during the years 1744–58 into his performance on the Haddington presbytery, again because he saw it as largely a stepping stone to a greater leadership role in the church. Consisting of sixteen ministers, one from each of the fifteen parishes plus a second charge from the parish of Haddington, the presbytery stood between the kirk session and the synod. Much of the business handled at its regular monthly meetings was routine: typically, it resolved discipline cases referred to it by the kirk sessions, it was responsible for finding ways to arrange parish funding for their poor, it surveyed and adjudicated matters relating to the ministers' glebes, it conveyed messages and policies from the General Assembly to the parishes, and it oversaw the proper management of the parishes with respect to ministerial behavior and the operation of the parish schools. Politically, Robertson probably found the presbytery not uncongenial but nonetheless a bit divided. Edward Stedman, former chaplain to the Earl of Hopetoun and the second charge in Haddington parish, was the active leader, and he provided important guidance for the young minister. In Carlyle's view, Stedman "was a man of excellent sense & great enlargement of mind, tho' he had the appearance of an old fashioned Presbyterian." He took it upon himself to draw Robertson out, though the latter responded very cautiously:

> Stedman very soon discovered Robertsons superiority & urged him to take a share in their debates at their monthly meetings when even on the most trifling subject and before a small audience the splendor of his [Robertson's] elocution could not be concealed. Stedman gave him confidence in himself and boldly predicted that he would one day be the leader of the assembly, and yet seven years past over his head before he made any distinguisht figure, or indeed before he had spoken either in the Synod which meets twice a year or in the General Assembly tho' he had been a member since 1744.[47]

In addition, a network of ministers connected by family ties and friendship supported Robertson, including Carlyle's father, William, from the parish of Prestonpans; Patrick Wilkie, first charge in Haddington and Stedman's father-in-law; John Hamilton of Bolton, who married

Carlyle's cousin Jean Wight and had John Home as his best man; and James Glen of Dirleton and George Murray of North Berwick, who were both friends of Carlyle. Less congenial, perhaps, were ministers such as Robert Blair of Athelstaneford, becoming famous for his poem *The Grave* (1743), with its notably evangelical themes and who was "dying slowly" and "so austere and void of urbanity as to make him quite disagreeable to young people"; James Witherspoon of Yester, whose soul was "buried beneath a mountain of flesh"; and Archibald Lundie of Saltoun, a "pious and primitive" old Scots Episcopalian who refused to sign the Confession of Faith but whose published synod sermon of 1727 strongly emphasized his belief that a minister's first commitment was to immediate parish duties.[48] Carlyle noted a distinct difference in social behavior between the two groups. As a divinity student visiting in east Lothian in the summer 1742, he found the presbytery dinners on meeting day stuffy and unwelcoming (for example, allowing only two bottles of "small Lisbon wine" no matter how many were attending). Subsequently, he and the other students set up a second meeting where they were joined by Stedman, Glen, and Murray, keeping up "an enlightened conversation until bedtime."[49] Between 1744 and 1758, the composition of the presbytery changed in a more liberal direction. About one half of the ministers were replaced by ministers such as John Home, Hew Bannatine, David Wark, Robert Dundas, Matthew Murray, and George Anderson, all of whom had Moderate leanings.

Robertson attended presbytery meetings in the 1744–58 period on average about 60 percent of the time, with a high of 75 percent in 1757 and a low of 30 percent in 1748. He also performed a minimum of presbytery duties, serving as clerk from June to December 1745, as moderator from December to June 1746–7 and in December–June 1753–4, as trustee of the Widow's Fund from 1752, and as elected parish representative to the General Assembly in 1746, 1751, 1753, and 1756. This rate of attendance and his involvement in other duties roughly matches that of most of the other members of the presbytery, although that level of performance was not impressive. The presbytery as a whole expressed its concern about its ministers' involvement in October 1752 when it passed a resolution stating that "the Presbytery taking under consideration, how much the attendance on y^r Meetings was Neglected, they agreed to revive their Antient practice of appointing those to Preach before the Presbytery, who were absent at any time without a Sufficient Excuse."[50] But Robertson's mediocre performance also reflects his developing involvement in wider church politics as well as more personal interests. His average attendance from 1744 to 1749 of 51 percent may be explained not only by a lack of interest and social distractions but also by the hardship caused by the death of both his parents in 1745 and a severe illness stretching from at least January to March in 1748 (a recurrence of rheumatic fever?). By the same token, his more active involvement from 1751 to 1757 (now averaging 67 percent attendance) may be explained by his engagement in the patronage issue[51] and the Douglas controversy requiring his keeping the presbytery in line with Moderate opinion, though it might also be alleged that Robertson's improved attendance was an attempt to cover his tracks regarding the bad management of Gladsmuir parish finances and to secure translation to Edinburgh to evade the fallout.[52]

Robertson's social network was significantly based on the Adam family, especially after the death of his parents in 1745. As William Adam (the architect's grandson) later commented, during these trying years "my grandfather's home was his [Robertson's] principal place of resort, and he was considered as one of my father's family."[53] Besides a respectable family heritage, the Adams provided Robertson with social standing and intellectual credentials. John Clerk of Eldin praised the Adam family for drawing "around them a set of men whose learning and genius have since done honour to that country which gave them birth."[54] The clerical students Robertson met at Edinburgh University were the heart of this network. Many were now settling into parish ministries as he was. Among them, Clerk names John Home, Alexander Carlyle, and Adam Ferguson. But to understand these friendships, it is helpful to describe briefly Robertson's social character. He was not a difficult friend, having "a Temper that was never Rufld" in Carlyle's view,[55] but he was often more admired than loved. His "Recluse and Studious Bent" together with his upbringing in a serious clerical household meant that he could be stiff and distant with others, lacking easy affability or intimacy so that he presented a formal, public face without revealing the personal thoughts and feelings behind it.[56] Writing from Holland in 1745 to the circle gathered at the Adams', Adam Ferguson described the serious observance of a Dutch Sunday, adding ironically that "every fellow sets on a form before his Door with perhaps Six Pair of Breeches on, and a tobacco pipe, smoking with as much Gravity and wisdom as the Minister of Gladsmuir himself."[57] But Robertson also responded warmly to people who were affable, lively, and open. John Home was a favorite of Robertson's throughout his life starting with their college days because Home possessed a "glowing complexion of mind," in Henry Mackenzie's description: his "temper was of that warm susceptible kind which is caught with the heroic and the tender, and which is more fitted to delight in the world of sentiment than to succeed in the bustle of ordinary life."[58] Carlyle said memorably that Home's "entry to a company was like opening a window and letting the sun into a dark room."[59] Home's enthusiasm affected how he saw his friends themselves, and Robertson said that Home invested his friends "with a sort of supernatural privilege above the ordinary humiliating circumstances. 'He never (said the Doctor) would allow that a friend was sick till he heard of his death.'"[60] Ferguson said that Home represented his own warmth of character in Young Norval in *Douglas*,[61] and it is surely no accident that in an Edinburgh rehearsal of the play Roberson read the part of the staid, dignified Lord Randolph.[62]

Home was ordained at Athelstaneford, just a few miles from Gladsmuir, in February 1747 after receiving his license to preach from the Edinburgh presbytery, having passed through his trials before the Haddington presbytery. But it soon became apparent that Home's mind, like Robertson's, was not on his parish duties. In a poem addressed to his friend Thomas Barrow dated November 1747, Home expressed the frustration he (and perhaps Robertson) felt with his situation just nine months after being ordained.

> You ask me Barrow how I brook,
>   The village life forlorn;
> And hold discourse with Swains that talk,
>   Of Cattle and of Corn.
>
> In such discourse I never join,
>   I have one Occupation;
> And very Strange, tho' true it is,
>   Only one Recreation.

Neither occupation nor recreation involved the ministry:

> All day I read, or walk alone,
>   Repeating as I go;
> In Latin Greek or English Verse
>   The Tales of war and woe.
>
> At Eve I trim the vestal fire
>   That Burns both night and day,
> From Verse to Prose, I often change;
>   And muse the Hours away.

Worse, he is in Athelstaneford, isolated in obscurity while his friends make their way in the world:

> On the wide Ocean of this World,
>   For various Ports you steer,
> Whilst anchored in a Sand lock'd Bay,
>   I ride inglorious here.[63]

As one might expect, in the eyes of his colleagues on the Haddington presbytery, Home neglected his ministry.[64] Most egregiously, between December and May 1749–50 and March to May 1757, Home disappeared from his parish to try to have first *Agis* and then *Douglas* staged in London. The first time he incurred the censure of the presbytery, which seemed baffled by his absence; the second time he returned to angry charges concerning his writing *Douglas*, and Robertson had to step in to stall presbytery proceedings so that Home would have time to resign his charge. Although it is claimed that Home was beloved by his parishioners,[65] it was probably not because he was a particularly effective minister.

As far as Robertson was concerned, Home had other virtues. His "love of letters, and his ardour for poetry" were perhaps bracing for Robertson during the years after his parents' deaths. Robertson may have been thinking about or even writing the *History of Scotland* at this time, and Home's enthusiasm for history ("Tales of war and woe") and other reading "of a kind to inflame the imagination and to dramatize, as it were, the passions" may have helped cultivate his interest in history. Plutarch was Home's favorite, "the author constantly in his hands,"[66] and we know that about the time of the death of his parents in 1745, Robertson read Enrico Davila's history of the civil wars in France, a work popular for its drawing of historical character.[67] Home was also close to the convivial Sir David Kinloch, who had recently moved into Gilmerton House with his new bride Harriet Cockburn. The house soon became "a great resort for John Home and his friends of the clergy."[68] Sir David was on friendly terms with David Hume and would entertain Smollett in 1753.[69] Together with Carlyle, Home also blazed the way to London in pursuit of literary fame, something Robertson would have to undertake as well. Home carried Carlyle's introduction to Smollett, who became a life-long friend; met William Collins, whom he inspired to write the *Ode on the Popular Superstitions of the Highlands*; and dealt (though unsuccessfully initially) with David Garrick. Robertson followed Home's lead and established acquaintance with Smollett and Garrick as well.

Ordained at Inveresk in 1748, just a few miles from Gladsmuir, Carlyle was, of course, one of Robertson's most enduring companions in the east Lothian vicinity. For Carlyle, Robertson was an iconic figure representing the scholarship and leadership to which the Moderates aspired.

> As the Leader of a party in the Management of Ecclesiastical Affairs, Robertson stands unrivaled for ability and Success. As at the Head of Learning in the first university of Scotland for Importance, the Conduct of the Principal was highly Meritorious.[70]

Carlyle saw himself as part of Robertson's achievement and worked with him consistently on the Moderate agenda, but he did not see himself as Robertson's agent but rather as his own man pursuing a parallel but distinct course. He had no problem criticizing Robertson. When, for instance, he was pursuing the abolition of the window tax for clergy in 1770 and Robertson told Mary Carlyle her husband was wasting his time, Carlyle had no problem telling her in return that "Robertson speaks nonsense."[71] The Carlyles and the Robertsons were on a familiar social footing with each other, as Mary indicates in a letter at this same time to her husband, who was still in London:

> Dr. Robertson, and wife, and daughters, surprised us yesterday in the middle of dinner: by a strange mistake their letter did not come; however, being Market Day they got a most excellent stake, and I gave him a Bottle of my best, and I realy believe he passed a very Comfortable day for no body presumed to interrupt him and he brayed incessantly; we were realy very happy and parted much better friends then ever we were before; they took a qualm I fin'd at having paid me so little attention this winter, and was in haste to do some thing before you appeared; however it is all made up now . . .[72]

The informal occasion is cordial and relaxed, though Mary's reference to incessant braying injects irony. One notices the same relationship between Carlyle and Robertson in the later *Autobiography*. Carlyle's admiration and loyalty are also tinged with suspicion and distrust, some of it sparked, perhaps, by Robertson's quietly supporting Carlyle's younger opponent Andrew Dalzel during Carlyle's losing campaign for the clerkship of the General Assembly in 1789.[73] In politics, Carlyle notes, Robertson was by some accused of "Fickleness" and even "Ingratitude." But rather than defend Robertson against such charges, Carlyle drew a different moral: "the Leaders of Conversation should not forget that their Words are Mark'd, and that [it] is sometimes better to be accounted Weak, Than Unstable and Inconsistant, for which the best Motives are seldom ascrib'd."[74] Carlyle's admiration never blinded him to the failings (real or perceived) of his friend.

Another member of the Adam–Robertson circle – and a particularly close friend to Robert Adam – was Adam Ferguson. He arrived at Edinburgh from St. Andrews in 1743 to study divinity and during his residency he quickly formed attachments with Robertson's circle. But in 1745 he was appointed deputy chaplain of the 43rd Highland Regiment on the basis of his knowledge of Gaelic and followed the regiment to the Netherlands. His earliest surviving letter, addressed to John Adam and dated just days before the Jacobites arrived in Edinburgh in September

1745, gives a sense of his attachment to the group: "I long exceedingly," he writes, "to hear from you . . . I am sure if you are sensible of the Pleasure it will give me to hear from you will not delay it Long."[75] Although he traveled on the Continent during his early years, he eventually held the chair of moral philosophy at the University of Edinburgh from 1764 to 1785, where he would become a (sometimes troublesome) ally for Robertson.

Robertson's ties to some of his other clerical friends were equally close, if not more so, compared to those with Home and Carlyle, but those ties are known in less detail. Hugh Blair, for example, whom Robertson had known probably from his time in the Divinity Hall about 1740,[76] was translated to Edinburgh Canongate from Collessie in Fife in 1743. He became a strong ally of Robertson, signing (though with some misgiving) the *Reasons of Dissent* of 1752 along with Home, Jardine, Logan, and others; he would become an important figure in Robertson's writing life later on, the two of them constantly exchanging their work for comments and adopting one another's writing practices.[77] Indeed, Carlyle notes that they "Liv'd in perfect Concord and the Daily Interchange of Friendly Offices During the 32 Years in which they were Members of the University of Edin[r]."[78] But their informal social contact prior to Robertson's move to Edinburgh in 1758 is not well documented; and in the 1740s, with Robertson in Gladsmuir and Blair at the Canongate Church before his move to St. Giles and busy establishing his reputation as a preacher, their interaction may not have been frequent after their college years. But Carlyle insists that travel from places like Gladsmuir or Inveresk was not an obstacle to friendship:

> It was peculiar to this City and to this Period, That [one] could arrive from the Country in the Afternoon, and be almost Certain of assembling Such Men as David Hume, and Adam Smith, and Blair, and Robertson and John Home and Ad. Ferguson, &c. &c. in a Tavern by 7 aclock which was the Hour of Supper in those Days and the chief time of convivial entertainment, till about the Year 1760.[79]

Though very amiable and a steady friend, Blair was retiring, Carlyle claiming he was "timid and unambitious, and withheld himself from public business of every kind."[80] Furthermore, his "infantine" conversation suggests he sheltered himself behind his literary labors as well the temperament of his wife, Katherine Bannatine, the daughter of James Bannatine and sister of Hew Bannatine. Katherine possessed a "Masculine Understanding," and she was "a Mate of a Superior and Decisive Mind, on which he could Rely for advice, in all his Doubts and Perplexities, which Occurred almost every Hour."[81]

Two other college friends were to play key roles in what would be called "Dr. Robertson's *administration*."[82] One was John Jardine, six years older than Robertson and "a hard-headed, jolly dog," in Boswell's estimation,[83] traits that would balance Robertson's lack of ease. The letters that Robertson wrote to Jardine are among the least formal in his correspondence, expressing both Jardine's openness and Robertson's comfort with him as an ally.[84] David Hume wrote from France that he yearned for the roughness of the Poker Club "and particularly the sharpness of Dr. Jardine" to counteract the lusciousness of French *politesse*."[85] Carlyle admired his worldliness: Jardine "had much sagacity, with great versatility of genius, and a talent for the management of men."[86] His first ministry was in Liberton in 1741 and then on to Lady Yester's (1750) and the Tron Church (1754) in Edinburgh. Marriage with Jean Drummond, the daughter of Provost George Drummond, in 1744 gave him a place within civic politics as well as the church, leading one critic to complain in 1763, when Jardine was dean of the Order of the Thistle

> The P[rovos]t, who dances, you know, to the whistle
> Of that arch-politician, the D[ea]n of the T[hist]le.[87]

The provost at the time was Drummond. Jardine's death in 1766 was a severe blow to Robertson because he lost a skilled ally and friend, but he soon found another effective manager, though of different disposition, in John Drysdale. He was three years older than Robertson but only two years ahead of him at university. In 1762, Robertson described him as

> among the oldest & most intimate of my companions [.] I can answer for his abilities, his unblemished character, & his goodness of heart. He is a good Scholar, & an excellent Preacher, & if you have not heard so much of him as of some other of his contemporaries, it is not because he has less merit, but because he is naturally shy & by some circumstance of his situation has been left much at home.[88]

Drysdale was licensed to preach in 1740 but spent the next several years serving as assistant minister to James Bannatine in the Trinity College Church in Edinburgh. He then moved on, securing a presentation to the parish of Kirkliston through the Earl of Hopetoun in 1748 and then marrying into the Adam family in 1749. His translation to Edinburgh in 1762 created a substantial fight between the Town Council and the Edinburgh ministers over rights of appointment, and Drysdale was so grateful for Robertson's support that "he resolved to give that eminent leader [Robertson] every assistance in his power, in support of what was called the moderate party in the church."[89]

Two other clergymen filled out the immediate circle around Robertson. Hew (or Hugh) Bannatine (d. 1769) was probably a college acquaintance for Robertson, and Carlyle met him in 1740 when he attended Divinity Hall when Robertson was there. Carlyle speaks highly of his sound good sense and judgment in life and in literary matters as well as his command of classical learning. Ranked among Carlyle's "Closest and most Discerning Friends, such as Ferguson and Robertson, and Blair,"[90] Bannatine enlisted alongside his ministerial friends as a volunteer in the Edinburgh brigade during the '45; he then went abroad sometime during 1745–7 as a tutor to James Johnston of Hilton, a major in the First Regiment of Dragoons "so much admir'd for his Beauty, and for his Many Duels";[91] and finally he returned to ordination at Ormiston in the presbytery of Dalkeith in 1747 followed by translation to Dirleton in Haddington presbytery in 1749, where he quickly settled in as one of the four (Carlyle, Home, Bannatine, and Robertson) in the circle of friends who lived in the country but would travel regularly to Edinburgh for suppers with the others living in town. He helped Robertson and Stedman to fend off the presbytery's effort to depose Home in 1757.[92] Less prominent in this group was George Logan, who replaced Bannatine at Ormiston after his translation to Dirleton in 1751. He, too, was an acquaintance from Divinity Hall, a volunteer for the college company, and helped to form Carlyle's "Chief Society" in the country.[93] Though Carlyle acknowledges Logan was "a Man of parts and Genius" particularly interested in mathematics and metaphysics, he also saw "he was of an Indolent and Dilatory Disposition."[94] That disposition included Logan's plagiarizing Carlyle's popular sermon delivered to the Haddington presbytery for his trials at the Dalkeith presbytery. The sermon had been successful at Haddington, but it backfired at Dalkeith, producing an investigation into its orthodoxy that Logan barely survived. Logan died in 1754 with a grieving Carlyle at his bedside.[95]

Among this group of college companions, we also catch glimpses of two shadowy figures that may or may not have been well known to Robertson. They lay outside the circle of clerical friends, but both possessed stimulating intellects. William McGhie and William Cleghorn appear incidentally among the college volunteers described by Carlyle offering to defend the city of Edinburgh in September 1745 when the Jacobite army was preparing to meet General Cope at Prestonpans. McGhie was a doctor and poet, whose medical studies coincided with Robertson's divinity studies in Edinburgh.[96] After the Jacobite invasion, during which he seems to have been a prisoner,[97] he moved to London's Grub Street and appears as a beloved member of Samuel Johnson's Ivy Lane Club,[98] which was begun in 1749, and, about this same time, a member of Tobias Smollett's circle, an important group for any Scot interested in literature. Carlyle, thinking McGhie one of the "steadiest" of the volunteers,[99] had recommended him to Smollett, who had on his own found him to be of "Value" and vowed to "cultivate his Acquaintance to the uttermost." Pursuing the friendship, Smollett found him to be a warm companion, though shy and reserved as a poet.[100] Unfortunately, we do not know Robertson's opinion of him because by the time Robertson made his first trip to London in order to secure a publisher for the *History of Scotland* and spend time with Smollett and his friends, McGhie had already been dead two years. William Cleghorn remained closer to home. He is most remembered for his having been elected as Professor of Pneumatics and Moral Philosophy at the University of Edinburgh over David Hume just a few months prior to his volunteering for the college company. Although his professorship brought him no fame, he appears to have been a high-minded rationalist, judging from Adam Ferguson's dialogue "An Excursion in the Highlands," and at one point he seems to share Robertson's view of the rational intellect as expressed in "De probabilitate historica": "the Almighty in superadding Intelligence to the Animal & Sensitive nature of Man gave him the Power of discriminating Excellence & Defect."[101] As a result, Cleghorn maintained that there is no need to assume the existence of a separate moral sense because moral discrimination is a matter of reason. Surprisingly for a rationalist and idealist, however, Cleghorn also shared much with John Home, Carlyle commenting that they were both "very fiery" in the face of the advancing Jacobites in the '45.[102]

The Jacobite invasion disrupted any plans Robertson might have had. At the time Charles Edward Stuart raised his standard at Glenfinnan on 19 August, Robertson had barely finished the first year of his parish duties. He had met regularly with the kirk session and the presbytery to conduct routine business and hold disciplinary hearings; he had reviewed with the session the state of the funds for poor maintenance, including airing the issue of a workhouse for the presbytery; and he had held his first Communion service on 28 July. Over the summer, Carlyle had been busy undergoing trials before the Haddington presbytery, which required his attendance, and, as the newest member of the presbytery, he was appointed to record the minutes from June to December. But word of Charles's landing reached Edinburgh by 8 August,[103] and the Gladsmuir kirk session meeting of 18 August was the last recorded until 4 May 1746. By 25 August, the Jacobite forces, having outmaneuvered Cope's, were beginning to make their way south toward Perth, Stirling, and Edinburgh. As this threat unfolded, the presbytery of Haddington suspended regular business on 10 September. What followed glowed with the martial and civic spirit of Marcus Aurelius, although mixed with a dash of comic opera.

The *Caledonian Mercury* for 12 September painted a picture of a city busy making orderly preparations and recruiting volunteers for defense:

> The Right Hon. The Lord Provost of this City is constantly employed in reviewing the Train'd Bands, and enlisting Recruits for his Lordship's Regiment, who come in every Hour in Numbers, and immediately enter upon Pay . . . So that the Lord Provost of Edinburgh, who is also Colonel of the Train'd Bands and City Guard, will speedily be in a Condition to put himself at the Head of a formidable little Army.
>
> The Gentlemen Volunteers of the Association are constantly exercised, in order to know the Use of the Firelock and Bayonet; and some of the Rev. Ministers file along with them.

The reality was rather different. Although Provost John Stewart had been warned in August that Charles had landed, the provost made little progress on defenses for the city, leading ultimately to charges of Jacobite sympathies for which he was tried but acquitted. Nor were a great many citizens eager to resist the invading Jacobites, and on 18 September the Town Council voted to disband the volunteers and offer no opposition. But an excited Carlyle arrived on 13 September to find the city "in great ferment and bustle."[104] He immediately joined along with his close companions Robertson, Home, McGhie, Bannatine, Cleghorn, Wilkie, Logan and others forming the "first or College Company" of volunteers to be commanded by former Provost George Drummond. The volunteers gathered on the 13th, drilled on the 14th, and on the 15th gathered in the College Yards to hear Drummond propose they join the two regiments of royal dragoons already in the city who had been ordered to engage the Jacobites in expectation that Cope's troops would arrive imminently. The volunteers "answered by an unanimous shout of applause."[105] They immediately marched up to the Lawnmarket, through the Luckenbooths, and down the Bow into the Grassmarket, along the way greeted with tears and ridicule from a divided city. In the Grassmarket, they were met by the loyal Hanovarian William Wishart, who believed resistance would be useless at this point and pleaded with them "to desist from this rash enterprise, which he said was exposing the flower of the youth of Edinburgh, and the hope of the next generation."[106] With some recruits already drifting away, the speech quelled the volunteers' ardor, and they were ordered back to the College Yards and dismissed. After a lively dinner at which the band debated courses of action, they took up their watch at the Netherbow Gate. The next day their civic spirit was dealt another blow when the two regiments of Cope's dragoons fled to Dunbar after an exchange of fire, and on the morning of the 17th the Jacobite army entered Edinburgh through the very gate the volunteers had watched and quickly took possession of the city.

Meanwhile, Carlyle, Cleghorn, and Robertson, accompanied by Robertson's cousin Fraser, remained determined to fight and decided to set off for Dunbar and join Cope's forces. But this plan, too, proved a comic failure. After dining at Carlyle's father's house in Prestonpans, they made their way on the Dunbar road to East Linton where Robertson and Fraser proposed to spend the rest of the night. In their great enthusiasm for battle,[107] Carlyle and Cleghorn pressed on to Dunbar, but they were not admitted to Cope's camp and had to make their way back to Linton where they begged lodgings from the local minister. When Robertson and Fraser greeted them in the morning, fresh and rested, Carlyle ruefully noted, "such is the difference between wisdom and folly."[108] On the 18th, the group made another visit to the camp, but it proved uneventful (except for Carlyle's observation of Cope's dejection), and they returned again to Linton through which, on the 19th, they saw Cope's army pass on their march toward Haddington and take their position in a field between Seton and Preston, near Prestonpans. On the morning of the 20th Cope's army marched to the battlefield, while the Pretender's forces, which had left Edinburgh on the 19th, managed to circle around Cope's position on the night of the 20th and attack from the east after dawn on the 21st. The battle was over quickly with Cope's troops in disorderly retreat, and Edinburgh, except for a pocket of resistance remaining at Edinburgh Castle, was now in Charles's hands.

Robertson as a named individual drops out of Carlyle's narrative after the camp visit on 18 September. He may well have been among the volunteers who followed the army to Haddington on the 19th, but it is unclear what he did after that. Carlyle returned to his father's house in Prestonpans on the 20th and the next day was able to see the edge of the battlefield where the "whole prospect was filled with runaways, and Highlanders pursuing them."[109] But events in the wake of the defeat give us a clue as to Robertson's actions. Carlyle's concerns were twofold as likely were Robertson's: his own personal safety and the security of his household. The Highlanders were said to be especially hard on captured volunteers, and Carlyle's father kept him out of sight and arranged for his departure to Holland on 9 October. He also spent time hiding valuables. Robertson's father, like the other Edinburgh ministers, had stopped preaching as much from a policy to put pressure on their parishioners by withholding the word of God as a desire for their safety and may have left the city altogether.[110] Robertson himself returned to his parish, about two miles to the east of Carlyle's house and in the opposite direction from the captured city, to keep out of sight, no doubt sharing Carlyle's assessment of the deplorable situation and the meanness of the Highland army:

> This view I had of the rebel army confirmed me in the prepossession that nothing but the weakest and most unaccountable bad conduct on our part could have possibly given them the victory. God forbid that Britain should ever again be in danger of being overrun by such a despicable enemy, for, at the best, the Highlanders were at that time but a raw militia, who were not cowards.[111]

Here Carlyle alludes to the origins of the militia issue that would occupy the Moderates, but his language, emphasizing the weakness and disorder of the British and the despicable character of the Highlanders, also calls attention to the kind of civic humanist thinking that underlay Robertson's earliest writing. Britain was defeated not only by its own weak character but also by slavish ignorance and tyranny.

From Robertson's point of view, the Jacobite invasion was an important moment because it impressed upon him the urgency of rebuilding the civic spirit of Britain.[112] From the point of view of the Presbyterian Church the events of the '45 were profoundly shocking, and parish ministers like Robertson were strongly advised of the terrible dangers posed. On 15 November, William Wishart issued on behalf of the commission of the General Assembly a "Warning and Exhortation" and sent it to all ministers with instructions to read it from the pulpit on the first Lord's Day. The Jacobite rebellion was a threat to religion and the state on a European-wide scale:

> We therefore do earnestly obtest all Protestants, all lovers of our religion, liberty and native country, to beware of the delusive arts which Romish emissaries from abroad, and the enemies of our constitution at home, have industriously and indefatigably used to destroy that glorious structure, which our gracious God reared up at the revolution, by King William of immortal memory.[113]

Major powers of Europe were behind this effort to replace Protestantism and liberty with Popery and arbitrary rule:

> But to complete our destruction, France and Spain, the avowed enemies of our country, not only of our religion, but of our trade and commerce, are called in to their [Jacobites'] assistance; who, whilst they are preparing to invade us at home, are distressing our trade abroad; with whom we are at open war, on the same principles on which war was waged in the reign of Queen Anne.[114]

Robertson and the Haddington presbytery shared these sentiments. Besides the injunction to read the "Warning and Exhortation" from the pulpit beginning in November, during September and October Robertson met regularly with the other members of the presbytery of Haddington, spending "a considerable time in prayer, upon account of the disorderly state of this country, thro' the present Rebellion."[115] As events moved toward a conclusion at the Battle of Culloden in April 1746, he together with the presbytery planned a Fast Day for 9 April in response to a call from the General Assembly to all presbyteries. At Haddington, the presbytery wished to address "the infalable [sic] tokens of God's displeasure against us in that detestable rebellion" in the tradition of the presbyterian jeremiad. The nation must engage in "solemn fasting, humiliation, & prayer" because the rebellion threatened the nation "with the loss of every thing dear to us as men or Christians, & which is avowedly supported by the united powers of Rome, France, & Spain the known & constant enemies of our Civil liberties & of our Holy protestant religion."[116] This was, indeed, a traumatic event that called for a response that would lay a proper intellectual foundation in church and state for Scotland's future as a civil society.

But however galvanized Robertson may have been by military and political events, the deaths of his father and mother on 16 and 22 November 1745 suddenly piled personal on top of national tragedy. We have no indication of how long they may have been ill, although the proximity of their deaths suggests they may have suffered some form of highly contagious pneumonia or influenza, perhaps arising from the stressful tumult of the Highlanders' occupation of the city from September to November. Their deaths left a deep mark on the twenty-five-year-old Robertson as suggested in a letter of 1759. He wrote to Margaret Hepburn to console her for the loss of her cousin Elizabeth Fletcher and suggested various remedies for distracting her from her sadness at her loss.

> I remember that on the greatest disappointment I shall ever meet with in human life
> (at least such I thought it at the time) I read all Davila's History. I frequently turned
> over several pages without knowing what I had been reading, but at other times it
> seized my attention, & I forgot every other thing.[117]

Although on its face this may seem rather tepid advice, for a man little given to intimate self-revelation it is a strong statement, and the fact that Robertson would recall his reading at the time some fourteen years later suggests the impact the event had on him.

Moreover, the loss of his parents may have left Robertson and his siblings in straitened circumstances. Of the eight Robertson children, five were between the ages of seventeen and twenty-five at the time of their parents' deaths, and three ranged between six and eleven. The provisions that were made for them are unclear. Were they to live with Robertson in the Gladsmuir manse? Or were some of the older children already established in Edinburgh, and could they have provided care? The usual explanation is that Robertson himself took on the responsibility for their care, making, in Stewart's eyes, a heroic sacrifice: "Undeterred by the magnitude of a charge, which must have appeared fatal to the prospects that had hitherto animated his studies, and resolved to sacrifice to a sacred duty all personal considerations, he invited his father's family to Gladsmuir, and continued to educate his sisters under his own roof, till they were settled respectably in the world."[118] Brougham adds that the eldest sister, Mary, superintended the family, and Stewart J. Brown notes Robertson relied on his modest stipend because they were without any other provision.[119] But the actual picture seems a bit more complicated. In April 1747, William Adam stepped in and along with Robertson made application for support to the newly established Widow's Fund managed by the Edinburgh presbytery. Their application stated that there were three children at home under the age of sixteen (Helen, Jean, and Eupham[120]) who accordingly "are entitled to draw out of the fund lately raised for a Provision to the Widows and Children of the ministers of this Church Two hundred and fifty pounds Sterling at Whitsunday next, but have no Tutors or Curators nominated by their Parents nor otherwise appointed for them." In June, Adam and Robertson agreed to act as trustees to the three children.[121] One wonders if some of the children might have stayed in Edinburgh with the Adams because in 1728 William Adam had moved his family to a house on the south side of the Cowgate near Niddry's Wynd, and, by 1745 he had built a new tenement there "clearly of considerable size and quality."[122] But with three or more children staying with the minister in Gladsmuir, the manse may have been rather crowded. Although built in 1725 and thus fairly new when Robertson occupied it, the manse was on a modest enough scale that it had to be enlarged considerably in 1841 because its then-occupant could not accommodate visiting ministers who came to assist him with communion.[123]

Even with assistance, Robertson's time must have been heavily taxed. The period from about 1747 to 1751 is the most obscure in Robertson's life because he left no writing from this time, and there is virtually no description of his activities apart from attendance at presbytery and synod meetings. There are records of his sister Margaret's marriage in 1750 and his own in 1751, and we know from presbytery minutes that he was seriously ill between January and April 1748. Brown speculates that his family burdens may have motivated him to advance himself in the church and the university,[124] and those burdens are certainly one dimension of his response to the Jacobite invasion. But intertwined with his personal concerns were concerns about the nation's future. Together, these personal and national motives prompted him to think seriously about writing history, and, fortunately, assistance was at hand. It is commonly assumed Robertson attended (and perhaps even plagiarized from) Adam Smith's lectures on rhetoric and the history of philosophy, which were being given in Edinburgh between 1748 and 1751.

No evidence has ever been cited to show that Robertson attended these lectures, though W. R. Scott concluded that "a considerable proportion of the younger ministers of Edinburgh ... attended" and "William Robertson ... was one of these."[125] Nor do we know the exact content of Smith's lectures. Scott argued that the lectures, which stretched over three years, consisted of at least one set on rhetoric and belles-lettres and one (probably in the last year) on civil law probably intended for students of jurisprudence. If the surviving version of Smith's rhetoric lectures from 1762–3 resembled the earlier ones,[126] Robertson may well have been quite interested in them, given his abiding concern with prose style as demonstrated by his Greek translation and by close attention to stylistic questions throughout his life. Like Smith, Robertson preferred Swift to Shaftesbury for style. In addition, one more tiny but tantalizing piece of evidence may speak to the pertinence of Smith's lectures: some time between 5 January and 15 July 1748, perhaps as he was recovering from his lengthy illness during that time, Robertson withdrew from John Gray's Library in Haddington a copy of Philippe de Commynes's *Memoirs*.[127] Traditionally considered a detached and impartial historian (qualities very important to Robertson) as well as a skeptic who exposed the realities behind the heroic fictions of historians like Froissart, Commynes might indicate a shared concern with the manner of writing history.[128] If Smith laid out the task of the historian in his Edinburgh lectures as he did in 1762–3, he would have confirmed Robertson's prior thinking about literary style as shown in his translation. Moreover, impartiality is an essential for historians, who ought to design their narratives "in view of narrating facts as they are without magnifying them or diminishing them."[129]

Scott claims that Robertson would have been more interested in the lectures on civil law and that the content of the lectures gave rise to friction between the two later on. Scott relies on John Callander of Craigforth's assertion that Robertson "borrowed the first volume of his History of Charles V" from the lectures on law, which contained the first outlines of the famous four-stages theory of history.[130] Ronald L. Meek points also to a document written by Smith in 1755 declaring that certain "leading principles," including the four-stages theory, were his property.[131] Smith said he drew up the document because he feared some unnamed person was going to steal them. Coupled with Callander's assertion, then, the evidence seems to point to Robertson as the would-be plagiarist. But the charge is difficult to accept at face value. It would not be until 1765, when he began writing the introduction to *Charles V*, that Robertson would compose anything that might be said to draw specifically on stadial ideas.[132] Robertson's interest in stadial concepts may owe more to Lord Kames's *Historical Law-Tracts* (1758) than to Smith's lectures,[133] and from clerical sources he already knew how providence brings about progress in human affairs, amply displayed in his sermon on *The Situation of the World* in 1755. Although lectures on rhetoric and jurisprudence would be of value to someone thinking about writing history, Smith's lectures were not Robertson's sole source for ideas.

Immediate political and ecclesiastical events, combined with his intellectual background, moved Robertson toward history along with Smith's lectures. In May 1748, with George Wishart moderating, the General Assembly sent the draft of an overture to the presbyteries seeking their opinion. In it, the Assembly sought to

> earnestly beseech and obtest all the ministers of this Church to be diligent in instructing the people committed to their care, in those principles of pure Christianity that are particularly opposite to the errors and corruptions of Popery and in the grounds and reasons of the Reformation, and the principles on which the late glorious Revolution and our present happy Establishment are founded.[134]

The overture received a mixed reception with many questioning whether ministers were capable of preaching on such politically charged topics, especially given the confused loyalties of the Rebellion. The 1749 Assembly therefore softened the language, lessened requirements, and only recommended such preaching. But Robertson appears to have been sufficiently sympathetic to the overture to become, in the midst of the 1748 Assembly, a member of the Old Revolution Club. To become a member, he had to echo the language of the overture by declaring "the Gratfull Sense he has of the Deliverance of the Kingdoms of Great Brittain & Ireland from Popery & Slavery" first by William and Mary and latterly by George II, to whom he swears his "Zealous Attachment." A history of Scotland, instructing its readers in how to think about Scottish politics and history, might help shore up the uncertain response to the Assembly's overture.

At the same time, within the church questions of rebellion and allegiance had become increasing urgent in the context of the patronage controversy. After 1740, cases of disputed ministerial appointments had accumulated, with fifty lodged with the General Assembly by 1750.[135]

Given the direction of Robertson's thinking from about 1740, it is easy to see why he felt this crisis urgently needed attention. In the same way that Whitefield's preaching and the Jacobite Rebellion undermined both social stability and the engagement of the church with current humanist thinking, so did the confusion over patronage appointments. From his perspective, the quality of appointments was often in the hands of those least able to judge candidates, and church appointments were crucial to building a modern society. This issue was not merely an abstract one for Robertson, as he discovered with the church appointment of his soon-to-be brother-in-law, James Syme in the parish of Alloa. This episode dramatizes just how much social disruption was at stake in the issue of church appointments.

Born in 1723, Syme was the same age as Robertson's oldest sister, Mary. We do not know when they met, but their wedding took place on 17 October 1751, just after his appointment at Alloa was settled. The presbytery of Stirling had granted him a license to preach in 1747, and his call to the parish of Alloa had come in early May 1750. But the call was disputed by the majority of parishioners supporting another candidate, James Skirvan. Syme was a worthy candidate for Robertson to support: he had completed an M.A. at King's College, Aberdeen, served as a tutor to young Sir Ralph Abercromby of Tullibody, near Alloa, and had the support of the principal heritor, George Abercromby. At first, the Stirling presbytery rejected both calls, but the decision was overturned by a special committee (called a riding committee) in August 1750 and the appointment of Syme approved. But trouble developed when the ordination edict was delivered on 16 September: the minister bearing the edict, John Warden of Gargunnock, was set upon by a group of colliers, his attendants beaten, and the edict taken from him. Then the protestors

> "rung the church-bell from morning to night, and in the afternoon displayed a flag from the steeple in token of victory, none offering to oppose them." To obviate the recurrence of this, four companies of soldiers were stationed in the town some time before the day of ordination, but he was settled without any disturbance.

Finally, on 21 November 1750, Syme was ordained at Alloa, with four ministers, three elders, and a small group of friends attending. No one came from the presbytery of Stirling. Among the friends were John Drysdale and Robertson.[136]

But the story does not end here because the legal repercussions for the protestors were severe, adding to the social damage. On 11 January the Lords of the Justiciary Court banished four protestors to the "plantations for seven years, to be computed from the time of their landing; with certification, that such of them as should return to Scotland within the time limited, should *toties quoties*, be whipped through Edinburgh, and re-transported for other seven years." Another "was banished Scotland for seven years, from and after 30th of January, and in case of his returning, to be *toties quoties* whipped through Edinburgh, and banished other seven years." Yet another "was fined 200 merks Scots to the private pursuers, and ordained to be kept prisoner in Edinburgh tolbooth, till the 15th of May next." Finally, the only woman sentenced

> was ordained to pass through Edinburgh on the 29th of January, her hands tied behind her back with a rope, the hangman walking immediately behind her, and holding the end of this rope in one hand, and his whip in the other, and then to be confined to the Edinburgh correction-house, at hard labour, till the 15th of May next.

No well-regulated church or civil society could tolerate such upheavals on an accelerating scale, and Robertson set about to address the problem.

Notes

1. *Scots Anticipation; or, A Summary of a Debate* (Edinburgh, 1779), p. 9. Robertson may also have been represented as a vulture. See Mossner, *David Hume*, pp. 391–2 and n. 1.
2. Clunie, "Account," p. 494. The details of the Gladsmuir parish are drawn from John Martine, *Reminiscences and Notices of Ten Parishes of the County of Haddington*, ed. E. J. Wilson (Haddington, 1894), pp. 174–99, and Patricia Coupe, *From Witches to Dragons: Life in an East Lothian Country Manse from the Covenanters to Gladsmuir Today* (n. p., 2012).
3. Sher, *Church and University*, p. 34.
4. *The Tryal of Witchcraft; or, Witchcraft Arraign'd and Condemn'd* (Glasgow, [1700?]).
5. Martine, *Reminiscences*, p. 187.
6. Robertson to Dalrymple, 4 January 1755, NLS MS 25,300, f. 63. The minutes of the Haddington presbytery do not record any punishment given to Purdie.
7. In 1773, Robertson again endorsed Dalrymple's efforts to quell superstition. He told Johnson that it was right for a man of known piety to "undeceive" those who still believed in the "fanatic" visions of Euphan McCullen (Boswell, *Life*, V, 39 and n.; Dalrymple, *Remarks on the History of Scotland* (Edinburgh, 1773), ch. XVI).
8. Even worse, Purdie was said to be very popular as a preacher, drawing "multitudes" to his communion services from surrounding parishes (David Louden, *History of Morham* [Haddington, 1889], p. 63).
9. *Life*, III, 334.

10. Ibid., III, 350. Boswell here is recalling Robertson's remarks some two weeks after their original conversation.

11. Ibid., III, 334–5.

12. "Account," in *Miscellaneous Works*, p. 178.

13. *History*, III, 37.

14. Stewart, "Account," in *Miscellaneous Works*, p. 197. See also Bower, *History*, III, 38.

15. NLS MS 3,980, f. 129.

16. "Principal Robertson," *Thistle, or Anglo-Caledonian Journal*, 1 (February 1836), p. 63.

17. "Agency," in *Miscellaneous Works*, p. 274.

18. *Mrs. Montagu, "Queen of the Blues": Her Letters and Friendships from 1762 to 1800*, ed. Reginal Blunt, 2 vols (London: Constable, n. d.), I, 145.

19. Islay Burns, *The Pastor of Kilsyth: or Memorials of the Life and Times of the Rev. W. H. Burns* (London: Nelson, 1860), p. 38.

20. Matheson, *Theories of Rhetoric*, p. 29.

21. *Lectures on Rhetoric*, II, 321–2.

22. Stewart reaches the same conclusion ("Account," in *Miscellaneous Works*, pp. 197–8).

23. *Recollections of the Table-Talk of Samuel Rogers* (New York, 1856), p. 45.

24. Cockburn, *Memorials*, p. 55; see also Stewart, "Account," in *Miscellaneous Works*, p. 195.

25. Ian Simpson Ross, *Life of Adam Smith* (Oxford: Clarendon Press, 1995), p. 85; Matheson, *Theories of Rhetoric*, pp. 236–8.

26. Quoted in Matheson, *Theories of Rhetoric*, p. 236.

27. Stewart, "Account," in *Miscellaneous Works*, p. 195.

28. NLS MS 25,411, f. 66.

29. Ibid., ff. 19–20.

30. See the useful summary of Walker's orthodox views in Ahnert, *Moral Culture*, pp. 107–8.

31. *Sermons on Practical Subjects*, 3rd edn, 2 vols (London, 1783), I, 82–3.

32. "Student Essay," in *Miscellaneous Works*, p. 13. The influence of Francis Hutcheson is also present. See his *Essay on the Nature and Conduct of the Passions and Affections*, ed. Aaron Garrett (Indianapolis: Liberty Fund, 2002), p. 132.

33. NLS MS 25,411, f. 64.

34. Walker, *Sermons*, I, 231.

35. Ibid., p. 227.

36. For helpful background on the relation of providential thinking to history in the period, see David Allan, *Virtue, Learning and the Scottish Enlightenment* (Edinburgh: Edinburgh University Press, 1993).

37. NLS MS 25,411, f. 61.

38. *The Confession of Faith* (Edinburgh, 1787), pp. 45–6.

39. NLS MS 25,411, ff. 69–70.

40. "Account," in *Miscellaneous Works*, p. 108.

41. Gleig, "Some Account," p. xviii.

42. *History*, III, 37–8.

43. "Robertson," in *Miscellaneous Works*, pp. 262–3.

44. Brown, "William Robertson," in *William Robertson*, p. 9.

45. Coupe, *From Witchcraft to Dragons*, pp. 40–1. I have been unable to locate in the Haddington presbytery minutes where Robertson is specifically reprimanded for his handling of sexual lapses.

46. NAS MS CH2/169/2, ff. 31, 40–1, 55.

47. "Copy scroll letter from Carlyle to Stewart," NLS 23,920, ff. 81–5.

48. *Autobiography*, pp. 103, 105.

49. Ibid., p. 72.

50. NAS MS CH2/185/12, p. 313.

51. On the level of the presbytery, Robertson's attendance was in part stimulated by his steering through the nomination of Robert Dundas to fill the vacancy in Humbie parish in 1754. Robertson had been so charged by a letter from Robert Dundas of Arniston of 6 August 1754 as recorded in the presbytery minutes. Dundas was a solid Moderate appointment, eventually marrying the daughter of Thomas Turnbull, the minister of Borthwick, who had proposed Robertson for the Gladsmuir parish and was a strong ally of both Robertson and his father.

52. Such a suspicion was put forward by the late Donald J. Withrington in an unpublished paper titled "Robertson's Early Ministry in Gladsmuir" at the conference on "William Robertson: Religion and the Historical Imagination in Eighteenth-Century Scotland," held at the University of Edinburgh, 22–23 October 1993. I am indebted to Withrington's paper.

53. Adam, *Sequel*, pp. 44–5; John Fleming, *Robert Adam and His Circle in Edinburgh and Rome* (Cambridge, MA: Harvard University Press), pp. 337–8.

54. Quoted in Fleming, *Robert Adam*, p. 5.

55. "Comparison," p. 278.

56. Stewart said that in the pulpit Robertson was "deficient in ease" though "interesting and impressive" ("Account," in *Miscellaneous Works*, p. 195). This formality was easily read as haughtiness. Benjamin Rush thought Robertson a "haughty Prelate," who was overbearing to inferiors and cringing to those above (EUL MS Dk.2.18[1], f. 113–14).

57. Ferguson to John Adam, 11 September 1745, in *Correspondence of Adam Ferguson*, ed. Vincenzo Merolle, 2 vols (London: William Pickering), I, 4. See also Jane Bush Fagg, "Biographical Introduction," ibid., I, xxiii.

58. *Account of the Life and Writings of John Home* (Edinburgh, 1822), p. 6.

59. *Autobiography*, p. 233.

60. Mackenzie, *Account*, pp. 7–8.

61. Ibid., pp. 6–7.

62. Sher, *Church and University*, p. 77.

63. EUL MS Dc.1.51, ff. 3–4.
64. Unfortunately, the kirk session minutes for Athelstaneford only date from 1770.
65. Gipson, *Life of Home*, p. 11.
66. Mackenzie, *Account*, pp. 30–1.
67. Robertson to [Margaret Hepburn], 12 January 1759, NLS MS 16,711, ff. 230–1.
68. Carlyle, *Autobiography*, p. 214.
69. Ibid., pp. 290–1.
70. "Comparison," p. 279.
71. Carlyle to Mary Carlyle, 24 April 1770, NLS MS 23,762, f. 63.
72. Mary Carlyle to Carlyle, 22 April 1770, NLS MS 23,762. f. 61.
73. See Carlyle's account in *Autobiography*, pp. 303–4.
74. "Comparison," pp. 279–80.
75. Ferguson to John Adam, 11 September 1745, in *Correspondence of Ferguson*, I, 6.
76. Blair was three years older than Robertson and accordingly was ahead of him in the university. Upon his completion of his MA degree in 1739 he remained in the university doing tutoring and probationary preaching for the next three years until his appointment at Collessie (Robert Morrell Schmitz, *Hugh Blair* [New York: King's Crown Press, 1948], p. 16).
77. Robertson to Andrew Dalzel, 28 August 1792, in Dalzel, *History of the University of Edinburgh*, 2 vols (Edinburgh, 1862), I, 96.
78. "Comparison," p. 281.
79. Ibid., p. 282.
80. *Autobiography*, pp. 305–6.
81. "Comparison," p. 278.
82. Stewart, "Account," in *Miscellaneous Works*, p. 185.
83. *Boswell's London Journal, 1762–1763*, ed. Frederick A. Pottle (New York: McGraw-Hill, 1950), p. 282.
84. Three of Robertson's letters to Jardine are University College London MSS: [Between 11 and 14 April 1756], 25 April 1757, and [16 March 1758]. A fourth letter is that of 20 April 1758 in Brougham, "Robertson," in *Miscellaneous Works*, pp. 278–9, where it is misdated as 1759. The tone is quite personal, and the salutations gradually migrate in the first three from "Dear Sir" to "Dear John" in the last one.
85. Hume to Adam Ferguson, 9 November 1763, in *Letters of David Hume*, ed. J. Y. T. Greig, 2 vols (1932; rpt. Oxford: Clarendon Press, 1969), I, 410.
86. *Autobiography*, p. 249.
87. Quoted in Richard B. Sher, "Moderates, Managers and Popular Politics in Mid-Eighteenth Century Edinburgh: The Drysdale 'Bustle' of the 1760s," in *New Perspectives on the Politics and Culture of Early Modern Scotland*, ed. John Dwyer et al. (Edinburgh: John Donald, n. d.), p. 189.
88. Robertson to Gilbert Elliot, 12 August 1762, NLS MS 11,009, f. 153.

89. Andrew Dalzel, "Account of the Life and Character of Dr. Drysdale," *Scots Magazine*, 55 (1793), pp. 366–7.
90. *Autobiography*, p. 425.
91. Ibid., p. 270.
92. Ibid., pp. 72n., 341.
93. Ibid., p. 231.
94. Ibid., p. 244.
95. Ibid., p. 315.
96. What little is known of of McGhie is summarized by Lewis Mansfield Knapp, *Tobias Smollett: Doctor of Men and Manners* (Princeton: Princeton University Press, 1949), pp. 80–2.
97. Archibald Cameron, *A Full and Authentic History of the Rebellion* (London, n. d.), p. 272.
98. W. Jackson Bate, *Samuel Johnson* (New York: Harcourt Brace Jovanovich, 1977), p. 266.
99. *Autobiography*, p. 131.
100. Smollett to Carlyle, 7 June 1748 and 1 October 1749, in *Letters of Tobias Smollett*, ed. Lewis M. Knapp (Oxford: Clarendon Press, 1970), pp. 9, 11.
101. "An Excursion in the Highlands," in *Manuscripts of Adam Ferguson*, ed. Vincenzo Merolle (London: Pickering & Chatto, 2006), p. 56.
102. *Autobiography*, p. 131.
103. James Grant, *Old and New Edinburgh*, 3 vols (London: Cassell, n. d.), I, 322.
104. *Autobiography*, p. 122.
105. Ibid., p. 125.
106. Ibid., p. 128.
107. When they stopped at an inn along the way to Linton, Cleghorn engaged in a "keen dispute" with a recruiting sergeant over whether a musket and bayonet was a superior weapon to a broadsword and target (ibid., pp. 139–40).
108. Ibid., p. 141.
109. Ibid., p. 151.
110. John Sibbald Gibson, *Edinburgh in the '45: Bonnie Prince Charlie at Holyrood* (Edinburgh: Saltire Society, 1995), pp. 30, 44, 50.
111. *Autobiography*, p. 157.
112. For discussions of this issue, see John Robertson, *The Scottish Enlightenment and the Militia Issue* (Edinburgh: John Donald, 1985), pp. 76–7; Sher, *Church and University*, pp. 37–44; and J. G. A. Pocock, *Barbarism and Religion: Narratives of Civil Government* (Cambridge: Cambridge University Press, 1999), pp. 265–7.
113. Morren, *Annals*, I, 75.
114. Ibid., I, 77.
115. NAS MS CH2/185/12, p. 251. The notes during 1745–6 are in Robertson's hand.
116. Ibid., p. 258.

117. Robertson to [Hepburn], 12 January 1759, NLS MS 16,711, f. 230.

118. "Account," in *Miscellaneous Works*, p. 107.

119. "Robertson," in *Miscellaneous Works*, p. 262; "William Robertson," in *William Robertson*, p. 10.

120. In the presbytery minutes Eupham is styled Eleanor. Perhaps in writing up the minutes the writer got the daughter's name confused with that of the deceased mother.

121. NAS MS CH2/121/16, pp. 152–3, 179.

122. Gifford, *William Adam*, p. 176.

123. Coupe, *From Witches to Dragons*, pp. 82–3, 111.

124. "William Robertson," in *William Robertson*, ed. Brown, p. 10.

125. Walter Robert Scott, *Adam Smith as Student and Professor* (1937; rpt. New York: Kelley, 1965), p. 63.

126. Ian Simpson Ross, *Life of Adam Smith* (Oxford: Clarendon Press, 1995), pp. 87–93. See Smith, *Lectures on Rhetoric and Belles Lettres*, ed. J. C. Bryce (1983; rpt. Indianapolis: Liberty Press, 1985).

127. NLS MS 16,480, f. 21. We do not know when Smith's lectures began in Edinburgh in 1748, but Robertson's withdrawal of Commynes from the library probably predates them. See Ross, *Adam Smith*, p. 86.

128. Smith's library contained a copy of the Paris, 1580, *Memoirs* (*Catalogue of the Library of Adam Smith*, ed. James Bonar [London, 1894], p. 24); however, Smith makes no reference to Commynes in his writings, though Robertson cites him a number of times in connection with his discussion of Louis XI in *Charles V*. For Commynes' refusal to exaggerate chivalric history, see Johan Huizinga, *The Autumn of the Middle Ages*, trans. Rodney J. Payton and Ulrich Mammitzsch (Chicago: University of Chicago Press, 1996), pp. 282–3. The Gray's library entry was never crossed through, perhaps indicating Robertson never returned the book.

129. Smith, *Lectures*, p. 101.

130. Scott, *Adam Smith*, p. 55.

131. *Social Science and the Ignoble Savage* (Cambridge: Cambridge University Press, 1976), pp. 110–11.

132. Ibid., p. 138.

133. See Chapter 4 below. Little has been said about Robertson's knowledge of Sir John Dalrymple's *Essay towards a General History of Feudal Property in Great Britain* (1757) as a possible source of stadial ideas. Dalrymple was a member of the Select Society, but there is no mention of the book in Robertson's known correspondence. He does cite it in the first edition of *Scotland* and again in *Charles V*. Like Kames, to whom the book is dedicated, Dalrymple sets up a three-stage evolution of society.

134. Morren, *Annals*, I, 109–10.

135. Brown, "William Robertson," in *William Robertson*, p. 12.

136. Morren, *Annals*, I, 185–6 n.

CHAPTER 4

Ministry and History, 1750–1759

In the 1750s, Robertson's attention moved from Gladsmuir to Edinburgh, a city about to undergo dramatic change, and Robertson was determined to contribute to that change. In 1752, Gilbert Elliot, who would be an important patron for Robertson, published *Proposals for Carrying on Certain Public Works in the City of Edinburgh* in which he captured the spirit of change at work in the city: he proposed constructing a merchant's exchange; administrative buildings for the town council, law courts, and an advocates' library; and an extension of the city both to the north and south, giving birth to Edinburgh's New Town. These proposals, made in the spirit of patriotism and the public interest in the wake of the Jacobite Rebellion, sought to develop the strength and prosperity appropriate to Edinburgh's new role in the reaffirmed Union:

> If the great objects of war and faction no longer present themselves, may they not find a more humane, and not less interesting exercise of their active powers, in promoting and cultivating the general arts of peace? In the reign of Queen *Elizabeth*, ENGLAND was but a forming state, as SCOTLAND is now. It was then that the spirit of the ENGLISH began to exert itself . . . In a lesser degree, the same disposition begins to discover itself in this country. Building bridges, repairing high-roads, establishing manufactures, forming commercial companies, and opening new veins of trade, are employments which have already thrown a lustre upon some of the first names of this country . . . [B]ut it is in prosecution of greater objects, that the leading men of a country ought to exert their power and influence. And what greater object can be presented to their view, than that of enlarging, beautifying, and improving the capital of their native country? What can redound more to their honour? What prove more beneficial to SCOTLAND, and by consequence to UNITED BRITAIN?[1]

To make this vision possible, the national culture had to be enlarged and beautified, and it is here that Robertson and his like-minded colleagues thought they had found their role. For them, the immediate issue was that church institutions had to be strengthened and practices regularized to make them effective parts of a well-ordered state. At the same time, the nation needed to know how to think about public affairs both in church and state. If Edinburgh were to emulate Elizabethan England in its public buildings, it would also need to shape its thinking about civil society to make those buildings meaningful. Reducing the chaos created by the patronage controversy was Robertson's immediate goal, but that task led to the broader one of showing Scotland the religious and cultural stance necessary for a successful civil society.

Alongside the city's new foundations, Robertson and his siblings were beginning to lay the foundations of their adult lives. In June 1750, at age twenty-five, Robertson's second oldest sister, Margaret, married Alexander Bruce, an Edinburgh merchant, taking up residence in Fairholm's Land in the middle of the West Bow.[2] In October 1752, his oldest sister, Mary, wed James Syme, the minister at Alloa. Elizabeth would not marry Archibald Hope, an accountant, until 1754, and Patrick, though he did not marry until 1769, was on his way to an established business. On 11 August 1751, Robertson himself, almost thirty, married his cousin Mary Nisbet, two years younger. In so doing, he married into a familiar and supportive family network. Mary was the daughter of James Nisbet, minister of the Old Kirk, Edinburgh, and his wife, Mary, was the daughter of David Pitcairn and the sister of Robertson's mother, Eleanor Pitcairn. Mary's siblings included brothers David, William, and Patrick (minister of Hutton on Dryfe and Corrie), and sister Janet. John Nisbet, a prominent Edinburgh Town Councilman, was also her brother and thus a useful political ally to Robertson making church appointments.[3] Mary's father, James, was brother-in-law to David Blair, father of poet Robert Blair, minister of Athelstaneford whom Robertson knew briefly during their service on the Haddington presbytery.

We do not know how or when William and Mary met, though given the close family ties they probably knew one another from an early age. Stewart says that marriage to Miss Nisbet "had long been the object of his wishes,"[4] and the proximity of the marriages of Robertson and his two sisters lends credence to the belief that Robertson postponed his own marriage until at least the eldest siblings were settled. From what little can be gleaned about her character, Mary Nisbet seemed ideally suited to be the family caretaker and helpmeet to a busy man of affairs who could be overbearing in company. We catch a brief glimpse of the family tea table in 1771 in Henry Marchant's diary: "At Breakfast His lady & Daughter [Mary] with two other young Ladies set a Table – His Daughter about 18 is very handsome & conducted the Tea Table with much Ease – His Lady was also very agreeable."[5] Mary's surviving correspondence includes several contributions to joint family letters together with a series of five letters of her own, written in June and July 1801, to her daughter-in-law, Isabella Cockburn, who had married William Robertson in 1796.[6] Mary Robertson was not a woman of letters: her command of spelling, grammar, and punctuation was shaky, and most of her expressed concerns were her family, relations, and household management. Her spoken language was wholly Scots and her manner unrefined. Her son James observed in a letter written from the spa at Buxton in 1786: "My mother owing to our living so much with great people is vastly improved in her manner, & language, & to tell the truth speaks the *English* with *fluency*."[7] But behind her everyday concerns and lack of social polish one can detect a sweetness – almost a naivety – of spirit that must have been very attractive to her family. Her comment on the death of her daughter Janet (Jenny), for example, is very touching. Jenny died in December 1789, and Mary wrote to her son William four months later that "I'm much oblig'd to you for your kind advices which I endeaver to follow but very many things occur have to mind me of my poor dear Jenny but I do every thing I can to conceal it I'm sure if you saw me you would think me a very good hipocrite as I wish to dwell on the many mercies I enjoy."[8] Such comments confirm William's sentiments on the death of his mother that he expressed in a letter of 13 March 1802 to his brother David:

> During all that long continued illness she preserved her faculties perfectly unim-paired & her fortitude & resignation never forsook her, & the same sweetness & gen-tleness & calm tranquility of temper for which she was always remarkable continued to the last moment . . . [N]othing can afford us so much satisfaction in our present afflicition as the reflection of having done every thing in our power for the comfort & happiness of so excellent a parent. The last words which my dear Father said to me were "be kind to your Mother" & I trust in God that I never forgot them.[9]

Even with allowance for William's filial piety, Stewart was correct in saying that Robertson's marriage "may be justly numbered among the most fortunate incidents of his life."[10]

The Robertson children followed quickly after the marriage. On 2 August 1752 their first daughter, Mary, was born, and, William, their first son was born on 15 December 1753. Four more children would be born to the Robertsons a few years later: Eleanor in 1755, Janet in 1756, James in 1762, and David in 1764. On the whole, it was a healthy, relatively long-lived family, with all the children but Janet living until well into the nine-teenth century (all of them dying between 1835 and 1845). The children would also go on to some measure of personal and professional success, prospering along with the city. Mary became the wife of Patrick Brydone, a socially well-connected traveler who wrote a *Tour through Sicily and*

Malta (1773) and provided Robertson some interesting scientific information. William would become procurator for the Church of Scotland and
Lord Robertson of the Court of Session, ultimately settling in fashionable
Charlotte Square. Eleanor married James Russell, writer to the signet,
and they remained in Edinburgh and close to the family. James and David
both pursued military careers, with James becoming general of the 92nd
Gordon Highlanders and David lieutenant-colonel of the 23rd regiment
as well as deputy adjutant general of what was then Ceylon. After marrying Margaretta Macdonald of Kinlochmoidart in 1799, David settled in
the north of Scotland, leading the life of an improving laird.

Alexander Carlyle proudly declared, "It was in this year, 1751, the
foundation was laid for the restoration of the discipline of the Church the
next year, in which Dr. Robertson, John Home and I had such an active
hand."[11] They laid the foundation by addressing a patronage dispute
from the presbytery of Linlithgow. The minister and the presbytery had
twice defied the order of the General Assembly to settle James Watson in
the parish of Torphichen, and it appeared in May 1751 that the General
Assembly meeting was prepared to allow the defiance to stand under a plea
of conscience. Shortly before the debate was to take place in the Assembly,
a "select company" of fifteen clergy and laymen came together in an
Edinburgh tavern to plan how to respond to what they saw as a serious
erosion of church discipline.[12] If Watson were not settled in accordance
with the choice of the patron, James Sandilands, Lord Torphichen, then
important consequences ought to follow for the minister and the presbytery. The "select company" included Robertson and his clerical allies
from the Edinburgh volunteers: Jardine, Blair, Home, and Carlyle, as well
as Jardine's father-in-law, leader of the volunteers, and recently re-elected
Lord Provost, George Drummond. They did not expect success at this
assembly, but, in Carlyle's words, "it was necessary to use every means
in our power to restore the authority of the Church, otherwise her government would be degraded and everything depending on her authority
would fall into confusion."[13] Home and Robertson were chosen to speak
on behalf of the measure, but it failed as expected. Robertson had made
an impressive speech that "not only gained the attention of the Assembly,
but drew the praise of the best judges,"[14] and he and five colleagues followed through by making up a substantial part of the riding committee
appointed by the Assembly to manage Watson's presentation. The strife
over patronage had thus given birth to the Moderate party.

Another disputed case followed several months later, when the parish
of Inverkeithing in the presbytery of Dunfermline refused a ministerial
appointment of the General Assembly. In March 1752, the commis-

sion of the General Assembly reversed an earlier opinion and declined to punish the presbytery, raising once again the threat of anarchy in making appointments. Following the narrow reversal of the commission's November ruling, Robertson and a group dissenting from the decision asked that it be debated at the upcoming General Assembly. The dissent-ers included many of those present at the original tavern meeting, and in March they published *Reasons of Dissent from the Sentence and Resolution of the Commission of the General Assembly* to be circulated prior to the May Assembly. The pamphlet is said to be primarily the work of Robertson but assisted by others among the group,[15] and this time the Moderates' measure carried in the General Assembly. This was an important moment for the Moderates because in it they confronted a basic philosophic issue at stake in the patronage controversy: how can the institutional church accommodate the claims of revealed truth?

Assuming that *Reasons of Dissent* is primarily Robertson's work, we can see how it dovetails with his religious thinking to this point, especially his concern with rational, publicly accessible foundations of thought. The task for Robertson, as it was for his father, was to navigate between the church as social institution and individual private judgment. Robertson first distinguishes human beings considered as individuals from human beings considered as members of society. The first "have no Guide but their own Understanding, and no Judge but their own Conscience."[16] But as members of society, there is the added obligation to "follow the Judgment of Society." Robertson then invokes the *Confession of Faith*, which makes a similar distinction between the "inward illumination of the Spirit of God" necessary to the understanding of the word and circumstances in the worship of God and the government of the church "common to human Actions and Societies, which are to be ordered by the Light of Nature and Christian Prudence."[17] Given this distinction, the conclusion is obvious:

> We allow to the Right of private Judgment, all the Extent and Obligation, that Reason or Religion require. But we can never admit, that any Man's private Judgment, gives him a Right, to disturb with Impunity, all publick Order.[18]

The constitution of the Church of Scotland ought to be maintained in what the authors take to be its ancient purity because it is the agreed upon arrangement for handling the light of faith alongside the light of nature. It echoes "De probabilitate historica": in the same way that the sum of human knowledge rests on both the light of nature and of faith, so the preservation of the true church depends on both the social institution and the illumination of the spirit. This conjunction assumes prior separation of the historical church from the spiritual church, but the true church must have both. Just as probable reasoning both guarantees the idea of a benevolent creator and is guaranteed by it, so church discipline and individual conscience guarantee each other. The discipline of the social institution is necessary for freedom of conscience to exist, and only freedom of conscience can give meaning to the social institution.

A history concerned with religious and political conflict in Scotland, especially in the wake of the Jacobite Rebellion, followed naturally. The early 1750s must have been filled with talk of history writing because the two soon-to-be leading historians of Britain, David Hume and Tobias Smollett, were in Edinburgh with history very much on their minds. Hume had returned to Edinburgh in 1751. In January 1753, he wrote to John Clephane that he was embarked on a history of Great Britain from 1603 to the present (though it would ultimately extend back to the Middle Ages), and he had already finished the reign of James VI and I.[19] There is no evidence that Robertson was personally known to Hume before 1757, but it would have been hard for Robertson to avoid knowing him. In 1752–3 Hume was very well acquainted with Robertson's colleague John Jardine, and he was a regular tavern associate of Carlyle, Blair, Smith, and Ferguson, and was likely joined on occasion by Home and Robertson who had to come in from the country.[20] Smollett was also in Edinburgh from June to November 1753 and talking convivially with many of these same people.[21] Smollett was already acquainted with Carlyle, and he had a warm regard for Home, Jardine, and Logan.[22] He does not mention meeting Robertson, though they would certainly meet in London in 1758, but once again Robertson probably heard plenty of talk about history. Smollett was then working on a history of the German Empire for the *Universal History*, and he was only a year away from plunging furiously into his *History of England*, which he completed in 1757.[23] He also may have planted the idea of a critical review in Edinburgh because he was to return to London and begin the *Critical Review* in 1755, the same year that Robertson, Jardine, Carlyle, and others launched the short-lived *Edinburgh Review*.

Another stimulus for the Scottish history may have come from an opponent of the Moderates. John Witherspoon was two years younger than Robertson, but well known to Carlyle and Robertson when they attended the university. He was the son of James Witherspoon with whom Robertson served on the Haddington presbytery. An evangelical, he waged a particularly coherent and compelling battle against the Moderate incorporation of worldly learning alongside Gospel teachings as well as against their embrace of a more benevolent, optimistic view of human nature drawn from Hutcheson. Witherspoon is said to have written a reply to *Reasons of Dissent* that followed shortly after its publication in 1752,[24] and probably in October 1753 he published a shrewd satire titled *Ecclesiastical Characteristics* just at the moment when Robertson announced to Dalrymple his prosecution of a Scottish history.[25] Witherspoon had in his sights ministers who, though claiming to be Christians, had diminished the central role of the Gospel message in favor of moral culture and who chose to pursue belles-lettres. Home's *Agis*, for which Home had temporarily abandoned his parish, is ridiculed as so perfect that "there will never be a tragedy published after it, unless by some body that is delirious."[26] Witherspoon was especially troubled by what he called in a later sermon "the unnatural mixture often to be seen of modern philosophy with ancient Christianity,"[27] and he makes jabs several times at "the saintship of Marcus Antoninus."[28] For Marcus' would-be translator, Witherspoon's comments may have struck home.

It is therefore of little surprise that Robertson wrote to David Dalrymple on 22 October 1753, "I intend to employ some of the idle time this winter in making a more diligent inquiry than ever I have done into that period of Scots History from the death of King James V to the death of Queen Mary."[29] He indicates that he had already been making some inquiries into Scottish history and had gathered some relevant material, whether on his own or drawing on his father's work. But to understand the place of Robertson's first history in his thinking we need to establish the context of other projects and issues that occupied him before the publication of his history in 1759. These gave his history shape and meaning as a contribution to public discourse about the place of the church and religion in modern commercial society. Then we can return to the *History of Scotland* and view it as the culmination of his thinking in the 1750s.

The first such project was his only published sermon, *The Situation of the World at the Time of Christ's Nativity*, which appeared in 1755. Important not only as the only sermon Robertson chose to publish, but also as his first public indication of his thinking about the nature of history, *Situation of the World* offers a rapprochement between the realms of reason and faith in history.[30] Preached on 6 January 1755 in Edinburgh as the annual sermon invited by the Society in Scotland for the Propagation of Christian Knowledge, the sermon was printed as usual with SSPCK sermons by Hamilton, Balfour, and Neill in Edinburgh. Robertson was a late substitution for John Erskine, who declined his invitation due to illness and asked to preach the next year.[31] But even Robertson's selection as a substitute was a sign of his growing prominence with the church and his stature as a preacher. Typically, SSPCK sermons addressed issues related to the spread of the Gospel in Britain and throughout the world, and Robertson's was no exception. He analyzed the historical factors that converged to make the moment of Christ's birth the most effective and propitious moment in history for this transforming event to occur. This theme is not a new one in Presbyterian theology: the declaration in the *Confession of Faith* that Christ was born in "the fullness of time" was a central idea as ministers traced the hand of providence in history.[32] One such minister, with whom Robertson's father served in London, was Robert Fleming, said to be a prime example of the "full extent of the connection in the Calvinist mind between history and prophecy."[33] Books 3 and 4 of his massive *Christology: A Discourse concerning Christ* examine in detail the issues surrounding his (and Robertson's) key contention: "That the *Time* of *Christ's coming* was *the Fulness of Time*, with respect unto the *concurring Circumstances* thereof, both as to *Men* and *Things*; which were such as never occurr'd before, nor since, if all these be considered together."[34] In keeping with his reforming spirit, Robertson made this traditional topic into "a very proper specimen of the great improvement that has been made in the art of preaching in this part of the united kingdom."[35]

Robertson begins the sermon with the separation of sacred from civil history: "sacred history, by drawing aside that veil which covers the counsels of the Almighty, lays open his designs to the view of his creatures."[36] Consequently, in this sermon, Robertson focuses not on doctrine alone but on doctrine "brought forth into action," which confirms "speculative opinions, by real and striking example." But historicizing doctrine in this way leads Robertson to employ a new strategy for articulating the conjunction of faith and reason. He considers the general law that "no perfection of any kind can be attained of a sudden"[37] and by this means bridges the gap between the permanence of revelation and the change of history. All the productions of the natural realm and all the changes in the moral realm are "gradual and progressive."[38] By the same token, revelation itself "was not poured in upon mankind all at once, and with its full splendor." Instead, "systems temporary and incomplete" will gradually but ultimately give way in the future to a "concluding and perfect revelation, which would *declare the whole council of God to man*." This striking description of progressive revelation in history (with its radical historicizing of St. Paul in Acts 20: 27) is crucial to Robertson's thinking about history. It strengthens the case for modesty of judgment with the assurance that all questions will ultimately be answered and all mysteries explained. What we know at any moment is part of a historical process that will evolve over time toward a promised fulfillment. Robertson has here

drawn on Newtonian ideas of the progressive course of nature, as inter-
preted by Maclaurin and Wishart (the latter also an admirer of Fleming[39])
to articulate his traditional topic from Galatians 4: 4 in a modern context,
bringing science and Scripture together.

The sermon had good circulation throughout the eighteenth century as
a reminder of the important role of sacred history alongside secular. Just as
various editions of Robertson's histories were published steadily throughout the century, so was what he called his "poor solitary sermon."[40] The
third edition (no copy of the second edition has been located) came out
in 1759 beside the *History of Scotland*. The year 1773 saw the fourth
edition published in Dublin, 1775 saw the fifth in Edinburgh done by
Balfour, and 1776 saw a German translation to go with *Charles V* and its
German translations. It was included in the three-volume *Scotch Preacher*
published between 1775 and 1779. Finally, it was published in conjunction with Thomas Cadell's edition of the *Disquisition on India* in 1791
by Elphingston Balfour in Edinburgh. These reprints are the work of
booksellers capitalizing on new publications, but when Robertson asked
Andrew Strahan about the status of his sermon in 1789, just as he was
starting work on the *Disquisition*, he seemed to see the sermon and the
history as companion pieces, one addressing civil and the other sacred
history.

Robertson also sought intellectual engagement in the wider community.
Like his sermon, these activities in the wider community were intended to
model polite ways of thinking in which one entertains new ideas without
necessarily relinquishing the realm of faith. Perhaps the most famous
example of his outreach was his role as a member of the Select Society.
On 22 May 1754 a group of fifteen prominent Edinburgh intellectuals
and professionals gathered in the Advocates' Library, among them David
Hume, Adam Smith, John Jardine, and Alexander Carlyle. Robertson was
not one of the original fifteen, but he was proposed at the meeting and
admitted as a member at the next meeting on 12 June.[41] Their purpose was
to form a debating society that would afford the members improvement
in philosophical inquiry and in the art of public speaking. Such societies
were common during the century, and this one seems, at first view, to
resemble in purpose the student club to which Robertson and Erskine
belonged in the 1740s. But the membership of the Select Society was
vastly different. Over its ten-year life from 1754 to 1764, the Select admitted 162 known members of whom over a third were advocates, almost a
third were from the army or business, and nearly another third were from
medicine, the church, or were gentlemen. Of the fourteen ministers who
were ultimately admitted, the five proposed at the first meeting comprised

the core of those supporting the *Reasons of Dissent*: Jardine, Carlyle, Home, Robertson, and Blair.[42] Thus the Select was very congenial to the Moderates' outlook. Many others found it to their taste as well, and Hume declared in 1755 that:

> It has grown to be a national concern. Young and old, noble and ignoble, witty and dull, laity and clergy, all the world are ambitious of a place amongst us, and we are as much solicited . . . as if we were to choose a Member of Parliament.[43]

Carlyle was equally pleased, claiming that the Select "improved and gave a name to the *literati* of this country, then beginning to distinguish themselves."[44]

Robertson was an active member of the Select. His volubility, range of intellectual interests, and oratorical skills already tested in the pulpit and the church courts perfectly suited him for such a society, and in the Select he had opportunity to engage topics pertinent to his historical interests. In 1755 he presided over a debate on the climate theory popularized by Montesquieu, a topic that surfaced several times for debate between 1754 and 1757. In 1757, the society debated luxury versus barbarity on 22 June, again on 29 June, and, at Robertson's request, extended the topic to 6 July when he presided. He presided again the next week on 13 July when the topic was naturalization of foreign Protestants. Because the Select proposed practical as well as academic topics, he even presided over a debate in 1760 on "promoting and supporting Publick Spirit" and abolishing vails (tips) given to servants as a social custom in Scotland.[45] The topic of vails in particular was widely discussed both in the Select Society and in Scotland at large in 1760, and those who opposed giving vails condemned them as inconsistent with a polite society because money corrupted the loyalty of servants and made their behavior mercenary. In this same spirit of social improvement, Robertson joined with Blair, Jardine, Ferguson, and others to organize a subsidiary of the Select Society. This was the Society for Promoting the Reading and Speaking of the English Language in Scotland, and it came on the heels of Thomas Sheridan's series of lectures on the topic delivered to enthusiastic audiences in Edinburgh. Their proposal was not couched in terms of the superiority of English over Scots but was based on the practical disadvantages the Scots face in their increasing interaction with English commerce and letters. To compete effectively with the south, Scots must learn to speak English with propriety to reap the "great and beneficial effects" of modern commercial society.[46] The authors proposed that a set of English schools be established, though the plan never materialized. But their aspiration for what they saw to be improvement by coupling emulation and competition was abundantly clear.

The importance of the Select Society for Robertson's career was considerable. In joining, he had become a member of a young, though established, group of intellectuals, professionals, and politically connected gentlemen. The average age was thirty-two (Robertson's age when he joined), most of them had common university training, and they belonged to the class of the ruling elite, either by virtue of wealth and position or by intellectual accomplishment. They were Scottish society's decision-makers, and they were confident of their role. Robertson always assumed a position of impartiality and independence throughout his career, but that position was ultimately dependent on the values embodied in the Select Society. As Roger Emerson has observed, "While . . . Dugald Stewart emphasized Robertson's independence and integrity, his principles would have been unheard and ineffective had he not spoken for the social and political elite in which he found a place."[47] The Select Society gave him that place: it broadened his reach beyond the church into secular society and at the same time helped to shape the tolerant conservatism[48] manifested in his clerical thinking. As a member of the Select Society, Robertson would no longer speak simply as a churchman; instead he would represent the church in society. Nor would he be simply an ivory tower historian; instead, his historical thinking would extend actively both to the church and to secular society. In short, he would be one of those cultural figures in the Select Society whose influence was "extensive and permanent in diffusing the taste for letters in Scotland, and in kindling the fire of genius, which then began to display itself in various works, which have done honour to the national character."[49]

His role with the *Edinburgh Review* was another step toward establishing cultural authority. Joining with other Select Society members including Smith, Blair, Jardine, Alexander Wedderburn, and James Russel, Robertson contributed eight reviews to the two issues of the journal that were published (four in each), the first issue covering January to July 1755 (published 26 August), and the second July 1755 to January 1756 (published in March 1756). The reviews were unsigned, making attributions a bit uncertain. In the preface of the 1818 reprint of the *Edinburgh Review*, James Mackintosh attributed eight articles to Robertson, six in history and two in literature. Of the six in history, Mackintosh specifically mentions Alexander Gordon's *History of Peter the Great*, David Moysie's *Memoirs of the Affairs of Scotland*, Robert Keith's *Catalogue of the Bishops . . . of Scotland*, and William Douglas's *State of the British Settlements in North-America*. Bower attributes Walter Anderson's *History of Croesus* to him, and Toussaint Rose's *Lettres de Louis XIV* is a plausible attribution on the basis of its content. In literature, the review of James Hervey's

Theron and Aspasio has a theological emphasis that makes Robertson a possible author, but the review of the fourth volume of Robert and James Dodsley's *Collection of Poems* is disputed, with Mackintosh giving it to Robertson and Bower to Blair. Robertson did know of the *Collection*, but the evidence comes later when he withdrew all six volumes from the Edinburgh University Library in 1769.[50]

These attributions contain some of the characteristic themes seen in Robertson's writing. The opening sentence of the preface of the first issue (presumably a joint effort and not attributed specifically to Robertson) picks up a major theme from *Situation of the World*, which had just been published the previous June: the purpose of the *Review* is to provide "a view of the progressive state of learning in this country."[51] Indeed, the preface as a whole lays out a view of the progress of Scottish cultural history from the sixteenth century to the present that echoed the vision of improvement in Elliot's *Proposals*. The *Review*'s narrative of progressive improvement describes how at first the promising greatness of George Buchanan's learning "soon gave place to the melancholy scene of disorder and violence that civil dissentions produced" during the reigns of Mary and James that Robertson was addressing. That tumultuous period was followed in turn by "a series of more deadful evils" in the form of oppression at the hands of Charles I, Cromwell, and Charles II.[52] Only with the Revolution was liberty re-established, but the Glorious Revolution could only be fulfilled by the Union, which brought a steady stream of improvements to North Britain. Today, the editors declare, Scots can compare their present advantages with the poorer conditions of the past, and they can see the sources of improvement: "If countries have their ages with respect to improvement, *North Britain* may be considered as in a state of early youth, guided and supported by the more mature strength of her kindred country."

Within this broad narrative, Robertson's articles assess the contributions of his authors to cultural progress, and in the process Robertson reveals his historical and cultural agenda. In keeping with his steady determination to stay out of partisan theological controversy, Robertson left books on religion to Jardine and Blair, preferring to concentrate on history and belles-lettres. With one exception, all six works of history Robertson reviewed fell short in one way or another of the "real objects of history, the characters of men and manners, the motives, the tendency and effects of public councils, the influence of foreign connections, and the variations of inferior policy" – in short, the coherent narration of cause and effect in the historical change of societies.[53] Robertson brings home his point repeatedly: Gordon's *History of Peter the Great* narrates only his military conquests and deals only slightly with civil transactions; Anderson's *Croesus* is dismissed as fiction disguised as history; Keith's *Catalogue of Bishops* is censured as a dry list of facts, though Robertson gives him respect because he is the author of *History of the Affairs of Church and State in Scotland*, a work that Robertson was at this time relying on heavily in writing his own history of Scotland; and Rose's *Lettres* fall well short of the illumination found in Voltaire's *Siècle de Louis XIV*. Although it is afflicted with "Lyric liberty" and "Pindaric wildness" in its composition, for Robertson only Douglas's *British Settlements* has genuine importance, pointing the way to one of the major preoccupations of his historical career: "The British empire in America has become a great and interesting object in history."[54] The two literary reviews sound complementary themes. Dodsley's *Collection* speaks to a major concern of the editors of the *Review*: attaining a proper English style in Scotland where "there is no standard of language, or at least one very remote."[55] The poems of Thomas Gray and Richard Jago reassure us that "the national taste still remains genuine and pure," and thus an appropriate model for style.[56] Robertson also admires Hervey's style and singles out his skill at natural description. But he takes issue with a theological point that bears on the importance of civic virtue and thus history. In Robertson's interpretation, Hervey takes belief in the imputed righteousness of Christ to be an assurance within the believer's own heart that a state of grace is free for all, if only one is simply conscious of it. But Robertson cautions that there must also be examination of our own hearts along with signs of regeneration to approach a state of grace. Conscious reflection and deliberate action, as well as subjective feeling, bring moral improvement.[57]

The progressive nature of history also crops up in a later review sometimes attributed to Robertson that was not published in the *Edinburgh Review*. On 15 March 1759, Robertson wrote to Smollett, at that time editor of the London-based *Critical Review*, asking to review Lord Kames's recently published *Historical Law-Tracts*.[58] Kames's book carried the date of 1758, but it was only advertised a few weeks before Robertson wrote to Smollett.[59] Sometime earlier, apparently, Robertson was in contact with Smollett and had asked or agreed to review the book. But because of Millar's demands for copy for the second edition of *Scotland*, Robertson explained in the 15 March letter that he had been unable to write the review of the book as he had promised for the March issue, and he asked Smollett either to extend the deadline to the April issue or, if that were not possible, see to the article himself. Robertson thought very highly of the book and wanted Smollett to give it careful treatment. The article duly appeared in the April 1759 issue. Although the style of the review seems to differ somewhat from Robertson's earlier reviews (perhaps as a result of Smollett's editing?), there are several plausible reasons for Robertson to promote the book. Both Kames and Smollett had given help of various kinds to Robertson in the past, and Andrew Millar certainly deserved well from him for the publication of *Scotland*.[60] But equally compelling was the content. The historical development of law clearly looks toward the introductory volume to *Charles V*, and in the spring of 1759 Robertson was weighing several options for the subject of his next history. It also marks Robertson's first public engagement with conjectural history, and the review makes a point of focusing on Tract I, dealing with criminal law, in which Kames lays out two concise expositions of the four-stages theory that Adam Smith had laid claim to in 1755.

This review also sheds doubt on John Callandar of Craigforth's claim that Robertson "borrowed" conjectural history from Smith's law lectures. Although in the *Historical Law-Tracts* Kames does not provide a detailed analysis of the four-stages theory, he does offer a convenient summary of the idea in the first tract, which deals with the progress of criminal law.[61] The review itself focuses on the criminal law tract for extensive summary and in the course of it gives substantial attention to the four-stages theory. Opening with a distinction between principles of natural law, which are unchanging, and the impact of government, which causes variations in laws, Robertson cites first the three-fold division stemming from Montesquieu of commonwealth, feudal kingdom, and despotism. The review points also to the four stages (hunting, pastoralism, feudalism, and commerce) that also profoundly affect the development of law.[62] At the end of the review, Kames's entire three-page note on the four stages of social development is quoted.[63] The author of this review embraces stadialism and is anxious that readers understand the tie between the four-stages theory and variation in criminal law as a model for the development of social institutions generally. If the author was Robertson, then we need to acknowledge Kames as an important influence on his historical thinking. That does not preclude the influence of Smith's formulations, though it may make us wonder if in fact Kames was the plagiarist that Smith feared and not Robertson.

A few years before he wrote the Kames review, the work of Kames, along with that of David Hume and John Home, had affected Robertson's thinking in much more politically charged ways. In 1755, some members of the Popular party launched an attack on Kames's *Essays on the Principles of Morality and Natural Religion* (1751), claiming, among other charges, that Kames denied free will and said freedom of action is a mere illusion. In 1753, the nearly eighty-year-old George Anderson, chaplain of Watson's

Hospital and a man of very combative temper, published *An Estimate of the Profit and Loss of Religion, Personally and publicly stated: Illustrated with reference to Essays on Morality and Natural Religion*, to open the attack on Kames, and he was soon followed during the 1755 General Assembly by John Bonar's *Analysis of the Moral and Religious Sentiments Contained in the Writings of Sopho and David Hume*, which pulled Hume into the furor as well. The controversy came during a busy year, politically and literarily, for Robertson and posed a challenge to his capacity for leadership because he was occupied on many fronts: in January 1755, he tried to quell an uproar about demonic possession within the Haddington presbytery and two days later delivered his fullest statement of Enlightened Christian thinking in *Situation of the World*; in April, the Haddington presbytery became suspicious about Home's absence from his parish to see to the staging of *Douglas* in London;[64] there was planning and writing for the *Edinburgh Review* as well as his history; and now in May, he and his Moderate friends had to argue (unsuccessfully) a settlement case in South Leith.[65] Nonetheless, Robertson still managed to score a notable success in the General Assembly by diverting the attack on Hume and Kames into a blunted, general Act against Infidelity and Immorality. Hume was sure more was to come, commenting "my damnation is postponed for a twelvemonth. But next Assembly will surely be upon me."[66]

George Logan's father, minister of Trinity parish in Edinburgh, died on 13 October 1755, and two days later Robertson, feeling it time to make his move from Gladsmuir, wrote to Gilbert Elliot, asking him to exercise his influence on his behalf with the Duke of Argyll and Lord Milton, who held the appointment. Robertson reminded Elliot that "I formerly mentioned to you my inclination to settle in a place where all my relations live, & my habits of friendship have been formed, & you was so good as to encourage me in that scheme," and he promised that "If a man may promise any thing upon his own future behaviour, I may venture to give assurances that I will neither disturb this town nor the Church with any irregular or Enthusiastic system either in preaching or in Church politics."[67] Although his appointment would suffer a long delay (in April 1756 he was still maneuvering to have his name put into the pool), the wheels were in motion to change Robertson's career significantly. But George Anderson was not deterred, as Hume had feared. In the 1756 General Assembly he launched another attack, this time focused on Hume's "most rude and open attacks upon the glorious Gospel of Christ"[68] with *Infidelity a Proper Object of Censure* published just a few days before the Assembly opening. Robertson and his Moderate colleagues were now faced with defeating an overture calling for a committee "to inquire into the writings" of Hume and to call him to appear before them at the next assembly. The debate was extensive and "very keen,"[69] but ultimately the Moderates prevailed, notably by using the Popular Party's argument of freedom of individual conscience against them and by making the case that Hume was not a declared Christian and thus outside Church jurisdiction.

The following year was to prove even more tumultuous with the eruption of the *Douglas* controversy. Robertson's role in it was notable, but, as before, it was played out against a backdrop of significant distractions. There was family grief. In August 1756, his wife Mary's father, James Nisbet, died from a skull fracture suffered in a fall down stairs, and six months later Mary's mother also died. Gladsmuir parish school and parish finances were in disarray. On 30 December 1756, the scandal involving William Pentland, the hapless Gladsmuir schoolmaster, surfaced: he was rebuked by the kirk session for his negligence, but this charge also implicated Robertson as minister. Moreover, the period 1756–7 was a time of severe upward pressure on grain prices, making it very difficult for the cash-strapped Gladsmuir parish to care for the poor. The session records show a great deal of time spent on devising schemes for poor support.[70] Even the first rehearsal of *Douglas* in Edinburgh on 4 December 1756 probably saw a tired Robertson reading the part of Lord Randolph because his daughter Janet was born just the day before the rehearsal.

But the rehearsal led to the first professional performance of the play at the Canongate Theatre on 14 December and from there to a prolonged political and cultural struggle within the church. In the view of John Jardine, "The ferment which this affair has occasioned is great. I don't remember to have seen any thing like it."[71] The controversy unfolded quickly after 14 December. On 4 January, Robertson attended a meeting of the presbytery of Haddington, which had received a letter from the presbytery of Edinburgh notifying them that Home had written and staged *Douglas*, that it had been acted "numerous times," and that the presbytery was to heed the "Admonition and Exhortation" against stage plays that would be published the next day. Home was absent from the presbytery meeting, having announced to his kirk session that he would be away for some time on business (i.e. in London arranging for the production of *Douglas* there, opening 14 March). After some deliberation, the presbytery did not seem eager to pursue the issue on its own and agreed to delay any further consideration of the matter until its 1 March meeting.[72] But by March, Home had not returned, and Robertson was charged with drafting a letter to Home informing him of the charges against him. Robertson volunteered to see that the letter was delivered, thus allowing a bit more time for delay.[73] Home stalled, first saying he would be present on 3 May but then telling the presbytery he would not be available until 9 May.[74] After the meeting, the presbytery simply passed the case on to the synod, and the synod, in turn, passed it back to the presbytery because there was no charge made. Home, however, had had enough, and after the meeting he told Jardine that he would resign his ministry at the next presbytery meeting (7 June), which he did.[75] While Home's case dragged on, Carlyle's attendance at the Edinburgh opening of *Douglas* came before the presbytery of Dalkeith, the spotlight quickly shifted, and once again Robertson played defense. First summoned by the presbytery in February, Carlyle was soon charged with attending the theatre and now brought his appeal of the case to the synod to be heard on 10 May. Robertson approached the case confidently, telling Jardine on 25 April, who was helping to develop a petition on Carlyle's behalf, "If the Petition you spoke of be presented, I have little fear of the Synod."[76] He was right. The Moderates planned their hearing strategy carefully the night before so that Robertson could speak from the floor on Carlyle's behalf, and the synod found the charges against Carlyle "not sufficiently clear and incontrovertible," sending the case to the General Assembly on the appeal of the presbytery. Robertson's appointment to the synod committee to respond to the appeal from the Dalkeith presbytery was a further benefit for Carlyle. The Assembly took up the case on 24 May, voting by a substantial margin to affirm the synod's sentence.[77]

With Home's resignation in June 1757, the *Douglas* controversy receded, and Robertson turned to other matters. One was his translation to Lady Yester's Chapel in Edinburgh, which had been hanging fire since August 1756 when it was initially approved by the Edinburgh Town Council under the influence of his cousin John Nisbet, then city treasurer and council member.[78] Four vacancies in the Edinburgh churches were to be filled, and four ministers had been elected to fill them: Robertson, John Erskine, Daniel MacQueen, and Henry Lundie.[79] In addition, on 2 March 1757, the Edinburgh presbytery decided Hugh Blair was to be translated from Lady Yester's to the New Church, later called the High Church, a very prestigious appointment in the Cathedral of St. Giles giving social prominence to Moderate views. But arranging the order and precedence of these appointments created great confusion, and on 30 March 1757 the presbytery agreed not to make a final decision until Whitsunday 1758, claiming that the roofs of Old and New Greyfriars needed extensive repairs first. In this interval of confusion, conservatives Patrick Cuming and John Hyndman chose to stir the pot, provoked by revenge for recent Moderate victories. Their most damaging action was to persuade the synod that Lundie should go to the High Church and Blair to the College

Church, a move that would lower the visibility of the Moderates along with the added benefit of thwarting Robertson's translation to Lady Yester's. Blair appealed the decision to the General Assembly, and after debate on 1–2 June, the sentence of the synod was overturned with Robertson being formally settled at Lady Yester's on 15 June. Robertson was extremely satisfied with the outcome of this latest struggle, as he explained privately to Gilbert Elliot on 24 June, just after returning from London:

> I was plunged at once into the depths of Kirk politics, the Edinburgh Clergy, who for the sake of trifles, are guilty of all the vices imparted to the great, had by a most wanton piece of injustice deprived Blair of the new kirk, & it cost us no small difficulty to overturn that deed, but I hope that, added to the play house folly last year, will make it easy for us defeat [sic] all Cumming & Hyndmans projects in time to come.[80]

But his public face appeared impartial. Despite his evident pleasure in the victory, when Robertson delivered his first sermon at Lady Yester's on 18 June, he chose a conciliatory text in view of the friction between the two parties. It was 1 Corinthians 1: 24 ("But unto them which are called, both Jews and Greeks, [we preach] Christ the power of God, and the wisdom of God"), showing (in Dalrymple's notes)

> that the Xtian Religion was the wisdom of God. 1. as it is delivered by an authority superior & more certain than reason. 2. as its precepts are most excellent. 3. as the motives to it are most cogent. 4. as the means of grace are provided to all those who seek to obey its precepts.[81]

By invoking "an authority superior & more certain than reason" that speaks to both Jews and Greeks, Robertson calls for peace and, at the same time, justifies the ways of God to the Popular party.

When he delivered his 18 June sermon at Lady Yester's, Robertson took pleasure in more than just his increasing stature as a minister and church leader, important as that was to him. He also had only a month earlier secured publication of his first major scholarly work, the *History of Scotland*, and from this watershed moment, as Dugald Stewart said, "the complexion of his fortune was changed."[82] At least since 1753, when he announced to Dalrymple his intention of writing the history, Robertson seems to have been steadily and rapidly (given all his political and social demands) composing the manuscript in chronological order. By August 1756, he appears to have reached 1586 and may have been working on the period of Elizabeth's proposing to try Mary for treason. In a letter to Dalrymple, he asks him for any information on the period he might have gleaned from Sir Alexander Dick's manuscripts, and the fact that he printed in the appendix to the history several letters from Dick's collection pertinent to the trial suggests his possible progress. He praises Dalrymple's critical comments on Walter Goodall's defense of Mary in *An Examination of the Letters Said to Have Been Written by Mary Queen of Scots to James, Earl of Bothwell* (1754), also suggesting his thinking about Mary's guilt.[83] A year later, in June 1757, he told George Ridpath he had reached 1589 (the conclusion of Book VII), although he "intends still to bestow a good deal of labour on it."[84] Just a month later he told Dalrymple he had reached 1600 and the problem of Gowrie's Conspiracy.[85] In September 1757 he was able to tell historian Thomas Birch, in a letter requesting his advice particularly on additional manuscript sources, "I have brought my work almost to a conclusion" and plan to bring the manuscript to London in the "winter."[86] In December he was confident enough in the completeness of his work to request from the Haddington presbytery a two- to three-month leave.[87]

The trip to London began in late February 1758 and proved to be as much for diversion from the fatigues of religious controversy as for work on his manuscript. He kept company frequently with Carlyle, who had also come to London for his sister Margaret's wedding, and, because it was Robertson's first time in the city, Carlyle said they "went to see the lions together."[88] Other familiar Edinburgh friends were in town, including Home and Ferguson, and together they regularly dined with John Dalrymple, Robert Adam, and Alexander Wedderburn.[89] Robertson and Carlyle were also often in company with physicians. Not only was Carlyle's sister marrying Dr. Thomas Dickson, but also Robertson's cousin, Dr. William Pitcairn, who had a well-established London practice, provided company and hospitality along with poet and physician John Armstrong. They visited Sir Gilbert Elliot, who was at the Admiralty, and they were able to see Dr. John Blair once again. Robertson met Smollett in person for the first time, with whom he "smoked Tobacco & drank punch for two days," and he became acquainted with figures who would be future correspondents and friends, such as David Garrick and Anglican Bishop John Douglas.[90] Robertson's sense of excitement and pleasure is best captured in two letters he wrote to Margaret Hepburn at Monkrigg, a niece of Lord Milton's who was a close friend of the Robertson household in Gladsmuir and a woman of some literary taste. He gave her a full account of his first experience of the London theatre, watching the first night of Home's tragedy *Agis* on 21 February, which was for him transporting:

> I cannot express the elegance & propriety with which the piece was performed. Perhaps I am no proper judge, as I still feel all the surprize & wonder of a Novice.

However all the old stagers tell me that never was any play acted so well on a first night. Garrick admirably played Lysander. There are some of the situations admirably adapted to his manner of acting, & I had no conception of such admirable power of expressing the strong passions. I was still more touched with the voice of Mrs Cibber who played Evanthe. There is a melody & tenderness in her voice, which is the pathetic itself; & tho' her person be not gracefull, nor her action so expressive as Garricks, her influence over me is at least equal to his.[91]

Writing again two weeks later, Robertson had immersed himself in enough drama to form his taste:

I long to see him [Garrick] in King Lear, where I am persuaded he will be great. From all I have seen of the stage, I am tempted to think that Tragic action is much more imperfect than Comic. I have been more moved with reading a good tragedy than I am by seeing it, but I never laughed by half so much at any Comedy as [fragment missing] ave done at seeing Garrick or Woodward or Shuter in their comic parts.[92]

Robertson was taking full advantage of this opportunity to adopt the literary polish of the capital, now even referring to himself ironically as "we English."[93]

But writing intruded on socializing and the theater. One important research task was enlisting Thomas Birch's help in gaining access to the manuscripts concerning the reign of Elizabeth compiled by Patrick Forbes. Two volumes of them had been published, and Robertson had seen them, thanks to Dalrymple, but there remained many more manuscripts that he had not seen. During March, Birch secured them from Philip Yorke, second Earl of Hardwicke and Viscount Royston, and, in all, Robertson says he was able to consult fourteen quarto volumes. As he ironically noted to Jardine:

I have got from this last [Lord Royston] a vast Collection of original papers. Many of them are curious. I am advised by several people to transcribe as many as will swell the book to a guinea price. The taste of this town is such, that such an addition will be esteemed very meritorious; & tho' it cost me little but the hiring an Amanuensis will add to the price in proportion to the increase of bulk. You see I begin to learn the craft of Authorship.[94]

Such favors gave Robertson an opening to share his manuscript with Lord Royston and other critics: "I have put my papers into the hands of several literary people, & besides them, I have got some persons of rank, & who lead the fashion in a town, where fashion governs every thing, to read them."[95] The list of readers was impressive, including Horace Walpole, the Earl of Bute, the speaker of the House of Commons Arthur Onslow, the Duke of Argyll, and George Lewis Scott, the preceptor to the Prince of Wales.[96] He found the task difficult because he had only one manuscript to show, the distances between houses in London were great, and important people were not often at home. But he persevered, received glowing recommendations, and was able to report extraordinary success to Jardine on 20 April:

> I have now brought my offers to a conclusion with Andrew Millar. After viewing the town, and considering the irresistible power of a combination of booksellers, I have agreed to sell him the property for £600. This, you see, is the sum I originally fixed upon as the full price of my work, and is more than was ever given for any book except David Hume's. You cannot imagine how much it has astonished all the London authors, nor how much Andrew Millar was astonished at the encomiums of my book which he got from people of rank. I have got some of the best puffers of England on my side. Mr. Doddington, Horace Walpole, Lady Hervey, and the Speaker are my sworn friends; and you will wonder, even in this great place, how I have got Mary Queen of Scots to be a subject of conversation. Every body here approves of the bargain I have made with Millar, and I am fully satisfied of the prudence of my own conduct; but of this I shall have full leisure to talk with you soon.[97]

The departure from London on 4 May, with visits before and after to luminaries such as Garrick, William Shenstone, and Lord Lyttleton, marked a truly triumphant return home.[98]

Having successfully fended off the last effort to derail the translations of the four ministers in the General Assembly in June, Robertson was busy with trying to clean up the last of his parish business before leaving Gladsmuir for Edinburgh. At the Haddington presbytery meeting of 13 June 1758, he asked that he be allowed, after his translation to Edinburgh had taken place, to hold kirk session meetings to sort out lingering problems with the parish poor funds, and the presbytery agreed.[99] Meanwhile, his translation was officially completed on the 15th, and on the 18th he preached his first sermon in Lady Yester's Chapel. Meanwhile, the Scottish history had to be finished and sent to London. On the 24th he wrote to Gilbert Elliot to thank him for the franking of "six parcells" of the manuscript because Millar "has been clamouring with all the impatience of a Bookseller."[100]

One source of assistance in this busy time was David Hume, who was in London during the fall of 1758. Hume was from the beginning a supporter of Robertson's work, telling Millar that the history is

> a Work of uncommon Merit. I know that he has employ'd himself with great Diligence & Care in collecting the Facts: His style is lively & entertaining: And he judges with Temper and Candor. He is a man generally known & esteemed in this

Country; and we look upon him very deservedly as inferior to no body in Capacity & Learning.[101]

Hume had advised Robertson to decline the offer of the Edinburgh booksellers and negotiate with Millar, and he had assured Millar not only of the quality of the history but also that it would not compete with his own history of the Stuarts, due to be published by Millar in the spring of 1759. While he was in London, Hume read the corrected sheets as they came from the press, calling Robertson's attention to several errors of fact and interpretation. In return for Hume's generous assistance, however, Robertson has been said to harbor a jealous fear of being overshadowed.[102] At some point, perhaps about the time Hume was completing volume two of the Stuarts in late 1756, he had asked Hume not to write on the 1485–1603 period for fear it would compete with his own history. Hume declined, saying that he

> could not write downward. For when you find occasion, by new discoveries, to correct your opinion with regard to facts which passed in Queen Elizabeth's days; who, that has not the best opportunities of informing himself, could venture to relate any recent transactions? I must therefore have abandoned altogether this scheme of the English History, in which I had proceeded so far, if I had not acted as I did.[103]

Robertson's jealous fear is plausible because his role of spokesman for Moderate impartiality was at stake. He was ten years younger than Hume, ambitious, and by far the lesser public figure. He could not afford to be dimmed by comparison, let alone stained with too close an association with a notorious skeptic. It was one thing to come to his assistance in the General Assembly, but another to be seen as a protégé or an inferior. Robertson even refused to follow up Hume's suggestions about altering his interpretation of the evidence about Mary to make her guilt more prominent. Robertson wanted at all costs to maintain the balance he had created in Mary's character because that impartial balance was crucial to maintaining the Moderate stance.[104]

By January 1759, the printing was virtually done, and advance copies were about to be sent out. On the 4th Robertson told Elliot that "I feel at present the utmost anxiety about the reception I shall meet with, but like a true desperado, I shut my eyes, think as little as I can, & rush forward."[105] It was perhaps not merely a coincidence that on the 14th, 21st, and 28th he delivered a series of three sermons at Lady Yester's on the topic of submitting to God's will, dwelling on points such as "God only chastens to mend, & that it is indeed from his goodness that he afflicts us," "bearing evil with a degree of contentment," and "better that his [God's] will than that ours be done."[106] But his patience was rewarded because his success could not have been greater. A month later, having received many letters of congratulation, Robertson's spirits were high. On 20 February, he wrote excitedly to Margaret Hepburn:

> It is now three weeks since my book was published, and to my great surprise, I have at once received from every person of taste as full and unreserved applause as my own vanity or your friendship could have wished. I have luckily made my appearance at a time when there is no faction in Parliament, and no business whatever to draw the attention of people of rank. A new book is as interesting an object in London as in Edinburgh, and all the great, the gay, and the busy have become at once my Readers. Prince Edward has made long extracts out of my book, the Princes's [sic] family talk of nothing else. I have letters from M[r] Walpole, M[r] Garrick, D[r] Warburton &c. &c. and even from my Bookseller which would fill you with wonder, and almost persuade you that I am a very great man. John Bull is exceedingly astonished to find that an untravelled Scotsman should write English with so much purity, and in order to account for this, he now firmly believes that I was educated at Oxford. The strongest circumstance in my fortune is the praise of the London authors, which I am told has likewise been bestowed with unusual profusion. What think you of that virtuous Heathen David Hume. Instead of feeling any emotion of envy on account of the success of an author, who had intruded into the province of History, of which he was formerly in possession, and who by writing on the same subject, was brought into direct comparison with himself, instead of this, he runs about praising my work, and enjoys the applause it meets with, as if it were bestowed on himself.[107]

As early as 27 January, Millar had told Robertson to prepare for a second edition, and it was duly published on 14 April with two more editions by 1761 and a total of fourteen by the end of his lifetime. Robertson had written one of the most widely read histories of his time, yet it treated a most unlikely topic: a narrative of parochial events occurring on the margin of Europe two centuries earlier and prompted by the recent struggles of presbyterian ministers. What was the basis of the appeal of the book? Critics point to the affecting story of Mary, to Robertson's care for documentary support that was greater than that of previous historians, or to narrative management. These are important qualities, but the work's intellectual center is Robertson's articulation of his Moderate vision, the successful conjoining of impartial historiography with Christian doctrine.

Robertson wished to write a history that would help to unify Scotland in the wake of the Jacobite rebellion. That meant negotiating the political division between Jacobites and Havoverians without compromising the vision of Scotland as a civil society. At the same time, he also had to navigate between the parties in the church, which had formed over the course of the 1750s and were polarized. On the one hand, the Popular party adhered to traditional Presbyterian doctrines, seeing them as the defining marks of the nation, and, on the other, the Moderate party sought to ensure "that organized and authoritative religion should remain within and not without the fabric of human society and sociability, subject always to society's magisterial and cultural authority."[108] Robertson could not manage a complete narrative that would show the emergence of the Moderate vision from the Presbyterian past without engaging in the very polemics that would undermine his principles.[109] What he could do was begin anew by imposing a new way of thinking about Scottish history and history in general. The conclusion of *Scotland* shows, not the end of a process of historical evolution, but a new beginning created by the Act of Union, which unleashed Scottish liberty and genius.

At the heart of Robertson's Moderate vision was an epistemology he had studied in earlier years and that he had adapted in his sermons. Along with Samuel Werenfels' *Dissertation concerning Meteors of Stile* was published his discussion of the problem of controversy, both philosophical and theological, which embraced the skeptical method of Descartes in order to defuse argument:

> For, let *Descartes's* Precept of disbelieving, tend even so much to *perplex* our Understandings, and by that means to *tempt* them to despair of knowing *any thing*, because *some things* are not to be understood; and to demand *Certainty*, where only *Probability* is to be had; Notwithstanding all this, I say, my Rule holds good, and has not one ill Consequence attending it. For, be the Controversy of ever so great Importance, what Harm is there in deferring to judg, whether it be concerning things really different, or only about Words *ill-express'd* and *misunderstood*, till I am more satisfactorily inform'd of the Matter; tho that shou'd not happen till Doomsday?[110]

The relevance of such thinking to Robertson's ideas in "De Probabilitate Historica" is apparent: in the realm of probability we cannot demand certainty. Werenfels excludes from the principle of deferral any truth upon which salvation depends. These are not subject to doubt, and common sense and the general experience of men suggest that such basic truths can be questioned only by willful paradox. But the realms of certainty and probability are in complete harmony, and truth will be known in time: "All our real Differences," Werenfels maintains, "are about Things merely probable." By claiming certainty in areas where only probability can be expected, people precipitate unresolvable controversy. "In uncertain and doubtful Matters, it's best totally to suspend our Judgment."[111]

In theological disputes, Werenfels adopted this same position. He rejected Catholicism because he argued that it assumed the infallibility of a human institution.[112] But dealing with controversy among Protestants was more complicated. First, Werenfels advocated reliability, not infallibility, of private judgment. Trusting one's own judgment before that of another is not pride in one's own knowledge; rather, it indicates fuller knowledge of the evidence supporting the opinion in question and the sincerity of the belief in it. Yet while the best path is to trust one's own determinations, one must also recognize the inherent limits of those determinations.[113] Second, while endorsing private judgment, Werenfels also cautions against the danger of public party attachment. "But of all things that are apt to deprave and distort the judgments of the most discerning, what is more so than that Party attachment, which has falsely prevailed among the Learned, especially in matters of Religion?" One should seek independence of party coupled with a candid recognition of the limits of individual judgment.[114] It is possible to see here Robertson's willingness to make a space for private judgment in *Reason of Dissent* as well as his constant insistence on presenting himself as impartial and above the fray of politics and party.[115]

These epistemological concerns are embedded in the structure and style of the *History of Scotland*. If narrative cannot describe the historical emergence of the Moderate temperament without pitfalls, the style of the book can show it in action. Robertson's goal in presenting Mary's character is to get beyond controversy, to quell disputes based on claims of absolute authority, and to avoid party attachments while stressing the limits of judgment. Mary's character cannot be simplified:

> Among historians, who . . . have either ascribed to her every virtuous and amiable quality, or have imputed to her all the vices of which the human heart is susceptible, we search in vain for Mary's real character. She neither merited the exaggerated praises of the one, nor the undistinguished censure of the other.[116]

When Robertson pulls her traits together, he piles them up in a long string of juxtapositions:

> Polite, affable, insinuating, sprightly, and capable of speaking and of writing with equal ease and dignity. Sudden, however, and violent in all her attachments; because her heart was warm and unsuspicious. Impatient of contradiction; because she had been accustomed from her infancy to be treated as a queen. No stranger, on some occasions, to dissimulation; which, in that perfidious court where she received her education, was reckoned among the necessary arts of government. Not insensible of flattery, or unconscious of that pleasure which almost every woman beholds the influence of her own beauty. Formed with the qualities which we love, not with the talents that we admire; she was an agreeable woman, rather than an illustrious queen.[117]

Reading Robertson's analysis of Mary's character, we enact an empirical discovery in a world governed not by certainty but by probability. There is remarkably little that we can absolutely determine about Mary; we must make probable judgments that are subject to constant revision. By contrast, consider the defense of Mary by Walter Goodall, depute-keeper of the Advocate's Library and clerk to the Select Society. Robertson knew Goodall and was keenly aware of his staunch Jacobite outlook.[118] His defense of Mary was passionate:

> For Mary Queen of Scots so far excelled all other sovereign Princes who ever yet appeared on the face of the earth, that, as if she had not been of mortal nature, all the arts and contrivances of her numerous and malicious enemies have not availed to fix upon her one crime, shall I say, not one single foible, either while on the throne, or in the jail, from her cradle to her grave, unless the want of omniscience or omnipotence shall be reckoned in her a defect.[119]

From this quasi-divine character radiates a series of implications for social structure and religious belief. She summons up the spirit of feudal hierarchy with its emphasis on dependence as opposed to the independence of commercial egalitarianism. Mary's character is revealed, not discovered by inference from evidence: we know her to be what she is immediately, intuitively, and absolutely. She embodies transcendent authority in both church and state.

The elaborate "Critical Dissertation concerning the Murder of King Henry, and the Genuineness of the Queen's Letters to Bothwell," which Robertson appended to the second edition, addresses Jacobite historians like Goodall in another way. Goodall had offered a cogent analysis of the Casket Letters, concluding that they were forgeries foisted upon the innocent Mary by the unscrupulous Earl of Moray. After a review of the evidence relating to Mary's involvement in the murder of Henry, Robertson concludes that only two judgments are possible: either Mary countenanced the murder without being involved in the crime, or she was directly involved in the planning of the murder and approved it. "Which of these conclusions is most agreeable to the evidence that has been produced," he writes in the final paragraph, "I leave my readers to determine."[120] In the face of uncertainty, Robertson defers judgment, but that does not mean no position has been taken. Although Mary is at least guilty in some degree, and that speaks to her extreme partisans like Goodall, even more important is the air of impartiality with which Robertson dismisses partisan opinion. By leaving his conclusions unstated, Robertson makes his readers consciously reflect on the basis of their knowledge, an act essential to a civil society.

This strategy extends to the cumulative effect of the entire history because Robertson asks his reader to see key events from multiple perspectives. Mary's death is a prime example. For a Marian defender like Thomas Carte, whom Robertson cites a number of times, the execution was one of the great instances of heroism in all of history:

> The patience, the constancy, and firmness, with which she endured all the hardships and indignities put upon her during her captivity, cannot be sufficiently admired; the *Christian* manner of her death was not unworthy of the best of men; and the intrepidity with which she met that kind of terrors, the genuine effect of innocence, was not surpassed by any of the heroes of antiquity.[121]

By comparison, Robertson's account is restrained, drawing on more temperate historians such as John Spottiswoode, Samuel Jebb, William Camden, and John Strype, and appending an objective, though not unsympathetic, letter from the Earls of Shrewsbury and Kent published in David Crawfurd's pro-Marian *Memoirs of the Affairs of Scotland* (1706). He admires her "calm but undaunted fortitude," and he expects his reader to sympathize with the response of those who witnessed the execution: "The rest of the spectators continued silent, and drowned in tears; being uncapable, at that moment, of any other sentiments but those of pity or admiration."[122] But this moment of sympathy is qualified by Mary's imprudence and folly the reader knows helped to create the situation. Mary is a victimized sentimental heroine: Robertson is unequivocal about Elizabeth's trial of Mary, calling it a scene of dissimulation and Elizabeth's denial of responsibility for Mary's death a "solemn farce."[123] But Robertson, through the course of the narrative, has also accumulated evidence to show Mary foolishly brought about her own undoing. Her impetuous trust in Elizabeth, her rash participation in schemes against Elizabeth's life, and her inability to outmaneuver Elizabeth on major issues are all narrated in detail, requiring the reader to qualify, but not to dismiss, Mary's heroic death. Because Mary is neither solely a guileless victim nor cunning manipulator, the reader can only understand her as a composite of innocence and guilt, nobility and folly, honesty and deception. Such a complex figure cannot be reduced to a simple, partisan judgment; instead, we defer final judgment, wishing, as Werenfels said, to be "more satisfactorily inform'd of the Matter."

Another touchstone in the *History* reveals Robertson's religious thinking in light of his Moderate stance. The characterization of John Knox was important enough for Robertson to send Dalrymple a copy of it by 1758 for his perusal, and it is a sensitive indicator of Robertson's attitudes for his readers.[124] On the one hand, Robertson sees him as driven by furious zeal:

His maxims . . . were often too severe, and the impetuosity of his temper excessive. Rigid and uncomplying himself, he shewed no indulgence to the infirmities of
others. Regardless of the distinctions of rank and character, he uttered his admonitions with an acrimony and vehemence, more apt to irritate than to reclaim This
often betrayed him into indecent and undutiful expressions with respect to the
queen's person and conduct.[125]

In a note to the eleventh edition of the *History*, Robertson added an eye-
witness description of Knox's preaching, for a moment reducing Knox
to almost a comic figure: "'e're he was done with his sermon, he was so
active and vigorous, that he was like to ding the pulpit in blads [beat the
pulpit to pieces], and fly out of it.'" Yet this mixture of comedy and zeal is
redeemed by his peculiar virtues:

> Those very qualities, however, which now render his character less amiable, fitted
> him to be the instrument of Providence for advancing the Reformation among a
> fierce people, and enabled him to face dangers, and to surmount opposition, from
> which a person of a more gentle spirit would have been apt to shrink back.[126]

The distinction of manner and matter in the description opens up a space
in which to reconcile evangelical and moderate views. Robertson histori-
cizes Knox so that he is deprived of his totemic status and shown to be his-
torically distant, a man of his time and not of the present time.[127] Yet what
is less noticeable is that by making Knox the instrument of providence
Robertson invests him with transcendent value. The faith he preaches is
true and unchanging, even though the manner in which he does so is no
longer appropriate. It was Robertson's insistence on unchanging religious
truth, despite his readiness to embrace historical change, that led Hume to
complain of "the godly Strain of his History."[128]

But few readers had such reservations about the book, and it became an
immediate success. Robertson's friend John Blair was so enthused he was
ready to wager that publisher Andrew Millar had said it sold comparably
to *Tom Jones*. Just the fact that Blair was willing to compare the success of
a work on Scottish history with a racy English novel shows the magnitude
of the *History*'s popularity.[129] By 1761, the book was in its fourth edition
with ten more to come over Robertson's lifetime. The reviews and comments from correspondents were glowing with praise of his dignified style,
clarity of narrative accuracy of information, and skill in exposition.[130] The
most knowledgeable review was Hume's, which appeared anonymously in
Smollett's *Critical Review*.[131] He understood exactly Robertson's intention and the political-religious context in which he was writing, judging
him to be an "impartial and accurate historian" and only demurring at the
character of Knox in which he found an artful apology interwoven with

his faults.[132] Robertson himself became identified with the Moderate cast of mind. In 1773, Boswell recorded a conversation among Robertson, Sir William Forbes, Johnson, and Patrick Murray, 5th Lord Elibank, who was a strong Jacobite until 1760. "'Mr. Robertson,'" said Elibank, "'the first thing that gave me a high opinion of you, was your saying in the Select Society, while parties ran high soon after the year 1745, that you did not think worse of a man's moral character for his having been in rebellion. This was venturing to utter a liberal sentiment, while both sides had a detestation of each other.'"[133] A later biographer recorded a similar anecdote involving Robertson's view of Mary and one of the major critics of that view: "It has been mentioned, as a fine instance of Dr. Robertson's propriety and dignity of feeling, that in his library was to be seen the picture of Mary, supported by his own portrait on one side, and that of Mr. [William] Tytler on the other."[134] The public (or at least a substantial part of it) seemed ready to embrace a book that showed a way toward a civil society, and Robertson's next historical task was to bring this modernized Scotland into conjunction with Europe.

Notes

1. ([Edinburgh], 1752), pp. 35–6.
2. *Directory of Edinburgh*, comp. Gilhooley, p. 58.
3. Sher, *Church and University*, p. 25.
4. Stewart, "Account," in *Miscellaneous Works*, p. 108.
5. Quoted in J. Bennett Nolan, *Benjamin Franklin in Scotland and Ireland 1759 and 1771* (Philadelphia: University of Pennsylvania Press, 1938), p. 176.
6. See Mary Robertson and Robertson to William Robertson, 26 May and 7 June [1789], NLS MS 3,944, ff. 8–9, 12–13; Robertson and Mary Robertson to Patrick Brydone and Mary Brydone, 4 November 1789, NAS WRH TD 77/142/4/300/19; Mary Robertson and Robertson to William Robertson, 5 April [1790], NLS MS 3,944, ff. 24–5; and Mary Robertson to Isabella Robertson, 17, 20, 23, 29 June, and 13 July 1801, NLS MS 3,946, ff. 48–9, 116–21, 132–3.
7. James Robertson to William Robertson, 31 October 1786, NLS MS 3,943, ff. 206–7.
8. Mary Robertson to William Robertson, 5 April 1790, NLS MS 3,944, ff. 24–5.
9. William Robertson to David Robertson, 13 March 1802, NLS MS 3,946, ff. 147–8.
10. Stewart, "Account," in *Miscellaneous Works*, p. 108.
11. *Autobiography*, pp. 255–6.
12. Ibid., p. 257.
13. Ibid., p. 258.

14. Ibid., p. 259.
15. See Sher, *Church and University*, p. 52; Morren, *Annals*, I, 231.
16. *Reasons of Dissent from the Sentence and Resolution of the Commission of the General Assembly, Met at Edinburgh March 11, 1752*, in *Miscellaneous Works*, p. 31.
17. Ibid., p. 33. See *Confession of Faith*, pp. 30–1.
18. *Reasons of Dissent*, in *Miscellaneous Works*, p. 35.
19. Hume to Clephane, 5 January 1753, in *Letters of Hume*, I, 170.
20. Carlyle, *Autobiography*, p. 288.
21. Knapp, *Tobias Smollett*, pp. 160–2.
22. Smollett to Carlyle, 1 March 1754, in *Letters of Smollett*, p. 36.
23. Knapp, *Tobias Smollett*, p. 163.
24. Sher, *Church and University*, p. 54.
25. Varnum Lansing Collins, *President Witherspoon: A Biography*, 2 vols (Princeton: Princeton University Press, 1925), I, 35, n. 9.
26. Witherspoon, *Ecclesiastical Characteristics, or the Arcana of Church Policy*, 2nd edn (Glasgow, 1754), p. 26.
27. *The Absolute Necessity of Salvation through Christ* (Edinburgh, 1758), p. 4.
28. *Ecclesiastical Characteristics*, p. 27. This reference appears in "The Athenian Creed," which was published in the second edition.
29. Robertson to Dalrymple, 22 October 1753, NLS MS 25,294, f. 7
30. History had an important place in Presbyterian thought: "the study of history could be seen as a devotional performance in its own right. It brought the audience into the closest possible contact with immediate prophetic evidence for the most valuable of spiritual truths" (Allan, *Virtue, Leaning and the Scottish Enlightenment*, p. 53).
31. NAS MS GD 95/2/7.
32. *Confession of Faith*, pp. 63–4. See Galatians 4: 4.
33. Allan, *Virtue, Learning and the Scottish Enlightenment*, p. 52.
34. *Christology: A Discourse concerning Christ*, 2 vols (London, 1705–8), II, 414.
35. John Jardine, review of *Situation of the World*, in *Edinburgh Review for the Year 1755*, 2nd edn (London, 1818), p. 37.
36. "Situation of the World at the Time of Christ's Nativity," in *Miscellaneous Works*, p. 6.
37. Ibid., p. 9.
38. Ibid., p. 10.
39. Wodrow, *Analecta*, IV,154; III, 255.
40. Robertson to Andrew Strahan (January or February 1789), Dunedin Public Library MS.
41. McElroy, *Scotland's Age of Improvement*, p. 49.
42. Roger Emerson, "The Social Composition of Enlightened Scotland: The Select Society of Edinburgh, 1754–1764," *Studies on Voltaire and the Eighteenth Century*, 114 (1973), pp. 291–329.
43. Hume to Allan Ramsay, April or May 1755, in *Letters of Hume*, I, 219.

44. *Autobiography*, p. 311.

45. NLS Adv. MS 23.1.1; Sher, *Church and University*, p. 227.

46. *Scots Magazine*, 23 (1761), p. 440.

47. Emerson, "Social Composition," p. 309.

48. The phrase belongs to Sher, *Church and University*, pp. 262–3.

49. Alexander Fraser Tytler, quoted in McElroy, *Age of Improvement*, p. 64.

50. EUL MS Da.2.5, 2 December 1769. The book could easily have been borrowed for someone else in the family.

51. "Preface," in *Edinburgh Review*, p. i.

52. Ibid., p. ii.

53. Review of David Moysie, *Memoirs of the Affairs of Scotland*, in "Eight Book Reviews from the Original Edinburgh Review, 1755–6," in *Miscellaneous Works*, p. 60.

54. Ibid., p. 83.

55. "Preface," in *Edinburgh Review*, p. iii.

56. "Eight Reviews," in *Miscellaneous Works*, p. 65.

57. Ibid., pp. 67–8. See also "The Larger Catechism," in *Confession of Faith*, pp. 233–8.

58. Robertson to Smollett, 15 March 1759, Massachusetts Historical Society MS.

59. See *Public Advertiser*, 28 February 1759.

60. Richard B. Sher, "Introduction to the *Miscellaneous Works*," in *Miscellaneous Works*, p. xxviii. I am indebted to Sher for identifying the letter and its circumstances.

61. *Historical Law-Tracts*, 2nd edn. (1761; rpt. Birmingham: Legal Classics Library), pp. 49–52 n.

62. "Review of Henry Home, Lord Kames, *Historical Law-Tracts*, 1759," in *Miscellaneous Works*, pp. 95–6.

63. Ibid., pp. 110–13.

64. NAS MS CH2/185/12, p. 333.

65. Morren, *Annals*, II, 65–6; *Diary of George Ridpath, Minister of Stitchel 1755–1761*, ed. Sir James Balfour Paul (Edinburgh: Edinburgh University Press, 1922), p. 11.

66. Hume to Allan Ramsay, June 1755, in *Letters of Hume*, I, 224.

67. Robertson to Elliot, 15 October 1755, NLS MS 16,693, ff. 95–6.

68. Morren, *Annals*, II, 86–7.

69. Ibid., II, 92.

70. Ibid., pp. 26–36. The parish seemed very preoccupied with poor relief between 1750 and 1757.

71. Jardine to Charles Erskine, undated but probably 11 May 1757, NLS MS 5,088, f. 3.

72. NAS MS CH2/185/12, p. 350.

73. Ibid., p. 351.

74. Ibid., pp. 352–3.

75. Jardine to Charles Erskine, undated but probably 11 May 1757, NLS MS 5,088, f. 3.
76. Robertson to Jardine, 25 April 1757, University College London MS.
77. Morren, *Annals*, II, 127–9.
78. In fact, Robertson said later that he owed his Edinburgh translation to Nisbet "alone" (Robertson to Elliot, 24 January 1766, NLS MS 11,010, f. 32). Robertson asked Jardine to enlist his help as early as April 1756 (Robertson to Jardine, between 11 and 14 April 1756, University College London MS).
79. The following summary of events is indebted to Sher, *Church and University*, pp. 96–9. The slow unfolding of Robertson's translation may be tracked in the minutes of the Edinburgh Town Council (ECA MS, SL1/1/72) for 11 August 1756, 19 August 1756, 1 September 1756, 13 March 1757, and 3 May 1758.
80. Robertson to Elliot, 24 June 1758, NLS MS 11,009, ff. 57–8. See also Robertson to Andrew Fletcher, 10 April 1758, NLS MS 16,707, ff. 98–9.
81. NLS MS 25,411, f. 50.
82. "Account," in *Miscellaneous Works*, p. 112.
83. Robertson to Dalrymple, 26 August 1756, NLS MS 25,294, ff. 37–8.
84. *Diary of Ridpath*, p. 143.
85. Robertson to Dalrymple, 26 July 1757, NLS MS 25,294, ff. 55–6, as well as 18 November 1757, NLS MS 25,294, ff. 57–8.
86. Robertson to Birch, 19 September 1757, BL Add. MS 4,317, f. 216.
87. NAS MS CH2/185/12, p. 360.
88. Carlyle, *Autobiography*, p. 349.
89. Ibid., p. 356.
90. Robertson to Jardine, [16 March 1758], University College London MS.
91. Robertson to [Hepburn], 22 February 1758, NLS MS 16,707, ff. 92–3.
92. Robertson to [Hepburn], after 16 March 1758, NLS MS 16,707, ff. 96–7.
93. Ibid.
94. Robertson to Jardine, [16 March 1758], University College London MS. Robertson did transcribe enough material to make an appendix of documents for *History of Scotland*, but none of them printed in the appendix is identified as coming from Royston's collections. Robertson was sufficiently intrigued with the manuscript collections he saw in London that, after publishing *Scotland*, he entertained the notion of publishing a separate volume of papers presumably devoted to the 1540–1600 period. See John Blair to Robertson, 27 February 1759, NLS MS 3,942, ff. 21–2, and Blair to Robertson, 30 June – 3 July 1759, NLS MS 3,942, ff. 38–9.
95. Robertson to Jardine, [16 March 1758], University College London MS.
96. Ibid.; Robertson to Fletcher, 10 April 1758, NLS 16,707, ff. 98–9; and Robertson to Jardine, 20 April 1758, in Brougham, "Robertson," in *Miscellaneous Works*, p. 279.

97. Robertson to Jardine, 20 April 1758, in Brougham, "Robertson," in *Miscellaneous Works*, p. 279.

98. Carlyle narrates their pleasant journey in *Autobiography*, pp. 359–95.

99. NAS MS CH2/185/12, p. 365.

100. Robertson to Elliot, 24 June 1758, NLS MS 11,009, f. 58.

101. Hume to Millar, 6 April 1758, in *Letters of Hume*, I, 273.

102. Mossner, *Life of Hume*, p. 397.

103. Hume to Robertson, 25 January 1759, in *Letters of Hume*, I, 294.

104. On Robertson's commitment to impartiality with regard to Mary, see Sher, *Church and University*, pp. 104–6, esp. p. 105 n. 59; and Karen O'Brien, *Narratives of Enlightenment: Cosmopolitan History from Voltaire to Gibbon* (Cambridge: Cambridge University Press, 1997), pp. 119–22.

105. Robertson to Elliot, 4 January 1759, NLS MS 11,008, ff. 80–1.

106. NLS MS 25,411, ff. 53–4.

107. Robertson to [Hepburn], 20 February 1759, NLS MS 16,711, ff. 234–5.

108. Pocock, *Narratives of Civil Government*, p. 270.

109. Ibid., pp. 273–4.

110. *A Discourse of Logomachys, or Controversy about Words . . . To Which Is Added a Dissertation concerning Meteors of Stile* (London, 1711), pp. 158–60.

111. Ibid., pp. 131, 168.

112. "Defense of Private Judgment," in *Three Discourses* (London, 1718), p. 32.

113. Ibid., p. 33.

114. Ibid., p. 63.

115. Early in his career, he told Elliot, "I grow every day more confirmed in the resolution of keeping my hands clear of all the dirty work which in this country goes by the name of politics. I see nothing a Clergyman can gain, but much that he must necessarily lose by meddling with them" (Robertson to Elliot, 24 June 1758, NLS MS 11,009, f. 59). As a historian, he maintained the same posture.

116. *History of Scotland*, in *Works of Robertson*, II, 179–80.

117. Ibid., p. 180.

118. See Hume to Robertson, February or March 1759, in *Letters of Hume*, I, 299–300.

119. *An Examination of the Letters Said to Be Written by Mary Queen of Scots*, 2 vols (Edinburgh, 1754), 1: xxvii.

120. *History of Scotland*, in *Works of Robertson*, II, 384.

121. *A General History of England*, 4 vols (London, 1747–55), III, 619.

122. *History of Scotland*, in *Works*, II, 179.

123. Ibid., p. 184.

124. O'Brien, *Narratives of Enlightenment*, p. 96 and n.10.

125. *History of Scotland*, in *Works of Robertson*, II, 44.

126. Ibid., II, 44–5.

127. Colin Kidd, *Subverting Scotland's Past: Scottish Whig Historians and the Creation of an Anglo-British Identity, 1689–c. 1830* (Cambridge: Cambridge

University Press, 1993), p. 192. See also Sher, *Church and University*, pp. 101–2, and O'Brien, *Narratives of Enlightenment*, pp. 126–7. In 1738 Robert Dodsley captured the implications of Robertson's critique of Knox in the *Art of Preaching* (3rd edn [Glasgow, n. d.], pp. 7–8):

> Some loudly bluster, and consign to Hell
> All who dare doubt one Word or Syllable
> Of what they call the Faith; & which extends
> To Whims without Use or Ends:
> Sure 'tis much nobler, and more like Divine,
> T' enlarge the Path to Heaven, then to confine:
> Insist alone on useful Points, or plain;
> And know, God cannot hate a virtuous Man.

128. Hume to Hugh Blair, March 1766, in *Letters of Hume*, II, 31.
129. Blair to Robertson, 30 June – 3 July 1759, NLS MS 3,942, f. 39. Blair asked Robertson to confirm that Millar had made the claim that the two books sold comparably, but Robertson's response is untraced. Blair should have lost the bet because over the first nine months *Tom Jones* sold 10,000 sets (Martin C. Battestin with Ruthe R. Battestin, *Henry Fielding: A Life* [London: Routledge, 1989], p. 452) while the *History of Scotland* sold about 3,200 sets covering the first three editions in 1759 (figure courtesy of Richard Sher).
130. For a laudatory account of the book's reception, see Stewart, "Account," in *Miscellaneous Works*, pp. 113–25. A listing of reviews may be found in Jeffrey Smitten, "Writings about William Robertson, 1755–1996," in *William Robertson*, p. 233.
131. *Critical Review*, 7 (1759), pp. 89–103. David Raynor makes the attribution of the review, based on internal evidence, in "Hume and Robertson's *History of Scotland*," *British Journal for Eighteenth-Century Studies*, 10 (1987), pp. 59–63.
132. Ibid., pp. 91, 102.
133. *Life*, V, 393.
134. Alexander Stewart, "The Life of Dr. William Robertson," in *Works of William Robertson*, 12 vols (London, 1822), I, xxxv–xxxvi. William Tytler was the author of *Historical and Critical Inquiry into the Evidence Produced by the Earls of Murray and Morton against Mary, Queen of Scots* (London, 1760) and several later editions. Tytler wished to adjudicate between critics of Mary like Robertson and Hume and proponents like Goodall, while Stewart takes Tytler to be the model of a polite critic but a critic nonetheless.

CHAPTER 5

"Innumerable Occupations," 1760–1769

In 1760, Robertson stood on the brink of a decade of personal achievement: lying ahead would be leadership of the the Moderates in the church, appointment as principal of the University of Edinburgh, and publication of what would be one of his most celebrated works. But the path toward these achievements was strewn with distractions in the form of competing choices and persistent demands made on his time. As a historian, his main concern over the decade was completing *Charles V*, but, as he complained to Baron Mure in 1761, "I would wish to apply my whole time to literary pursuits, which is at present parceled out among innumerable occupations."[1] Early in the decade, he and his Moderate colleagues advocated for a Scottish militia, and he helped Robert Adam ready his lavish folio on the palace of Diocletian for publication. He would be elected principal of the University of Edinburgh in 1762, a post he naively expected to be a sinecure but which turned out to be not only demanding but one that he grew to love. In the church, he faced constant struggles between the Moderate party and the Popular party, requiring constant negotiation on patronage and related issues because neither party gained a permanent, stable majority. He moved from Lady Yester's Chapel to Old Greyfriars in 1761 where, although he now had a collegiate ministry, he still had demands of preaching and parish duties. In the midst of these demands, he faced decisions on what to do to capitalize on the success of *Scotland* and what to do with the Earl of Bute's request for a history of England. His family continued to grow with the births of two more sons, James (1762) and David (1764), even as his health suffered under the pressure of work, with an onset of what was most likely pneumonia in 1765 at an important moment in writing *Charles V*.

Throughout this network of conflicting demands, there runs a unifying theme: the modernizing of Scotland. *Charles V* would describe the broader historical process underlying this theme, in which the major states of Europe had become near equals and had remained so for two centuries.[2] The condition of near equality made conquest and universal empire impossible, introducing instead a principle of emulation based on exchange. He described this principle in his later sermon on the Glorious Revolution:

> All the civilized nations of Europe may be considered as forming one extensive community. The intercourse among them is great, & every improvement in science, in arts, in commerce, in government introduced into any of them is soon known in the others, & in time is adopted and imitated.[3]

Alongside the structural transformation of states was the transformation of religion brought with the Reformation. For a cleric in the Church of Scotland, the Reformation was a second Revelation, bringing "a revolution in the sentiments of mankind, the greatest, as well as the most beneficial, that has happened since the publication of Christianity."[4] But in Robertson's view, the Presbyterian ministry faced a difficult task in promulgating the true faith in the context of states which have acquired a new "internal vigour."[5] The Moderates did not simply adopt an Erastian position and accommodate themselves to rising secularity; they were concerned to make the church an equal partner with the state. The church would cooperate with the state as shown by the Moderates' patronage policy, but it would also maintain its independence, as shown by the *Reasons of Dissent.*[6] This balance of support and independence requires religious toleration and an educated, polite clergy willing to embrace secular knowledge and play a role in civic leadership. Accordingly, as principal, Robertson improved the breadth of learning among the faculty, the resources of the university library, the quality of the medical school, and the condition of the university's buildings. Writing history, practicing ministry, and administering the university were all directed toward creating a civil society that would allow Scotland to take a place in Britain and Europe.

Even in some of his apparently incidental activities, Robertson's focus remained on the problem of modernisation. A good example is his part in advocating for a Scottish militia, which began in the 1750s and extended into at least the early 1760s. As the Moderates formulated their thinking about a modern society in the 1750s they encountered an apparent contradiction. Although feudal society had to be rejected, the Scottish martial tradition at the heart of feudal society had become associated with a free and independent citizenry, especially in the work of Andrew Fletcher of Saltoun. Robertson and his friends embraced this martial spirit. They had taken up arms readily in 1745 (however briefly), and plays like Home's *Douglas* and *Agis* evoked the Scots martial spirit as part of their patriotic appeal, with Robertson's enthusiastic endorsement. When Robertson attended the London performance of *Agis* in 1758, he said the play was engaging and admired particularly the patriotic spirit of Home's epilogue, alluding to the Seven Years War: "France yet shall tremble at the British sword, / And dread the Vengeance of her antient Lord."[7] For Robertson, it was "to the times," and he noted with pleasure that the lines were "repeated twice with infinite applause."[8] Likewise in the *History of Scotland*, Robertson could dramatize "military virtue" because in his view it "has always been the characteristic of the Scottish nation."[9] For instance, the daring attack on Dunbarton Castle in 1571 by Captain Thomas Crawford of Jordan Hill is a stirring narrative.[10] Crawford, "a gallant and enterprising officer," one night managed to scale the castle situated "on top of a high and almost inaccessible rock, which rises in the middle of a plain." Robertson narrates the climb up the scaling ladder, including Crawford's cool handling of a soldier who fainted on the ladder, blocking the ascent. Rather than throw him off, Crawford had him bound to the ladder and had the troops climb over him. Crawford was amply rewarded for his "valour and good conduct," and "as he did not lose a single man in the enterprise, he enjoyed his success with unmixed pleasure." But more was at stake with the militia than literary representation.

Government had a long-standing reluctance to arm Scottish counties following the Jacobite conflict, and the confusion and gloom prevailing at the start of the Seven Years War brought the militia into focus. A threatened invasion by France in 1756 and the prospect of relying on foreign mercenaries for defense added further pressure. In May 1756 William Pitt and George Townshend introduced and pushed through Commons a bill that would establish a national militia for the whole of the United Kingdom. When the bill was defeated in the Lords, a second bill was introduced in June 1757, but, except for two regiments raised from Highland clans, it ignored Scotland. Robertson and his Moderate colleagues actively supported the Militia Bill because, as Robertson wrote later, the establishment of a Scottish militia was a crucial test of the character of Scottish society and "certainly of more importance to Scotland than any [issue] that has happened since the Union."[11] The nation was threatened with a military challenge plus a possible invasion from France and needed self-defense, as Adam Ferguson had argued in his *Reflections Previous to the Establishment of a Militia* (1756). With British forces encountering severe setbacks at the beginning of the war, Robertson, Carlyle, and Home were members of a General Assembly committee to draft a strongly worded address to the king that was approved by the commission of the Assembly in November 1756, but it was not published in the *London Gazette* and

ultimately failed to reach the king because it was deemed too openly critical of government, claiming (in italics) that "calamities . . . (though justly
merited by a sinful nation) *do not seem to have been brought upon this land by
any signal efforts of the wisdom or courage of our enemies.*"[12]

The issue arose again in 1759–60 when Admiral François Thurot
evaded Commodore William Boys' blockade, appearing off the coast of
Scotland in mid-October 1759, and was assumed to be planning an invasion. Robertson wrote to Townshend on 25 October that the Edinburgh
presbytery approved an address to the king in which

> we assure his Majesty, that from our knowledge of the principles & spirit of the great
> bulk of our people, that they ardently desire to be enabled to repell the insults of the
> enemy, & if they shall be entrusted with arms we are persuaded they will employ
> them in defence of his person & government.[13]

Carlyle followed with a letter on 15 November to Townshend in which he
said the Synod of Lothian and Tweeddale had also approved an address
that carried with little opposition.[14] On 6 February, Carlyle published
his successful pamphlet, *The Question Relating to a Scots Militia*, which
Robertson edited. Robertson laughingly said that he added a paragraph
that accounted for the pamphlet's success.[15] Gilbert Elliot introduced a
bill in spring 1760, but all in vain – the bill was roundly defeated on 15
April. Robertson wrote bitterly to Elliot:

> You will easily conceive the astonishment & concern of your friends in this country
> upon the miscarriage of the Militia Bill. Besides all the other advantages of the
> measure, I am fully convinced that it would have proved the most effectual security
> of the present government in this part of the kingdom, & it vexes one to see more
> done in one day to sower & alienate the minds of the people, than the attention of
> many years will be able to counterballance.[16]

But he was determined to persist, telling Elliot that an "address in a
vigorous strain" from the General Assembly would have some weight,
and "it may be procured." On 20 May the General Assembly approved
it, affirming the desire of all Scots to repel the king's enemies "with such
Vigour as their Principles of Religion and Loyalty would naturally have
inspired."[17]

The defeat of the Scottish militia bill in April 1760 did not end the
militia agitation for the Moderates. In 1762 Ferguson founded the Poker
Club, dedicated to "poking" the fire for a militia, and periodic agitation
continued, especially during the American war, but a bill was not passed
until 1797. Robertson, though a founding member of the club and cer-

tainly sympathetic, does not seem to be again directly involved, although the value of "military virtue" remained embedded in his histories. Early in his review of feudal society in the first book of *Charles V*, Robertson observes that "Force of mind, a sense of personal dignity, gallantry in enterprize, invincible perseverance in execution, contempt of danger and of death, are the characteristic virtues of uncivilized nations."[18] He was even more explicit in the *History of America*: among the virtues of the savage state, Robertson finds the Native Americans possess "the spirit of independence," a degree of fortitude making them superior to threats of danger and death, and a "zeal for the honour of their tribe, and . . . love of their country, which prompts them to brave danger that it may triumph, and to endure the most exquisite torments, without a groan, that it may not be disgraced."[19] These are precisely the qualities that underlie military virtue and whose spirit he found in a Stoic philosopher like Marcus Aurelius.[20] Feudal society fails because it warps these virtues, exercising them only in a context of tyranny, brutality, and chaos. But commercial society, by fostering liberty, law, and manners to the exclusion of military virtue, runs the danger of what he called "lethargy."[21] As Carlyle explained, "our eager pursuit of trade, together with the softness that luxury induces, and the contempt of military honours which wealth begets" lead to reliance on standing armies and vitiate our civic spirit.[22] "Lethargy" for Robertson produces a country like India in which "their effeminate appearance, their unwarlike spirit" result in European nations seeing them as inferior and open to conquest.[23] The solution for Scotland must be to establish a creative tension, in Carlyle's words, "to mix the military spirit with our civil and commercial policy."[24] A militia is a means to a very necessary social end.

Similar themes emerged in another project dating from the 1750s that engaged Robertson's time. His cousin Robert Adam published in 1764 the *Ruins of the Palace of the Emperor Diocletian at Spalatro in Dalmatia*, a collection of over seventy engraved plates in folio depicting the remains of the emperor's private residence after he resigned the empire in 305. The project took initial shape during Adam's journey to Italy in 1754–7 when he realized that to establish himself in England as an architect he ought first to publish an imposing folio that would define his taste.[25] Although he had several other sites in mind, Spalatro (or Split) presented itself as both affordable and undocumented. His expedition visited there in the late summer of 1757, he had several drawings in hand, and he composed a preface. But distrusting both his writing and his classical knowledge, in 1757 he called on Robertson to revise the preface. He was delighted with the result:

> I cannot enough express my Surprize & admiration of Willie's Preface. It is beauti-
> fully said & in a few Lines contains the full Sence of what woud have taken many
> pages from any other Historian of this Age but himself. If any thing can make
> me think more highly of his abilitys than I did from his History it is the masterly
> Penning of my Preface.[26]

Robertson had sharpened, condensed, and focused a diffuse travel narrative titled "Reasons and Motives for Undertaking the Voyage to Spalatro
in Dalmatia" that was merely accompanied by pictures. He turned it into
an argument for the genius of ancient architecture for which the illustrations now served as examples.[27] Robertson probably also had at least a hand
in the book's proposal, dedication, and description of plates. Proposals
for the book were published on 26 January 1760.[28] James Adam visited
Italy in 1760–3, overseeing the engravings under the direction of Charles
Louis Clérisseau, and Robertson went to London in September 1760 and
perhaps again in 1761 to assist with editing.[29] Printed by William Strahan
and with a subscriber list that contained virtually all the Moderate literati
and their allies, the book appeared in 1764 to a very positive reception.

Although Robertson's role is nowhere acknowledged in the book,
Adam's publication may have helped shape his view of Charles V's reign.
As monarchs, Diocletian and Charles V had much in common, as Gibbon
noted:

> The parallel of Charles the Fifth [and Diocletian] . . . will naturally offer itself to our
> mind, not only since the eloquence of a modern historian has rendered that name
> so familiar to an English reader, but from the very striking resemblance between
> the characters of the two emperors, whose political abilities were superior to their
> military genius, and whose specious virtues were much less the effect of nature than
> of art.[30]

Both had abdicated their thrones at a relatively young age, and both had
worn out their constitutions "with wars and journies [sic], the cares of
royalty, and their application to business." But Robertson and Adam both
find George III superior to these great figures because he is not consumed
by conquest. The dedication of the *Ruins* to George III concludes:

> At this happy Period, when Great Britain enjoys in Peace the Reputation and Power
> she has acquired by Arms, Your Majesty's singular attention to the Arts of Elegance,
> promises an Age of Perfection that will compleat the Glories of your Reign, and fix
> an Aera no less remarkable than that of PERICLES, AUGUSTUS, or the MEDICIS.[31]

In his dedication of *Charles V* to the king, Robertson delivered a version of
this same praise of managing arms and arts:

Your Subjects cannot observe the various calamities, which that Monarch's [Charles V's] ambition to be distinguished as a Conqueror, brought upon his dominions, without recollecting the felicity of their own times, and looking up with gratitude to their Sovereign, who, during the fervor of youth, and amidst the career of victory, possessed such self-command, and maturity of judgment, as to set bounds to his own triumphs, and prefer the blessings of peace to the splendor of military glory.[32]

Adam's plates (and Gibbon's allusion to artificial virtues) also carry a cautionary theme for George III's less martial "Age of Perfection." Robertson easily saw that the pictorial message of so many of the plates is decline and fall because Adam and Clérisseau "took every opportunity to charge the archaeological and geometrical data contained in the plates of *Spalatro* with an emotive, picturesque power."[33] That emotional power includes a sense of fallen greatness. The plates echo Piranesi, with whom Adam associated during his Italian journey, showing heroic Roman ruins juxtaposed to an unheroic and oriental present. The introduction reinforces this elegiac visual motif:

The inhabitants of Spalatro have destroyed some parts of the palace, in order to procure materials for building; and to this their town owes its name, which is evidently a corruption of Palatium. In other places houses are built upon the old foundations, and modern works are so intermingled with the ancient, as to be scarcely distinguishable.[34]

Such an elegiac note concerning change and decline reminds us of what happens when an empire becomes lethargic, devotes too much attention to elegance, and loses its sense of civic and military virtue.

The collaboration between Robertson and Robert and James Adam was successful enough that he was called upon later by another Adam brother, John, the oldest of the four Adam brothers and Robertson's contemporary from the Dalkeith Grammar School. John proposed to publish a project originally begun by his father, William, to document his architectural work with a book of plates. William was not able to bring the project to publication and it appears that John resumed it shortly after William's death in 1748. He added to the plates that William had printed so that by 1764 he was ready to think about publication. He called upon Robertson to approach Andrew Millar. Their negotiations were successful enough that on John's instructions Robertson drafted an agreement in the fall of 1765 during a London visit, not only committing John to delivery of 750 copies of 160 folio copper plates by Christmas 1766 but also committing Robertson to the revision of "an Explanation or Description of the said Plates."[35] Perhaps fortunately for Robertson, given the importance of completing *Charles V* along with his roles as minister and principal, the deal fell through. Millar issued proposals for the book in spring 1766 and may have found the market for it lacking. But it also appears that John could not follow through with delivery of the copper plates because of an ownership dispute. In the end, the book did not appear until 1811 when it was published by Adam Black with no preface or explanation of the plates.

Alongside these smaller projects, Robertson had to decide on the subject of a major work he hoped would capitalize on the history of Scotland and establish him as Britain's leading historian. He seemed to know early on what he wanted to do because it was signaled in the parcels of manuscript sent to Millar after his spring 1758 trip to London. The germ of *Charles V* appears in the close of Book I of *Scotland* where Robertson adds a brief "view of the political state of Europe" at the beginning of the sixteenth century, noting the concept of a balance of power: "A thorough knowledge of that general system, of which every kingdom in Europe forms a part, is not less requisite toward understanding the history of a nation, than an acquaintance with its peculiar government and laws."[36] Although Robertson already saw a connection between the *History of Scotland* and *Charles V*, he also thought it well to canvass the opinions of his friends. Upon his return to Edinburgh, he apparently discussed possible topics with Dalrymple, who then wrote to Horace Walpole on 5 July 1758, asking his opinion of what Robertson should pursue.[37] Following the publication of the *History of Scotland*, John Blair urged him to write a history of England, an idea backed by Charles Cathcart, the king's representative to the General Assembly, the Earl of Bute, and the king.[38] But as 1759 progressed other ideas were floated. Horace Walpole disliked Robertson's idea of Charles V but endorsed a history of Greece, which Hume had first raised, and added his own suggestions of a history of learning or of a history of humanity comprehending the reigns of the five good Roman emperors.[39] Hume also disliked the reign of Charles V and discouraged Robertson's suggestion of the age of Leo X while recommending a collection of modern lives in the manner of Plutarch or the history of Greece.[40] By the end of April, Robertson may have had enough suggestions, and Ferguson told Elliot that "I have not heard from Robertson what he is meditating for the Subject of further Works he probably declines being troubled with many opinions."[41] In October Robertson told Charles Townshend that he had settled on Charles V and was about to begin writing, and in December he wrote Thomas Birch that he had "begun to labor seriously" and enclosed a list of over 70 books he wished to consult.[42] Despite all the canvassing and suggestions, Robertson never let go of his original intention.

He knew from his university days that the age of Charles V marked a key turning point in Western history because it not only was the beginning of the modern European state system but also, and more importantly for the Church of Scotland, the advent of reformed religion. But the age was also compelling and colorful in itself. In his letter to Walpole of 20 February 1759, describing his interest in the topic of Charles V, Robertson echoes Voltaire's *Essai sur les moeurs*:

> The Emperor Charles V, though neither the most pleasant nor the most perfect character of that age, is on account of the extent of his dominions, & the length of his reign, the most proper person for occupying this capital place. I have therefore some thoughts of writing the History of his Reign. The events are great & interesting. The struggle of the Spanish Cortez for their liberty; the Reformation in Germany; the wars in Italy; the revival of letters; the conquest of the new world; the rise of the Piratical States in Barbary, & the Emperors expedition against them; his wars with the Turks; the rivalship between Charles & Francis; their intrigues with Henry VIII are all splendid objects in History. The inferior characters too are good, Leo X, Luther, the Constable Bourbon, the Marquis de Pescara, &c., are pleasant or (which is as lucky for an Historian) strange figures. The field is wide, & I shall have many books to read, but as I shall not be plagued with the endless controversies which perplexed me in my last work, I am not dismayed at mere labour.[43]

Robertson's fascination with the dynamism and grandeur of the age indicates the great attraction the sixteenth century held for him. But behind that surface, Robertson also saw a transformative moment in history. Charles V was the central figure of his time not only because he was the most powerful and, in some ways, heroic figure but also because he was the catalyst for what Robertson called "a remarkable change" across all the major kingdoms of Europe.[44]

When Europe had not yet acquired a system of states with sufficient "vigour" and awareness of their own strength, great leaders like Charles V and Francis I could aspire to absolute power. But, beginning with Charles VIII's invasion of Italy in 1494, that very aspiration created the system that eventually limited their desires: "The advantages possessed by one state, were counterbalanced by circumstances favourable to others, and this prevented any from attaining such superiority as might have been fatal to all."[45] If Scotland were to assume a place in this system of kingdoms, then it would have to understand the history of this "remarkable" transformation from a feudal to a commercial stage.

The concept of a balance of power had a long history, reaching back to Thucydides' discussion of the relation of Athens and the Spartan league through Polybius to Guicciardini's analysis of the power relations of the Italian states. More recently, Hume had written an important essay on the balance of power in 1752.[46] For Robertson, there are two related themes to discuss: the first, developed in the "View of the Progress of Society," is the progressive improvement of the states of Europe toward a common level of strength and refinement; the second is Charles V's ambition, which rather than an extensive empire produced a set of states held in counter-balance with each other by their relative equality of power. In the same way that the romantic ideals surrounding Mary give way to the rationality of commercial society, so Charles's vast, destructive ambitions of military conquest ironically give way to a group of more provident states that are now internally strengthened and that can now give attention to their social improvement.

The balance of power is only one dimension of the story of Charles V; the other is the Reformation. Robertson's handling of the Reformation is distinctive and tells us much about how he does and does not bring religion and history together. He does not mention the Reformation in the "View of Society," which focuses on government, laws, and manners. He introduces it early in Book II[47] in connection with the very first act of Charles's administration, calling the Diet of Worms in 1521. His nearly sixty-page introduction to the Diet is devoted almost exclusively to describing secular causes of the Reformation, including the sale of indul-gences by Leo X, the powerful advocacy of Luther and Zwingli, and the political missteps made by the court of Rome. He also provides an analysis of the special circumstances that conspired to turn an abuse of indulgences into an entire reformation of religion and a breaking of papal power. The schism of the fourteenth century, the worldliness of popes such as Alexander VI and Julius II, the invention of printing, and the revival of learning, which brought an intellectual awakening, were coupled with resentment stemming from oppressive immorality, exorbitant wealth, excessive power, and greed to produce "a revolution in the sentiments of mankind, the greatest, as well as the most beneficial, that has happened since the publication of Christianity."[48] He also rules out, as an explicitly religious historian might not, discussion of the theological doctrines of the Reformation.[49] He frames this secular account of what is, for the Church of Scotland, a second Revelation, with two explicit allusions to "that Divine Providence which, with infinite ease, can bring about events which to human sagacity appear impossible."[50] The largely secular tenor of his discussions of the church does not change through the course of the nar-rative. Given Robertson's restraint in handling the specifically religious aspects of his history, one might ask how he intends us to respond to his acknowledgments of divine intervention. Are they merely polite touches or are they something more significant?

Religion was never far from Robertson's mind. In all his thinking, there is a mutual implication of religion and history, sometimes explicit but always already there.[51] Just ten days after writing to Birch confirming his intention to write on Charles V and "the first establishment of the present political system of Europe," Robertson delivered a series of three sermons on successive Sundays based on Daniel 4: 34–5, dealing with Nebuchadnezzar's realization of God's providence.[52] On 23 December, he preached on what is implied in God's providence: "God preserves us. [T]here *is* no created being independent [*sic*]; perhaps there *cannot* be, the preservation of all things is a *daily* creation." A week later, he took up this theme in the context of sacred history, showing

> how the providence of God overrules the actions of men. 1. By inspiring them with other sentiments than their own. 2. By disposing of events in such manner as to make men alter their purposes, as in yᵉ case of David when he meant to kill Nabal, or by disappointing their purposes, as in yᵉ [case?] of Sennacherib. He observed that yᵉ scriptures contained the history of providence, which in other historys is less Clear, in Common life less discernable, because in profane history & in common life we read in interpretation.

Finally, on 6 January, he concluded the series by showing what inferences and motives are to be drawn from dwelling on providence:

> 1. That we do not live in a world of anarchy, & confusion. 2. That we have by yᵉ light of reason and more so by revelation, knowledge of what is fit & certainty of God protecting us. 3. That from a good conscience here & the hopes of a life of glory for ever, we may be secure in whatever befalls us & trust in the Providence of God.

Reading *Charles V* in light of his sermons lends much greater weight to his sparing reference to divine intervention. Providence is always a subtext because we read profane history like *Charles V* "in interpretation": that is, we read the words of a limited interpreter of history always against the unmediated truth of Scripture. As he argued in his student essay, history depends on probable reasoning, which, in turn, is sanctioned by God because probable reasoning is a source of knowledge. For Robertson, then, historiography puts the careful narrative of events foremost but it is congruent with divine providence. For example, when Charles's ambitious plans are overturned with the Treaty of Passau in 1552, Robertson reminds us that "so wonderfully doth the wisdom of God superintend and regulate the caprice of human passions, and render them subservient towards the accomplishment of his own purposes."[53] Then he reinforces his point by describing the "miserable plight" of Charles's troops as they make their way over the Alps after their final defeat at the hands of Maurice of Saxony and noting how it was "very unlike the pomp with which Charles had appeared during the five preceding years as the conqueror of Germany."[54] Turning back to the defeat of the Elector of Brandenburg in 1547, which launched Charles's German conquest, one finds Charles "seated on a magnificent throne, with all the ensigns of his dignity, surrounded by a numerous train of the princes of the empire."[55] The contrast with the humiliated, defeated elector prompted in everyone's mind "serious reflections . . . upon the instability and emptiness of human grandeur,"[56] exactly what has now beset Charles. Moments of moral reflection like this one force a shift in perspective for readers, pulling them out of civic history and into a providential history. Proper judgment of Charles's fate requires reason, but reason also implies faith.

Understanding the importance of *Charles V* to Robertson's sense of his career helps us appreciate his confusion and uncertainty about what to do with the requests urging him to write a history of England. Some have implied that Robertson used them to manipulate the patronage system, promising to write the history but in the end just keeping the positions he gained by making the promise.[57] It is true that he gained a great deal through Lord Bute, and he certainly did not write an English history, but his decision-making process was complicated. Robertson had quickly declined John Blair's proposal to write the history, saying he did not wish to rival Hume. But the proposal flattered and intrigued him.[58] A few weeks later, he wrote an excited letter to Gilbert Elliot, declaring "I am perfectly astonished at my own success, & what at first I ascribed to the influence of a few men of taste, to the good-nature of the English, & to the idleness of the people of rank who have no faction in parliament to amuse them, I now modestly consider as the effect of some extraordinary merit in myself which I did not formerly attend to sufficiently."[59] The sudden success of *Scotland* had opened a door to patronage, and now was his chance to go through it. He went on to wonder whether "Amidst all this run of luck it was impossible not reflect [sic] whether it might not be possible to make some advantage of it." His first thought was to secure a chair of history in the university, but he ran into problems of funding for the position.[60] He then requested a recently vacated deanery of the Chapel Royal, but Bute gave that appointment to Jardine while presenting Robertson with the slightly lesser appointment of Chaplain in Ordinary.[61] But that appointment was soon followed by the letter from Cathcart of 20 July 1761 assuring him of Lord Bute's full support for the English history and the king's favorable backing of the project. Robertson, caught off guard, later told Elliot he "had been so little accustomed to see Kings or Ministers attend to any literary concern, or think of making provision for any man of letters, that I was a good deal surprized at a proposal so unexpected."[62]

Thus began a series of perplexed negotiations.[63] Bute's initial desire was to have Robertson, like John Home before him, leave the ministry, move to London, and live on a government sinecure to write his history of England, and there was much in the offer that was attractive, particularly, as he stated in his reply to Cathcart on 27 July 1761, "to have it in my power to apply myself wholly to my studies." Moreover, "This the encouragement your lordship mentions will put it in my power."[64] But certain conditions had to be met: Robertson wished to stay in Scotland and to delay the English history. His age (forty) was a consideration. Robertson was no longer young, unattached, and able to move at will to a new country with its strange manners and mode of life. In addition, as he pointed out to Baron Mure a few months later, with a wife and four children (and a fifth, James, who would be born in two months), "I must consider not only what would be agreeable to myself, but what may be of advantage to them."[65] Then there was his church. Robertson wanted "to be considered only as a Man of Letters, with a Clerical character."[66] Although he would like to be released from the burden of regular preaching, he was not inclined to resign from the Church of Scotland. One wonders, too, if Robertson was not leery of Bute as a patron. He probably knew from Home that Bute could be demanding and keeping some distance between them might help insure Robertson's independence and preserve his leadership role.[67] Finally, there was the problem of the partially completed manuscript of *Charles V*. By July 1761 Robertson said he was more than one-third finished with the book, and he speculated that it would take another two years of work to complete it. That would mean that he probably would not begin work on an English history until 1764 at the earliest, and by that point, though no one could know it in 1761, Bute would be out of power, ironically making the whole project of the English history moot.

Baron Mure was able to craft a proposal that met Robertson's requests. Robertson would be able to stay in Scotland, apart from spending a few months in London; he would resign his parish but would retain his chaplaincy as a member of the church, receiving instead a pension of about £200 per year; and he would be given the next vacant university principalship in either Edinburgh or Glasgow.[68] With that arrangement in place, the drama shifted to possible university appointments, and Robertson particularly had his eye on the aged John Gowdie at the University of Edinburgh, who, as Robertson observed, "is taken so ill that his life is despaired of."[69] On 19 February 1762 Gowdie died, and the candidates for his post immediately appeared. Daniel MacQueen and Patrick Cuming came forward for the Popular party, and Robertson and several of his friends, including Blair, Ferguson, Jardine, and George Wishart for the Moderates. Ferguson was the only serious contender, but Bute's strong commitment to Robertson was the deciding factor. For Robertson, it seemed an ideal post, and on 10 March 1762 he was elected principal.

Robertson told Elliot that he thought the post a sinecure, making it even more suitable for someone with his historical commitments. By August, he had discovered the truth: "I need not tell you how many avocations from study arose from the discharge of the Ministerial office in Edinburgh, & how much this will be increased by entering on the office of Principal . . . of a College, which has been several years without a Head, & has not had one who attended to its affairs of a very long time."[70] This discovery complicated his ongoing negotiations with Bute because Robertson had not yet found the financial support he felt necessary for sustained work on *Charles V*. Robertson therefore wrote to Elliot in August, asking his help in persuading Bute to give Robertson the post of Historiographer Royal for Scotland with a £200 stipend so that he could give up his ministry. Negotiations stretched into April 1763 when Robertson put his most fully detailed request before Cathcart.[71] The Historiographer stipend was now set at £250 plus the salaries from the principalship and the chaplaincy. In addition Robertson estimated his expenses for books and copying to be "four or five hundred pounds." In the end, Bute simply stuck with £200 for the Historiographer post and nothing more, and Robertson took the offer, perhaps in part because Bute fell from power in May and the prospects for patronage were suddenly limited. The Historiographer appointment was signed on 6 August 1763, but that was essentially the last act in the drama. Robertson never did write an English history, although he toyed briefly with the idea of a history of the Restoration and Queen Anne periods in 1778,[72] but he retained all the fruits of patronage: his chaplaincy, his principalship, and his post as Historiographer Royal for Scotland, in addition to his salary as minister of Old Greyfriars.

Robertson does not come off well in these difficult negotiations. He gained a great deal of money, increasing his income from £139 in 1761 (after his translation to Old Greyfriars) to almost £500 in 1763. To be sure, his appointment as principal was momentous for the history of the university, but at the same time he appears greedy and opportunistic. Requests seemed to keep escalating: first to live in Scotland, then a pension to replace the ministry, then the principalship, then the position as Historiographer – all coming in a matter of months. But it is also important to remember what Robertson did not do in response to Bute's surprising offer of support for the writing of *Charles V*, a project to which he was very deeply committed.[73] He did not accept the sinecure offer and move to London but chose to stay in Edinburgh and Scotland. His reasons were complicated, but had he been solely interested in personal gain and social ambition such a move was necessary. Moreover, he did not wish to resign from the Church of Scotland, though he did wish to resign his ministry. But in the end, he did not resign it, even though Bute put up £200. Did greed motivate him, or did he wish to remain actively involved in the church? His identity as a churchman was essential to his personal life as well as to his historical vision, and at least in his own mind, he could not be a man of letters without bringing to that role a clerical character.

Although Bute himself failed in his role as Maecenas providing patronage for Robertson's English history, Robertson's career steadily moved forward. One event was temporary but symbolic. In 1763, as a sign of his ascendency to a leadership position in the General Assembly, Robertson was appointed moderator for the meeting in May. It was an annual appointment by a vote of the members of the General Assembly, and among his duties, the moderator was required to compose several official Assembly documents and deliver the opening sermon at the next year's meeting. Robertson's sermon was never printed, and no record of it remains. His name is attached to three official documents: a largely pro forma response to the king's annual letter supporting and approving the meeting of the General Assembly, a congratulatory address on the Treaty of Paris ending the Seven Years War, and a congratulatory address, again largely pro forma, on the birth of the king's son, George Augustus, the future George IV. Robertson's comments on the Treaty of Paris, however, bear his impress because they anticipate the central theme of *Charles V*, particularly the history's concerns with the balance of power and the important role of commerce in civil society, and they do so in the context of the church:

> By a definitive Treaty with your Enemies, the great Objects for which War was undertaken are attained; the Possessions of chief Consequence to *Britain* are secured; new Sources of Commerce are opened; and Territories are added to your Crown, more extensive and of greater Value, than have been acquired by any Nation since the Division of *Europe* into great Kingdoms, and the Establishment of a Balance of Power, have put a Stop to the Rapidity of Conquest; and as your Majesty can now turn your whole Attention towards the Cultivation and Encouragement of the Arts of Peace, which, even under the Pressure, and amidst the Avocations of War, you did not neglect, these, under your royal Patronage, must revive and flourish, and *Britain*, as it is the greatest, will become the most polished and illustrious Nation in Europe.[74]

This is a splendid moment for Robertson: in the context of the Church of Scotland, he endorses the progress of commerce, empire, and civil

society, and his projected *Charles V* will show how that new age had come
to be.

Robertson's appointment as principal came to mean more to him than
he imagined it would. At the laying of the foundation stone of the long-
sought Old College in 1791, he looked back over his three decades as
principal and offered a concise view of the university's mission, putting it
at the heart of the Moderates' goals:

> May [God] continue to protect our University, the object of whose institutions is to
> instil into the minds of youth principles of sound knowledge, to inspire them with
> the love of religion and virtue, and to prepare them for filling the various stations in
> society with honour to themselves, and with benefit to their country.[75]

The office of principal could be no mere sinecure because it meant too
much for the Moderates' Enlightenment values. The university was a
catalyst for the social and intellectual transformation of the city. Add to this
broad vision the fact that the university was from its founding in 1594, the
"tounis college." It was under the jurisdiction, financial control, and leadership of the Edinburgh Town Council, making it closely tied to the civic
interests of the city. It was also subject to the scrutiny and approval of the
church,[76] which had been demonstrated clearly, Robertson would recall,
when in 1745 Hume was denied a professorship by the Edinburgh presbytery, whose membership at the time included the elder William Robertson.
What Robertson realized was that the university was a vital component that
would bring together the commercial interests of the city and the religious
mission of the church under the auspices of learning, which benefits both.

Although Robertson was elected principal in March 1762, he did not
assume the post until November.[77] But once in position, he showed the
same kind of practical entrepreneurial spirit that marked his grandfather's
career, and his efforts were to have a very significant impact on the university, starting with the library. In December, Professor George Stuart
(father of Gilbert Stuart, who would become something of a nemesis to
Robertson), chose to resign as Keeper of the Library. Although he had
compiled a three-volume catalogue, he had never been able to put the
library into proper order, and his departure from the library opened the
way for changes.[78] Robertson appointed James Robertson, professor of
Hebrew, as librarian, who recruited Duke Gordon as under-librarian,
and together they would make an effective team to develop the library,
ultimately producing a definitive catalogue. Robertson also firmed up the
collection of matriculation fees, giving the library an expanded source of
income independent of the Town Council; initiated development of the
medical collections ("one of the few things," he noted, "wanting to render

Medical Education more compleat here than in any part of Europe"), and requested an increase in the funds granted by the Town Council for fires to warm the 1617 building that housed the books.[79] On the heels of these initiatives, Robertson proposed the creation of a natural history museum to house the university's collections. Writing to the Town Council in 1765, he demonstrated his shrewd grasp of the university's situation by couching his argument not only in terms of education but also the local economy and civic pride: the creation of a museum "would lend greatly to complete the plan of Medical Education, on account of which so many Strangers resort hither to the no small emolument both of the Professors & Citizens."[80] The museum could be created at minimal expense, by fitting up the room in the 1617 building vacated by printers who had had a lease on it. Although the project was completed, the first professor appointed as keeper, Robert Ramsay, was ineffectual, and it was not until John Walker's appointment in 1779 that the museum was fully developed. More successful was the building of a new anatomy theatre that Robertson backed in 1764.[81] Alexander Monro *secundus* had offered to reimburse the £300 cost himself out of his fees from his very popular anatomy lectures. The theater accommodated 200 students to observe demonstrations plus Monro's collection of specimens, and its success was shown when Monro had to add a gallery in 1783.

These projects show Robertson's ambition, but they also reveal a major problem he faced: dilapidated buildings and lack of space. The time seemed right for a major undertaking. As a result of Robertson's initiatives, there had been much recent discussion about rebuilding the college and expectations were high at the moment.[82] Also, the principal, who had just written a bestselling history of his country and who was on the verge of publishing another major history, was the right person to carry the project forward. Thus, on 4 December 1767, Robertson discussed with the Senatus Academicus the future of the college and specifically a new college building, with the meeting recommending the creation of a joint committee composed of members from the university and the Town Council. The Town Council agreed, and the committee met on the 19th and filed their report on the 23rd. Because the cost of the project could not be funded from city resources, private donors would have to be approached. The best opportunity was during the current session of Parliament (destined to run until March 1768 and resume in May and June), when "the most wealthy and considerable persons both of our Country and of the Southern part of the Island are assembled at London."[83] A list of prominent figures was prepared, who would act as independent trustees, and Robertson drafted and published a subscription paper titled a *Memorial Relating to the University of Edinburgh* at the end of

January 1768. The scope of the project was substantial. A note appended to the subscription paper describes the cost:

> It is proposed to erect sixteen schools and teaching-rooms, so as to accommodate the professors of the several arts and sciences, together with a public hall, museum, and library-room. According to a survey and estimate by a skillful architect, these sixteen schools or teaching-rooms may be built for about 6500£, and the above-mentioned public hall, museum, and library-room, may be finished in a decent and proper manner, and the chymical laboratory, anatomical theatre, and public schools, may be fitted up, for the additional sum of 8500£ or thereabout.[84]

Fraser points out that a further £10,000 would have been needed for professors' houses, bringing the total subscription to £25,000.[85] Despite the glowing report in the March *Scots Magazine* that the subscription "goes on successfully," it never reached enough to cover the first phase of the project, the sixteen teaching-rooms. For the next two decades, Robertson had to be content with piecemeal repairs to what he termed, echoing a Jesuit priest, "Hae miseriae nostrae."[86]

Alongside his efforts to patch and rebuild college facilities, Robertson enhanced the college's faculty. Under William Carstares fifty years earlier, the university had discarded the regent system in which a single professor would oversee all four years of a single class in favor of professors who specialized in a particular discipline. But despite the growing importance of specialized academic expertise in faculty appointments, Robertson still had to work closely with the Town Council, considering not only the candidates' academic accomplishments but also their place in the Moderates' vision of education and their acceptability to the Town Council. Robertson's successful development of the faculty was aided by having two of his closest allies in place within the university: Hugh Blair and Adam Ferguson. Blair was named Regius Professor of Belles Lettres in April 1762 on the heels of Robertson's appointment as principal in March but before he had been officially approved for office on 11 November. Ferguson was also already in place, having been appointed to the natural philosophy chair in 1759, although that is not where he would remain. A third favorable event was the resignation of Patrick Cuming, the sixty-seven-year-old professor of ecclesiastical history and opponent of the Moderate agenda in both the church and the university, as already shown by his attack on Home's *Douglas*. Cuming had gained considerable power during Gowdie's principalship, but the appointment of Robertson clearly showed him the future, and Cuming resigned in favor of his son, Robert. That left the way clear for Robertson to move ahead to reshape the university's faculty with the Town Council's backing.

His first task was to strengthen the moral philosophy chair. Just a few weeks into his tenure, Robertson wrote to Elliot explaining a plan:

> You know of how much importance the Class of Moral philosophy is in the Scotch College. Unfortunately your friend Mr Balfour tho' a man of great integrity, & well-skilled I am told in his own profession of law, teaches that class in such a manner that it has dwindled to nothing, which is a cruel circumstance to the College, & a real & essential loss to the country, as there are more Gentlemen & Clergymen educated here than in any other College.[87]

Moral philosophy was not something of interest only to divinity students; it was central to the mission of the university, as he made clear in his foundation stone speech of 1791. Unfortunately, James Balfour of Pilrig had turned the class into a sinecure, had done little to distinguish it outside the classroom, and had the added disadvantage of being a critic of Hume. Impatience for his removal circulated through the Town Council, and in 1759 had emerged as a "double scheme," which Robertson resurrected in his letter to Elliot. Balfour would vacate moral philosophy to become sheriff depute, Ferguson would move to moral philosophy, and James Russel, surgeon, Select Society member, and Moderate ally, would fill Ferguson's position in natural philosophy. By 1764 Robertson adroitly brought the "double scheme" to pass, with the change that Balfour now would become Professor of the Law of Nature and Nations, which Robert Bruce had conveniently vacated to become a Lord of Session. It was so smoothly done Blair crowed to Hume, "Is not this clever?"[88] Although Russel died only nine years into his tenure, he made interesting innovations in the natural philosophy curriculum; Ferguson taught successfully until he developed wanderlust in 1772.

Robertson's next major appointment – and one of his best – was the distinguished chemist Joseph Black, whom he lured from the University of Glasgow. Robertson was personally invested in securing the appointment because Black was brilliant, convivial, and a solid Whig. Writing his father in June 1766 just after accepting the appointment, Black said Robertson was the "Warmest & and most usefull" of his friends assisting in the move.

> Dr.Robertson who misses no opportunity of improving the Medical College at Edinburgh has for several years past been striving to bring me into it & in some hard struggles which he and Dr. Cullen had to keep out other Candidates he often did me the honour to declare that he did not act from friendship or attachment to any Person but solely to promote the Prosperity of the College.[89]

Robert Cullen, who was to be one of Robertson's close personal friends, was important to this scheme because he chose to move to the Institutes of

Medicine chair, leaving the Chemistry chair for Black, making the move all the more attractive. As a coda to these early appointments of the 1760s, Robertson was able to create the first chair of *materia medica* in the university and fill it with Francis Home, a successful physician who would follow Cullen as president of the Royal College of Physicians of Edinburgh from 1775 to 1777.

Robertson's success in securing control of the direction of the university was matched by his management of the church, but Robertson had to learn from experience. Anti-patronage sentiment had received a boost with the controversial settlement in his Edinburgh parish of John Drysdale.[90] What looked to be a reasonable settlement, at least in terms of Drysdale's credentials, became, through the Moderates' and Robertson's mishandling, "one of the keenest contests ever agitated in Scotland, respecting the right of presentation."[91] In August 1762, Robertson wrote to Elliot in the wake of John Hyndman's death that Drysdale would, in his estimation, be the most effective replacement for the man who had been his closest aide in forwarding the Moderate agenda. Earlier Hyndman had been the associate of Patrick Cuming in leading opposition to the Moderates, but Robertson had managed to persuade him to join with the Moderates to add his political skill and to embarrass his opponent Cuming.[92] In choosing Drysdale as Hyndman's successor, Robertson clearly wanted someone who could act effectively in a subordinate political role. Drysdale was also well connected: he was a close friend of James Oswald of Dunniker, one of the leading opponents of the Moderates, as well as being related to the Adams by marriage. But the Moderates, led by Robertson, made the mistake of attempting to bypass the Edinburgh General Sessions in an effort to avoid opposition to the appointment, relying instead solely on the Town Council for approval. Although some Moderates, like Carlyle,[93] argued that the right of appointment rested solely with the Town Council and had been extended to the General Sessions simply as a courtesy to involve the city's ministers in the choice of their colleagues, the move elicited popular outrage at the procedure. Only after the House of Lords affirmed the Town Council's right of appointment was Drysdale duly confirmed by the General Assembly in 1764.

Two years later, the controversy over the Schism Overture built on the Drysdale "Bustle," alleging that Moderates were abusing the law of patronage and forcing members to secede from the church with their practice of rejecting popular election of ministers in favor of the choice made by lay patrons. Robertson himself solicited votes. Writing to his friend George Lawrie, minister of Kilmarnoch, for example, he was blunt:

You have heard I dare say of the Schism Overture, & know by whom it was framed, & against what men & what Measures it was intended. I am persuaded it would occasion great disorder & dissension in the Church. I beg therefore that you would endeavour to secure us from your Presbytery moderate & reasonable men who will attend. You know the way of attaining this, & I trust that both from publick spirit & from private friendship you will exert yourself.[94]

But by the time of Assembly, Robertson was ill, probably suffering his usual chronic congestion, and Blair confessed to Hume that the "Church [is] in a Tottering State."[95] The moderator for this Assembly was James Oswald of Methven, whom Carlyle thought to be "a respectable clergyman of the Church of Scotland,"[96] but who also supported the overture against the Moderates, a position he made clear in his sermon opening the Assembly and in his 1767 *Letters concerning the Present State of the Church of Scotland*. The debate opened on 30 May, with Oswald making a temperate and reasonable assessment of the overture and urging the Assembly to approve it. Robertson replied that investigation of schism would stifle diversity of religious opinion, an argument leading to one of his more famous statements on religious tolerance when he said that "as in the works of nature, for example in a bed of flowers, great part of the beauty arises from the variety in shape, size, and colour; so, in the moral world, the differences of opinion in religion, the various sects, and opposite modes of worship, constituted a remarkable beauty in the system upon the whole."[97] But the debate was long, starting at 10:00 in the morning and not concluding until 9:00 at night, and it was, as Morren noted, "deliberate." In the evening, the drama of the occasion was heightened when John Jardine died of a heart attack after the debate and in the midst of the voting. Jardine had carefully tallied the votes beforehand and expected victory, but just as the roll call reached the decisive point, Carlyle saw that Jardine "had tumbled from his seat, and being a man of six feet two inches, and of large bones, had borne down all those on the two benches below him, and fallen to the ground."[98] Jardine was carried outside but died very quickly. Carlyle returned to the Assembly, and in order to calm the house and conclude the voting, said there was hope for Jardine's recovery. In the end, the Moderates prevailed in rejecting the overture 99 to 85, as Jardine had predicted. The Overture was a watershed moment for the Moderates. Carlyle called it a "deadly blow to the enemies of presentations"[99] because the defeat of the Popular Party's challenge, although not giving the Moderates a dominant hand, did give them a pronounced leadership role in church management at least until the end of the 1770s when Robertson laid aside his leadership position.

Meanwhile, amid his "innumerable occupations," Robertson continued to grapple with the writing of *Charles V*. The project had started smoothly. In February 1760 Robertson said he was "making progress," and by January 1762 the project seemed well in hand, with Robertson telling James Edmondstone, "I propose not to exceed the size of two volumes in quarto, I have already got through more than one-half of it, but as I write slowly, & have many avocations, I shall not be ready for the press sooner than two years hence."[100] His avocations increased with his appointment as principal, and by July 1762 Boswell said the book "will not be ready for the press for some time."[101] In 1762–3, the complications of the "Drysdale Bustle" intruded, but Hugh Blair still predicted he would finish by summer 1765.[102] Unfortunately, summer 1765 saw Robertson sufficiently ill to cancel a proposed trip to Paris to visit Hume.[103] By October 1765, Robertson had recovered but now added his own reason for delay, having decided to expand his history by adding the "View of the Progress of Society in Europe," which became now the first volume of the history though the third written.[104] We do not know exactly what prompted him to add the book or when he chose to do it. The first letter mentioning it in his known correspondence was written to Thomas Birch:

> I have met with many interruptions in carrying on my Charles V partly from bad health, & partly from the avocations arising from performing the duties of my office. But I am within sight of land. The historical part of the work is finished [i.e. volumes two and three], & I am busy with a preliminary book in which I propose to give a view of the progress in the State of Society, laws, manners, & arts from the irruption of the barbarous nations to the beginning of the sixteenth century. This is a laborious undertaking, but I flatter myself that I shall be able to finish it in a few months.[105]

But he again misjudged his time. Robertson soon discovered that the estimate he gave Birch of "a few months" was far too optimistic because the "preliminary book," by which he probably meant something about the length of Book I of *Scotland* or one of the narrative books from *Charles V*, was growing to double their length and quadruple the length if the "Proofs and Illustrations" are included. Hume told Millar in October 1766 that Robertson "talks of being ready Winter after this" and is "just now finishing an introduction" so that anticipated publication was pushed back to winter 1767–8.[106] But it was not until May 1768 that Robertson finally arrived in London with his completed manuscript.

Although it may have delayed the publication of the book, the "View of Society" quickly became the most celebrated feature of the work. It has also created some confusion about Robertson's design of the history as a whole. Some critics have seen a momentous change in historiography signaled in its pages with the introductory volume representing a new way of writing history that is "masterly, with its retrospect over the dark scene of the Middle Ages, and the gradually dawning light. The author gives us a wonderful story of the steady progress that was taking place in Europe."[107] But this gesture toward historicism, with its sense of organic transformation over time, is not sustained because the narrative of the two following volumes does not show the same "broad skill": "It proceeds in a somewhat narrow perspective from one action to another, and though making clear enough distinctions between practical interests and human passions as motives, it is deficient in any large ideas which would draw the whole together."[108] Others see Robertson as "a somewhat reluctant stadial historian" and the introduction to *Charles V* as an expanded version of the introductory chapter of *Scotland*, with a conventional focus on politics, diplomacy, and the consequences of the feudal system.[109] Yet there seems at first glance little reason for Robertson to be reluctant or cautious. He was familiar with the conjectural thinking of Smith, John Dalrymple, and Kames. In addition to these earlier sources, there were more recent ones because he was close to the writing of Blair's *Critical Dissertation* on Ossian (1763) and Ferguson's *Essay on Civil Society* (1767).[110] Given this exposure to conjectural thinking, why didn't he engage it more directly and fully?

The short answer is he was writing the reign of Charles V, not the progress of Europe. As his process of composition indicates, Robertson added a separate, preliminary discussion to an already completed narrative. Thus he understood the "View of the Progress of Society in Europe" to be what he called it: a view or survey preparatory to the main narrative history of Charles V's reign, not a fully developed conjectural history. The "View" is organized into three complementary sections, which follow each other in chronological order. The first deals with the internal government, laws, and manners of the European nations as they evolved from the collapse of the Roman Empire to about the fourteenth century. The second treats the national forces required for foreign operations, in other words the external relations of the European nations at the beginning of the fifteenth century. The third analyzes the variations in the constitutions and forms among the nations at the start of the sixteenth century. The only section that deals directly with the categories of conjectural history is the first, and Robertson signals his departure from narrative history:

> It is not my province to give a minute detail of the progress of government and manners in each particular nation, whose transactions are the object of the following history. But, in order to exhibit a just view of the state of Europe at the opening of

the sixteenth century, it is necessary to look back, and to contemplate the condition of the northern nations upon their first settlement in those countries which they occupied. It is necessary to mark the great steps by which they advanced from barbarism to refinement, and to point out those general principles and events which, by their uniform as well as extensive operation, conducted all of them to that degree of improvement in policy and in manners which they had attained at the period when Charles V began his reign.[111]

In his well-known definition of conjectural history, outlined in his life of Adam Smith, Dugald Stewart conflates two different ideas. One is the notion of steps in a gradual transition from rudeness to refinement, the other a mode of analysis in which "known principles of human nature" are used to describe stages in the process.[112] The first issued in the notion of defined stages of development, as in the four-stages theory of Smith and Kames, the other in analysis of modes of subsistence. In the "View," Robertson does not map distinct, defined stages of progress, but he does analyze causes of change in terms of material and social causes as well as principles of human nature. The "View" displaces human agents in favor of material and social causes and general principles of human behavior. In contrast with this view, and in tension with it, is the "History of Charles V"[113] itself, a detailed narrative of characters, motives, and events, forming, for Robertson, a distinct but reliable form of history.[114] But since the analysis of the "View" is preparatory or introductory to the narrative books, which he wrote first, the history as a whole is still primarily humanist history, not conjectural history. Robertson had synthesized the innovative methods he found in Montesquieu, Smith, Dalrymple, Kames, Blair, and Ferguson, but he confined those methods in *Charles V* to a subordinate position because he was writing a different kind of history.

With his whole manuscript finally completed, probably in the early months of 1768, and choosing to pass up the General Assembly meeting (which had little pressing business this year[115]) Robertson set off in company with Hugh Blair for London to negotiate its sale with William Strahan. They left Edinburgh early in May 1768, arriving in London about the 14th when Boswell wrote excitedly to William Temple: "D[r] Robertson is come up loaden with his Charles the V. Three large Quartos. He has been offered 3000 guineas for it. To what a price has literature risen!"[116] In contrast to his earlier trip to negotiate *Scotland*, Robertson did not need to knock on many doors. Carlyle reports glowingly that Robertson was a celebrity:

Dr. Robertson was introduced to the first company in London, as all the people of fashion, both male and female, were eager to see the historian of Queen Mary, who had given them so much pleasure. He did not disappoint their expectation, for though he spoke broad Scotch in point of pronunciation and accent or tone, his was the language of literature and taste, and of an enlightened and liberal mind.[117]

He wasted little time getting his work into circulation. From his lodgings in New Bond Street on 17 May he replied to Elizabeth Montagu's request to see his new work, sending her two sections of the history and promising her the first section of the "View," which had not yet arrived, because "he is very ambitious of knowing her sentiments" regarding that part in particular.[118] He and Blair also circulated in society, dining with Garrick and at least twice with Boswell together with such notables as Samuel Johnson, Thomas Percy, John Douglas, Bennett Langton, Thomas Davies, and Alexander, Earl of Eglinton. Most important of all, he successfully negotiated an agreement for *Charles V* that was astonishingly lucrative.[119] We do not know who offered the £3,000 that Boswell mentioned, and there may have been a bidding war. Robertson declined the £3,000 offer, to the wonder of William Temple, who wrote Boswell on 27 May (increasing pounds to guineas): "Has Dr Robertson refused the 3000 guineas? It is indeed glorious encouragement, & does honour to the sense & taste of our times."[120] But the price was to rise even higher. That same day Robertson accepted an offer from Strahan for £3,400 plus £400 for a second edition. For some reason, Strahan responded the same day by upping his offer to £3,500 and £500 for a second edition.[121] The terms of payment were to be settled later, and on 5 July, when Strahan had traveled to Edinburgh, they closed the negotiations. Robertson later sought to invest some of the money. In 1769 he tried to purchase property near Dalmeny Park, the seat of Lord Roseberry, but was outbid: "I have missed Leuchold," he wrote; "Lord Roseberry had set his heart upon it, and purchased it at three thousand four hundred pounds; a price which so far exceeded any calculation, that it would have been ridiculous in me to have given it. This is unlucky, as the place suited me so well. But I could not afford to buy it at such a rate."[122]

Before the book was published on 9 March 1769, a number of other matters had to be settled. In August 1768 Robertson received permission to dedicate the book to the king, though William Breton, the king's secretary, cautioned him not to make the dedication florid, and Robertson contented himself with declaring George's wisdom superior to that of Charles V.[123] The other task was securing a good French translation. As early as 1762, he could see the importance of translation, telling Edmonstone: "As the History of Charles V will probably be more interesting to foreigners than that of a small & detached kingdom like Scotland, I should wish much that it might be soon translated."[124] But he had not previously taken much care about securing a translation. The French translation of the *History of Scotland* had occurred without Robertson's participation, the history simply falling into the hands of Nicholas Bresset de la Chapelle, who published his translation in 1764. Hume even had to let Robertson know in spring 1765 that the translation was out.[125] Worse, Hume added that La Chapelle "was much out of Humour & with Reason, for never hearing from [Robertson]."[126]

But *Charles V* had to be different, and Robertson mobilized a social network in a deliberate quest to create cultural value for the book. His task proved a complicated and frustrating example of the difficulty of dealing with translation. But in the end the process was successful because the French translation of *Charles V* became as much of a landmark as the original text. Robertson's best connections were through Hume and their friend Andrew Stuart, both of whom had ties to Baron D'Holbach's *salon*. In May 1768, just as Robertson left Edinburgh for London, he gave a letter to Andrew Stuart to be sent to D'Holbach, asking his help in locating a proper translator. Robertson's letter is untraced, but in his cover letter, Stuart observes: "In conversing with [Robertson] these last few days he exprest an anxiety about the Translation of it into french, that the history which is as much calculated for other Countries as for Britain might be translated by some able hand well acquainted both with the English & french Languages."[127] D'Holbach wrote back saying he had asked Jean-Baptiste-Antoine Suard, a well-established journalist, editor, and man of letters, to undertake the task and proposed Robertson send sheets of the history to Suard as they were printed.[128] Despite his evident anxiety, Robertson did not write Suard to confirm the arrangement until 4 August and only did so after being chastised by Hume, who knew this opportunity should not slip away.[129] Despite the delay, Robertson amply expressed his satisfaction with the choice of Suard, and his long relationship with his translator was underway.

For Robertson's purpose, Suard was an excellent choice. Through the D'Holbach *salon*, Hume had made Suard's acquaintance during his time in Paris as embassy secretary in 1764–5.[130] In 1766, Suard had translated Hume's account of his quarrel with Rousseau, and Hume was extremely pleased with it.[131] At the same time, Suard had established himself as a very credible spokesperson for English literature generally, particularly though his journalistic work on the highly influential *Journal étranger* and the *Gazette littéraire de l'Europe*, which had included extracts from Robertson's *History of Scotland* as well as Hume's *History of England*.[132] Suard's personal philosophy resonated with that expressed in Robertson's histories, particularly in *Charles V*, because the book dealt with the progress of improvement and refinement. For Suard, polite society (*le monde*) represented something more than just a genteel, comfortable environment:

> *Le monde* was an ideal of sociable living, not a hierarchical establishment . . . *Le monde* stood for the elite not within the regime of estates and orders but within *la société civile*: the people who provided a model of communication for everyone else who wished to cultivate the bonds sociability. *Le monde* was thus a component of Suard's philosophy and not merely the privileged ground of his existence.[133]

To Suard, "Robertson's image of modernity must have looked like a vast salon – a network of 'correspondence' and 'communication' yielding increasing 'refinement.'"[134] How then could Suard resist such a carefully packaged request for translation, one that was presented to him in the context of D'Holbach's *salon* via a network of well-connected gentlemen from Britain whose literature he was working diligently to promote? Working in this context was the very embodiment of sociability.

Despite so much promise, the translation got off to a bad start. The plan, as D'Holbach had proposed, was to send Suard the sheets of the book as they came off the press, and the printing of the book was underway at Strahan's press by early fall of 1768, with Hume in London dispatching packets of sheets to Suard. But Robertson was anxious. He wrote to Hume on 7 October, urging him to keep Suard on task because printing was proceeding faster than expected and he wanted Suard to beat any other translator.[135] By the end of November, Hume wrote that a great part of the printed book had been delivered to Suard and that he would "supply him [Suard] regularly."[136] But then only silence came from France. On 31 January 1769, Robertson wrote testily to Hume:

> Have you heard what progress M. Suard has made? He may be a good writer, but he is rather deficient in politeness. I have written to him twice,[137] & in as civil terms as I could employ, but he has never made me any return, which as I am an Original & he but a translator, is a great neglect of my superior dignity.[138]

A letter from Suard to Robertson dated 19 January 1769 probably arrived shortly after Robertson wrote Hume, but it only added to Robertson's worries. In it Suard was full of praises of *Charles V*, especially the first volume, but he also confessed that he was "peu laborieux, fort dissipé."[139] More upsetting, he said he had abandoned the work on volume two to begin work on the introductory volume. Robertson had been adamant that Suard was to complete volumes two and three before working on the preliminary volume because Robertson, who knew its importance to his project, wished to polish it up to the last possible minute. In response to the 19 January letter, Robertson wrote an angry letter to Suard, which is untraced, and Hume also wrote Suard on 10 March 1769, the moment the English *Charles V* was published, restating Robertson's concerns about his lack of progress.[140]

Finally, a letter dated 2 November 1769 arrived from Suard, full of apologies.[141] He claimed to have written Robertson twice, answering his letters of 4 August 1768 and the untraced letter of fall 1768, but both Suard's letters had miscarried. We do not know what Robertson's response was to this letter because at this point there is a gap in their correspondence until September 1771, when Robertson sent Suard a cordial letter, thanking him for a copy of the translation which had appeared some eight months earlier.[142] There was likely not much, if any, correspondence between them because he confessed he was no less negligent than Suard at maintaining their relationship. With the completion of the translation, Robertson could afford to be generous in his praise. He softened his earlier view about the relation of author and translator: "I . . . cannot express how much I am indebted to you for the care and elegance with which you have executed a work which I am sensible must have been very disagreeable to you, because it was below you."[143] Then he acknowledged that if the book meets with a favorable reception in Europe, it will be primarily because of Suard's elegant translation, and he adds that he always felt that the book, especially the preliminary volume, was better suited to a French audience.

The critical reception of *Charles V* in Britain was certainly favorable but was not immune to criticism.[144] Most of the published reviews acknowledged the importance of the book, sometimes in high-flown terms. Owen Ruffhead was typical in claiming "this admirable work may be justly ranked among the capital pieces of historical evidence."[145] But even Robertson's critics allowed merit. At the end of a detailed and sharply critical examination in the *Critical Review*, William Guthrie grudgingly admitted:

> Notwithstanding the inaccuracies we have noted, this history has great merit. The stile is, for the most part, pure and elegant; the narrative clear and concise; and as often as the author exerts himself in obtaining the best information, the facts may be depended on.[146]

Even Robertson's soon-to-be arch-enemy, Gilbert Stuart, congratulated the public (without irony) upon "this very valuable acquisition to the world of letters."[147] The personal comments were equally complimentary. Horace Walpole, who had originally advised against the topic of Charles V, now freely admitted he was wrong: "You knew better than I did, of what you was capable; & I am ready to balance the account between my first discernment & my want of it in the second Instance, by freely confessing how much you was in the right not to take my Advice."[148] John Douglas echoed many others in declaring that "Your first Volume is looked upon as a Production superior to every thing that hath ever appeared in our Language," while John Blair called attention to specific merits:

> I must tell you then that your History is most universally approved of, the first Volume however has the greatest Number of admirers and tho many of the particulars were known piecemeal before, yet they are delighted to find them so happily ranged & delivered *uno ore*. One Gentleman has read the whole 3 volumes already three times over & likes it still the better. Your reflections please him exceedingly & yet they rise always naturally from the Subject whereas some other Historians *se puisent en raisonements*. The *Ministry of Cardinal Ximenes* & the *Conduct of Luther* are favorite Passages.[149]

Sales of the book also said something about its reception.[150] Strahan had printed 4,000 quarto copies at the relative high price of £2 12s. 6d., and Blair reported that 2,600 of them had been sold in the first month, though sales diminished rapidly, and Strahan did not believe a second edition was warranted until 1772. But that was only the beginning. Over the course of Robertson's life, there were five editions of *Charles V*; in 1785, when he began a major revision of his works, 3,541 quarto copies were in circulation, not to mention thousands of octavo copies, copies printed in Ireland, Scotland, America, and France, plus abbreviated versions and "beauties." By the end of the century, *Charles V* had become one of the most widely circulated historical works of its time. It would be eclipsed during the nineteenth by changing historical methods and increased access to sources, but for Robertson the book was a huge economic, intellectual, and reputational success.

Notes

1. Robertson to Mure, 25 November 1761, in Stewart, "Account," in *Miscellaneous Works*, p. 137.
2. *History of the Reign of the Emperor Charles V*, in *Works of Robertson*, IV, 303, 305.
3. "Sermon on the Glorious Revolution," in *Miscellaneous Works*, p. 182. See also *Charles V*, in *Works of Robertson*, IV, 303.
4. *Charles V*, in *Works of Robertson*, IV, 104.
5. Ibid., IV, 305.
6. This position is argued well by Ahnert, *Moral Culture*, ch. 3.
7. "Epilogue," *Agis: A Tragedy* (London, 1758), rpt. *The Plays of John Home*, ed. James S. Malek (New York: Garland, 1980), [p. 72].

8. Robertson to [Margaret Hepburn], 22 February 1758), NLS MS 1,670, f. 93.

9. *History of Scotland*, in *Works of Robertson*, II, 252.

10. Ibid., II, 15–17.

11. Robertson to Townshend, 23 February 1760, Clements Library, University of Michigan MS, Townshend Papers 295/3/22. In this discussion, I am indebted to John Robertson, *Scottish Enlightenment and the Militia Issue* (Edinburgh: John Donald, 1985), ch. 4.

12. Morren, *Annals*, II, 100.

13. Robertson to Townshend, 25 October 1759, Clements Library, University of Michigan MS, Townshend Papers 295/3/21.

14. Sher, *Church and University*, p. 224.

15. Carlyle, *Autobiography*, p. 419.

16. Robertson to Elliot, 30 April 1760, NLS MS 11,009, f. 70.

17. *Principal Acts of the General Assembly of the Church of Scotland* (Edinburgh, 1760), p. 8. Morren, *Annals*, II, 189–90, notes that the vigorous tone of the address caused it to be received coolly by the king.

18. *Charles V*, in *Works of Robertson*, I, 23.

19. *History of America*, in *Works of Robertson*, II, 220–2.

20. See NLS 3,955, Book II, v, and VII, vi.

21. The word is Robertson's in Robertson to Townsend, 25 October 1759, Clements Library, University of Michigan, MS Townshend Papers 295/3/21.

22. *Question Relating to a Scots Militia*, pp. 13–14.

23. *Disquisition on India*, in *Works of Robertson*, p. 332.

24. *Question Relating to a Scots Militia*, p. 5.

25. The development of the project is described by John Fleming, "An Adam Miscellany: The Journey to Spalatro," *Architectural Review*, 123 (1958), pp. 103–7.

26. Robert Adam to James Adam, 1 November 1757, NAS MS GD 18/4843. Adam's reference to Robertson's history indicates he had read the manuscript of *Scotland*.

27. A. A. Tait, *Robert Adam: Drawings and Imagination* (Cambridge: Cambridge University Press, 1993), p. 104.

28. *Caledonian Mercury*, 6 and 16 February 1760.

29. On the 1760 visit, see Fleming, "Journey," p. 105, n. 25. See also James Adam to Nelly Adam, 25 November 1760, NAS MS GD 18/4877. In September 1761 we know that Robertson was in London and present at a meeting of Adam Smith and Samuel Johnson at William Strahan's (Boswell, *Life*, III, 331–2; Ross, *Adam Smith*, pp. 191–2; and J. A. Cochrane, *Dr. Johnson's Printer: The Life of William Strahan* [Cambridge, MA: Harvard University Press, 1964], p. 163). It seems likely he would have visited with the Adam household, especially since in March James had written that Robertson and his brother ought to collaborate on the explications of the

plates before he put together a final dummy copy (Fleming, "Journey," p. 106, n. 39).

30. *History of the Decline and Fall of the Roman Empire*, ed. David Womersley, 3 vols (London: Penguin, 1994), I, 391–2.
31. *Ruins of the Palace of the Emperor Diocletian at Spalatro in Dalmatia* (London, 1764), p. iv.
32. *Charles V*, in *Works of Robertson*, I, [vi].
33. Eileen Harris, *British Architectural Books and Writers 1556–1785* (Cambridge: Cambridge University Press, 1990), p. 78.
34. *Ruins*, p. 3.
35. Quoted in Harris, *British Architectural Books*, p. 99. Throughout this paragraph I am indebted to Harris's account.
36. *History of Scotland*, in *Works of Robertson*, I, 87–8.
37. Dalrymple to Walpole, 5 July 1758, NLS MS 1,738, f. 3.
38. See Blair to Robertson, 6 February 1759, NLS MS 3,942, ff. 15–16; Blair to Robertson, 27 February 1759, NLS MS 3,942, ff. 21–2; Carthcart to Robertson, 20 July 1761, NLS MS 3,942, ff. 40–1.
39. Walpole to Robertson, 4 March 1759, NLS MS 3,942, ff. 25–7; Hume to Robertson, 8 February 1759, in *Letters of Hume*, I, 296–8.
40. Hume to Robertson, 7 April 1759, in *Letters of Hume*, I, 314–16.
41. Ferguson to Elliot, 27 April 1759, NLS MS 11,015, f. 10.
42. Robertson to Townshend, 25 October 1759, Clements Library, University of Michigan, MS, Townshend Papers 295/3/21; Robertson to Birch, 13 December 1759, BL Add. MS 4317, ff. 228–9.
43. Robertson to Walpole, 20 February 1759, Mitchell Library, Cowie Collection, University of Glasgow MS 407C. See Voltaire, *Essay on Universal History* (Edinburgh, 1777), II, 213–14.
44. *Charles V*, in *Works of Robertson*, IV, 305.
45. Ibid., IV, 304; see also I, 132–3.
46. "Of the Balance of Power," in *Essays, Moral, Political, and Literary*, ed. Eugene F. Miller (Indianapolis: Liberty Fund, 1985), pp. 332–41. For a useful comparison, see Frederick G. Whelan, "Robertson, Hume, and the Balance of Power," *Hume Studies*, 21 (1995), pp. 315–32.
47. As the history was written, Book II would have been the first he wrote if he wrote the narrative in chronological sequence, which he seems to have done.
48. Ibid., II, 104.
49. Ibid., II, 159.
50. Ibid., II, 104, 160.
51. I am indebted to others who have noted Robertson's linking of civic and religious. Pocock has spoken of Robertson's habit of "contextualizing ecclesiastical history within civil" (*Narratives of Civil Government*, p. 286). See also O'Brien, *Narratives of Enlightenment*, pp. 122–8, 141–8; Phillipson, "Introduction," in *Works of Robertson*, I, lvi–lx; and Phillipson, "Providence

and Progress: An Introduction to the Historical Thought of William Robertson," in *William Robertson*, pp. 55–73.

52. Robertson to Birch, 13 December 1759, BL Add. MS 4,317, ff. 228–9; Dalrymple's notes on Robertson's sermons, NLS MS 25,411, ff. 62–3.

53. *Charles V*, in *Works of Robertson*, IV, 93–4.

54. Ibid., IV, 72–3.

55. Ibid., III, 419.

56. Ibid., III, 420.

57. See, for example, James L. McKelvey's influential article "William Robertson and Lord Bute," *Studies in Scottish Literature*, 6 (1968), pp. 238–47.

58. The letter in which Robertson declines Blair's proposal of 6 February 1759 is untraced. Blair discusses Robertson's refusal in his response of 27 February (Blair to Robertson, NLS MS 3,942, ff. 21–2).

59. Robertson to Elliot, [early March 1759], NLS MS 11,008, ff. 92–3.

60. Robertson to Elliot, 7 February 1761, NLS MS 11,009, ff. 79–80, and Elliot to Robertson, 3 March 1761, NLS MS 3,942, ff. 42–3, and Elliot to Robertson, 2 July 1761, NLS MS 3,942, ff. 44–5.

61. Robertson to Elliot, 25 June 1761, NLS MS 11,009, ff. 81–2, and Elliot to Robertson, 2 July 1761 NLS MS 3,942, ff. 44–5.

62. Robertson to Elliot, 7 August 1762, NLS MS 11,009, f. 149.

63. I am indebted to the more detailed accounts of this affair in Jeremy J. Cater, "The Making of Principal Robertson in 1762: Politics and the University of Edinburgh in the Second Half of the Eighteenth Century," *Scottish Historical Review*, 49 (1970), pp. 60–84; McKelvey, "William Robertson and Lord Bute," and Sher, *Church and University*, pp. 112–17.

64. Robertson to Cathcart, [27 July 1761], in Stewart, "Account," in *Miscellaneous Works*, p. 135.

65. Robertson to Mure, 25 November 1761, in ibid., p. 136.

66. Robertson to Elliot, 15 February 1762, NLS MS 11,009, ff. 105–6.

67. Carlyle was aware of Bute's "insatiable vanity," which required incessant flattery from Home (*Autobiography*, p. 377, and Gipson, *Home*, p. 22). Robertson's own "Great Love of Dissertation" (Carlyle, "Comparison," p. 278) indicated his own substantial vanity, which would not have done well in a role subservient to a personality like Bute's.

68. Sher, *Church and University*, p. 113.

69. Robertson to Elliot, 15 February 1762, NLS MS 11,009, ff. 105–6.

70. Robertson to Elliot, 7 August 1762, NLS MS 11,009, f. 151.

71. Robertson to Cathcart, 9 April 1763, BL Add. MS 38,200, ff. 295–7.

72. Robertson to Robert Waddilove, [3 July 1778], in Stewart, "Account," in *Miscellaneous Works*, pp. 162–3.

73. Brown, "William Robertson," in *William Robertson*, p. 23.

74. "The General Assembly's Congratulatory Address to the King," in *Miscellaneous Works*, p. 119.

75. "Address of Principal Robertson on Laying the Foundation Stone of the Edinburgh College, 1791," in Brougham, "Robertson," in *Miscellaneous Works*, p. 319.

76. The formal mission of the university from the beginning was the training of clergymen, a charge that was symbolized by the requirement that the university principal be a minister. But by the 1750s law and medicine had become so important that fully half the enrolled students were in those non-divinity areas.

77. Sher, *Church and University*, p. 136, n. 183.

78. William Zachs, *Without Regard to Good Manners: A Biography of Gilbert Stuart 1743–1786* (Edinburgh: Edinburgh University Press, 1992), p. 5.

79. Robertson to George Drummond, 22 December 1762, Edinburgh City Archives MS Bundle 12, Shelf 36, Bay C; C. P. Finlayson and S. M. Simpson, "The History of the Library 1710–1837," in *Edinburgh University Library 1580–1980: A Collection of Historical Essays*, ed. Jean R. Guild and Alexander Law (Edinburgh: Edinburgh University Library), pp. 56–7; [Alexander Monro *primus*? to Robertson], 31 December 1762, Glasgow University Library MS Cullen 612/12.

80. Robertson to James Stuart, Lord Provost, 30 April 1765, Edinburgh City Archives MS, Bundle 16, Shelf 36, Bay C.

81. Andrew G. Fraser, *The Building of Old College: Adam, Playfair, & the University of Edinburgh* (Edinburgh: Edinburgh University Press, 1989), pp. 41–3.

82. Edinburgh Town Council Minutes, 23 December 1767, Edinburgh City Archives MS SL 1/1/83, pp. 294–9.

83. Ibid., p. 290.

84. "Memorial," in *Miscellaneous Works*, p. 137.

85. Fraser, *Old College*, p. 92.

86. Boswell, *Life*, V, 42.

87. Robertson to Elliot, 8 January 1763, NLS MS 11,009, ff. 163–4.

88. Quoted in Grant, *Story of the University of Edinburgh*, II, 315.

89. Joseph Black to John Black, 30 June 1766, in *Correspondence of Joseph Black*, ed. Robert G. Anderson and Jean Jones, 2 vols (Farnham: Ashgate, 2012), I, 187.

90. Sher, *Church and University*, p. 135.

91. Bower, *History*, III, 86.

92. Richard B. Sher "Moderates, Managers and Popular Politics in Mid-Eighteenth Century Edinburgh: The Drysdale 'Bustle,'" in *New Perspectives on the Politics and Culture of Early Modern Scotland*, ed. John Dwyer et al. (Edinburgh: John Donald, n. d.), pp. 185–6. Sher's study is an excellent analysis of this very complicated controversy.

93. See, for example, his *Faction Detected* (London, 1763).

94. Robertson to Lawrie, 17 March 1766, NAS MS GD 461/113/1 (typescript copy).

95. Quoted in Sher, *Church and University*, p. 131.

96. *Autobiography*, p. 97.

97. Morren, *Annals*, II, 331–2. It is easy to overestimate the liberality of this statement, making it important to keep the immediate context of the argument in mind. He is replying to an overture that would restrict Moderate views, not embracing all possible shades of religious difference.

98. *Autobiography*, p. 490.

99. *Autobiography*, p. 491.

100. Robertson to Townshend, 23 February 1760, University of Michigan MS, Clements Library, Townshend Papers, 295/3/22; Robertson to Edmondstone, 4 January 1762, NLS MS 1,005, ff. 5–6.

101. Boswell to Dalrymple, July 1762, in *Letters of James Boswell*, ed. Chauncy Brewster Tinker (Oxford: Oxford University Press, 1924), I, 17.

102. Blair to Hume, 15 November 1764, NLS MS 23,153, No. 54.

103. Blair to Hume, 1 July [1765], NLS MS 23,153, No. 53.

104. The "View of Society" is not numbered among the twelve books of the history but is a separate preliminary. Book I begins physical volume two.

105. Robertson to Birch, 8 October 1765, BL Add. MS 4,317, f. 233.

106. Hume to Millar, 8 October 1766, in *Letters of Hume*, II, 106.

107. Friedrich Meinecke, *Historism: The Rise of the New Historical Outlook*, trans. J. E. Anderson (New York: Herder & Herder, 1972), p. 194.

108. Ibid., p. 195.

109. O'Brien, *Narratives of Enlightenment*, pp. 132–6 (esp. p. 133), and Nicholas Phillipson, "Providence and Progress," in *William Robertson*, pp. 60–1. I am indebted particularly to O'Brien's discussion of Robertson and stadial history. See also Mark Salber Phillips, *Society and Sentiment: Genres of Historical Writing in Britain 1740–1820* (Princeton: Princeton University Press, 2000), p. 90. The term *stadial* overlaps with *conjectural*, and I prefer to use the latter term because it is broader.

110. In March 1758, during Robertson's sojourn in London to sell the manuscript of *Scotland*, Ferguson, who was at nearby Harrow as tutor to Lord Bute's sons, mentioned to Gilbert Elliot his thoughts about his current work: "I have begun to revise the Paper you saw, & I am changing it to a Dissertation on the Vicissitudes incident to Human Society, & propose when that is done to write two more on the History of Manners, & on the History of Literature" (Ferguson to Elliot, 19 March 1758, in *Correspondence of Ferguson*, I, 27). During Robertson's visit, Ferguson would join him, Carlyle, Home, Wedderburn, John Dalrymple, and Robert Adam at a coffee house on Wednesdays to discuss such ideas (Carlyle, *Autobiography*, p. 356). Some years later, in 1766 when the *Essay* was being readied for publication, Hume read the manuscript on the enthusiastic recommendation of Robertson and Blair, but he was very disappointed, urging them to give the manuscript "another Perusal, with more Severity and less Prepossession" (Hume to Hugh Blair, 11 February 1766, in *Letters of Hume*,

II, 12). In the fall of 1759, Robertson was one of the literary figures whom Home first approached after "discovering" Macpherson's translations of Ossian. He enthusiastically endorsed publication as soon as possible (Sher, *Church and University*, p. 244). In June of the following year, Robertson was again one of a group who undertook to finance Macpherson's expedition to the Highlands in search of more poems (ibid., p. 246). When Blair sent his completed manuscript of the *Dissertation* to Becket and DeHont, Robertson had read and judged it so that Blair said he based his estimation of his work "upon the opinion of two such allowed good Judges of the value of Literary property to a Bookseller, as Mr. David Hume & Dr. Robertson" (Blair to Thomas Becket, 19 August 1762, quoted in R. W. Chapman, "Blair on Ossian," *Review of English Studies*, 7 [1931], p. 81).

111. *Charles V*, in *Works of Robertson*, I, 13–14; see also I, 125.
112. Stewart, "Account of the Life and Writings of Adam Smith," in Smith, *Essays on Philosophical Subjects*, ed. J. D. Wightman and J. C. Bryce (1980; rpt. Indianapolis: Liberty Press, 1982), pp. 292–3.
113. Ibid., I, 147.
114. Robertson thought character essential to historical writing and to *Charles V*. See Neil Hargraves, "Revelation of Character in Eighteenth-Century Historiography and William Robertson's *History of the Reign of Charles V*," *Eighteenth-Century Life*, 27 (2003), pp. 23–48.
115. Carlyle, *Autobiography*, p. 520.
116. Boswell to Temple, 14 May 1768, in *Correspondence of Boswell and William Johnson Temple 1756–1795*, ed. Thomas Crawford, 2 vols (Edinburgh: Edinburgh University Press), I, 236.
117. *Autobiography*, p. 519.
118. Robertson to Elizabeth Montagu, 17 May [1768], Huntington Library MS 4,654.
119. Richard Sher treats the sale of *Charles V* in "*Charles V* and the Book Trade: An Episode in Enlightenment Print Culture," in *William Robertson*, pp. 164–95 (esp. pp. 166–7).
120. Temple to Boswell, 27 May 1768, in *Correspondence of Boswell and Temple*, I, 238–9.
121. *Letters of David Hume to William Strahan* (Oxford: Clarendon Press, 1888), p. 158, n. 7; Robertson to Strahan, 27 May 1768, NLS MS 3,942, f. 63.
122. Robertson to William Mure, 14 December 1769, in *Caldwell Papers*, II, pt. 2, pp. 160–1). Perhaps complicating the situation for Robertson was the financial failure of Patrick Nisbet, his wife's brother. Robertson loaned him £60 in May (Nisbet to Robertson, 15 May 1769, NLS 3,942, f. 98), and a year later Carlyle hinted matters had worsened considerably: "Poor Dr Robertson, is some poorer than he was by the failure of the Nisbets" (Carlyle to Mary Carlyle, 23 March 1770, NLS MS 23,762, f. 36).
123. William Breton to Robertson, 9 August 1768, NLS 3,942, ff. 67–8.
124. Robertson to Edmonstone, 4 January 1762, NLS MS 1,005, f. 5.

125. Hume to Hugh Blair and others, 6 April 1765, in *Letters of Hume*, I, 495–6.
126. Ibid., I, 499.
127. Stuart to D'Holbach, 12 May 1768, NLS MS 8,262, ff. 235–6.
128. D'Holbach to Robertson, 30 May 1768, NLS MS 3,942, ff. 65–6.
129. Robertson to Suard, 4 August 1768, Yale University MS. See also the French translation of Robertson to Hume, 2 August 1768, in Charles Nisard, *Mémoires et correspondances historiques et littéraires inédits, 1726–1816* (Paris, 1858), p. 104. The original English version of Robertson's letter is untraced.
130. Mossner, *Life of Hume*, p. 480; and Alfred C. Hunter, *J.-B.-A. Suard: Un Introducteur de la littérature anglaise en France* (Paris: Champion, 1925), pp. 115–16. See also Hume to Suard, [November 1763 – March 1764], in *New Hume Letters*, ed. Raymond Klibansky and Ernest C. Mossner (Oxford: Clarendon Press, 1954), pp. 79–80.
131. Hume to Suard, 5 November 1766, in *Letters of Hume*, II, 101–4.
132. See Hunter, *Suard*, ch. 6. He notes that these two journals "exercé une influence hors de proportion avec la brièveté de leur vie et la maigreur de leur contenu" (p. 89).
133. Daniel Gordon, *Citizens without Sovereignty: Equality and Sociability in French Thought, 1670–1789* (Princeton: Princeton University Press, 1994), p. 139.
134. Ibid., p. 159.
135. Reference courtesy of David Raynor. See also Hume to Robertson, [ante 7 October 1768], in *Letters of Hume*, II, 193–5.
136. Hume to Robertson, 27 November 1768, in *New Hume Letters*, pp. 185–7.
137. Robertson refers to his letter of 4 August 1768 and to a second letter (untraced) probably written sometime in the fall 1768.
138. Robertson to Hume, 31 January 1769, in R. B. Sher and M. A. Stewart, "William Robertson and David Hume: Three Letters," *Hume Studies* (1985), pp. 75–7.
139. Suard to Robertson, 19 January 1769, NLS MS 3,942, ff. 73–4.
140. Hume to Suard, 10 March 1769, in *Letters*, II, 195–6.
141. Suard to Robertson, 2 November 1769, NLS MS 3,942, ff. 101–2.
142. *New Monthly Magazine*, 13 (January to June 1820), pp. 7–8.
143. Ibid.
144. For a listing of reviews, see Smitten, "Bibliography of Writings about William Robertson," in *William Robertson*, p. 235.
145. *Monthly Review*, 41 (1769), p. 94.
146. *Critical Review*, 28 (1769), p. 415. For the identification of Guthrie as reviewer and discussion of his attitude, see John Douglas to Robertson, 21 April 1769, NLS MS 3,942, ff. 91–2.
147. *London Magazine*, 38 (1769), p. 156.
148. Walpole to Robertson, 7 March 1769, NLS MS 3,942, f. 87.

149. Douglas to Robertson, 21 April 1769, NLS MS 3,942, f. 91; Blair to Robertson, 13 April 1769, NLS MS 3,942, f. 89.
150. Publishing details in this paragraph are from Sher, "*Charles V* and the Book Trade," in *William Robertson*, pp. 175–6.

CHAPTER 6

Achievement and Decline, 1770–1780

The publication of the glamorous second edition of *Charles V* in spring 1772 was a landmark in Robertson's career. The edition itself symbolized his new stature:

> The frontispiece of the first volume portrays not Charles V ... but William Robertson, looking appropriately dignified in clerical gown and wig ... [T]he overall effect is to give prominence to the book's author rather than its subject.[1]

The Scottish minister now shared with stage with Diocletian and George III, who also bore comparison to Charles V. An important member of the Republic of Letters, Robertson received praise and solicitations from all over Europe and America. Following in 1777 would be the *History of America*, which Robertson considered his most laborious and ambitious history and which added luster to his standing as a historian as well as money in his account. In the church, "Dr. Robertson's administration" held, if not hegemony, at least a measure of control, but the Moderates survived challenges until the end of the decade. The university continued to prosper, although no major building projects were undertaken until the late 1780s. The college's reputation was high. An English visitor like Edward Topham could overlook the poor facilities and shabby students to claim Scottish education superior to that of England: "There are few places where a polite education can be better acquired than in this city; and where the knowledge requisite to form a Gentleman, and a Man of the World, can be sooner obtained." Scots students "are always well stored with such acquisitions as render them more serviceable in society; and from which the most common occasions of life may reap some advantage" – a perfect restatement of the Moderate vision of education.[2] International prestige arrived when Princess Dashkov, the close friend of Catherine the Great and a leading figure of the Russian Enlightenment, brought her son to enroll in the college in 1777. Over the course of the 1770s, Robertson also saw three of his children launched into the world: William completed his education as an advocate and secured a position as procurator in the church; James (at age sixteen) joined the army, was soon posted to Madras, and would go on to a notable military career; and Eleanor married John Russell, a solid, reliable Writer to the Signet. The Russells remained close to the Robertsons over the coming years.

But as he told David Garrick, "Every man must pay a price for his fame."[3] He would not finish what could have been a more extensive history of colonization in the New World because of bad health and political circumstances. Attacks on his historical works and his personal character mounted as the American crisis polarized the political atmosphere. In the General Assembly, serious and protracted controversies erupted concerning patronage and the American rebellion. He confronted violent opposition to his stance on Catholic penal laws, and that, coupled with a prolonged and debilitating illness and political pressures inside and outside the Moderate party, led him to resign his role as church leader. The college effort to raise the funds for a new building failed, and, despite an opportunity, it even failed to build its much-needed observatory, in part through his negligence. His health broken, a major historical project gone, and his leadership position compromised, he would withdraw from politics and lay aside writing during the early 1780s. Although his health and vigor would return in the mid-1780s, the close of the 1770s was also the close of Dr. Robertson's administration.

But in 1770, he embarked on his next historical project with confidence. When he explained in his preface to *Charles V* that he omitted the story of the Spanish empire in America because it formed an "episode, disproportionate to the principal work,"[4] he actually had in view something much larger than just filling a gap with the Spanish story. Non-Hispanic colonization of the New World was also a topic of great interest for him, dating at least from his review of William Douglas's *Summary, Historical and Political, of the First Plantings, Progressive Improvements, and Present State of the British Settlements in North-America* for the 1756 *Edinburgh Review*, where even at that early date, he believed "The British empire in America has become a great and interesting object in history."[5] Nor was he interested in cataloguing the deeds of the Europeans alone:

I found that the discovery of the new world; the state of society among its ancient inhabitants; their character, manners, and arts; the genius of the European settlements in its various provinces, together with the influence of these upon the systems of policy or commerce in Europe, were subjects so splendid and important, that a superficial view of them could afford little satisfaction.[6]

The solution was to write a broad history that would not only allow him to complete the Spanish story, but also pursue his interest in conjectural history, examine the development of the British colonies along with those of the Portuguese, and survey "the settlements of the various nations of Europe in the West India islands."[7] Such a comprehensive project fit the trajectory of Robertson's career as a historian, which had gradually widened in its scope from nation to empire as Britain began to grapple with the legacy of the Seven Years War from the 1750s onward. Robertson was reaching toward a global view of history.

The Edinburgh University borrowing register suggests work began on the *History of America* shortly after the publication of *Charles V*. Robertson withdrew seventeen titles relevant to the New World history between 9 December 1768 and 1 January 1772, but on the latter date he also withdrew an additional dozen titles.[8] Composition proceeded steadily, though as he complained to Suard, "slowly,"[9] up to the outbreak of the American rebellion. The first glimpse of Robertson engaged with the project comes in April 1770 when Andrew Dalzel reported to Robert Liston the challenges Robertson confronted gathering materials and making arrangements to locate documents in Spain.

> When he heard of your having been at Madrid, he exprest great regret that he had not known of your intention before you set out for that City; for as the best materials for the American History are contained in Spanish Authors he finds it absolutely necessary to have recourse to Spain for procuring such books. He told me that the only Correspondence he had with Madrid was by means of [Andrew] Balfour the Bookseller in this place, & that Balfour's method of corresponding was not all clever, or Satisfactory. He therefore regretts much that he had lost the opportunity of your being in the Spot, as you would probably have found out a proper person for furnishing him with the books he wanted.[10]

But it was not until his spring visit to London in April and May 1771, when he waited on Thomas Robinson, Lord Grantham, the British ambassador to Spain, that he established an information network. Robertson's goal, as he explained to Grantham, was "to see every thing the Spanish have published concerning America."[11] Unfortunately, as he later reported in his preface to the *History of America*, he fell far short of seeing everything because he could not gain access to the closely guarded Archivos de Simancas where, tantalizingly, were stored 873 large bundles of documents relating to the Spanish colonies, but Grantham and his chaplain, Robert Waddilove, still proved to be valuable agents providing books, manuscripts, and answers to questionnaires for which Robertson was deeply grateful.[12]

He probably began writing by the fall 1770, but a year later he told Suard that he had not yet written enough to tell if the book would "prove a curious and entertaining work."[13] As always, there were distractions that slowed his pace. One was preparation for the publication of the second edition of *Charles V*. After spending six weeks in April and May 1771 in London, he returned to Edinburgh in time to attend the General Assembly and then spent the summer months correcting his first edition, sending the corrections to Strahan in early August. The corrections were "not very considerable, but will render it [the second edition] more accurate."[14] Because Strahan was distressed by the appearance of Irish and even American reprints of the first edition, he not only sought improved accuracy, but also a more elegant format for the new edition comprised of four octavo volumes and featuring four new frontispiece engravings. Perhaps at Strahan's instigation, during his London visit Robertson sat for a portrait painted by Sir Joshua Reynolds.[15] Robertson was proud of the result and pointedly reminded Strahan to secure an engraving of it for the book.[16] In fact, illustrations for the book may have been in Robertson's mind for a while because in 1769 Thomas Hervey, eccentric politician and writer, had recommended using Lucas Vorsterman's engraving of Reubens' copy of a then-lost Titian portrait of Charles V to begin Book I.[17] Being himself "not much conversant in any branch of vertu," he wrote Horace Walpole, "the Prince of Virtuosi," in summer 1771 to get advice on other pictures.[18] Walpole recommended for volume III Titian's Francis I from an engraving in the famous Crozat Collection.[19] The fourth engraving, which began volume IV, was the death of Charles V, taken from an original painting in the collection of George Scott and engraved by Isaac Taylor, one of the leading London book illustrators.[20] Scott was a mathematician and preceptor to the children of the Royal family during the 1750s, as well as one of the critics Robertson enlisted in 1758 when he was handing round the manuscript of the *History of Scotland*.[21]

In August 1773, progress on the *History of America* was again interrupted. The occasion was Samuel Johnson's tour of Scotland, in company with Boswell. For Robertson, meeting Johnson on his home ground gave him a chance to enjoy his celebrity, and Boswell, who had long thought about bringing Johnson to Scotland, used Robertson as another attraction for Johnson to entice him to come. Boswell was always ambivalent about Robertson, alternately admiring him and sneering at him, giving readers both Robertson's dignity and vanity.[22] In the course of a letter sharply reminding Robertson to provide a Latin inscription for his picture of Mary, Queen of Scots, abdicating her crown, Boswell, rather incongruously, given his sharp reminder, also asks Robertson for an invitation for Johnson:

> Our friend M^r. *Samuel Johnson* is in great health & spirits; and I do think has a serious resolution to visit Scotland this year. The more attraction however the better; and therefore though I know he will be happy to meet you there, it will forward the scheme, if in your answer to this, you express yourself concerning it with that power of which you are so happily possessed, and which may be so directed as to operate strongly upon him.[23]

Robertson obliged with a clerical touch that Boswell could send along:

> I wish he [Johnson] would make the experiment. He sometimes cracks his jokes upon us; but he will find that we can distinguish between the stabs of malevolence, and the rebukes of the righteous, which are like excellent oil, and break not the head [Psalm 141: 5]. Offer my best compliments to him, and assure him that I shall be happy to have the satisfaction of seeing him under my roof.[24]

Robertson had first met Johnson in September 1761 during a brief London visit with the Adams to work on the Spalatro publication and perhaps to meet with Bute to discuss patronage proposals. Robertson told Boswell the meeting was at Strahan's just after Johnson had had an unpleasant meeting with Adam Smith. Before Robertson arrived, Strahan had admonished Johnson not to treat Robertson the way he had Smith. "'No, no, Sir, (said Johnson) I warrant you Robertson and I shall do very well,'" and they did, Robertson saying, "'he was gentle with me the whole evening; and he has been so upon every occasion that we have met since. I have often said (laughing) that I have been in great measure indebted to Smith for my good reception.'"[25] Robertson eagerly met Johnson on 15 August over wine, and in the conversation that followed Boswell smugly recorded several Johnsonian rebuttals of opinions Robertson aired.[26] The next day, after breakfast, Robertson accompanied Johnson, Boswell, and others on a tour of major sights around the city. Johnson took a jab at Presbyterians before St. Giles, saying "'Come, (said Dr. Johnson jocularly to Principal Robertson) let me see what was once a church!'"[27] But Robertson must have been delighted with Johnson's pleasure in the university library, upon which he had spent considerable effort, though he was embarrassed by the state of the college buildings, which he had been unable to improve. They moved on to Holyrood, where Boswell said he was "much entertained while Principal Robertson fluently harangued to Dr. Johnson, on the spot, concerning scenes of his celebrated History of Scotland."[28] When Johnson returned to Edinburgh in November after touring the Highlands, Robertson joined him at breakfast, greeting him with a line from his favorite poet, Virgil, but Johnson later said to Boswell that "'to see a man come up with a formal air and a Latin line, when we had had no fatigue and no danger, was provoking.'"[29] But, at the end of his visit, after a supper at Blair's (where Robertson was a guest), which included discussion of subordination and government, Johnson very much approved of the two Moderate leaders, telling Boswell, "'Sir, these two doctors are good men, and wise men.'"[30]

A few days after Johnson's departure for the Highlands, Robertson returned to thinking about *America*, explaining to Suard that the work would be three quarto volumes and that "Above a third part is finished," including "a long disquisition concerning the manners & customs of the rude nations of America, upon which I have bestowed much time and attention."[31] At this point, Robertson is still thinking in terms of a history of colonization, not just the Spanish portion alone. The disquisition on the Indians occurs in Book IV, halfway through the Spanish portion, and it would be about one-third the way through a work of twelve books occupying three quartos. The Spanish portion would occupy two volumes (Books I–VIII) with the third volume (Books IX–XII presumably) devoted to the British colonization of North America, the Portuguese colonies in South America, and the various settlements in the West Indies.[32] Two years later events in the American colonies derailed his plans. He may have completed the Spanish portion sometime in the spring or summer of 1775 and begun work on the British portion in the late summer or fall.[33] His letter to William Strahan of 6 October, written several months after the battle of Bunker Hill, betrayed growing uncertainty about the future of his project: "It is lucky that my American history was not finished before this event. How many plausible theories that I should have been entitled to form, are contradicted by what has now happened."[34] But, despite misgivings, he persevered, working on the British portion in November 1775, April 1776, and June–July 1776, finally laying the manuscript aside on 8 July, four days after American independence was declared. At the end of August, he explained to Sir Robert Murray Keith his motives for publishing the Spanish portion now:

I had determined to defer publishing any part of my History of America untill the whole was completed. But the unfortunate situation into which we have got with our Colonies obliges me to alter that resolution. It is impossible to give any description of their political or commercial situation, or to venture upon any speculation concerning them while the contest between us remains undecided. Instead of a History, one could write only the conjecture or fabulous pamphlet of the day. In whatever way the dispute terminates, a new face of things must be introduced into British America. The Colonies must either become independant [sic] States, or be induced to a more perfect dependance [sic] than formerly. It becomes necessary then to wait for some time before one can publish any thing thing [sic] concerning them. When that period may arrive is uncertain, & in the mean time, a juncture when the attention not only of G. Britain but of all Europe is turned to America, & which renders every publication concerning it interesting, will be lost. This has induced me to seize the occasion that presents itself, & to publish this winter the first two volumes of my Work.[35]

Four years later, Robertson revived the project, working on the British portion in 1780 and 1781. But to write successful history and not polemics, in Robertson's view, one must know the outcome of events to explain what had actually happened, and the future direction of the former colonies was still uncertain. In addition, writing in an atmosphere of controversy and partisanship, which was certainly prevalent during and after the Revolution, was something he disliked as he knew from writing the *History of Scotland*. The failure still nagged at him in 1784 when he wrote to Keith: "Alas America is now lost to the Empire & to me."[36] Although Robertson was certainly pleased with his work on Spanish colonization – especially because of his use of original source material – and he had more than fulfilled his obligation to complete the story of *Charles V*, the suspension of the entire project was a major blow to his aspirations as a historian.

Strahan bought the manuscript of the Spanish portion for £2,667 (a bit below the price for *Charles V* but certainly a good price)[37] and published the book on 28 May 1777. His investment was largely a success. Robertson had written what most critics agree is his master work, an accomplishment perhaps the more surprising because in writing it, Robertson moved outside the European sphere with its tradition of civil history and moved toward other areas of the globe whose human cultures did not share that history. Although Robertson attempted to contain his new history within the civil history of Europe by telling the story within the context of European colonization, he nonetheless had to embark upon a different form, bringing narrative history and conjectural history more closely together than he had done in *Charles V*. Robertson focuses his attention in three main areas: the exploration and conquests of Columbus, Cortes, and Pizarro; the description of native life and culture; and the nature and extent of the civilizations of the Aztecs and Incas. Book I is an introduction tracing the history of navigation from earliest times up to the time of Columbus. It functions as a background summary in the same way as did the opening chapter of the *History of Scotland* and the more elaborate first volume of *Charles V*. Books II and III cover the voyages of Columbus, with Books V and VI treating Cortes and Pizarro. Book IV breaks the narrative with a description and analysis of Native Americans, which is counterbalanced with Book VII describing the Aztecs and Incas as forms of civilization to be examined against those of Europe. The history concludes with Book VIII on the effects of Spanish policies on the colonies from the sixteenth to the mid-eighteenth centuries, drawing the American story back into a Eurocentric context. The contents are diverse: tales of chivalric boldness and romantic delusion among the conquistadores, the presentation of a stage of society (savagery) prior to the European experience of *Charles V*, the anomaly of Aztec and Inca empires that somehow lack civil histories, and contemporary analysis of problematic colonial policy. The history of America posed the most difficult and obscure set of challenges Robertson had yet encountered to think through historical events in terms of probable reasoning and assurances of providence.[38]

Wherever Robertson turned in his history, he faced uncertain information, poorly explored territory, or striking facts that seem to overpower explanation. The *History of America* is permeated with a sense of disjunction, in which the particular displaces the general.[39] Robertson relies on his carefully balanced analyses of characters, events, and cultures, but now they lead to a sense of bafflement or openness before something seemingly inexplicable, and that sense leads him back, at the deepest level of the history, to rely on the basic principle of deferral of judgment. Consider the typical handling of the so-called degeneracy thesis of Cornelius de Pauw, who argued that climate is at least the primary, if not the only, cause of the degeneracy of the human species in the New World.[40] For Robertson this monocausal explanation cannot begin to account for the facts: "The operations of men are so complex, that we must not attribute the form which they assume, to the force of a single principle or cause."[41] The cause is overdetermined, and explanation at this point must be deferred. Or we can turn to the treatment of Bartolomé de las Casas, the "Apostle of the Indians." For some, such as the abbé Raynal, he was a saint, "interposing between the American and the Spaniard," in order to save the native people from destructive slavery.[42] But for Robertson, Las Casas was difficult to judge because his circumstances were unique. Robertson concludes that Las Casas deserves great praise for his "humane activity" on behalf of the Indians, but, in the same sentence, he heavily qualifies this praise by saying Las Casas negated his own efforts through rashness, imprudence, and an inability to understand his own situation in the colonial effort.[43] How can judgment of such a man reach final closure? In the words of Samuel Werenfels, "In uncertain and doubtful Matters, it's best totally to suspend our Judgment, especially when we are in danger of wronging others, by ascribing to 'em Opinions, which are none of theirs . . . For like fond Lovers, they can't spy the Faults of their Mistress, their darling Opinions."[44]

Or consider the absence from America of the story of providential improvement that Robertson tells in *Charles V*.[45] Robertson never explains why the conjectural development of society he suggests in the *View of Society* did not occur in the New World. He carefully evokes the image of humanity gradually peopling the earth from the time of Eden:

> We know, with infallible certainty, that all the human race spring from the same source, and that the descendents of one man, under the protection, as well as in obedience to the command of heaven, multiplied and replenished the earth . . . We cannot trace the branches of this first family, or point out with certainty the time and manner in which they divided and spread over the face of the globe.[46]

Yet the peoples of the New World, even the apparently improved Aztecs and Incas, remain outside this narrative and to some appear to be a separate and detached branch of humanity. The huge distance between the "infallible certainty" of the divine plan and the uncertainty of human reason in understanding the unfolding of that plan takes us to the ultimately mysterious conjunction of religion and history. Human beings lessen that distance with rational investigation, such as the Russian voyages of discovery of 1741 that confirmed a land passage from the Old World to the New.[47] But as he observed in a sermon, "Reason's feeble hand endeavors to withdraw the vail which is between us and the unknown world of spirits – but she is not able. Her discoverys are imperfect."[48] Religion and history, the sacred and the secular, will move closer together as knowledge expands because we know that history unfolds within a providential plan. But we do not have direct knowledge of that plan because, as creatures living in profane history, we can only interpret – not know – the cause and course of events. We cannot

> penetrate into the mysteries of the divine administration. To discern and to worship a superintending power, is an evidence of the enlargement and maturity of the human understanding; a vain desire of prying into futurity, is the error of its infancy, and a proof of its weakness.[49]

The *History of America* is a story of many failures:[50] the failure of the Native Americans to progress beyond savagery; the failure of Incan and Aztec cultures to develop technology; the failure of the Spanish to develop successful colonial policy to stem the brutal conquest and exploitation of native peoples; the spread of a false religion across South America; and, most sweepingly, the failure of European theory to compass the features of the New World as a whole. As Robertson lamented:

It is not attending to any single cause or principle, how powerful and extensive
soever its influence may appear, that we can explain the actions, or account for the
character, of men. Even the law of climate, more universal, perhaps, in its operation than any that affects the human species, cannot be applied, in judging of their
conduct, without many exceptions.[51]

Yet in this admission lies the redemption of the story of failure. In a congratulatory letter, Edmund Burke praised Robertson for his judgment:
"You have employed Philosophy to judge on Manners; and from manners
you have drawn new resources for Philosophy."[52] Robertson does not
solve mysteries; instead, he offers a way to think about them. They are
challenging and provocative precisely because we cannot fully explain
them by the light of nature, but we have the assurance that they will be
explained in time.

Because the *History of America* was conceived as a part of the *History of
Charles V*, Robertson was concerned again to secure continental translations.[53] Once again he approached Suard, though without the need of the
careful diplomacy used to secure the translation of *Charles V*.[54] By 1772
Suard was not just a translator of Robertson but a well-placed foreign
agent or ambassador sending information and conducting some research
on his behalf. His attentions included charging the abbé André Morellet
with delivering a copy of abbé Raynal's recently published *Histoire
philosophique* to Robertson during Morellet's upcoming visit to London
to be sure the historian had the latest and best information.[55] Although
Robertson had a copy in hand when the book and Suard's letter arrived,
he was grateful and agreed with Suard that it was a valuable acquisition.
In his turn, Robertson sought Suard's help with a number of particular
research problems connected to the writing of the *History of America*.
Robertson wanted a copy of Charles Marie de La Condamine's journal
of his voyage down the Amazon, wished to verify a claim made by Pierre
Kalm about Indian relics in Canada, and needed information about
Cardinal Granville's papers in Besançon.[56] Suard wrote back, following
up on each one of Robertson's requests, and even offering an introduction
to La Condamine, for which Robertson was especially grateful (though
La Condamine died before Robertson could be introduced).[57] Robertson
replied with profuse thanks "for all the trouble you have been pleased
to take on my account."[58] In 1776 they agreed on a translation of the
History of America to be handled in much the same way as was *Charles V*.
Suard shared the work of translation with the abbé Morrellet and Henrik
Jansen, and their collaboration was a success, perhaps greater than Suard's
Charles-Quint.

Translations in other European languages spread Robertson's fame during the 1770s. Translations appeared in Italian and German[59] (with other languages such as Polish and Hungarian following later), though Robertson did not secure one in Spanish. Robertson was especially disappointed by this failure because he took special pride in his "care for the honor of the [Spanish] nation . . . which I have respected more than some other foreign writers because I have sought to know it better."[60] In August 1777, Ramón de Guevara y Vasconcelos, with the backing of Pedro Rodriguez Campomanes, a great admirer of Robertson for his moderation and impartiality toward Spain, proposed to the Royal Academy of Madrid that they sponsor an annotated translation of the *History of America*. The Academy agreed with Guevara y Vasconcelos' assessment, and they especially liked Robertson's not following what they perceived as an anti-Spanish bias in previous historical treatments. A membership in the Real Academia de la Historia was immediately forthcoming, which Robertson accepted. The translation was completed in late 1778, but the Council of the Indies, under the leadership of the minister of the Indies, José Gálvez, read Robertson's impartiality as criticism of and an insult to Spanish honor. He submitted the manuscript to an anonymous outside reviewer (possibly Juan Bautista Muñoz, the Royal Cosmographer of the Indies), who concluded that Robertson had indeed impugned Spanish integrity, leading Gálvez to persuade Charles III to suspend the whole project. By December 1778, the translation was dead, and the English edition was banned throughout the Spanish empire.

But in Britain, both public and private comments were overwhelmingly positive.[61] The *Critical Review*, for example, ran a lengthy and generally laudatory piece, not only acknowledging the continuing excellence of Robertson's works but also suggesting a new dimension in Robertson's historical writing:

> But the art and ability of the author are scarcely less conspicuous than the dignity and importance of his subject. The striking light in which he has delineated his capital figures, and the glowing colours with which he has adorned them, do great honour to the vigour of his imagination; while the dexterous arrangement of his materials, equally display his discernment and his taste.[62]

Phrases like "vigour of imagination" and "glowing colours" were not present in earlier reviews, and they suggest that Robertson found in the discovery of the New World an excitement that well suited his ambitious and enterprising character. But *America*'s reception was not without controversy and criticism. The so-called Black Legend, the belief in the inherent inferiority and barbarism of Spanish culture, was still prevalent in mid-eighteenth-century Britain. Although Robertson attempted to judge impartially between the Spanish and their critics, he failed to persuade all those convinced of Spanish ruthlessness. One reader printed a letter to Robertson in which the author sharply attacked his portrayal of figures like Cortès and Pizarro as heroic asserting they were nothing more than savage pirates.[63] Horace Walpole objected strongly to what he saw as Robertson's sneering treatment of Bartolomé de Las Casas.[64] Robertson showed Las Casas' devotion to the Indians but also saw him from a Spanish perspective as well. Robertson was being impartial, but Walpole was appalled:

> Two expressions have shocked me. Speaking of that indefatigable good man Las Casas, who labored to rescue the poor Americans from the tyranny of their conquerors, the Doctor calls it a bustling activity, and says he was ashamed to show his face after the final termination of his splendid schemes. What epithets for so humane a design![65]

The danger in impartiality for Robertson was taking a wide, comprehensive view of a historical process that was mixed in character when some of his readers wished for a polemic. His critics could and did seize upon one point or another, but Robertson, as he did in his two earlier histories and his published sermon, was committed to an inclusive survey. Neither the deeds of the conquistadores nor the humane deeds of Las Casas ought to be judged in isolation.

Unable to continue with his history of British America, Robertson's colonial history was put aside. Strahan visited him in Edinburgh during August 1777, and he may have sensed Robertson was uncertain what to pursue, or perhaps Robertson raised the subject of another history. In any event, Strahan wrote him on 8 January 1778, proposing a new project:

> It hath just now occurred to me, as you are in a manner obliged to make a Pause in the Prosecution of the History of America till our Colonies there are in a way of Settlement, and may wish to make some profitable use of your Time in the Interim, to mention to you a Continuation of Hume's History to the Accession of the late King. Perhaps this may be agreeable to you, and if it is I see no sort of Impropriety in your undertaking it.[66]

Robertson entertained the idea and discussed it with various friends, such as Gibbon (encouraging) and Walpole (discouraging), during his visit to London in the spring.[67] By summer he felt quite confident that he had the requisite materials at hand and could manage the volatile subject matter:

> I hope to write a history which may be both entertaining and instructive. I know that I shall get upon dangerous ground, and must relate events concerning which

our political factions entertain very different sentiments. But I am little alarmed
with this. I flatter myself that I have temper enough to judge with impartiality; and
if, after examining with candour, I do give offense, there is no man whose situation
is more independent.[68]

But by the beginning of the following spring, he complained to Gibbon
that ill health and other factors (doubtless including the turmoil surrounding the attempted repeal of the anti-Catholic penal laws) had prevented
him from working on the project.[69] By the fall matters had worsened.
He told the Earl of Hardwicke that he had been "much distressed with
Rheumatick pains" since the spring of 1778, and "the perpetual languor,
which this occasioned, made it very improper . . . to labour hard."
Although his health was improving, he added, "many circumstances"
have conspired to discourage him from carrying on the English history.[70]

If Robertson faced controversy in his historical writing, he encountered
it even more directly in the church during the 1770s. As he wrote in 1779
to Henry Dundas, it was a time in which "a spirit of fanaticism and disorder is spreading among our Order."[71] The dramatic Moderate victory
in the 1766 Schism debate may have momentarily quieted but did not
end Popular party opposition to patronage. Presentations continued to be
disputed at an increasing rate with over one-third of all those occurring in
the second half of the century taking place in the decade between 1766 and
1775.[72] Perhaps the most notable disputed presentation since those of the
early 1750s, and certainly the most protracted, was the case of the parish of
St. Ninian's. The case began in 1766 with the decision of the presbytery of
Stirling to deny David Thomson's translation to St. Ninian's. His patron,
John Stewart of Allanbank, appealed to the General Assembly, but the
presbytery repeatedly managed to evade the orders from the Assembly
to ordain Thomson. The issue was debated in the 1771 Assembly, where
Boswell had occasion to argue for the first time before the church court
and, sniping at Robertson, later wrote up a summary of the debate published in the *London Magazine* following the 1772 Assembly.[73]

Robertson knew the debate would be difficult. Writing to a Moderate
ally, Thomas Hepburn, before the 1771 Assembly, Robertson carefully
advised him on the precaution of bringing copies of commissions to
avoid challenges, and he informed him about the importance of electing
Thomas Chalmers as moderator.[74] In a rare defeat for the Moderates (one
of only two such elections during the 1770s), Chalmers lost to the Popular
party's candidate, Robert Walker, indicating something of the opposition's strength. The debate was acrimonious, but it offers a good example
of the steadfast opposition Robertson's leadership and policies met in the

church courts. Speaking toward the end of the debate, as was his custom, Robertson attempted to argue from an impartial position:

> Let us . . . if possible suspend for a moment that spirit of party which, there is no denying, actuates this Assembly to an amazing degree, and I am afraid renders it difficult, very difficult, for us to treat any subject with the becoming moderation and temper of dispassionate enquiry.[75]

Then, drawing on concepts he applied to the nations of Europe in *Charles V*, he made the unfortunate argument that translation opens the possibility of ambition and emulation for churchmen: "Many wise and good men have wished that we had a little more room for ambition, that we had some establishments of higher advantage than any which he was at present, in order to stimulate a laudable emulation to excel."[76] Andrew Freebairn, minister from Dunbarton and, in Boswell's view, "the great champion of the popular party," launched a withering attack, asserting "the true ambition, the honour, and the glory of a minister of the Church of Scotland, should be a faithful and conscientious discharge of the duties of that office, the importance of which spreads as wide as the eternal concerns of mankind."[77] The gulf between these two radically different approaches to ministry – ministry as profession and as faith – was simply unbridgeable in debate. In the end, the motion to reverse the decision of the Stirling presbytery passed by only two votes. The bitter case was not resolved: it returned to the Assembly each year until 1775 as members of the presbytery refused to implement the sentence of the Assembly until they were finally rebuked by the church.

The Popular party, under the impetus of dynamic figures like Andrew Crosbie, had also begun to develop an association between patronage and illiberal government.[78] Crosbie argued on largely secular grounds for freedom of conscience in making presentations on the grounds of civic rights and benefits.[79] Although Crosbie's position did not prevail in the Assembly, it did help fuel the Popular party's political support for the American Revolution. The 1776 Assembly was widely expected to be very contentious with respect to approving a loyal address because "a considerable number of the clergy were for addressing the King, to recall the troops from America, and to put an end to so unnatural a war."[80] But Robertson's management and the Popular party's fear of appearing disloyal combined to change the outcome. When the issue came forward on 27 May, Robertson moved the creation of a committee, of which he was to be a member, to draft an address, which he felt "breathed a spirit of mildness becoming the church of Scotland, and at the same time shewed their loyalty to his Majesty."[81] The Popular party objected to terming the conflict a "dangerous and unnatural rebellion," but it made a concession to the opposition, praying that God "may bless the humane means employed by your Majesty to recall our fellow-subjects to a sense of their duty, and to put a speedy period, without effusion of blood."[82] The address was approved unanimously, and subsequent addresses until 1782 were passed with equal acceptance, but behind Robertson's parliamentary tactics was more than a desire to please the government or to quell dissension in the Assembly. There was a considered worldview that encompassed the economic and political dimensions of empire as well as the moral and religious.

Beginning with the Stamp Act crisis in 1766, Robertson saw the problem of American independence in terms of a balance of forces reflecting his political as well as religious preoccupations. In a letter to William Strahan written just after the Commons repealed the Stamp Act, Robertson, echoing William Pitt's words, declared, "I rejoice, from my love of the human species, that a million of men have some chance of running the same great career which other free people have help before them."[83] At the same time, he does not see independence coming sooner than it should, and he trusts that Britain will retain supremacy "as long as it ought to be preserved." Likewise, almost a decade later, he repeats this view again to Strahan. The colonies will one day attain independence, but "not just now . . . At the same time one cannot but regret that prosperous growing states should be checked in their career. As a lover of mankind, I bewail it; but as a subject of Great Britain, I must wish that their depend- ence should continue."[84] Robertson admired the spirit of liberty and independence, but that spirit must be contained within a larger, stable system to control change. His political thinking about the colonies was influenced by Thomas Pownall's *Administration of the Colonies*, a book he knew as early as 1769.[85] In concert with William Pitt's policies, it postu- lated a kind of Newtonian harmony in the colonial system in which the mother country acted as the center of gravity: "Great Britain, as the center of this system, must be the center of attraction, to which these colonies, in the administration of every power of their government, in the exercise of their judicial powers, and the execution of their laws, and in every opera- tion of their trade must tend."[86] But, like Newton's vision of the cosmic system, this colonial system could not be merely static. It evolves with "a temper and spirit which remember that these are our people, our breth- ren, faithful, good and beneficial subjects, and free-born Englishmen, or by adoption, possessing all the rights of freedom."[87] It had to be stable yet it had to progress because, as Robertson had declared in *Situation of the World*, under God's providence the "advance [of all things] towards their final and complete state is gradual and progressive. This holds with regard to all the productions in the natural, and all the changes in the moral world."[88]

But Robertson did not think of colonial affairs only in these large, political terms. He also addressed the moral complexity of the "unnatural rebellion" as it was experienced in individual lives. On 26 February 1778, during his trip to London from February to May in part to see to the publication of the second edition of *History of America*, he delivered a fast-day sermon, probably at the Scots Church at London Wall where his father had been a ministerial assistant to Robert Fleming. The invitation was likely extended by Henry Hunter, an Edinburgh graduate and recipient of a doctorate of divinity there in 1771. Notes to the sermon survive in the hand of an anonymous parishioner, and they reveal the dilemma Robertson had in addressing the Revolution. On the one hand, the sermon invokes an image from Marcus Aurelius to enforce Pownall's notion of the importance of a unified whole: "Let us devoutly Pray that they [the colonists] may return to their duty – that the Hands and the Feet, may no longer Rise up against the Head."[89] On the other, he deplored the self-destruction of one part of the empire being pitted against another and appeals for moral reformation, using a familiar moral homily.

> We *Here* are not called upon to Deliberate and give Counsel, we are placed in a more humble Sphere, but there is not one of the least of us who is not capable of contributing by private conduct to the General Good, when reformation *begins* it must be in the Hearts of Individuals, from that spread to families, Provinces and Kingdoms.[90]

This appeal to personal toleration and forgiveness gives moral and religious depth to his position on the American Revolution, which may not be apparent in his historical thinking or in his political maneuvering.

An opportunity to secure one facet of the church's administration as well as to advance his eldest son's interest appeared in 1776 with the anticipated retirement of David Dalrymple, son of Hew Dalrymple of Drummore, as procurator of the church. But the campaign, though ultimately successful, was damaging to Robertson himself, proving so exhausting that it began his downward slide toward serious illness and, at least at the outset, personally embarrassing. The procurator gave legal and fiscal counsel to the General Assembly, and Dalrymple had held the position from 1746 to 1777, when he became a lord of session as Lord Westhall. Robertson's son William was a plausible candidate for the post. Indeed, Robertson admitted that he "had sometimes looked forward in my own thoughts to this office for the young man," and when Henry Dundas told Robertson of Westhall's impending elevation and of his desire to support

William for the position, Robertson seized the opportunity.[91] William was only twenty-two when the campaign started, which Robertson knew was a disadvantage, but William had recently completed his training as an advocate, he was the son of a prominent minister and thus attuned to the needs of the Assembly, and the post of procurator would give him a solid first step toward legal distinction. He had also taken steps to acquire some social polish: he may have had some modest pretentions to fashionable literary taste,[92] and, after William had been called to the bar in spring 1775, his father told Garrick that he was sending his son to London "in order to look about him for two months, & to rub off corners."[93]

The campaign had a bad start caused by Westhall's not resigning the procurator post immediately upon his elevation. Robertson began the campaign by assuming that Dalrymple would soon relinquish his procuratorship, and Robertson wished to act quickly to forestall other candidates. His task was to line up the clergymen who were already commissioned to attend the 1776 Assembly, which would begin on 23 May, in case there was a sudden election, or, if there were no election, he would at least have begun to influence the selection of commissioners for the 1777 Assembly. But Robertson had acted only with Dundas's backing and had neglected to seek the support of his greater patron, Lord Arniston, Dundas's brother-in-law. Dalrymple was reluctant to resign, causing a hastily arranged election,[94] and Henry Dundas himself, in his role as Lord Advocate, wanted time to process the appointment.[95] Robertson had thrust himself forward without proper consultation and had triggered a free-for-all. Shortly after the 1776 Assembly he had to give Lord Arniston a groveling apology:

> No event in my life has ever given me more pain, than that I should have been the cause, however innocently, of an awkward situation betwixt Your Lordship & my Lord Advocate. I am anxious to explain my own conduct, & to remove any unfavourable conception you may entertain with regard to it. I am conscious of such a sincere respect for Your Lordship that I cannot forbear any longer to attempt placing myself again on my former ground in your opinion, & if you will give me leave I shall pay my respects at Arniston [sic?] on monday. I am so much shattered by the fatigues of the Assembly, & by the severe bout of canvassing occasioned by the premature activity of some young Candidates, that I cannot propose waiting upon Your Lordship sooner. In the meantime, I hope you will permit me to say that however desirable the office at which I have been aiming may be to my Son, I would rather relinquish it forever, than fail in any expression of that respect & attachment which I owe to your Lordship, & most sincerely feel.[96]

Dalrymple stayed on through the 1777 Assembly as procurator. Robertson persevered in this effort, and he and Henry Dundas successfully secured the position for William in 1778 after fending off most other contenders

and finally securing a concession of the election from the strongest opponent, Henry Erskine.[97]

Not all of Robertson's church dealings were so public, and besides his
political dealings in the Assembly, he also had routine activities in the Old
Greyfriars kirk session as well as preaching. Although these duties were
attenuated compared to Gladsmuir by virtue of his many avocations and
illnesses, they still played a role in his work life. We catch a glimpse of
Robertson as Edinburgh minister through the testimony of someone who
knew him in his church role for a very long time: John Erskine. Erskine
joined Robertson as colleague minister of Old Greyfriars in 1767 and
knew him over a span of twenty-five years. Their relationship is sometimes characterized with an anecdote. The nineteenth-century Scottish
theologian Islay Burns described his father's impressions of the two men:

> I find express confirmation in these memoranda [of his father] of that characteristic
> anecdote in which tradition has embodied, and as it were enshrined, the distinc-
> tive character and spirit of these two distinguished men. "The Rev. Principal," so
> he relates the story, "one forenoon had advanced the position, that 'so great is the
> beauty of virtue, that if perfect virtue should appear in a human form, all would fall
> down and worship her;' and the sounder colleague in the afternoon said, in allusion
> to this, 'That perfect virtue did appear once, and only once in a human form, – and
> was crucified.'"[98]

This moderate vs. evangelical opposition omits the warm regard the two
men shared and the value Erskine attached to Robertson's work. Although
they were cast, in contemporary opinion, in the roles of leaders of opposed
parties, Robertson and Erskine held many religious and cultural values in
common.[99] But even more important than these in assessing Robertson's
churchmanship were Erskine's personal observations about his colleague's
work and beliefs because they reveal that behind Robertson's concerns
with church politics, college affairs, and the writing and publication of
history lay a stable, unwavering acceptance of traditional Presbyterian
belief. Erskine admired his sermons on the evidence and the duties of
Christianity but found his lectures on the text "perhaps more useful"
because they often showed

> that the divinity and atonement of Christ, the depravity of human nature, the insuf-
> ficiency of repentance and reformation to expiate the guilt of sin, and to purchase the
> divine favour, and the necessity of the influences of the Spirit, were doctrines clearly
> asserted in the sacred oracles; and that the Scriptures urged against them, admitted
> an easy and natural interpretation, consistently with their truth.[100]

For Erskine, such traditionalism is captured particularly in Robertson's
recommendation to young ministers of Thomas Vincent's edition of the

Shorter Catechism, particularly its discussion of the imputed righteousness of Christ.[101] Vincent asserts that justification is based on faith and
not works, and it derives from God's free grace and not merit.[102] Indeed,
Erskine never wavered in his assessment of Robertson. In a letter to John
Rylands written a month after Robertson's death, he wrote: "He was by no
means a favourer of the modern socinean or Arian schemes, or of giving
up subscription to articles of faith."[103] Although we discover laxness in his
parochial tasks and worldliness in his ambitions, he adhered to a sincere,
ultimately traditional, core of belief.[104]

However sincere his faith, it did not translate into the diligent attention that Erskine gave to his ministry. The relevant parish registers
for Old Greyfriars before 1776 are lost, and those kept after 1776 to
Robertson's death are little more than records of approving elections
and appointments, but they show Erskine's regular beside Robertson's
very irregular attendance. But Robertson did not escape parish duties
or frustrating adjudication. One such episode was recorded between
November 1775 and February 1776, just as he was beginning his ill-fated
history of British America and just before his exhausting canvass for the
procuratorship. In this instance, we see Robertson working in concert
with his colleague minister as they attempt to resolve a complicated,
time-consuming charge of fornication lodged against Marion Creighton,
servant to Robert Dalgleish, a pill-maker in Edinburgh, in which she
claimed to have given birth to an illegitimate child. Robertson faced in
Edinburgh the same difficult, sometimes sordid, cases that he had faced
in Gladsmuir, despite his more elevated clerical status and international
reputation as an historian. Appearing before the Old Greyfriars session
on referral from the West Side Kirk (because the suspected fornication had taken place there), Creighton alleged that Dalgleish was the
father. The first meeting was 8 December with Robertson as moderator
admonishing Creighton "with Suitable Exhortations to tell the truth and
nothing but the truth as in the Sight of God."[105] Creighton again asserted
that Dalgleish was the father, though she changed a detail in her story,
saying "there was no bed in the Room where her Mistress found her,
and Robert Dalgleish, but an Easie Chair in place of a Bed in which they
were found." Dalgleish was summoned and denied the charge so that the
session, having heard both, "reasoned at some length," ordering each
one to submit a written account of their story together with witnesses
to be called. Robertson missed the next two meetings, returning on 5
January, with Erskine as moderator, and the session "sat long," reaching
no conclusion and simply adjourning for ten days. On the 15th, with
Robertson as moderator, the session finally concluded that the charges

against Dalgleish were not sufficiently established and referred it to the Edinburgh presbytery with the recommendation that the charges be dismissed. But the presbytery remitted the case, and on 5 February, with Robertson moderating, the session returned to the case and sought to depose Creighton's mother as well as Dalgleish's witnesses. Dalgleish protested the eligibility of Creighton's mother as a witness, but the session did not act on the protest and ordered an extract of it to be sent to Creighton to answer. But on 26 February, with Erskine moderating, the case finally fizzled out: neither Dalgleish nor Creighton appeared; Creighton failed to answer the extract; the helpless session referred the matter back to the presbytery to act as they saw fit; and the case disappeared from the session records.

Robertson's ministry also drew him into civic contexts. As a minister, Robertson had weighed schemes of poor relief in Gladsmuir, and he maintained that interest at Old Greyfriars. Edinburgh's charity workhouse was in financial crisis in the early 1770s because of failing public support and high costs, with several schemes proposed to remedy the problem, one of which was backed by Sir William Forbes in 1774. Forbes was a very generous benefactor and manager of numerous charitable projects in Edinburgh, including serving as one of the managers of the Charity Work-House. He was also a member of a small committee appointed by the city magistrates to address the chronic underfunding of the workhouse. Robertson was likely an active member of the committee, and Hume was asked to join and probably did.[106] The committee produced two reports, and both documents proposed reliance on a mandatory tax (to be shared by the Court of Session and the general population), though they did not abolish voluntary contributions to be taken at the church door.[107] Robertson seems to have sought outside advice, and received some from Lord Kames with his essay on "Public Police with Respect to the Poor," which was published in his *Sketches of the History of Man* in 1774 and revised for the second edition in 1778. In that essay, Kames takes a strong position against levying a tax for the maintenance of the poor, arguing that public charity maintained solely by taxation is immoral in its effects because such taxation diminishes voluntary charity and breeds idleness. He concludes that public institutions such as foundling hospitals, charity schools, and poor houses should be replaced by allowances to poor families and that if any tax must be levied to maintain the poor, it should rely equally on voluntary and mandatory contributions. Kames told his publisher, William Creech, that he had addressed the revised version of the essay to Robertson,[108] but Robertson did not appear to welcome the advice. His comments to Forbes when he forwarded the manuscript indicate that he was rather cool toward some of its ideas, perhaps because they undercut his more institutionally oriented solutions.[109]

In spite of the disappointing collapse of the building fund scheme launched in 1768, the 1770s showed the university to be gaining stature. Yet it was a victim of its own success because increasing numbers of students put pressure on the university's physical plant, which one visitor termed "a most miserable musty pile scarce fit for stables"[110] and in which Robertson himself had said, more decorously, there was "no room or building . . . that has any degree of academical decency."[111] To be sure, Robertson had made some head way in at least accommodating students in the 1760s by constructing (with the help of Professor Monro) and then twice enlarging a new anatomy theatre and by adding a story on the 1642 library building with the help of the Town Council.[112] But the 1770s and 1780s were to show substantial growth with the student population doubling from around 500–600 in 1768 to a thousand or more by 1789,[113] putting ever greater pressure on space and facilities. Unfortunately, given the constraints of the Town Council, the principal could only respond with piecemeal changes. Between 1770 and 1775 he wrote a steady stream letters to the Town Council requesting constant repairs and expansions, and these describe the endless building problems Robertson faced. They include repaving the College yard ("Were you to see the College yards in winter or during rainy weather you would be convinced that some alteration is requisite"); expanding Joseph Black's classroom ("The number of Students of Chemistry has increased so much that Dr Black's class cannot contain them"); repairing the roof belonging to the soon-to-retire Humanity Professor George Stuart ("the roof . . . is so insufficient that it is necessary to repair it") and then enlarging the Humanity classroom, upon Stuart's retirement in 1775 for the newly appointed Humanity Professor John Hill; covering the expense of transporting "the natural productions & other curiosities" from Captain Cook's 1775 voyage because "the University have no funds for defraying that expence"; meeting the request from newly appointed Logic Professor John Bruce for "proper Benches" so that students can take lecture notes and "to have the Room, which at present is in disrepair, whitened and painted."[114] Robertson also requested repairs to his own house in 1772 and again in 1775.[115] One major accomplishment was the construction of a new chemistry classroom and laboratory in 1781 for Joseph Black, who needed space for his increasing chemistry students. His move to new quarters then allowed the Natural History Museum to gain space for its growing collections. There were also extracurricular demands on facilities. The Speculative Society, founded for the improvement of public speaking and debate in 1764, had lobbied for space within the College in which to build their own hall, which the Town Council granted in 1769; by 1775, the Society further requested space for a hall lobby. Robertson supported the requests as part of his effort to develop student debating societies, and his son William became a member the Speculative in 1770. But space was always at a premium, and other student societies did not secure a permanent place in the College.[116]

One setback for the College was the failure to construct an observatory, and the story of this failing shows the austere and unstable fiscal environment in which Robertson operated as principal, some of the instability in this case being of his own doing.[117] Early pressure for an observatory came from Colin Maclaurin, who finally obtained permission from the Town Council to build an observatory within the College in 1742. But work was delayed because of the disruption of the '45, and Maclaurin was said to have overworked himself in fortifying the Edinburgh walls, resulting in his death in spring of 1746. The project was now in limbo because there was no one to push it forward. But thanks to a donation from the Earl of Morton, subscription lectures given by Maclaurin himself before his death, and interest payments on the account, when Robertson became principal, £490 was available to fund it. Unfortunately, he and Alexander Monro, the professor of anatomy, had both signed bonds loaning most of the money to the professor of mathematics, Matthew Stewart, for his personal use, but Stewart, forced by ill-health, retired in 1772 bankrupt. As Stewart's estate was being sorted out to see what his creditors could recover, Thomas Short, a mathematical instrument-maker, appeared in Edinburgh in 1776 with a scheme to put a large reflector telescope on Calton Hill in an observatory open for public admission. The remains of the College's fund that could be recovered together with Short's efforts to raise a subscription and the Town Council's renewed commitment, led to a ceremony to lay the foundation stone of the new observatory on 25 July 1776 with city officials, including Robertson as principal, in attendance. But this new effort, too, was doomed. Overly ambitious plans, plus cost overruns, led to a partially completed structure that was not finished until 1792 and even then was unusable for serious research. Not until 1811 would a serious proposal be put forward and pursued to establish an observatory for scientific research.

Robertson also had his hands full with numerous faculty changes. There were significant losses: the distinguished John Gregory, professor of the practice of physic, died suddenly at the age of 49, and the much beloved John Stevenson, professor of logic and rhetoric, retired. The latter was replaced by the relatively undistinguished John Bruce, while the former's position brought improvement when William Cullen moved to the chair of the practice of physic and James Gregory came from Aberdeen for the theory of physic.[118] Working with the Town Council, Robertson steadily strengthened the faculty: Allan Maconochie (later Lord Meadowbank) purchased the public law chair of James Balfour of Pilrig; Andrew Dalzel purchased his chair from Andrew Hunter for £300 but had the ability to revive a failing Greek program; Dugald Stewart, who initially replaced his father, Matthew Stewart, in mathematics, later moved to moral philosophy to become one of the most distinguished teachers in the University; John Robison was specifically recruited by Robertson for the natural philosophy chair; and John Walker, professor of natural history, brought new life to natural history and the museum collections.[119] Robertson had to step in to preserve Adam Ferguson's position because Ferguson had become restless in his position as Professor of Moral Philosophy and in 1772 formed plans to go to India.[120] Robertson immediately began seeking help from his friends to resolve the problem.[121] The India scheme did not materialize, but in 1774 Ferguson did accept a position as tutor to the 5th Earl of Chesterfield and went to the Continent, leaving his class in the hands of John Bruce and giving his children and his pregnant wife to the care of Joseph Black and the Robertson household. During his absence, the Town Council, in hopes of appointing James Beattie to oppose Hume's skepticism, declared the moral philosophy chair vacant, and Robertson and his friends again had to rally support to have the move rescinded, a move that offended Beattie's supporters like David Garrick.[122] Boswell noted in April 1772 that

> he [Garrick] praised Beattie highly and said he would ride to Edinburgh to serve him. He said Dr. Robertson's persecuting Beattie for having attacked Hume had hurt the Doctor's character a good deal in England. "What?" said he, "here is a writer who is throwing loose those moral ties by which men are restrained from cutting one another's throats or picking one another's pockets" (acting it admirably all the time). "There comes another writer who attacks him. And shall a reverend clergyman persecute that writer who stands boldly forth on the side of religion?"[123]

Robertson's London visit in the spring of 1778 was a welcome interlude coming between the demands of the university, church, and writing and before the anti-Catholic riots and his protracted bouts of sickness that ensued. Boswell dined with him along with Johnson at Allan Ramsay's, where Robertson cheerfully disagreed with Johnson's harangue against wine drinking. When Johnson "with a placid smile" refused to argue, Robertson said, "(holding a glass of generous claret in his hand.) 'Sir, I can only drink your health.'"[124] William Adam also offers a pleasant picture of Robertson in the London social scene, finally meeting Gibbon, with whom he had been corresponding and whose work he greatly admired. Adam arranged the dinner on 15 March, and "the two historians, the baronet [Sir Adam Ferguson], who was a very well informed man, and a fine scholar, and Mr. ['Fish'] Crawford, who had literature and habits of society, made a very agreeable party." Gibbon enjoyed it enough to have a rebound party in a week, and Adam recorded a conversation on public speaking, Charles James Fox, the leading opponent of Lord North's American policies, saying to Robertson, "'Now, Doctor, I suppose it is as easy for you, you must be so much master of the topics, to preach a sermon without particular preparation, as it is for me to make a speech on the American War.' 'Not quite so, Mr. Fox, says the Doctor, 'I must take care to be a little circumspect and considerate in my doctrine.'"[125] Unfortunately, Robertson did not see what was coming upon his return to Edinburgh, for the General Assembly coming up in May would show him the limitations of circumspection and consideration in the face of personal animus and mob agitation.

Although Robertson was not involved in the development of the bill to abolish the Catholic penal laws, he said he was sympathetic to the relatively modest reforms contained in the proposal. The idea for the bill may have originated with Sir John Dalrymple, but Henry Dundas, named Lord Advocate in 1775, embraced it as a way to advance religious toleration and to bolster manpower for the military effort in America by recruiting Catholic Highlanders for the army. The bill easily passed in Parliament, and Dundas casually proposed a separate bill for Scotland taken up in the fall of 1778. Opposition followed quickly. Driven by strong popular sentiment from the urban poor and provincial synods, it was, according to one historian, "the first political movement in modern Scotland organized from below."[126] "No Popery" sentiment tapped the anger of a populace upset by the course of the war in America and by the economic dislocations it caused to trade with the colonies.[127] Ministers like Alexander Carlyle at first supported these defenders of the Protestant faith in the spirit of their own stout defense of the church against Popery in 1745.

When the operations of the famous committee [the Committee for the Protestant Interest] extended themselves to my parish, I was weak enough (never suspecting the consequences which followed) to be somewhat proud of the spirit shown by the people. I was much pleased with the Whipmen of Fisherrow, who declared that they would endure all that could be inflicted by scorpions and whips, rather than renounce the Protestant faith. I was truly delighted with the Butchers of Musselburgh, who like their worthy forefathers, would resist unto blood, rather than embrace the Romish superstition. I was charmed with the Journeymen Tailors of Newbigging, whose venerable ancestors had saved a remnant from the shears of popish persecution.[128]

Like Carlyle, Robertson, too, at first took a complacent view of the resistance. In the Assembly debate of 28 May 1778, he denied that the Protestant religion was in any danger from the bill:

> [that] the whole country was alarmed; . . . he could by no means agree was the case. His intercourse with society was, perhaps, as extensive as that of most gentlemen in the house; and he could not find that any alarm had been taken.[129]

He dismissed concerns that disturbances in Glasgow had no reasonable basis because there was nothing in the bill that should cause alarm.

But as fall progressed into winter matters became uglier. On 18 October, a Glasgow crowd attacked a Catholic comb-maker and stoned a Catholic who had heard mass in his house.[130] On the 27th, James Adolphus Oughton, the commander in chief of forces in Scotland, wrote to warn Robertson about the danger implicit in the Glasgow incident:

> The still Voice of Reason, and the mild persuasives which Wisdom, Justice, Humanity and Piety suggest may be listen'd to at first; and, at least, obviate the Effects, though seldom powerfull enough to remove rooted Prejudices: but the Exertions of legal Authority tend to aggravate and inflame; and when the Spirits of Men are worked up to a certain Pitch, and a blind mob becomes the Executioners of blind Zeal no One can foresee what Calamities may ensue.[131]

Disturbances spread to Edinburgh. On 30 January 1779, a mob gathered outside the house of Vicar Apostolic George Hay, pelting the house and breaking windows. Three days later the mob inflicted greater damage:

> At length on the 2d of February 1779, the mob assembled, and, with the assistance of five hundred sailors from Leith, proceeded to their work of destruction. Repeated applications were made to the Lord Provost for protection against the rioters, but he was deaf to all entreaties. The Duke of Buccleugh, and some other officers, fired with indignation at such daring excesses, hastened, with a few troops, to the spot, seized the most forward of the incendiaries, and would have dispersed the mob, but the authorities positively refused to allow him to proceed, and the work of destruction went on. The chapel and house were soon reduced to ashes, and the rabble then spread themselves over the city, burning and destroying everything belonging to Catholics which came in their way.[132]

Among the onlookers in front of Hay's library was Boswell, who tried to stop the rioters but was shouted down.

> It hurt me to see a large book, perhaps some venerable manuscript, come flaming out at one of the windows. One of the mob cried, "They" (i.e., the papists) "burnt us. We'll burn them." Another cried, "Think what they did to our worthy forefathers." It was striking to see what one has read of religious fury realized.[133]

Boswell prudently retired from the scene and went up Calton Hill for a better view of the conflagration.

The next day Robertson and his family met the mob's fury. Rioting continued into 3 February 1779 when the mob sacked the chapel in Blackfriars Wynd and threatened Robertson's house along with Andrew Crosbie's. In the words of the *Scots Magazine*, "At night they seemed to intend an attack upon the house of Principal Robertson; but by that time some troops of dragoons had arrived in town, and a party of the fencibles were posted in the college-court; so that the mob could not come near the house."[134] Dugald Stewart offers a more dramatic scene:

> Some of us too are able to bear testimony, from what fell under our own immediate observation, of the firmness and tranquility which Dr. Robertson displayed at a very critical juncture, when, after repeated acts of successful and unpunished outrage, committed in different parts of this city, a furious populace threatened an attack on his house, and were only restrained by a military force, from sacrificing his life to their vengeance.[135]

Boswell, this time "'inflamed' with port," confronted the ugly temper of the mob when he tried to disperse it but had to be dragged away before he was hurt.[136] On 4 February an observer wrote: "Principal Robertson was Obliged to Fly to the [Edinburgh] Castle for Safety as were Several Popish familys whose houses they have Abused in Short if things were to go on an universale Flame woud be all over Scotland in a twinckling."[137] A death threat accompanied the Robertson family's flight to the castle:

> Rev[d] Sir,
> If you consult your own safety and y[t]. of your family take refuge in Ed[r]. Castle along with D[r]. Hay alias His Grace the Archbishop of S[t]. Andrews & remember y[t]. y[e]. death of Sharpe y[e]. apostate is still no murder in the opinion of 20000 people inhabitants of this city of Ed[r]. who are soon to be reinforced by y[e]. inhabitants of Glasgow – take this warning from one who once esteemed you much & therefore wishes to save your life – we are resolute & determined – our plan is laid – our officers are chosen of which now I am one – we are furnished w[t]. every necessary viz; arms, ammunition, &c., &c. – we are therefore to resist unto blood – our plan is laid over all Scotland – therefore save yourself & thank me when you have burnt this. *Vincere vel Mori*.[138]

Other such letters appeared after the event. One, dated 19 February, promised an ongoing threat to his life:

Sir
> I am very lately come to this City, where I purpose to stay about six months.
>
> I have heard so much of your base Character, and what you have don to destroy the Church of Scotland, and also to re establish Popery in this nation, as I am a mortle enemie to all such principles' and practices, and especially to all such traitors as you are, I have now a pair of pistols, well loaded, which I purpose to give you the contents of one of them [remainder of MS torn away].[139]

For a man whose highest values included the rule of law and the maintenance of social order, watching fires burning in the city, enduring threats to his life and the safety of his family, and his Presbyterian faith transformed into bigotry and violence, these riots were shocking. He had seen the effects of the Porteous Riots, but the anti-popery riots lashed out directly at him and the civil society he had sought to build.

At the same time, Robertson's role as a public figure invited other attacks. The most strident and persistent began in 1777. Gilbert Stuart, the historian and the eldest son of George Stuart, the holder of the chair of Humanity and the College Librarian until his retirement in 1775, was furious when he was not appointed to the professorship of Public Law (filled by Alan Maconochie) and launched a frenetic campaign of character assassination against Robertson, whom he suspected of having personally blocked his appointment. Because Robertson had been Maconochie's guardian since1762, Stuart alleged personal bias.[140] Further disappointment followed in 1779 when Stuart was denied the professorship of Universal Civil History in favor of Alexander Fraser Tytler, and again Stuart accused Robertson of personal intervention. In a series of at least half a dozen publications appearing between 1778 and 1782, Stuart attacked Robertson's reputation as a historian, his role in the church, his political behavior, and his moral character. Stuart's hatred of Robertson lasted for the rest of his life. Even on his death bed in August 1786, suffering severe dropsy, Stuart declared, as his physician drained his abdomen, "'Bottle these fluids and send them to Principal Robertson to use as a purge.'"[141] A broadside Stuart published perhaps around the time of the February 1779 Edinburgh riots shows his virulence:

> He is fond of the reputation of Subtility, and he has obtained it. – Incapable of esteeming any body, and unworthy of being the object of esteem himself. – He gives flattery, and takes it. – The half-hearted, who adore Literature, and fancy him some thing, form circles around him; in the midst of which he sits gaping for applause, and swoln with vanity. – Yet he observes with regret the decline of his fame. – The admirers of Queen Mary, can see little in CHARLES the 5th, and still less in AMERICA.[142]

An angry Robertson later described the events of 1778–9, saying that when he was fighting on behalf of "religious liberty," Stuart was working to "expose me to popular odium and personal danger."[143] Robertson shared his anger with members of his family. Perhaps at this time, his son William became so involved in the affair that he fought a duel with Stuart. Brougham appears to be the only source of this story, though he does claim to have spoken to Stuart's second. In any event, Brougham tells us that no one was hurt:

> An accommodation having taken place on the field, I have heard Stuart's second say that he was obliged, knowing his friend's [Stuart's] intemperate habits, to oppose the proposal which he made with his usual want of conduct, and indeed of right feeling, that all the parties should dine together on quitting the field. That second, an able and honourable man, always admitted Stuart's unjustifiable conduct towards the historian, one of whose nieces he (the second) afterwards married.[144]

The unnamed second was Brougham's father, for, on 22 May 1778, he had married Eleanora Syme, the daughter of Robertson's sister Mary and the Reverend James Syme.[145] It is also worth noting, in the interest of plausibility, that William himself was no stranger to duels. In a letter to his parents written from London in 1780, he describes in knowledgeable detail the duel between Captain William Fullerton, later to be a good family friend, and Lord Shelburne over an exchange of personal insults in the House of Commons.[146]

The single-minded attacks on Robertson, especially their characterization of his views of Catholic relief, obscured the complexity and difficulty of his actual position.[147] Robertson was not an unqualified champion of universal religious toleration or even of complete toleration for Catholics in Britain. His histories and his actions during the '45 amply demonstrate his distrust of Catholics as potential agents of a foreign power and believers in a false religion.[148] Of course, it is equally clear that Robertson also wished to stretch the boundaries of his faith and its institutions in order to make it more tolerant and more broadly world-affirming. The speech on the penal laws, which he gave to the 1779 General Assembly, explains his motives for supporting the bill for Catholic relief. It falls into two parts, the first describing Robertson's personal experience of events, the second focusing more impersonally on the issue of the day, which was deliberation on a resolution to establish an extraordinary commission to guard against the danger of popery.

What emerges from the first part is his reluctance to support Dundas's bill because, although he had "observed with pleasure, the rapid progress of liberal sentiments in this enlightened age," he also was "well acquainted with the deep-rooted aversion of Britons to the doctrines and spirit of Popery."[149] He had no part in developing the measure; he first learned about it from the newspapers. He was skeptical, believing the bill to be "premature" because it might grant too much. But after reading it, he could support it because "the relief given to Papists appeared to me neither too great nor too little."[150] It only restored to Catholics the fundamental "rights of a man" formulated by Locke – life, liberty, and property. He sided with substantial majorities in favor of the bill when it was debated in synod and assembly, but his views changed once he perceived the strong popular opposition because he always believed "that, in legislation, the sentiments and dispositions of the people for whom the laws are made, should be attended to with care."[151] He went so far as to be the only "private person" who lobbied in London for repeal of the bill that he had initially favored. But violent abuse overwhelmed this conciliating approach:

> What is the recompense I have received? My character as a man, as a citizen, and as a minister of the gospel, has been delineated in the most odious colours: I have been represented as a pensioner of the Pope, as an agent for Rome, as a seducer of my brethren to Popery, as the tool of a king and a ministry bent on overturning the Protestant religion.[152]

Turning from his apologia, Robertson skillfully builds on the experience he has described. Just as he was a victim of the fears of the populace, so the assembly should not let those fears prevent them from adopting a sensible resolution regarding the supposed danger of popery in Scotland. The number of Catholics in Scotland is small, their wealth is insignificant, and their ministry is poorly supported. Why then should the assembly pass resolutions that will only further alarm the people? Instead, they should work to quiet those fears by taking steps within the already established structures for safeguarding the Protestant faith in Scotland. Robertson proposed a slightly modified version of the resolution before the Assembly, and won a compromise version, adopted unanimously. Although there were repercussions from the events of 1778–9, the question of Catholic relief in Scotland was quieted until 1793 when relief measures were accepted. But by then Robertson was at the end of his life.

The General Assembly of 1780 was the last one that Robertson attended. His resignation from the leadership position that he had created was sudden, putting the Moderates into disarray. Carlyle described the impact of Robertson's choice:

> The Principal . . . has abdicated the Government of the Church which leaves us at a Loss for some time. By means of his Great Abilities for Debate (for no Man ever

excelled him in the Inside of a Court) he created himself a new office, for he has not only been the Leader in Ecclesiastical Affairs, but the Assembly Orator for 20 Years.[153]

Exactly how the resignation was made known or with whom it may have been discussed is not known. In any event, Robertson's motives were complex, involving both personal and public factors. Immediate considerations were the riots themselves and illness. The ugliness of the anti-Catholic riots in Edinburgh was enhanced in Robertson's mind when the Gordon Riots broke out in London from 2–13 June 1780, coinciding with the last three days of the General Assembly. As he did when trying to write the history of the American colonies in the face of the war and its effects on the public, Robertson felt his strategies for handling political conflict – temperance, conciliation, and candor – were no longer viable. As he told Robert Waddilove in 1778, he writes to an audience that can read with impartiality.[154] Although he still had persuasive authority within the General Assembly (as indicated by the impact of his speech on Catholic relief),[155] a dangerous gap had opened up between the Assembly and the provincial synods, most of which supported the anti-Catholic agitation. More important, perhaps, he had been through an exhausting and difficult personal experience that had challenged his deepest values and had threatened the safety of his family. The stress of this ordeal, compounded by his rheumatic illnesses that were to plague him into the early 1780s, added to his sense of helplessness in the face of impossible personal and political demands.

All of Robertson's many tasks as historian, church leader, and principal were conducted during the later 1770s against a backdrop of steadily declining health, much of it brought on by overwork. Robertson suffered frequently recurring colds or pneumonia accompanied by congestion and resulting in periods of deafness. But the very end of the 1770s and the early years of the 1780s brought a crisis. Writing in 1784, Robertson said, "I laboured beyond my strength, [during] the time of publishing the History of America. This brought upon me a violent Rheumatick fever, which shattered my constitution so much that it cost me three years attention, & three journeys to Buxton, to re-establish my health."[156] The prelude to the crisis he describes began in June 1776 when he complained that he had been "shattered by the fatigues of the Assembly," especially by the canvass for the procurator position on behalf of William. Matters did not improve in the coming months. On the eve of the publication of the *History of America* in May 1777, he wrote to Lord Grantham, apologizing for his bad state of health: "I am still a good deal shattered, but I have made shift to struggle forward to the conclusion of my work."[157] His illness was serious enough that he complained to three correspondents of his "bad state of health" and fits of "languor," with the result that this "unlucky indisposition" finally forced him to postpone his intended trip to London until the next year.[158] He seems to have improved over the course of 1778, enjoying an interlude in London, but in February, March, and April of 1779, his health again deteriorated,[159] and he barely recovered to deliver his speech on the penal laws. This series of illnesses may have been streptococcal infections that, in his case, developed into an inflammatory disease. In the fall of 1779 he told the Earl of Hardwicke he was "much distressed with Rheumatick pains" since he had been in London in late winter and spring 1778.[160] Fall 1779 to 1782 is the period of Robertson's withdrawal from public life. He said he was ill off and on (sometimes severely) at least from September 1780 into fall 1781 and then again for several weeks in late winter and spring 1782.[161] He managed a trip to London in June 1781 to receive a pension of £200 from the king but had to leave London abruptly for Buxton before returning home.[162] He visited the spa at Buxton each year from 1780 to 1782.[163] Although the records are fragmentary, such prolonged bouts of debilitating illness, the accompanying deafness, and recovery efforts could easily have been important factors in his retirement.[164]

Less immediate but still important causes included political issues from within and without the Moderate party. Sir Henry Moncrieff Wellwood recalled a conversation he had with Robertson in 1782 concerning subscription to the Confession of Faith. Members of the Moderate party urged him to adopt stronger positions than he thought prudent or feasible.

> But there was one subject, which, for some years before he retired, had become particularly uneasy to him, and on which he had been more urged and fretted than on all the other subjects of contention in the Church; the scheme into which many of his friends entered zealously for abolishing subscription to the *Confession of Faith and Formula*. This he expressly declared his resolution to resist in every form. But he was so much teased with remonstrances on the subject, that he mentioned them as having at least *confirmed* his resolution to retire.[165]

Wellwood's observation is confirmed not only by the underlying conservative principles in Robertson's religious thinking, but also by John Erskine's identical comment based on his long acquaintance with Robertson: "He constantly discouraged schemes for abolishing or altering the subscription to that formulary, required of ministers and preachers of the church of Scotland, though suggested or supported by men, whose characters he respected, and who had ability and inclination to assist his measures of church policy."[166]

There was also his relationship with Henry Dundas, the major political figure in Scotland and the presumed patron of the Moderates. Here again knowledge of exact circumstances are obscure, but Carlyle pointed out that Robertson had a difficult time dealing with the Arniston family.[167] He was alienated from the first President Dundas until 1753, and he "deserted" Henry Dundas in 1782, apparently to secure for William control of church patronage. But it has also been argued that Robertson was never committed to Dundas because his family connections were all with the Whigs, through the Dalzels, Clerks of Eldin, Adams, and Broughams.[168] Moreover, Robertson had long held that the church must be independent of politics and that he had always been wary of becoming entangled in secular politics. That was one motive behind the *Reason of Dissent* in 1752. If the church were subordinate to its own rules and maintained its own system of order, it could remain free of direct political interference in its operations and appointments. With Dundas's bungling of the Relief Act in Scotland, Robertson felt he had been put in an untenable position. He was not consulted but had to read that the act would be extended to Scotland in the newspapers. On a personal level, he was, as he implied in the Relief Act speech and as he demonstrated throughout his career, suspicious of Catholicism. But he was now forced to support the act even in the face of national hostility, although at the same time he lobbied as a "private person" against the measure with the ministry in London. Dundas had subjected the church to an unnecessary, embarrassing, and ultimately mortifying political struggle. Although the surviving correspondence between Dundas and Robertson is courteous, this clumsy intrusion into church matters must have offended Robertson because it completely undermined one of his key maxims of church government: "Never wantonly to offend the prejudices of the people, and rather to endeavor to manage, than directly to combat them."[169] He may have thought Dundas would not long survive, and it was time to leave a sinking ship.[170]

Notes

1. Sher, "*Charles V* and the Book Trade," pp. 176–7.
2. *Letters from Edinburgh, Written in the Years 1774 and 1775* (London, 1776), pp. 218, 220.
3. Robertson to Garrick, 14 March 1775, Folger Library MS PN 2598/G3/F5/copy 4/Ex-ill.
4. *Charles V*, in *Works of Robertson*, I, xiv.
5. "Reviews from the *Edinburgh Review*," in *Miscellaneous Works*, p. 82.
6. *Charles V*, in *Works of Robertson*, I, xiv.

7. *History of America*, in *Works of Robertson*, I, vi.

8. EUL MS Da. 2.5.

9. Robertson to Suard, 21 February 1773, in *New Monthly Magazine*, 13 (January to June 1820), p. 9.

10. Dalzel to Liston, 15 April 1770, NLS MS 5,513, ff. 183–4. This note is actually written at the bottom of a letter of the same date from Edward Maccormick to Liston, f. 183.

11. Robertson to Grantham, 21 February 1772, Bedfordshire Record Office MS L30/14/331/1. Jeremy Black has reprinted the correspondence with Grantham in "The Enlightenment Historian at Work: The Researches of William Robertson," *Bulletin of Hispanic Studies*, 65 (1988), pp. 251–60.

12. *History of America*, I, pp. viii–x.

13. Robertson to John Craufurd, [Autumn 1770], EUL MS Gen. 1,732/1; Robertson to Suard, [September 1771], *New Monthly Magazine*, 13 (January to June, 1820), p. 8.

14. Robertson to Strahan, 7 August 1771, Bodleian Library 25,435, f. 308. Transcription courtesy of David Womersley.

15. The portrait is in the Scottish National Portrait Gallery, SPNG 1393.

16. Robertson to Strahan, 7 August 1771, Bodleian Library 25,435, ff. 307–8.

17. A copy of Vosterman's engraving is in the British Museum, object number 1891,0414.957.

18. Robertson to Strahan, 7 August 1771, Bodleian Library 25,435, ff. 307–8. Robertson's actual request is untraced, but the results of his inquiry Robertson sent to Thomas Cadell, 6 September 1771, Bodleian Library MS 25,435, ff. 312–13.

19. The painting is in the Louvre INV 753. The engraving may be found in *Recueil d'estampes d'après les plus beaux tableaux et d'après les plus beaux dessins qui sont en France dans le cabinet du roy*, 2 vols (Paris, 1729–42), II, 58 and plate.

20. I am unable to identify the painter of the original. Robertson's son William saw the picture (or a copy of it) in a church in Brussels during his Continental tour in 1783 (NLS MS 3,943, ff. 174–5). This engraving was changed in later editions.

21. Robertson to Jardine, [16 March 1758], University College London MS.

22. On Boswell's relationship with Robertson, see Richard B. Sher, "Scottish Divines and Legal Lairds: Boswell's Scots Presbyterian Identity," in *New Light on Boswell: Critical and Historical Essays on the Occasion of the Bicentenary of the "Life of Johnson,"* ed. Greg Clingham (Cambridge: Cambridge University Press, 1991), pp. 28–55.

23. Boswell to Robertson, 15 April 1773, Yale University Library MS.

24. Robertson to Boswell, post 15 April 1773, quoted in Boswell, *Life of Johnson*, V, 15.

25. *Life of Johnson*, III, 331–2. See also Ross, *Life of Smith*, pp. 191–2, and Cochrane, *Johnson's Printer*, p. 163.

26. Boswell, *Life of Johnson*, V, 32–8

27. Ibid., V, 41.

28. Ibid., V, 42–3.

29. Ibid., V, 392.

30. Ibid., V, 397.

31. Robertson to Suard, 28 August 1773, State Historical Museum (Moscow), Fonds Orlov Dossier 22n. 123.

32. But it must be noted that his son William, who may have been privy to his father's intentions, wanted to publish the British portion as an independent fragment and not a continuation of a larger history. John Playfair persuaded him and Andrew Strahan that the manuscript should be styled Books IX and X of the *History of America*. See William Robertson to Strahan, 5 October 1795, NLS MS 3,944, ff. 181–2; Strahan to William Robertson, 9 October 1795, NLS MS 3,944, f. 183; and William Robertson to Strahan, 6 November 1795, NLS MS 3,944, ff. 189–90.

33. A major portion of the manuscript of British America survives as NLS MS 3,965. It is missing perhaps the first 15–30 pages, and the first extant installment is dated 4 November 1775 (f. 287).

34. Robertson to Strahan, 6 October 1775, in Stewart, "Account," in *Miscellaneous Works*, p. 161.

35. Robertson to Keith, 26 August 1776, BL Add. MS 35,350, f. 60.

36. Robertson to Keith, 8 March 1784, BL Add. MS 35,350, f. 70.

37. Richard B. Sher, "Boswell on Robertson and the Moderates: New Evidence," *The Age of Johnson: A Scholarly Annual*, 11 (2000), p. 210 and n. 20.

38. One reviewer complained of too much thinking: "The History of America . . . is all alive, and animated with theory . . . Every circumstance, however simple and obvious, is adorned with speculation" (*Critical Review*, 44 [August 1777], p. 128).

39. David Womersley, "The Historical Writings of William Robertson," *Journal of the History of Ideas*, 47 (1986), pp. 503–6. I am also indebted to the more extensive discussions in O'Brien, *Narratives of Enlightenment*, ch. 5; Phillipson, "Providence and Progress," in *William Robertson*, pp. 61–71; and J. G. A Pocock, *Barbarians, Savages and Empires* (Cambridge: Cambridge University Press, 2005), chs 10–11.

40. See, for example, *Recherches philosophiques sur les Américains*, 3 vols (Paris and Berlin, 1770), I, 4. Robertson had long-standing interest in the topic, which he had first encountered in Montesquieu. It was debated at the Select Society at its first meetings in December 1754, February 1755, and, with Robertson presiding, March 1755 (NLS MS Advocates' 23.1.1).

41. *History of America*, in *Works of Robertson*, II, 141–2.

42. *Philosophical and Political History of the Settlements and Trade of the Europeans in the East and West Indies*, trans. J. O. Justamond, 6 vols (1798; rpt. New York: Negro University Press, 1969), III, 197.

43. *History of America*, in *Works of Robertson*, I, 336.

44. *Discourse of Logomachys*, p. 168.

45. Pocock , *Barbarians, Savages and Empires*, p. 200.

46. *History of America*, in *Works of Robertson*, II, 26, 27–9.

47. Ibid., II, 43–7.

48. Dalrymple's notes on Robertson's sermon of 27 January 1760, NLS MS 25,411, f. 64.

49. *History of America*, in *Works of Robertson*, II, 198.

50. O'Brien, *Narratives of Enlightenment*, p. 156.

51. *History of America*, in *Works of Robertson*, IV, 230.

52. Burke to Robertson, 9 June 1777, NLS MS 3,943, ff. 17–18.

53. In this discussion, I am indebted to John Renwick, "The Reception of William Robertson's Historical Writings in Eighteenth-Century France," in *William Robertson*, pp. 145–63.

54. Robertson was approached very soon after the publication of Suard's translation of *Charles V* by Pierre Le Tourneur offering to translate the American portion when it was completed (Le Tourneur to Robertson, 20 November 1771, NLS MS 3,942, ff. 110–11). But Robertson may have doubted his ability because when Suard recruited him to assist with *Charles-Quint*, his work was so poor Suard had to redo it (Hunter, *Suard*, p. 117).

55. Suard to Robertson, 6 April 1772, NLS MS 3,942, ff. 118–19.

56. Robertson to Suard, 21 February 1773, in *New Monthly Magazine*, 13 (January–June 1820), pp. 9–10.

57. Suard to Robertson, 25 June 1773, NLS MS 3,942, ff. 127–9; see also Suard to Robertson, 8 July 1774, NLS MS 3,942, ff. 152–3.

58. Robertson to Suard, 28 August 1773, State Historical Museum (Moscow), Fonds Orlov Dossier 22n. 123.

59. See Gianfranco Tarabuzzi, "Le traduzioni italiani settecentesche delle opera di William Robertson," *Rivista storica italiani*, 91 (1979), pp. 486–509; and especially László Kontler, *Translations, Histories, Enlightenments: William Robertson in Germany, 1760–1795* (New York: Palgrave Macmillan, 2014).

60. Robertson to Campomanes, 31 January 1778, quoted in Jorge Cañizares-Esguerra, *How to Write the History of the New World: Histories, Epistemologies, and Identities in the Eighteenth-Century Atlantic World* (Stanford: Stanford University Press, 2001), p. 177. I am indebted to Cañizares-Esguerra's discussion, pp. 171–82.

61. A list of reviews may be found in Smitten, "Bibliography of Writings about Robertson," in *William Robertson*, pp. 237–8.

62. *Critical Review*, 44 (July 1777), pp. 127–8.

63. *Gentleman's Magazine*, 48 (1778), pp. 11–14.

64. Walpole to Lady Ossory, 15 June 1777, in *Correspondence of Walpole*, ed. W. S. Lewis et al., 48 vols (New Haven, CT: Yale University Press, 1937–83), XXXII, 358.

65. Walpole to William Mason, 10 June 1777, in ibid., XXVIII, 314.

66. Strahan to Robertson, 8 January 1778, NLS MS 3,943, f. 59.

67. Gibbon to Robertson, 14 January [1779], NLS MS 3,943, ff. 61–2; Walpole to Mason, April 1778, in *Correspondence of Walpole*, XXVIII, 386–90.

68. Robertson to Waddilove, [3 July 1778], in Stewart, "Account," in *Miscellaneous Works*, p. 163.

69. Robertson to Gibbon, 10 March 1779, BL Add. MS 34,886, ff. 108–9.

70. Robertson to Hardwicke, 27 November 1779, BL Add. MS 35,350, f. 62.

71. Robertson to [Dundas], 15 November 1779, Public Record Office MS SP 54/47, ff. 354–5.

72. Richard Sher and Alexander Murdoch, "Patronage and Party in the Church of Scotland, 1750–1800," in *Church, Politics, and Society: Scotland 1408–1929*, ed. Norman Macdougall (Edinburgh: John Donald, 1983), pp. 199–201.

73. Frank Brady, *James Boswell: The Later Years 1769–1795* (New York: McGraw-Hill, 1984), pp. 14–15; Richard Sher, "Scottish Divines and Legal Lairds," pp. 41–9.

74. Robertson to Hepburn, 18 February 1771, Bibliothèque de Lille MS 855, f. 513.

75. As reported by Boswell in "Debates in the General Assembly of the Church of Scotland," *London Magazine*, 42 (April–August 1773), p. 239.

76. Ibid.

77. Ibid., pp. 239–40. Boswell also cites this passage as being the central issue in Robertson's church role in his "Sceptical Observations upon a Late Character of Dr. Robertson," which appeared in the June 1772 issue of the *London Magazine*.

78. John R. McIntosh, *Church and Theology in Enlightenment Scotland: The Popular Party, 1740–1800* (East Linton: Tuckwell Press, 1998), ch. 4.

79. *Thoughts of a Layman concerning Patronage and Presentations* (Edinburgh, 1769).

80. *Scots Magazine*, 38 (1776), p. 271.

81. Ibid., p. 272.

82. Ibid., p. 273.

83. Robertson to Strahan, [post 22 February 1766], in Stewart, "Account," in *Miscellaneous Works*, p. 161. Robertson echoes William Pitt's famous speech of 14 January 1766 in which he declared "I rejoice that America has resisted. Three millions of people, so dead to all feelings of liberty, as voluntarily to submit to be slaves, would have been fit instruments to make slaves of all the rest" (quoted in *Prologue to Revolution: Sources and Documents on the Stamp Act Crisis, 1764–1766*, ed. Edmund S. Morgan [Chapel Hill, NC: University of North Carolina Press, 1959], p. 139). On Robertson's admiration of Pitt, see Robertson to Jardine, 20 April 1758, in Brougham, "Robertson," in *Miscellaneous Works*, p. 279.

84. Robertson to Strahan, 6 October 1775, in ibid., pp. 160–1.

85. Robertson withdrew the book on 4 October 1769, 12 October 1775, and 24 October 1780 (EUL MS Da. 2.2–4).

86. Pownall, *Administration of the Colonies* (London, 1765), p. 36. See also G. H. Guttridge, "Thomas Pownall's *The Administration of the Colonies*: The Six Editions," *William and Mary Quarterly*, 26 (1969), pp. 32–4.

87. Pownall, *Administration*, p. 38.

88. *Situation of the World*, in *Works of Robertson*, pp. 9–10.

89. "Notes for a Fast Day Sermon on the American Revolution, 1778," in *Miscellaneous Works*, p. 142. See Robertson's translation of this image in the *Meditations*, in ibid., p. 16.

90. "Notes for a Fast Day Sermon," in ibid, p. 141.

91. Robertson to [Robert Dundas of Arniston], 30 April 1776, NAS/WRH/RH/4/15/5.

92. See, for instance, an epistolary poem written in 1774 addressed to him by a J. R., jr., containing fashionable motifs such as "pleasing melancholy," an "Ivy mant'led Cell," and "solitude" (NAS MS GD 98/1073, Volume II, 43).

93. Robertson to Garrick, 14 March 1775, Folger Library MS PN 2598/G#/F5/copy 4/Ex-ill.

94. Westhall to Robertson, 16 May 1776, NLS MS 3,942, ff. 222–3 and 225–6.

95. Dundas to Robertson, 9 May [1776], NLS MS 3,953, ff. 16–17.

96. Robertson to Robert Dundas of Arniston, 7 June 1776, NAS MS WRH/RH/4/15/5.

97. Robertson to Maccormick, 11 July [1777], Bayerische Staatsbibliothek MS.

98. *The Pastor of Kilsyth: or, Memorials of the Life and Times of the Rev. W. H. Burns* (London, 1860), p. 39.

99. For a detailed and sympathetic analysis of Erskine's perceptions of Robertson, see John McIntosh, "Principal William Robertson, the Popular Party and the General Assembly," *Records of the Scottish Church History Society*, 43 (2014), pp. 31–49.

100. "Agency," in *Miscellaneous Works*, p. 275.

101. Ibid., pp. 264–5.

102. *Explicatory Catechism; or an Explanation of the Assemblies [sic] Shorter Catechism* (Edinburgh, 1713), pp. 94–8. He may have qualified his endorsement in his review of Hervey's *Theron and Aspasia* in the *Edinburgh Review*, but he did not doubt it. See Chapter 4 above.

103. Erskine to Rylands, 8 July 1793, EUL MS 99.14, no. 58. Reference courtesy of Richard Sher.

104. By "traditional," I refer to his embrace of the transcendent role of faith. See Ahnert, *Moral Culture*, pp. 100–2, for a helpful summary of Robertson's attitudes.

105. Old Greyfriars Kirk Session Records, NAS MS CH2/128/3.

106. Hume to Forbes, 3 March 1774, in *Further Letters of David Hume*, ed. Felix Waldmann (Edinburgh: Edinburgh Bibliographical Society, 2014), p. 84.

107. The situation of the workhouse is described in *Scots Magazine*, 36 (1774), pp. 109–11.

108. Kames to Creech, 2 May 1775, NAS WRH/RH/4/26/1.

109. Robertson to Forbes, 29 May 1775, NLS MS Acc. 4,796, Box 3, Folder 1.

110. Henry Marchant, quoted in Horn, *Short History*, p. 79.

111. "Memorial," in *Miscellaneous Works*, p. 132.

112. Horn claims that there was a "rise in student numbers" behind the construction of Monro's theater (*Short History*, p. 79), but Grant claims that the number of students in 1768 approximately matched that at the end of the seventeenth century (*Story of the University of Edinburgh*, II, 492). Either way, the facilities were certainly in need of improvement.

113. Grant, *Story of the University of Edinburgh*, II, 492.

114. Robertson to Anthony Ferguson, 15 July 1771, Edinburgh City Archive MS; Robertson to Thomas Elder, 19 November 1771, Edinburgh City Archive MS; Robertson to Thomas Grieve, 6 October 1772, Edinburgh City Archive MS; Robertson to William Trotter, 1 May 1775, Edinburgh City Archive MS; Robertson to William Trotter, 7 August 1775, Edinburgh City Archives MS; John Bruce to Robertson, 5 October 1775, Edinburgh City Archives, McLeod Bundles 11.

115. Edinburgh Town Council Minutes, 89 (26 August 1772), p. 291, and 93 (6 September 1775), pp. 40–1.

116. Fraser, *Building of Old College*, p. 44.

117. In this discussion, I am indebted to D. J. Bryden, "The Edinburgh Observatory 1736–1811: A Story of Failure," *Annals of Science*, 47 (1990), pp. 445–74.

118. Roger L. Emerson, *Academic Patronage in the Scottish Enlightenment: Glasgow, Edinburgh, and St Andrews Universities* (Edinburgh: Edinburgh University Press, 2008), pp. 338–9, 305.

119. Ibid., pp. 262, 336, 328, 348–9, and 307–8.

120. Fagg, "Biographical Introduction," in *Correspondence of Ferguson*, I, xliii–xlv.

121. John Home to James Edmonstone, 18 February 1772, NLS MS 1,005, ff. 15–16.

122. Emerson, *Academic Patronage*, pp. 345–6.

123. *Boswell for the Defence 1769–1774*, ed. William K. Wimsatt, Jr, and Frederick A. Pottle (New York: McGraw-Hill, 1959), pp. 124–5.

124. Boswell, *Life of Johnson*, III, 335–6.

125. Adam, *Sequel to the Gift of a Grandfather* (n. p., 1839), pp. 50–1.

126. Fry, *Dundas Despotism*, p. 73. See also Fry's account of motives leading to the outbreak of violence in Scotland, pp. 67–73.

127. Robert Kent Donovan, *No Popery and Radicalism: Opposition to Roman Catholic Relief in Scotland, 1778–1782* (New York: Garland, 1987), pp. 187–8.

128. Quoted in Fry, *Dundas Despotism*, p. 73.

129. *Scots Magazine* 40 (1778), p. 270.

130. Donovan, *No Popery*, p. 14.

131. Oughton to Robertson, 27 October 1778, NLS MS 3,943, ff. 80–1.

132. Hay, *Works*, ed. Right Rev. Strain, 7 vols (Edinburgh, 1871–3), I, xxii–xxiii.
133. *Boswell's Edinburgh Journals 1767–1786*, ed. Hugh M. Milne (Edinburgh: Mercat Press, 2001), p. 333.
134. *Scots Magazine*, 41 (1779), p. 108.
135. Stewart, "Account," in *Miscellaneous Works*, p. 187.
136. Brady, *Later Years*, pp. 183–4.
137. William Kerr to Thomas Kennedy, 4 February 1779, NAS MS GD 27/6/35.
138. Unidentified Correspondent to Robertson, [3 February 1779], NLS MS 3,943, ff. 86–8.
139. Unidentified Correspondent to Robertson, [19 February] 1779, NLS MS 3,943, f. 89.
140. Zachs, *Without Regard to Good Manners*, p. 206, n. 32. In this discussion, I am indebted to Zach's account of the relationship of Stuart and Robertson.
141. Ibid., p. 185.
142. *Character of a Certain Popular Historian* ([Edinburgh ?], 1779).
143. Somerville, *My Own Life*, pp. 275–6.
144. Brougham, "Robertson," in *Miscellaneous Works*, p. 308.
145. The elder Henry Brougham was a Westmoreland squire of modest means. He had arrived in Edinburgh perhaps in late 1777 or early 1778, seeking consolation for the death of his fiancé (Chester W. New, *The Life of Henry Brougham to 1830* (Oxford: Clarendon Press, 1961), p. 3; and Grant, *Old and New Edinburgh*, II, 168). He had been referred to David Stuart Erskine, Lord Buchan, for an introduction to Edinburgh society (Brougham, *Life and Times*, I, 16–17), and quite possibly through Buchan encountered Gilbert Stuart because Buchan was one of Stuart's patrons. He stayed in Mrs. Syme's lodging house in the Cowgate, where he met Eleanora.
146. William Robertson to Robertson and Mary Robertson, [23 March 1780], NLS MS 3,943, ff. 118-21.
147. In one print dated 1 April 1779, Robertson is shown as a front man for the pope, and he addresses an armed, sympathetically portrayed highlander, saying of the popish bill, "It's quite harmless now, Sawney" (John Miller, *Religion in the Popular Prints 1600–1832* (Cambridge: Chadwyck-Healey, 1986), plate 82 (BMC 5534)). Robertson alludes to the print in "Speech on Catholic Relief," in *Miscellaneous Works*, p. 152. Mark Goldie in "The Scottish Catholic Enlightenment," *Journal of British Studies*, 30 (1991), pp. 20–62, provides background to the print and identifies Robertson.
148. For a vigorous argument that Robertson was staunchly anti-Catholic, see Alexander Du Toit, "'A Species of False Religion': William Robertson, Catholic Relief and the Myth of Moderate Tolerance," *Innes Review*, 52 (2001), pp. 167–88.
149. "Speech on Catholic Relief," in *Miscellaneous Works*, p. 144.
150. Ibid., p. 145.
151. Ibid., pp. 149–50.

152. Ibid., p. 152.

153. Quoted in Sher, *Church and University*, pp. 295–6.

154. Robertson to Waddilove, [3 July 1778], in Stewart, "Account," in *Miscellaneous Works*, p. 162.

155. Wellwood maintains that Robertson's authority in the General Assembly was undiminished in 1780 and that he may simply have wished to resign when his authority was at its height (quoted in Stewart, "Account," in *Miscellaneous Works*, pp. 236–7).

156. Robertson to Keith, 8 March 1784, BL Add. MS 35,350, f. 70.

157. Robertson to Grantham, 19 May 1777, Bedfordshire Record Office MS L30/14/331/4.

158. Robertson to Edmund Burke, 5 June 1777, Fitzwilliam MSS, Sheffield City Libraries, Wentworth Woodhouse Muniments, Bk 1/973; Robertson to Gibbon, 5 June 1777, BL Add. MS 34,886, f. 97; Robertson to Strahan, 31 May [1777], Yale University Library MS.

159. Robertson to Gibbon, 10 March 1779, BL Add. MS 34,886, ff. 108–9; and William Robertson to Unidentified Correspondent, 15 April 1779, NLS MS 3,943, ff. 98–9.

160. Robertson to Hardwicke, 27 November 1779, BL Add. MS 35,350, ff. 62–4.

161. Robertson to Home, 21 September 1780, NLS MS 124, ff. 86–7; Robertson to Charles Wallace, 20 November 1780, Edinburgh City Archives, SL 12/25 (Letterbook), p. 103; Robertson to Maccormick, 20 April 1781, NLS MS 583, ff. 390–1; Blair to Strahan, 28 June 1782, NLS MS 3,408, ff. 1–2. These are periods of illness indicated by his correspondence, but there may well have been others.

162. Robertson to [William Strahan], 23 July 1781, Princeton University Library, Elizabeth Montagu Papers, Box 1, Folder 34.

163. On 8 March 1784, Robertson told Robert Murray Keith that he had been to Buxton three times (BL Add. MS 35,350, ff. 70–1). The visits of July 1781 and July 1782 are documented, and it is possible he visited in 1780 because he reported himself "languid & deaf" to Home and Carlyle, reminding them that since "you are publick Speakers I can call upon you in English *to raise your voices*, or in Scotch *to speak up*" (NLS 124, ff. 86–7), and there is a large gap in his correspondence from 17 June to 21 September in which he could have gone to Buxton for treatment. He also alluded to having been in Buxton fairly recently in a letter to Robert Orme of 1 February 1781 (in Robert Orme, *Historical Fragments of the Mogul Empire* [London, 1805], pp. xxxix–xl).

164. Clark concludes, on the basis of the letter to Keith, that "health alone could not account for his retirement" ("Moderatism and the Moderate Party in the Church of Scotland, 1752–1805," unpublished thesis, Cambridge, 1964, p. 409, n. 4). As the subsequent narrative suggests, I attribute more weight to health factors than Clark seems to do.

165. Quoted in Stewart, "Account," in *Miscellaneous Works*, p. 237.

166. Erskine, "Agency," in *Miscellaneous Works*, p. 264.
167. *Autobiography*, p. 308.
168. Clark, "Moderatism and the Moderate Party," pp. 408–9.
169. Quoted in Wellwood, *Account of Erskine*, p. 465.
170. Fry, *Dundas Despotism*, p. 76.

CHAPTER 7

Last Years, 1781–1793

Robertson retired into a world where the American Revolution had awakened public opinion, creating partisan divisions at all levels. Thomas Somerville observed that the failure of the war in America produced a "great change" in British society: "the discussion of this subject not only engaged the attention of the public bodies of men, but became a principal subject of conversation in every company, and often excited angry debates, which impaired the pleasures of social life, and weakened the confidence of friendship."[1] During the early 1780s, political instability added to the tension. The fall of Lord North's administration in March 1782 brought eighteen months of confusion as the government staggered through three administrations, which Boswell picturesquely described as "that extraordinary fluctuation of Ministers whom we have . . . seen, like the visions of Macbeth: 'Come like shadows, so depart.'"[2] The fluctuation concluded in December 1783 with the king's dismissal of the coalition of Charles James Fox and Lord North and the rejection of Fox's India Bill. One temporary casualty in this confusion that affected Robertson was Henry Dundas, who, between August and December 1783, was replaced as Lord Advocate by the liberal Henry Erskine taking the post. Although no serious damage to Dundas's interests resulted from this four-month hiatus, it encouraged those like the Earl of Buchan (Henry Erskine's brother) and his protégé Gilbert Stuart who saw Robertson as the vulnerable representative of an entrenched establishment. Robertson shared the deep national concern in the midst of uncertainty, Boswell terming it "the most interesting period since the Restoration."[3] In March 1784, on the eve of Pitt's sweeping victory, Robertson wrote to Robert Murray Keith that "The wretched state of our publick affairs for four months past, which must render us the scorn of all Europe, has afflicted me so much, that I hardly possess myself sufficiently to apply myself to study as usual."[4] But a conservative, more united, government emerged when William Pitt the Younger, who had become Prime Minister upon the fall of the Fox–North

Coalition, gained a stunning victory in the general elections of March 1784, supported nationally by a wave of relief at ending several years of instability.

In such an atmosphere of confusion and partisanship, even a seemingly beneficial project, such as establishing a scholarly society, created controversy. In 1782–3, Robertson led the effort to establish the Royal Society of Edinburgh. Although Stewart and Brougham pass over this seemingly uncontroversial achievement, it is in fact a revealing instance of the cultural divisions he faced in his last years. The establishment of the Royal Society does not begin with Robertson but with John Walker, who was appointed professor of natural history at Edinburgh in late 1779, replacing the recently deceased Regius Professor and Keeper of the Museum, Robert Ramsay, who had not lectured on natural history for years.[5] Walker, church minister at Moffat, had edged out his rival candidate, William Smellie, the editor of the *Encyclopaedia Britannica* and an established naturalist. But Walker was not immediately in a position to give up his ministry in Moffat and only delivered his first lectures in the spring of 1782. In the interim between Walker's appointment and his first course of lectures, the Earl of Buchan stepped forward as the patron for a course of lectures on the philosophy of natural history to be delivered by Smellie. Buchan did so under the auspices of his newly established Society of Antiquaries of Scotland, which had met for the first time in 1780. Although Buchan ultimately withdrew the plan,[6] Walker wrote to him opposing the idea of the lectures as infringing on his prerogative as professor, and in March 1782 drafted a counterproposal for a single Royal Society of Edinburgh that would subsume both the SAS and the Philosophical Society of Edinburgh. It was likely Walker's draft that Robertson alluded to in the November 1782 meeting of the Senatus Academicus when he said he had in hand a "Sketch of a memorial" that would become the basis of the petition for a charter for the RSE.[7]

But Buchan was interested in far more than just patronizing Smellie's lectures. As he wrote in the petition for a royal charter, the SAS was "a society for investigating antiquities, as well as natural and civil history in general, with a view to the improvement of the minds of mankind, and to promote a taste for natural and useful knowledge."[8] Such a commitment to knowledge was not only beneficial to humankind, it was also patriotic. Buchan later declared that "I consider the elucidation of the first dawn of History in my Country as no mean [or] frivolous employment adapted to the plodding Antiquary only, but to the Historian and the Patriot."[9] To give Scottish antiquarians the stature he felt they deserved, Buchan submitted his petition for a royal charter on 21 May 1782, which was duly referred to Henry Dundas as Lord Advocate. Dundas, in turn, consulted the university faculty and no doubt included Robertson as well, and he quickly realized that there would have to be negotiations between Buchan and Robertson because the university faculty already had in hand Walker's sketch of a memorial that proposed the creation of a single society. November 26th was set as the date for a personal meeting between Robertson and Buchan.

Robertson himself approached the whole topic of antiquarian research with biases already in place. At the outset of the *History of Scotland* Robertson divides Scottish history into four segments, the first of which, the period up to 995, he defines as "the region of pure fable and conjecture, and ought to be totally neglected, or abandoned to the industry and credulity of antiquaries."[10] Although in subsequent years Robertson treated antiquaries like Lord Hailes and Sir William Hamilton with great respect, his whole historical outlook was focused on the moral uses of modern history in the shaping of a civil society, a far cry from Buchan's yearning for a romantic past:

> This misfortune is ours; and such has been the accumulation of disgrace and discomfiture that has fallen on us . . . since the last wretched twenty-four years of the British annals, that I turn with aversion from the filthy picture before my eyes, and look back for consolation to the times which are past. It was in seeking . . . for such opiates to the watchful care of a good citizen in a falling empire, that I fell into antiquarian research.[11]

Likewise, we have seen that Queen Mary for Robertson was "an agreeable woman, rather than an illustrious queen,"[12] and Buchan's sentimental adulation of her as "a beautifull and injured Queen"[13] was clearly not something Robertson would readily embrace. Compounding the problem, in Robertson's view, was the fact that the members of the SAS were not gentlemen. Not only was Buchan himself a radical Whig, which alone made him suspicious to the conservative Robertson, but he also had drawn his Society's members from the margins of the intellectual community Robertson inhabited.[14] Roberson would certainly have agreed with Andrew Dalzel's observation that Buchan "had admitted such a number of ragamuffins into the Society of Antiquaries, that the respectable members are resigning very fast, and joining the University and Faculty of Advocates in an application for a Royal Charter for a new Society."[15]

Buchan's attitudes alone would make the meeting difficult, not to mention his almost pathological vanity and arrogance,[16] but matters were made worse for Robertson by Buchan's role as the patron of Gilbert Stuart at whose hands Robertson had already suffered abuse. Stuart sent Buchan and the SAS a copy of his recently published *History of Scotland, from the Establishment of the Reformation, till the Death of Queen Mary* (1782), pointing out particularly that his account differs "most essentially" from Robertson's *Scotland*. Also in 1782, Stuart published anonymously in London a shilling pamphlet titled *Critical Observations concerning the Scottish Historians Hume, Stuart, and Robertson*, which was filled with personal invective against Robertson.[17] Stuart juxtaposes passages from Robertson's *History of Scotland* with his own narrative and contrasts Robertson's writing with Hume's, concluding that Robertson's fame,

> like the flame expiring in the socket, hastens to its dissolution. His admirers among the clergy of Scotland, have waited long for his apotheosis, like the Jews for their Messiah. A more melancholy task now employs their humanity. They try to sooth the peevishness of their desponding idol; hold up to it the milk of adulation, and, vainly credulous, think to fit to its itching brows the reluctant and uncomplying laurel.[18]

Such a diatribe must have been difficult to take for a man who had been struggling with persistent illness, who could no longer exercise church leadership, and who had been forced to lay aside his most ambitious historical work.

The meeting between Buchan and Robertson on 26 November 1782 was, naturally, a complete disaster. We have only Buchan's account of the meeting, given to William Charles Little in a letter, and no indication of what Robertson himself thought about it. But Buchan's account is clear. Between his arrogance and Stuart's venom, as well as Robertson's protective attitude toward the university and his long-standing concern for natural philosophy as part of the curriculum, the two could hardly inhabit the same room. Buchan opened the meeting with a personal barb:

> I asked the Reverend Minister why he has accepted of the honour of being a member of the Antiquarian Society & had chosen to make his opposition at this Time, when those who perceived his reputation declining & his rival Gilbert Stuart bringing him over the Coals attributed his attack to the impotent rage of a disappointed Author? He grew pale, trembled, and said Posterity would determine the Controversy.[19]

Buchan moved on to address his more substantive charges that the university had not handled the museum collection responsibly and that there was no good reason why Walker should have a monopoly on natural philosophy. Finally, he claimed that the real reason for opposition to the SAS was that it was associated with radical "Whiggery," but the Society "would Judge for themselves whether it was right for them to disperse like a Vile Mob at the waving of his hand." Robertson did not respond to the attack:

"The Historiographer blush'd & grinn'd a Ghastly Smile." Robertson had, no doubt, realized the hopelessness of the situation and abided by his usual policy of avoiding polemics. Buchan closed his letter with some social snobbery of his own, dismissing Robertson as "An obscure Priest the Brother of an obscure Goldsmith in Edinburgh."

Four days later, on St. Andrew's Day, the Senatus Academicus met, rejecting the application of the SAS and endorsing Robertson's proposal for a single royal society that would subsume both the Antiquarian Society and the Philosophical Society. Robertson apparently expanded and revised Walker's draft of a proposal, presented it on 2 December for approval by the senate, and forwarded it to Dundas, who invited Buchan to respond. In February, Buchan made a credible argument against the main claims of the petition for the RSE, claiming that there was no reason Scotland could not support two scholarly societies and that Walker had nothing to fear from SAS lectures. He capped his argument by threatening a legislative visitation to look into the mishandling he saw in the museum's collections. Buchan's response, plus a political position slipping with the election of a more Whiggish government in 1783, led Dundas to approve both petitions. Robertson accepted the compromise, saying that Dundas really had no choice, although the settling of the affair did not stop Stuart from launching another salvo of attacks on Robertson in conjunction with the second edition of his *History of Scotland*, which appeared in 1783–4, by printing as an appendix the inflammatory letters written in connection with his presentation of his *History of Scotland* to the SAS.[20] Robertson's patience had been tried enough, and it may have been in 1783–4 that Robertson consulted William Adam about filing a lawsuit for slander against Stuart. Adam explains that "he wrote to me very anxiously, proposing to have redress in a court of law. I never had seen him so much bent upon anything."[21] Adam wisely persuaded Robertson not to pursue a suit.[22] With the charters approved, the two societies proceeded to meet, but the Royal Society of Edinburgh, with more resources and more established members, soon came to dominate the scene. By the end of the decade, the SAS had become moribund, and Buchan resigned as a member.

Antagonism was also evident within the church in the form of a renewed attack on patronage. In the wake of the fervor over the American Revolution, there was a sudden upsurge in the number of disputed calls. In the period 1776–80 there were just three such cases, but from 1781 to 1785 there were twelve.[23] The fall of Lord North's government in March 1782 and its replacement by that of the more liberal Marquis of Rockingham, just prior to the General Assembly, offered hope that Popular protests might at last be heard. In the 1782 Assembly meeting, the foremost Popular speaker, Henry Erskine, led debate in favor of a proposal for the Assembly to offer its congratulations to the king for having discarded North and embraced Rockingham, but the Moderates managed to defeat the measure after lengthy debate. In 1783, with Erskine's appointment as Lord Advocate only two months away and the Moderate majority still holding, the Synods of Perth, Stirling, and Fife filed an overture to abolish the patronage law established in 1712 and return to the Act of 1690 in which local heritors and gentry were consulted in moderating calls. Again the Moderates prevailed, but only by the narrow margin of eighty-seven votes to seventy-eight. Better organized at the 1784 Assembly, and with Pitt having swept the general elections a month earlier, the Moderates again rejected overtures to abolish the 1712 law, though this time by a large majority. In addition, without a vote, they deleted the instructions to Commission asking the Assembly to apply to the king to redress the grievance of patronage – an instruction that Robertson had deliberately not removed in order to placate Popular sentiment. Carlyle captured the tenor of the 1784 Assembly:

> . . . the Wild Brethren are completely routed, and Fanaticism has received a greater blow than ever it did in our time. To say the truth, such was the spirit of the clergy that even the prudence and political timidity of our friend the Principal could not have restrained them had he been their leader. He has, however, marked the most sincere joy upon this occasion, and I say that he, like King William, trained the army which was afterwards victorious.[24]

It remained for Robertson himself to take the field. One last Popular effort to make an appeal to Parliament came before the Edinburgh General Sessions in August 1784, and Robertson felt called upon to defend his position. The General Sessions dealt with matters such as poor relief, public order, and other secular concerns of the church in which Robertson remained interested. But the application to Parliament, involving issues of both church and state, struck him as a matter of such great importance that he laid aside temporarily his resolution to retire from church courts. The terms of the debate were to Robertson's advantage because during the final stages of the long-standing patronage dispute the Popular party had shifted from a theological argument to a much more secular one, making it even more difficult for them to match Robertson's political knowledge and skill.[25] In his opening remarks, he disputed two points made by the Popular party: that secession from the church was due to the law of patronage and that there were more violent settlements after 1752 than before that date. The second claim, Robertson said, was simply inaccurate, and the first was misleading because the Seceders wanted popular choice by the congregation at large and not by heritors or kirk sessions, as the application requested. Robertson then shifted away from patronage itself, which had been often debated, and moved to parliamentary procedure and its implications. His political mastery awed the writer for the *Caledonian Mercury*: "The Principal, in the most elegant speech we ever remembered to have heard, displayed a knowledge of mankind, and of the Constitution of this country, which astonished the audience, and to which no pen but his own could do proper justice."[26] An application for patronage relief, he argued, had no chance of success in Parliament because it would not be supported by the ministry, the opposition, or the people at large. Far from being a harmless proposal worth trying, the real danger in seeking relief from patronage lies in the inevitable demand for full democratic choice: "I think the people right – once admit, that, in a constitution connected with the state, any share falls to an heritor or elder, I see no cause why every individual should not be entitled to the same privilege." To drive his point home, Robertson then contextualized the application in terms of the events of 1778–9:

> Not long ago, Sir, the trump of sedition sounded through the kingdom on this very head. Your good sense and moderation then effectually quelled it. Shall we now resume so factious a traffic? We have been told that there is no danger in the attempt [to make application to parliament]. Sir, it is an easy matter to alarm the populace but who is he that can compose them? "He who saith to the roaring sea, thus far shalt thou come, and no farther: he only can still the noise of the sea, the noise of the waves, and the will of the people."

The resolution was defeated in the General Sessions, though it resurfaced in the 1785 Assembly only to be defeated once more by a substantial margin of thirty-five votes. From that point on, although a handful of cases came to the Assembly before Robertson's death, patronage, as he had formulated it, was never seriously challenged. It would reappear in the nineteenth century as a cause leading to the Disruption, but by that time it operated in a different context.[27]

    This speech is a sign that Robertson's retirement had allowed him time to recover his health, reanimate his historical interests, and give attention to family matters. By 1783, he was getting stronger: he took a "Highland jaunt" during the month of August, and then, in his letter of 8 March 1784, he announced to Robert Murray Keith that "as I am in more firm health just now, than I have been for several years, I do mean to resume my pen."[28] One reason he felt ready to write again was that he had never completely laid aside his habits of study. In spite of the disappointment of the history of British America and the irritating attacks of Stuart, Robertson impressed the young Lord Brougham with his steady engagement with scholarship:

> His whole life was spent in study, I well remember his constant habit of quitting the drawing-room both after dinner and again after tea, and remaining shut up in his library. The period of time when I saw this was after the "History of America" had been published, and before Major Rennell's map and memoir appeared,[29] which he tells us first suggested the "Disquisition on Ancient India." Consequently, for above ten years he was in the course of constant study, engaged in extending his information, examining and revolving the facts of history, contemplating ethical and theological truths, amusing his fancy with the strains of Greek and Roman poetry, or warming it at the first of ancient eloquence so congenial to his mind, at once argumentative and rhetorical; and all this study produced not one written line, though thus unremittingly carried on.[30]

Considering that Brougham was born in 1778, the accuracy of his observation is questionable, but his description does suggest how it was that Robertson was able to re-engage his historical writing after a hiatus when a less committed writer might have retired into silence.

Family affairs also occupied him during the early years of his retirement. The death of his sister Margaret in May 1781 must have added to his prolonged "nervous, deaf & languid" condition that he reported to Gibbon on 12 May.[31] Although we do not know how close his relationship with Margaret may have been, Robertson's efforts in the 1770s to secure a position for her son Alexander suggests some active tie between them. His own sons needed advancement as well. "It is my fate," he said to Robert Orme in 1781, doubtless with mixed feelings, "to be the father of a military family."[32] He was concerned particularly about his son James. At the end of December 1780, Robertson, then in very poor health, had written to John Craufurd, asking if he should approach Lord Macartney, who was about to leave for Madras as governor of Fort St. George, to see if he could do something for James, who was stationed there. That something, he hoped, would be "of essential benefit to him & give me some chance of seeing him once more before I go."[33] But nothing came of his request. On 20 April 1781, his worries probably increased. Robertson told Joseph Maccormick he had received that morning a letter from James, still in Madras, describing how he had just "escaped from the cruel fate of many of his Brother officers, who have been cut off by Hyder [Ali]."[34] Ali's attack was particularly savage and effective, the government in Fort St. George reporting, "'The disaster which has befallen us is such as cannot be paralleled since the English had possession in India.'"[35] At the same time, David also received his father's help. On 1 December1780,

Robertson wrote Charles Jenkinson, Lord Liverpool, seeking his support for an ensign's post for David. Liverpool complied and in February 1781 Robertson could report to Orme that David was now with William Fullarton's 98th Regiment, about to sail to Madras where he would join his brother.[36]

The three daughters of the family were likewise making their choices of life. Eleanor, the second eldest daughter, had married John Russell, a writer to the signet, in 1778, but Janet, the youngest, had ongoing health problems, remained unmarried at home, and died in 1789 at the young age of 33. The eldest daughter, Mary, at least one observer speculated, seemed likely to marry Dugald Stewart. William Drennan, a friend of Stewart's, dined with the Robertsons during a visit to Edinburgh in September 1782:

> D. Stewart supped along but paid his attentions chiefly to Miss Robertson, a lady with whom as the world says and indeed as it appears he is going to be connected . . . He is in good health and high reputation, is at present tutor to Lord Ancrum, eldest son of the Marquis of Lothian, a genteel young man for which tuition he gets £250 and it was obtained by Dr Robertson's interest with the Marquis, it is very natural for the people to suppose that he intended Stewart for his son-in-law. Miss Robertson is a sensible, handsome girl with at least £1,000 fortune, paints well (herself I mean) and will no doubt render Dugald the happiest of men.[37]

But a year later Stewart married Helen Bannatyne. Drennan could have misread Stewart's behavior, the romance may have faded, or perhaps Robertson himself was hoping to arrange something that was never to be. It is unclear where Mary met her eventual husband, Patrick Brydone, a man seventeen years her senior, and, to judge by William Ward's print of Andrew Geddes' 1818 portrait of him, not an attractive man. A founding member of the Royal Society of Edinburgh with a keen interest in the properties of electricity, Brydone would certainly have known Robertson through the Society. Brydone also knew William Fullarton, who had traveled with him through Sicily and Malta, and Fullarton, in turn, was not only James's commanding officer but also a friend of William's.[38] Married on 4 April 1785, Patrick and Mary settled into his estate at Lennel near Coldstream. The marriage was a happy one for the family as a whole because the Brydones became a major support for the family, with Lennel a frequent retreat. Brydone would become a good friend to Robertson, and later the principal declared warmly that "I never am more at my ease, or more happy than under your roof, & I need not add that Mrs Robertson is no less so."[39] Besides welcome hospitality, Brydone provided various acts of friendship, assisting Robertson with the sale of the Spanish books he had previously offered to the Faculty of Advocates, experimenting with electricity in an attempt to relieve the principal's deafness, and exchanging books.[40]

Despite his improving health in 1783–4, it was not until a year and a half later that Robertson actually proposed to Andrew Strahan a particular writing project. Writing to him on 17 October 1785 to express condolences for the death of William Strahan, Robertson said he had been approached by Campbell Denovan, a printer working in Edinburgh's Lawnmarket, about reprinting the *History of Scotland*. Robertson rejected the idea because the term of copyright with Strahan did not expire until 1788, plus he was alarmed that John Murray, the London printer, "when here got a sheet of a pirated Edition on coarse paper printed here," and suggested to Andrew to pursue damages. "If you have it in view," he continued, "to print any new Edition of Scotland soon, please let me know, & I shall revise the whole, & make what may be considered an authentic Edition, which has got the last polish from the hand of the Author." He then expanded his request in a postscript: "Let me know always before you send a new Edition of any other of my Books to press."[41] Thus began Robertson's thorough revision of all his histories, all to be published between 1787 and 1788. Separate pamphlets of "Additions and Corrections" to *Scotland* and *America* were printed to be bound in previously published editions along with new editions of each of the three histories in which the changes were incorporated into the text. In the spring of 1788, the eleventh edition of *Scotland*, the sixth edition of *Charles V*, and the fifth of the *History of America* were also gathered together by Strahan and Cadell into a limited, uniform edition and presented to Robertson's closest associates, such as Edward Gibbon. Although these revisions were not in fact the very last ones, they were Robertson's most systematic attempt to update his work and respond to his critics.

Two matters were uppermost in Robertson's mind as he negotiated with Strahan and Cadell about the revised edition: the format of the books and his approach to his critics. Strahan replied on 21 November and encouraged Robertson's proposal for revision, and at the end of December Robertson told him he had begun revision of *Scotland*.[42] He added a caveat, insisting that he did not wish to labor on revision "unless you agree to print a handsome Edition." Toward that end, he suggested that "if it be not inconsistent with your interest" that they print a small quarto edition alongside the more modest but marketable octavo. He also planned to include a frontispiece of Mary, telling the Earl of Hardwicke:

> My Proprietors propose to prefix a print of Queen Mary to the Quarto edition, executed by some capital Artist. I am at a loss which of her Portraits I ought to copy.

I have been informed that the Dowager Lady Warwick has an excellent portrait of that Queen, which probably came from the family of Hamilton. I flatter myself that Her Ladyship will allow me to have a drawing made from it.[43]

As tutor to George Greville, second Earl of Warwick, whose mother, the Lady Dowager, was Elizabeth Hamilton, Robertson could easily believe that using their portrait, with its association with two noble families, would add further luster to the appearance of the book.[44] His approach to his critics also stressed the noble quality of the new edition. He explained to Hardwicke, in words that he would adapt a year later as the substance of his preface to the eleventh edition of *Scotland*:

I purpose to make a general review of the whole, & to consider every thing that has been published on that period of history since my first Edition. I flatter myself that Your Lordship thinks more kindly of me than to suppose that I will enter into any of those angry controversies, which bigots & party-writers have carried on about the disputed events in Queen Mary's reign. All I intend is, wherever I have fallen into any error, I shall instantly, without any observation or reasoning, correct it. Wherever I find my own ideas to be just & well-founded, I shall without taking notice of what either writers have published, suffer them to remain, adding in some particular places, such illustrations as I think necessary.[45]

This is the same strategy Robertson followed as often as possible in other facets of his career. He maintains the work's dignity, and thus its authority and impartiality, by refusing to engage in partisan disputes. Like the physical format of the book, its narrative is a monumental, self-contained structure, immune to idle tampering.[46]

Cadell issued two sets of *Additions and Corrections* for the edited histories: the first, published in 1787 and based on the 1781 octavo edition of the *History of Scotland*, and the second, published in 1788 and based on the 1778 quarto edition of the *History of America*. The *History of Charles V* was also updated but not sufficiently to warrant a separate set of additions and corrections. In the twenty-three additions and corrections to *Scotland*, Robertson did not engage in any polemics and completely ignored his most vociferous recent adversary, Gilbert Stuart, allowing for no discussion that would illuminate the conceptual gap between their interpretations of history. As Stuart's most recent biographer explains, Stuart emphasizes "the language of the heart" rather than the "language of reason" in order to break down historical distance between reader and historical character.[47] Robertson's insistence on dignity and impartiality as the key principles of historical writing depended on critical distance between narrative and reader, carefully controlling all suggestions of a "language of the heart." But Stuart immersed his reader in an "ideal presence,"[48] raising strong emotion and creating close identification between character and reader. Robertson also dismissed John Whitaker's *Mary Queen of Scots Vindicated*, which appeared in 1787, as simply a "ponderous work" filled with "all the acrimony of personal enmity."[49] But Robertson ignored even politer critics, such as lawyer William Tytler, whose *Inquiry into the Evidence against Mary, Queen of Scots*, had first appeared in 1759 and was currently in its third edition with a fourth due in 1790. Tytler pursued a line of argument developed by William Goodal in the 1750s claiming the incriminating letters attributed to Mary were forged, but the only new authority Robertson cites in his unshaken belief in their genuineness is David Dalrymple's commentary on Tytler, *Miscellaneous Remarks on the Enquiry into the Evidence against Mary, Queen of Scots* (1784). By and large, Robertson's additions to *Scotland* either illustrate his assertions more concretely or correct or clarify points of fact in the narrative from documentary sources. He does not attempt to reinterpret any of his evidence but simply gives a higher polish to his history.[50]

The additions and corrections to *America* respond more directly to one of Robertson's chief critics: the Jesuit priest, Francesco Saverio Clavigero (Robertson's Italian version of his name). Seven of the twenty-four additions and corrections are addressed to Clavigero, though Robertson found little of value in his *Storia antica del Messico* (1780–1), which he read in Robert Cullen's translation (1787). "Upon perusing his work," Robertson writes in an addition to his preface to *America*, "I find that it contains hardly any addition to the ancient History of the Mexican empire." As for Clavigero's claim that Robertson's interpretation of Mexican history is "mistaken" in some points and is "misrepresented" in others, Robertson declares:

> When an Author is conscious of having exerted industry in research and impartiality in decision, he may, without presumption, claim what praise is due to these qualities, and he cannot be insensible to any assertion that tends to weaken the force of his claim. A feeling of this kind has induced me to examine such strictures of M. Clavigero on my History of America as merited any attention, especially as these are made by one who seemed to possess the means of obtaining accurate information, and to shew that the greater part of them is destitute of any just foundation.[51]

Here again Robertson places himself above polemics by assuming the dignity of history and asserting rather than arguing the validity of contrary evidence.[52] He fails to understand Clavigero's fervent effort to establish a history based in the New World and to defend creole culture, claiming he was misled by "the abundance of his zeal for the honour of his native country" and "the improbable narratives and fanciful conjectures" of his mentors, Juan de Torquemada and Lorenzo Boturini.[53] As with the additions and corrections to *Scotland*, these also aim strictly to clarify matters of fact rather than re-conceptualize or reinterpret.

After the difficult birth of the Royal Society of Edinburgh, Robertson found time to maintain at least a modest presence: he was listed in the *Transactions* as at least a nominal president of the Literary Class until his death; John Maclaurin, Lord Dreghorn, asked him to review his "Dissertation to Prove that Troy Was Not Taken by the Greeks" before he presented it to the society in 1784; he submitted a memoir on printing he received from France in 1786; and he wrote the dedication of the first volume of *Transactions* to the king for the Duke of Buccleugh.[54] But more significant were the editorial revisions and unpublished preface he wrote for the geologist James Hutton because they indicate Robertson's thinking about new scientific discoveries and their relationship to religion. Hutton had lived in Edinburgh since the 1760s, and Robertson knew him as a friend of Adam Smith, Joseph Black, and John Playfair. Robertson and Hutton were both members of the Oyster Club, and certainly they knew each other through the RSE because Hutton was an active member from the beginning. In 1785, Hutton wrote an *Abstract . . . Concerning the System of the Earth*, a summary of his longer work presented to the RSE in March and April and outlining his revolutionary thinking about the age of the earth. The *Abstract* was printed about 1790, but the manuscript itself has vanished. But it was probably Robertson who recast Hutton's original ideas into the *Abstract*'s stylistically attractive form.[55] Robertson also assisted Hutton by drafting a revision of a preface intended for the full "Theory of the Earth," which appeared in the first volume of the RSE's *Transactions*. Hutton may have worked on the preface as early as July 1785, and Robertson wrote his revision of it between that date and July 1787. In this case, the manuscript of the preface does survive, and it is in Robertson's handwriting. It was never printed because Hutton decided not to use a preface at all for the "Theory," perhaps believing that raising religious issues, as the preface does, would only stimulate opposition.[56]

Robertson's work shows how willing Robertson was both to embrace science and yet to accommodate it to sacred history, just as he had done with sacred and secular history.[57] Hutton knew his geological theories had the potential to contradict Mosaic chronology, for example when in the *Abstract* he claims "that, with respect to human observation, this world has neither a beginning nor an end,"[58] and he did not want the reception of his scientific theories to be sidetracked by religious controversy. Robertson could foresee the theological danger because his son-in-law Patrick Brydone was the author of a famous passage challenging traditional Christian chronology. In the *Tour through Sicily and Malta*, a book reprinted into the 1790s, Brydone recorded a conversation he had with geologist Guisseppe Recupero about the age of Mount Etna:

> Recupero tells me he is exceedingly embarrassed, by these discoveries [the lowest strata on Etna must be at least 14,000 years old], in writing the history of the mountain. That Moses hangs like a dead weight upon him, and blunts his zeal for inquiry; for that really he has not the conscience to make his mountain so young, as that prophet makes the world.[59]

The passage had upset Boswell and Johnson and led James Beattie to complain to Lord Hailes about Brydone's apparent jabs at Mosaic history and to deplore the fashionable praise of Voltaire even among the clergy.[60] To forestall such complaints, Robertson told Hutton in the cover letter, "the stile is rendered a little more Theological," providing a very concise (less than 350 words) yet masterful statement of his Moderate view of Enlightenment science and its place in religious thought.

Robertson first separates the realms of religion and science, but by the conclusion of the preface he finds a way to reunite and harmonize them. The opening paragraph is Moderatism in a nutshell:

> It is not the end of Revelation to instruct mankind in speculative science; to communicate to them a history of Nature; or to explain the true system of the Universe. Intent upon inculcating the religious doctrines which we ought to believe, & the moral virtues which we are required to practice, it rests satisfied with describing the phenomena of nature not according to philosophic truth, but as they appear to our view.[61]

The second paragraph argues that in the Mosaic account the term *day* cannot be taken in the literal sense as "our measure of time which is days, & years." Instead, it simply must "signify an indefinite period, & is employed with a view of conveying to us the idea that things were called into being successively, & in perfect order & arrangement." The third paragraph reintroduces biblical chronology by claiming that after the appearance of humans in the sixth period or day, "the sacred writings contain a chronological history of mankind, & of the events which have happened on the habitable globe." The research in the "Theory of the Earth" relates only to the "ancient operation of this earth," predating the appearance of human beings, and it demonstrates the effect of these operations "in preparing it [the earth] to be such an habitation for Man & other Animals as infinite wisdom & goodness destined it to be." Although religion and science occupy different realms, an invisible divine hand working for human benefit remains present in natural geological processes.

This expansive vision of infinite wisdom and goodness operating in a world without beginning or end appears in a comparable form in Robertson's religious and political thinking of the late 1780s. On 5 November 1788, Robertson along with the rest of clerical Britain celebrated the centenary of the Glorious Revolution, and contrary to his usual practice, he wrote out this sermon. A draft of it survives, though it is not a draft quite ready for publication, and Robertson inserted additional comments spontaneously as he delivered it. After Robertson's death, Lord Brougham asked Lord Robertson to see the manuscript and wondered why it was never published. "His answer was that he wished to avoid giving it publicity, because, in the violence of the times [the1790s], the author of it would be set down for a Jacobin, how innocent soever he was at the day of its being preached."[62] This may have been Robertson's thinking as well. John Erskine, for example, said that Robertson was concerned about the commemoration "perhaps from the fear that on such an occasion, whig principles would be zealously inculcated."[63] That is, Robertson feared radical "whig" sentiments like those he had seen brandished during the anti-Catholic furor of several years earlier. Yet the draft and its preservation suggest an interest in publication. Just a couple of months after the sermon's delivery, he told Andrew Strahan he felt sorry for *The Situation of the World*, "my poor solitary sermon[.] I have rather been an unnatural parent. It is still naked as it was born; & I am afraid I shall never give it a companion."[64] Although affairs in France could still appear very hopeful to Robertson in early 1789,[65] pulling him toward publication, he also may have thought it best, as he did with the American revolt, to see the outcome of the upheaval clearly before committing the sermon to print. By 1793, the Revolution and its repercussions had lost their luster, and he referred, in a letter to Bishop John Douglas, to "the wild tenets of the present day," and to John Drysdale's sermon, "On the Distinction of Ranks," as an antidote against them.[66] Drysdale had urged his parishioners to "cease to complain of the conduct of Providence, and learn, to our happy experience, that the Lord of all the earth has done right *in making poor, and making rich; in bringing low, and lifting up* (1 Samuel 2: 7)," a religious theme that modifies Robertson's more optimistic views in the centenary sermon.[67]

Despite his later caution, Robertson, in 1788, could be fervent about the spread of events. His youthful and earnest passion impressed the ten-year-old Brougham, who attended the sermon's delivery at Old Greyfriars with his grandmother (Robertson's sister Mary):

I well remember his referring to the events now going on on the Continent, as the forerunners of far greater ones which he saw casting their shadows before. He certainly had no apprehension of mischief, but he was full of hope for the future, and his exultation was boundless in contemplating the deliverance of "so many millions of so great a nation from the fetters of arbitrary government."[68]

In keeping with Robertson's "boundless" exultation, the sermon itself reaches toward a vision of God's infinite wisdom and goodness working through time, reaching back not just to 1688 but to the citadel of Jerusalem and ahead to the moment when future generations across the Christian world shall dwell in "that happy time" of religious unity and political liberty.[69] As God made the physical earth a fit habitation for human beings, so He has built political and religious institutions for human benefit.

The sermon itself offers his most extended comment on contemporary British government and society. The central image of the sermon comes from its text, Psalm 48: 12–13, praising the building of Zion: "Walk about Zion, & go round about her; tell the towers thereof, mark well her bulk-warks [sic], consider her palaces, that ye may tell generations following: for this God is our God forever & ever."[70] The sermon begins with two major divisions, the first treating the growth of rights and liberty in civil government, the second the growth of rights and toleration in religion. The division reflects the same division of civil and sacred history – the realm of reason and that of faith – Robertson posited in the *Situation of the World*. In civil history, 1688 brought the curtailing of monarchical power, the strengthening of the influence of the people, and new freedom of expression through freedom of the press. Knowledge of these rights now extends so widely that "There never was any extensive society in which knowledge was so generally diffused, & in which so great a number of men are in the habit of reasoning & inquiring concerning what is best & most beneficial to the society."[71] Robertson sees similar expansion of the "religious right of men" in 1688 where the great struggle was for the right of individual conscience, the right to "be regulated by the dictates of our own reason & conscience, or by what we conceive to be the injunctions of his [God's] word." He reviews in particular the history of the Covenanters in the seventeenth century, whose plight is gradually relieved by provisions of the Revolution of 1688 and the Union of 1707. The sermon then turns to a peroration in which civil and religious history join in a climactic vision in which "a view more enlarged & more noble opens to us."[72] Europe forms one extensive community, and, as one European nation improves, the others (France being the unnamed but most important recent example) follow suit. Like Zion, British institutions were found to be "beautiful & our situation on the sides of the north, the joy of the whole earth, men saw it & they marveled."[73] Across Europe, and again especially in France, the result has been a "wonderfull revolution in the sentiments of nations."[74] But at this point, Robertson the minister backs away slightly from his glorious vision, a move that implies Carlyle's saying he was "Dazzled by the Splendour of the French Revolution" is exaggerated.[75] For Robertson, only God knows what the results of this revolution are going to be. *If* (Robertson's word) the spirit of toleration spreads across Europe, then we may see "that happy time, when there shall be but one faith one baptism, & one hope of our calling," but at this point human knowledge ends, and we can only "join wise & good men of every age in considering this [the great revolution in sentiment] as the work of God & not of man."[76] Progress occurs incrementally over long periods of time, and human beings have only limited time in which to witness progress. Good can be accomplished and applauded, Zion can be built, but the final direction of events is unknowable to humans and rests in the hands of Providence.

Just a year later, Robertson celebrated another important occasion. On 19 October 1789 he called a special meeting of the Senatus Academicus to announce that "the Town Council had come to the Resolution to have the foundation stone laid of a new building for the University [what is now known as the Old College located on South Bridge], designed by Mr. Robert Adam Architect, on the 16th day of next month."[77] Although Robertson did not live to see the building completed, he took great personal satisfaction in seeing the need he had put forth in the 1768 *Memorial* finally brought to fruition. Provost James Hunter Blair had put forward proposals late in 1784 for the building of South Bridge, and in response to that plan James Gregory proposed rebuilding the university somewhat along the lines of that suggested in the *Memorial*. Subscription forms began to circulate, and in 1790 advertisements for subscriptions appeared in London newspapers. This time the financial backing for the plan was more substantial than it had been in 1768, and construction began in 1789 and proceeded for a few years. By the time of Robertson's death in 1793, however, building had effectively ceased with only a portion of the structure completed, a casualty of Robert Adam's death in 1792 and the outbreak of war with France in February 1793. The university building would not be finished until 1826–7, and then according to the design of William Playfair.[78]

But the laying of the foundation stone on 16 November was a spectacle celebrating the Enlightenment in Edinburgh. In the view of the *Scots Magazine*, it was "one of the most brilliant and numerous that ever was exhibited in this city."[77] Before an estimated thirty thousand spectators, a procession of professors, students, magistrates, and freemasons walked together with the university's mace carried before them to the site of the new building. The principal, following Lord Provost Thomas Elder and the magistrates and members of the Town Council, was accompanied by Andrew Hunter, Professor of Divinity, and Thomas Hardy, Professor of Church History, emphasizing the traditional pre-eminence of divinity within the university. The procession chanted verses to the tune of "The Hero Comes," Henry Carey's popular song from his 1734 oratorio *Britannia; or the Royal Lovers*, written to celebrate the marriage of Princess Anne to William, Prince of Orange. The tune provided a political subtext celebrating the Hanoverian monarchy, and the new lyrics echoed imagery from Robertson's earlier *Memorial*:

> Long, long, dishonour of our Isle
> Neglected lay the Muse's pile;
> Her fav'rite walls neglected lay,
> Rude, mean, and moud'ring to decay.

Francis, Lord Napier, the Grand Master of the Freemasons, presided over the ceremony. After setting the stone in place with traditional Masonic tools, he invoked the blessing of the "Great Architect of the Universe," and in keeping with Masonic ritual he poured wheat, wine, and oil over the foundation stone with an accompanying prayer. After Lord Napier had delivered his celebratory speeches, Robertson delivered his reply.

Lord Brougham had the manuscript (or a copy of it) in his possession in 1845 when writing his biography, but it has since disappeared, though Brougham at least reprinted what he had as an appendix. Acknowledging the support of the monarch as well as the magistrates and members of the Town Council, the principal praised his colleagues, whose "abilities and assiduity in discharging the duties of their respective offices" have resulted in making the university not only "a seat of education to youth in every part of the British dominions, but, to the honour of our country, students have been attracted to it from almost every nation in Europe, and every state in America."[80] It was fitting, he continued, that Lord Napier, whose ancestor was Thomas Napier, the distinguished mathematician, laid the foundation stone of "this new mansion of science." Robertson might also have mentioned that Napier, as representative of the Freemasons, also represented a long and important association between the leadership of Edinburgh and the Masons that included leading politicians such as George Drummond and Sir William Forbes as well as successful merchants such as Robertson's brother Patrick. He then turned to his own sentiments, and with considerable understatement he acknowledged his "own peculiar felicity" to have lived "to witness an event so beneficial to this University, the prosperity of which is near to my heart, and has ever been the object of my warmest wishes."[81] After a closing prayer, the procession returned to Parliament Close to the tune of James Thomson's "Rule Britannia," singing of rebirth:

> The stone we've seen first plac'd by Napier's hand,
> Whose future pile aloft shall rise,
> Whose fame shall spread through every distant land,
> And, raised by time, shall reach the skies.

There followed a grand dinner at the Assembly Rooms in George Street, where 300 noblemen and gentlemen attended and were surely encouraged to subscribe to the building fund.

All this commemorative writing may have helped Robertson toward his last book. He was surprised by it himself: "No man had formed a more decided resolution of retreating early from publick view, & of spending the eve of life in tranquility of professional & domestic occupations." Yet now "I step forth with a new work when just on the brink of three score & ten."[82] The book was a very personal statement (for a man not given to public self-disclosure), and he ended it with an uncharacteristically personal touch: "If I might presume to hope that the description which I have given of the manners and institutions of the people of India could contribute in the smallest degree, and with the most remote influence, to render their character more respectable, and their condition more happy, I shall close my literary labours with the satisfaction of thinking that I have not lived or written in vain."[83] Robertson felt a paternal bond with this book, telling Gibbon that "like other parents I have a partial fondness for this child of my old age." But his fondness was not widely shared. Seldom referred to as a triumph even by his contemporaries, *The Disquisition Concerning the Knowledge the Ancients Had of India* is the least read and least discussed of his four histories, and only recently has it acquired respect.[84] The work is not a full history of the West's relationship with India, and it omits important aspects of Indian history and culture, but it is a moving and thoughtful coda to Robertson's historical career, possessing liberality and humane awareness. In this sense, the book is of a piece with his other valedictions of his last years, suggesting the breadth and humanity of his final vision of history.

Published on 4 June 1791, the manuscript had been submitted to Strahan and Cadell in November 1790, and Robertson probably began it two years earlier in July 1788, as indicated by the university's borrowing registers. Robertson acknowledged the inspiration of James Rennell's *Memoir of the Map of Hindoostan* in the revised edition of 1788. He also admired the last two volumes of the *Decline and Fall of the Roman Empire* (1788), with their push toward the Orient in sweeping surveys of the relations among medieval Europe, Byzantium, and Islam. Having read them through twice, he told Gibbon: "I know no example in any age or nation of such a vast body of valuable & elegant information communicated by any individual."[85] He looked at India against the backdrop of the abbé Raynal's *Philosophical and Political History of the Settlements and Trade of the Europeans in the East and West Indies,* which he first encountered in 1773, one critic observing that readers of the *Disquisition* will "often trace the stolen footsteps of our author" in Raynal's "snow."[86] The year 1788 also marked the opening of the trial of Warren Hastings on 15 February, with his friend Edmund Burke playing a leading role. Robertson also had contact with ambitious India hands such as Sir John Macpherson, a controversial figure allied with Hastings. It is unclear how well acquainted with Macpherson Robertson was, but in 1770 the historian appeared comfortable with imperial efforts in India, commenting jovially, "We all flatter ourselves with hopes that you are to return with a sound constitution & a full purse."[87]

But the deepest personal connections to India were through Robertson's sons James and David. After arriving in 1782, David was forced to leave India for health reasons, travelling over parts of Africa and Asia, returning to Edinburgh in 1785 able to "tell of the Turks & Saracens," and then residing in Yverdun, having become a captain in the 23rd regiment.[88] But David returned to the East as Deputy Adjutant-General of what was then Ceylon from 1801 to 1803, and wrote in 1799 a military report on the country's agriculture, natural resources, and military defense, concluding, in his father's vein, that if current development policies are followed the native peoples will be freed "from these bonds of Servitude and those remains of feudal barbarism that oppressed them 'and froze the general current of their Souls.'"[89] James's career was equally successful. He was in high favor with Sir Eyre Coote for conduct under his command, and he enhanced his reputation on the night of 18 October 1791, at the siege of the fort at Nundydroog, which Tipu Sultan's forces held. The lead article in the *London Chronicle* for 5–7 April 1792 carried the news that James led the charge by the grenadiers of the 36th and 71st regiments into the fort once its wall had been breached:

> On getting possession of the fort, Capt. Robertson, with a benevolence that does honour to his feelings as a man, and a promptitude of exertion, which gives a lustre

to his military character as an officer, to prevent irregularity and confusion, and avoid that indiscriminate slaughter which too frequently, and often unavoidable, marks the consequences of a storm at all times, but particularly in the night, directed his first attention to the establishment of order among the gallant troops under his command; and such was the wonderful success that attended his endeavours, that although there were 200 women in the fort, not one of them received the least injury.

To prevent even more bloodshed, James permitted members of the enemy garrison to escape down the mountain so that only about forty of the enemy were killed. Within the Robertson family, James's heroism was a significant event. His brother William tried to imagine what the family must be feeling:

It is impossible for me to describe the joy & exultation which I feel, which has been heightened by thinking of the pleasure & delight which you & my Mother must feel on seeing a son deservedly so dear to you distinguishing himself by every thing which can exalt the character of a soldier. I wish I could witness the scene of domestic happiness which this news must occasion at Lennell [sic], if I could envy you for any thing it would be for the feelings of a Father at this time.[90]

In a moment of parental pride (and perhaps to whet the public appetite for his *Disquisition*), Robertson wrote Andrew Strahan on 15 April, asking him to insert in the *Chronicle* a paragraph identifying James as the historian's son, a task Strahan duly performed.[91]

Like Robertson's two previous histories, the *Disquisition* is divided between narrative and conjectural history. Occupying about 50 percent of the book, the narrative is in four parts, three devoted to chronological divisions of the subject and one to general observations on the whole period to 1498. The chronological boundary of 1498 was determined for him: "Of all the occurrences in the history of the human race," the discovery of America and the navigation of the Cape of Good Hope are among the most important because they brought dramatic changes to trade and culture in both East and West.[92] A descriptive appendix follows, taking up about 25 percent of the work treating the manners, customs, institutions, and learning of the Hindus. Notes and illustrations to the narrative and the appendix, often lengthy and wide ranging, treating contemporary and historical issues, comprise the remaining 25 percent. The book lacks the grand narrative architecture of his previous histories, but it bears the title of a disquisition, not a history, suggesting it is investigative and even fragmentary, though not lacking coherence.[93]

The narrative lays out an unbroken record of commercial contact with India, exhibiting "such a view of the various modes in which intercourse with India had been carried on from the earliest times, as might shew how much that great branch of commerce has contributed, in every age, to increase the wealth and power of the nations which possessed it."[94] The narrative layers one mode of contact between East and West on top of another, like geological strata, building up India not only as a desirable but also a necessary trading partner for any commercial nation. In the ancient world, first contact was only possible by land, though the Phoenicians eventually created sea routes, and Alexander not only made India known to the West, but he also was the first foreign presence to occupy the country. With the collapse of his empire, no European power had the means to hold territory in India again until the arrival of the Portuguese, but other nations quickly intervened. Egypt obtained control of all commerce and from this monopoly "derived that extraordinary degree of opulence and power for which it was conspicuous" and increased commerce with India to an extent "astonishing even to the present age."[95] In the seventh century, Europe had to manage trade through Islamic merchants who controlled the eastern Mediterranean until the crusades brought a rapid increase of wealth to Italy, and Genoa and Venice gained control of Indian trade.[96] As the "spirit of commerce" revived in the thirteenth century, other European nations entered the field, and with the discovery of direct sea routes to India, keen competition for trade followed.[97] Here the narrative ends, but the British reader would easily infer that the Battle of Plassey in 1757 had inaugurated their own phase of Indian commerce.

At the beginning of his appendix, Robertson asks the obvious question behind this narrative of contact: what caused nations throughout history to engage so extensively and persistently in trade with India? Raw material did not drive this trade (pepper excepted); instead, it was the "superior improvement of [India's] inhabitants," and only a survey of the "institutions, manners, and arts" will explain "the eagerness of all nations to obtain the production of their ingenious industry."[98] India's superior polish and sophistication was irresistibly attractive because a desire for progress dwells in all human societies. Humanity began its "career of improvement" in the East, and India is "one of the first countries in which men made any considerable progress in that career."[99] To demonstrate this contention, Robertson covers six topics in the appendix: social structure, political constitution, laws, arts, science, and religion. Arguing for the high state of early Indian culture, Robertson sometimes goes counter to received opinion. For example, his discussion of social structure overturns the negative connotations of caste. Abbé Raynal is typical in arguing that:

> The distribution of the Indians into casts, each superior to the other, is a mark of the deepest corruption, and the most ancient system of slavery. It discovers an unjust

and disgusting pre-eminence of the priesthood over all other ranks of society, and a
stupid inattention to the first legislator, to the general good of the nation.[100]

For Robertson, the caste system is an early sign of the division of labor,
and thus "one of the most undoubted proofs of a society considerably
advanced in its progress."[101] He concedes that the caste system stifles
individual genius, but because "the arrangements of civil government are
made, not for what is extraordinary, but for what is common," the caste
system was the best means for providing for the needs of all the members
of society.[102] The caste system additionally brings expertise: workers concentrate efforts on allotted tasks, and highly sophisticated workmanship
results.

But his willingness to accept Indian culture has limits, especially with
religion. Robertson is a long way from acknowledging that the Hindu
religion is true in the same sense as Christianity is true.[103] What he does
acknowledge is that the Brahmins in particular attained, through their
sophisticated science, a sense of the divine that parallels that of the Stoics,
whom he admired from the earliest portion of his career.[104] His strategy is
as much as possible to compare, not judge, to stretch Eurocentric assump-
tions gently rather than attack them forcefully. For example, he does not
call for missionary Christianizing of India at a time when pressure for
such action was increasing.[105] To see how tactful Robertson's approach
is, consider just one small example of the challenge posed by Hinduism to
Mosaic chronology, a challenge he would take seriously given his thinking about Hutton's geology. On the one hand, Enlightenment critics of
religion like Voltaire accepted Hindu chronology, arguing it showed the
existence of a civilization older and more refined than that of the Hebrews
and thus cast doubt on the biblical account of creation.[106] On the other,
the mainstream British public, though "willing to accept a sympathetic
portrayal of Hinduism . . . were not prepared to accept claims for its
antiquity which could be subversive of Christianity."[107] To bridge this
gap, Robertson reviews the details of the chronology issue in Note LXVII,
first quoting a lengthy description of the four Hindu eras from Nathaniel
Halhead and then observing that "nothing can be more extravagant in
itself, or more repugnant to our mode of calculating the duration of
the world, founded on sacred and infallible authority," than the Hindu
chronology.[108] That claim of truth asserted, Robertson then assumes a
delicately balanced stance:

To me it appears highly probable, that when we understand more thoroughly the
principles upon which the factitious aeras or Jogues of the Hindoos have been

formed, that we may be more able to reconcile their chronology to the true mode of computing time, founded on the authority of the Old Testament.[109]

As he did in the preface for Hutton's "Theory of the Earth," he personalizes the statement ("to me"), situating it in the perspective of a limited perceiver; he acknowledges that we do not have adequate information about Hindu chronology to make an informed judgment; and he concludes with a neatly bracketed claim for the truth of Mosaic chronology, for, after all, if Mosaic chronology were absolutely true, it would not matter what information we had about Hindu chronology. By means of such skillful rhetoric, Robertson engages Indian culture seriously and gives it a measure of parity with Western values.

This account of Robertson's thinking in the *Disquisition* has so far omitted one important negative feature of Indian culture: its lack of change, even stagnation. The image of an immutable India Robertson would have encountered in Montesquieu and, more closely at hand, in the work of his own one-time protégé John Logan,[110] and it appears repeatedly in the *Disquisition*. India is "a country where the manners, the customs, and even the dress of the people are almost as permanent and invariable as the face of nature itself."[111] Robertson explains that India had arrived early at a high stage of civilization but then remained unaltered at that stage until the Europeans, now the embodiment of progress, arrived in the fifteenth century.[112] For Logan, the country's immutability means its complete separation from Europe. Defending Warren Hastings against charges of cruelty, Logan appealed to the vast gulf between India and Britain:

> We have now the experience of ages to demonstrate, that any attempts to introduce European maxims and manners among the Asiatic nations, must be forever in vain. Nature, and long-established habits stronger than nature, fix insurmountable obstacles in the way. IMMUTABILITY appears to be the characteristic of Asia, and its forms, like the laws of the Medes and Persians, are incapable of change. The manners of the Persians and Indians of this day originate from the same spirit, and exhibit the same appearance, that prevailed among their ancestors at a period too remote for historical research. With an astonishing attachment to their own usages and customs, they have an inveterate and invincible aversion to those of the Europeans. Asia and Europe have been in contact for three thousand years; and although many innovations and improvements have passed from the former to the latter, not a single trace can be found of one custom, originally European, having been adopted by the nations of Asia.[113]

Given that Indian culture is unalterably opposed to British ideas, policy in India must rest upon force: "Our possessions in Asia were gained by the sword, and, if they are to be retained, must in all future ages be held by the sword."[114]

Although at first glance Robertson may seem to endorse Logan's call for force in his praise of James's heroism and Macpherson's full purse, his actual position is more nuanced. He urges peaceful respect for Indian culture, but he does not deny that the British have a military role in India, which is to preserve trade through dominion.[115] Respecting Indian culture means working with it to preserve justice, order, and stability. Robertson does not spell out the practical policies his position entails (although, as he pointed out to Henry Dundas, he did intend his book to inform legislative opinion[116]), but his position is close to that of his friend Colonel William Fullarton in his *View of the English Interests in India*, who argues that Britain must maintain a strong military presence in India if there is to be a presence at all because inconsistency produces only destruction.[117] A strong military will provide well for the inhabitants by building a productive environment and will aid British commercial interests. But this presence should rest on the stability and historical longevity of Indian culture:

> The mode of restoring prosperity to your territories is, in my opinion, extremely simple. These countries experienced the refinements of civil polity and regulation suited to their condition, ages before they even heard the name of European. You have only to restore the general form and tenor of the Indian jurisprudence; and where that system, over-rating the pretensions of superior casts, tends to the violation of natural law and public welfare, there the rigor of Gentoo enactments should be mitigated, without destroying the established order and gradations of the country. Protect the poor from the oppression of the great, restrain the despotic violence of the native leaders, and let everyone within the limits of the English influence feel that he is safe in his property, his person, and his life. If this were actually the case, the husbandman, the labourer, the manufacturer, and the merchant would very soon fly from every corner of Indostan, to take shelter under a government that respected the sacred rights and established institutions of their ancestors, while it afforded personal security and independence, the offspring of an English polity.[118]

Fullarton and Robertson share a Eurocentric perspective, but it is one that rejects the extremes of subjugation by force to secure empire or abandoning all pretensions to it. His son James at Nundydroog, showing military heroism coupled with humanity, represented for Robertson the preservation of trade by dominion.

Robertson's "speculations" on India seem to be leading him into new territory.[119] The commercial relations of Europe with India imply the possibility of commercial relations that are global. Under British leadership, perhaps, there can develop a system or network in which nations and peoples are tied together:

> The commercial genius of Europe, which has given it a visible ascendant over the three other divisions of the earth, by discerning their respective wants and resources, and by rendering them reciprocally subservient to one another, has established an union among them, from which it has derived an immense increase of opulence, of power, and of enjoyments.[120]

This is an imperial plan, and Raynal had already described the sad results of empire. But Robertson does not acknowledge them. He prefers instead to assume the civilizing power of commerce in which the effect of these evolving commercial networks is "familiarizing and reconciling men of hostile principles and discordant manners to one another."[121] In addition, we must always assume that sanctioning the benefits of commerce is the "progressive plan of Providence." Robertson's description of Europe's "commercial genius" echoes his description of the operations of Providence in his first published sermon. According to that plan, Providence creates "one vast society, closely cemented by mutual wants; each part contributing its share towards the subsistence, the pleasure, and improvement of the whole."[122] In both commerce and religion,"systems temporary and incomplete might serve to introduce that concluding and perfect revelation, which would *declare the whole council of God to man*."[123]

Robertson worried a good deal about the format of the book, being reluctant, as he told Strahan, to "descend from the dignity of an Quarto Author to the humble rank of Octavo" and making sure the bulk of the quarto justified the price by using fewer lines per page and thicker paper.[124] As the book began printing, he wrote to Suard asking if he would translate it using the same technique of the sheets being forwarded as they were printed so the two version would be almost simultaneous, but Suard, devastated by the French Revolution, said he could not comply but did find another translator, who published the French version in 1792.[125] Periodical reviews were mixed, with some offering somewhat tepid praise befitting Robertson's stature, but others were more sharply critical.[126] Robertson was pleased with the responses to the publisher's copies he sent to friends, especially with the warm praise of James Rennell.[127] He seems never to have elicited a comment from Gibbon, despite a reminder.[128] In the end, Strahan and Cadell were relieved that the book did not damage Robertson's reputation.[129] They gave Robertson £1,111 2s. 6d., which was based on length – that is, five-sixths of one-half the price for *America*.[130]

With the book out, he moved on to other tasks, undertaking no major projects but busying himself with small final revisions of his histories. On the heels of the printing of *India*, Robertson added "two papers" to the cheap edition of *Scotland* to give it an advantage over a pirated edition recently published by a combination of Edinburgh booksellers, and in the fall of 1791, he sent Strahan two parcels of revisions for the seventh edition of *Charles V*.[131] In 1792, he sent Strahan some further revisions, and Strahan announced in November that *Scotland* would enter its fourteenth edition and the *Disquisition* its second.[132] These were to prove the last editions of his histories Robertson could be said to have supervised. Robertson was still sought after as a literary mentor by aspiring authors. He gave a good deal of support to Thomas Somerville, a clergyman twenty years his junior, who was seeking publication for his first major history, *The History of Political Transactions, and of Parties, from the Restoration of King Charles the Second to the Death of King William*. In February 1791, Robertson, in the midst of the printing of the *Disquisition* and securing engravings for the two accompanying maps, took time to read a portion of Somerville's manuscript and to write to Andrew Strahan recommending it.[133] Strahan quickly issued a contract in March for £500, a generous amount for an unknown writer.[134] In January 1793, Robertson discussed with Somerville the possibility of a second history, this time on the reign of Queen Anne, and supplied him with notes on papers he had seen in the Duchess of Buccleugh's collections. It was a dramatic moment for Somerville:

> He opened his desk, and cut out from his common-place book the sheets containing the notes, and delivered them into my hands. I felt assured that they were the latest pledge of his regard, for the wan complexion and wasted frame of this excellent man precluded the hope of my ever seeing him again.[135]

The dead also had to be memorialized. When John Drysdale died in 1788, he did not signify that his sermons should be suppressed even though he himself never chose to publish any of them, and in late summer 1792, Andrew Dalzel, Drysdale's son-in-law, consulted Robertson, who promised to "read them with the utmost attention, and put down on paper every observation, great and small, which occurs to me, while you have full liberty to adopt or to reject or alter them as you think best."[136] Although Dalzel gave the editorial credit to Rev. William Moodie of St. Andrew's Church, Edinburgh, Robertson took some pride in the published sermons, telling Bishop Douglas not only that Drysdale was "the companion of my youth & my intimate friend through the whole of his life," but also that in his sermons "the doctrines of Religion are ably illustrated, & its duties enforced with a strength of argument, an earnestness & fervor which, I should think, must make a deep impression upon all who read them."[137]

Robertson still maintained a public presence in his last few years. He continued to preach, and John Erskine said it was "with as much distinctness and vigour as ever, though his deafness deprives him of the pleasures of society."[138] His backing was still sought for some of the reform controversies that roiled Edinburgh in the early 1790s. In 1789, John Skinner, Episcopal bishop of Aberdeen, was defeated in his campaign in Parliament to remove penal laws on nonjuring Episcopal clergy, and for his second attempt in 1791 he elicited support from Robertson, who wrote on his behalf to John Douglas. For Robertson, who had long maintained cordial ties with Scottish Episcopalians, it was a natural extension of Catholic relief: Douglas was sufficiently impressed with the liberality of Robertson's sentiments that he passed the letter along to the Archbishop of Canterbury to support Skinner's cause, which prevailed finally in the spring of 1792.[139] At this same time, Robertson may have been caught up in the Test Act controversy, although evidence is not clear. In 1790, Thomas Somerville launched his campaign in Parliament to abolish the Test Act as it applies to the Church of Scotland, requiring anyone having employment in England to take communion in the Church of England. The controversy split the Moderates in the General Assembly and Robertson's own loyalties, with Carlyle leading the anti-repeal side and William Robertson, as procurator, playing an active role on the other. Both Carlyle and the procurator spoke strongly on the issue, and William also drafted a committee *Memorial* laying out the case for repeal, which one committee member said showed the influence of William's father.[140] But Robertson never publicly declared his views.

When Robertson's university colleagues could see that his end was near, they offered him one final honor at the instigation of Dugald Stewart and Andrew Dalzel. On 4 March 1792, Dalzel wrote to Robertson reporting on a dinner with "a numerous company of Professors" to which Robertson was invited but could not attend because of illness (probably liver failure as indicated by his jaundice) and his plans to visit the Brydones at Lennel to recover. Stewart suggested to Dalzel just minutes before the dinner that the company, in recognition of Robertson's work as a historian, his long tenure as principal, and particularly his contributions to the university library, have him sit for a portrait to be done by Henry Raeburn, who was emerging as Scotland's leading portrait painter.[141] Robertson's formal response was delayed because he had contracted a cold on top of his already seriously weakened condition and primarily because he learned on 6 March of the death of his cousin and admired friend Robert Adam, which afflicted him greatly. After remaining for some time in Edinburgh to be with the Drysdales, he replied to Dalzel from Lennel on 9 April that he was deeply touched: "No honour ever conferred upon me was more pleasing or acceptable to me," and he would "with much pride" sit for Raeburn on his return to Edinburgh. "I hope," he continued, "I shall not show a new face to my old friends, but, instead of the suspicious yellow, shall present an honest red and white."[142]

The picture itself, which presently hangs in the room of the Academic Senate, certainly shows a sick man: frail and a bit hunched in his chair with slight hints of jaundice.[143] Yet his face still shows strength of character: he embodies reasonableness and judgment combined with determination and authority. The symbols of his power and accomplishments are distributed around him: dressed in black in a black academic gown with brilliant white Presbyterian preaching bands that stand out in stark contrast; on his left, the university mace lying prominently displayed across his desk along with quills and books. In the foreground is a copy of Tacitus, in the background a set of Robertson's works with *Scotland* and *Charles V* showing. On his right, on the floor beside his chair, rest three books: Lodovico Muratori's *Antichita italiane*, Jeronimo Zurita y Castro's *Anales de Corona de Aragon*, and Jeronimo de Blancas's *Commemtarios de la Cosas de Agaron*. The choice may seem surprising, but Robertson (and Gibbon as well) admired the Renaissance historian Muratori as the great practitioner of more scientific historiography, the first historian to pay close attention to the precision and accuracy of evidence.[144] Zurita and Blancas, likewise, were noted for their technical expertise as well as founding the tradition of Spanish historiography. Both figure notably in *Charles V*. Although an early work of Raeburn's, the portrait is vivid, capturing Robertson's career and character more deeply than does Reynolds's earlier, rather more glossy rendering.

This final academic honor was timely because Robertson's health was failing quickly. Over the summer of 1792, the Robertsons took Grange House, a small castellated tower house about a mile and a half from the center of Edinburgh. It was sufficiently removed from the city that Robertson could retreat to the country easily and regain strength yet still be accessible to the town. By October he could tell Brydone that "All here are well & I continue to gain ground," though he was still undergoing active treatment:

> I had a first conference with Dr. Black, who has ordered for me some Carminative drops to expel the flatulence. I had occasion to write the Minister of Newbattle yesterday, & have (sub rosa) made inquiry concerning the wise-woman in his parish.[145]

The juxtaposition of scientific and folk medicine suggests that Robertson was trying all measures, and the measures had success such that by

February 1793 Brydone could tell Cadell Robertson was "wonderfully well."[146] At the end of March he was busy making revisions to India and wrote to his London bookseller for a copy of William Hodges's *Travels in India in the Years 1780, 1781, 1782, and 1783*, which had just been published, adding "I am very desirous of seeing his Travels, before I send off a corrected copy of My Disquisition . . . which goes soon to the press."[147] But on the first of April his final illness struck:

> I have had a return of my disease, which has distressed & enfeebled me a good deal. It began on the first of the month, but for three or four days, it begins to abate & I feel much easier. I had no pain or sickness, but my bowels were affected, & I was very averse to any kind of effort.[148]

He felt better ten days later, again ordering a book on India, but confessing he was "still very feeble."[149] Probably about this time he summoned the strength to entertain visitors, including "two gentlemen from New York." They were so anxious for an interview that he

> rallied all his powers to entertain his guests, and to inspire in their minds a feeling of kindness towards the parent land of the late colonists; and, on their rising to take leave, he said to them, in accents at once dignified and pathetic "When you go home, tell your countrymen that you saw the wreck of Dr. Robertson."[150]

On 4 June, when Robertson was confined to his couch and had difficulty talking, Stewart saw him for the last time, and Robertson requested that he write his life. He died on 11 June at Grange House, and his funeral took place on the 15th with Blair, Erskine, and eleven others in attendance. He was buried in Old Greyfriars churchyard next to the Adam tomb, with a lengthy inscription commemorating his achievements. On the tomb are two memorial tablets, one for William Robertson and the other for David Robertson.

Two of the people who knew Robertson best left comments on his last weeks of life that capture the admiration and criticism Robertson's character elicited. The idealistic close of the appendix to John Erskine's funeral sermon is one of these:

> He bore the severe and tedious distress, which issued in his death, with remarkable patience and serenity, and with expressions of gratitude to God, for the many comforts with which, for a long series of years, he had been blessed. Among these, he mentioned to me, with peculiar emotion, the tender affection of his wife and children; their kind and sympathizing attention in his hours of languishing and pain; their respectable characters in life, and the comfortable situation in which he left them. In one of his last conversations with me, he expressed his joy in reflecting, that his life on earth had not been altogether in vain; and his hopes, that, through the

merits of Jesus, the God, who had so signally prospered him in this world, would, in another, and better world, be his portion and happiness.[151]

The other is Alexander Carlyle's report to John Macpherson in India about their old friend, offering a more realistic assessment:

> To begin with Robertson, whom you shall see no more. In one word, he appeared more respectable when he was dying than ever he did even when living. He was calm and collected, and even placid and even gay. My poor wife had a desire to see him, and went on purpose, but when she saw him, from a window, leaning on his daughter, with his tottering frame, and directing the gardener on how to dress some flower-beds, her sensibility threw her into a paroxysm of grief; she fled upstairs to Mrs. Russell and could not see him. His house, for three weeks before he died, was really an anticipation of heaven.[152]

Sir John replied to Carlyle's account, assuring him it was "worth volumes of Sermons."[153]

Notes

1. *My Own Life*, pp. 198–9.
2. *Letter to the People of Scotland* (Edinburgh, 1783), p. 8.
3. Ibid., p. 41.
4. Robertson to Keith, 8 March 1784, BL Add. MS 35,350, ff. 70–1.
5. Emerson, *Academic Patronage*, pp. 306–8.
6. Smellie would publish the basis of his lectures as the *Philosophy of Natural History*, 2 vols (1790–9). It is ironic that in light of the furor to ensue, Robertson would read the prospectus for the book in 1786 and the proofs in 1789, telling Smellie that "it will be an useful, entertaining, and popular book" (Robertson to Smellie, October 1786, in Robert Kerr, *Memoirs of the Life, Writings, & Correspondence of William Smellie*, 2 vols (Edinburgh, 1811), II, 288–9; see also Robertson to Smellie, 28 April [1789] and 13 January [1790], in ibid., II, 300–1).
7. EUL MS. Da. 31.5, pp. 306–10.
8. "The Humble Petition of the Society of Antiquaries of Scotland," rpt. in *English Review*, 1 (1783), p. 426.
9. Quoted in Iain Gordon Brown, *The Hobby-Horsical Antiquary: A Scottish Character 1640–1830* (Edinburgh: National Library of Scotland, 1980), p. 15.
10. *History of Scotland*, in *Works of Robertson*, I, 5–6.
11. Quoted in Brown, *Hobby-Horsical Antiquary*, pp. 29–30.
12. *History of Scotland*, in *Works of Robertson*, II, 180.
13. Buchan to Gilbert Stuart, 18 April 1783, EUL MS Dc.1.24. No. 19.
14. Roger L. Emerson, "The Scottish Enlightenment and the End of the Philosophical Society of Edinburgh," *British Journal for the History of Science*, 21 (1988), p. 52.

15. Quoted in ibid., p. 43.
16. The term "pathological" belongs to Steven Shapin, "Property, Patronage, and the Politics of Science: The Founding of the Royal Society of Edinburgh," *British Journal for the History of Science*, 7 (1974), p. 15.
17. Stuart publicly denied authorship, but the pamphlet has been identified as his. See Zachs, *Without Regard to Good Manners*, pp. 166–72.
18. *Critical Observations concerning the Scottish Historians Hume, Stuart, and Robertson* (London, 1782), p. 53.
19. Buchan to Little, 26 November 1782, EUL MS Gen 1429/16/4.
20. *History of Scotland*, 2nd edn, Appendix II, pp. 151–9.
21. *Sequel to the Gift of a Grandfather*, p. 53.
22. Evidence points to the threatened lawsuit occurring in 1783. Adam tells us that Stuart was resident in London at the time the lawsuit was discussed, and Stuart had returned to London in 1783 (Zachs, *Without Regard to Good Manners*, p. 171). Adam himself was called to the English bar only in 1782. Finally, Adam says that Robertson, "soon after" the consultation, sent him copies of his revised histories, which were under way in 1785–6 and published in 1787–8.
23. Sher and Murdoch, "Patronage and Party," p. 200.
24. Quoted in Meikle, *Scotland and the French Revolution*, p. 39.
25. McIntosh, *Church and Theology*, p. 150.
26. *Caledonian Mercury*, 21 August 1784.
27. Sher and Murdoch, "Patronage and Party," pp. 197–8.
28. William Robertson to Robertson and Mary Robertson, 23 August 1783, NLS MS 3,943, ff. 155–6; Robertson to Robert Murray Keith, BL Add. MS 35,350, ff. 70–1.
29. That is, between 1777 and probably 1788, the latter being the publication date of the second edition of James Rennell's *Memoir of a Map of Hindoostan*, which Robertson consulted.
30. "Robertson," in *Miscellaneous Works*, p. 259.
31. Robertson to Gibbon, 12 May 1781, BL Add. MS 34,886, ff. 117–18.
32. Robertson to Orme, 1 February 1781, in Orme, *Historical Fragments*, pp. xxxix–xl.
33. Robertson to Craufurd, 28 December 1780, NLS 10,782, ff. 152–3. The phrase "before I go" is cryptic. Is Robertson anticipating his own death?
34. Robertson to Maccormick, 20 April 1781, NLS 583, ff. 390–1.
35. Quoted in Colonel H. C. Wylly, comp., *A Life of Lieutenant-General Sir Eyre Coote, K.B.* (Oxford: Clarendon Press, 1922), p. 186.
36. Jenkinson to Robertson, 16 January 1781, BL Add. MS 38,308, f. 67; and Robertson to Orme, 1 February 1781, in Orme, *Historical Fragments*, pp. xxxix–xl.
37. Drennan to Sam McTier, September [17]82, in *Drennan-McTier Letters*, ed. Jean Agnew and Maria Luddy, 3 vols (Dublin: Women's History Project in

association with the Irish Manuscripts Commission, 1998), I, 61. I am grateful to Richard Sher for calling these letters to my attention.

38. William Robertson to Robertson and Mary Robertson, [23 March 1780], NLS MS 3,943, ff. 118–21. See also Fullarton's two undated letters to William in NLS MS 3,953, ff. 24–7.

39. Robertson to Brydone, 29 September [1790], NAS MS WRH TD 77/142/4/305/1.

40. Robertson to Brydone, 14 April 1785, NAS WRH TD 77/142/4/306/22; Robertson and Mary Robertson to William Robertson, 7 June [1789], NLS MS 3,944, ff. 12–13; Robertson and Mary Robertson to Patrick and Mary Brydone, 4 November 1789, NAS WRH TD 77/142/4/300/19.

41. Robertson to Andrew Strahan, [17 October 1785], Duke University Library MS.

42. Robertson to Strahan, 24 December 1785, Duke University Library MS. Strahan's letter of 21 November is untraced.

43. Robertson to Phillip Yorke, 30 January 1786, BL Add. MS 35,350, ff. 72–3.

44. On Robertson's relationship with the Warwick family, see Robertson to William Mure, 19 March 1765, in *Caldwell Papers*, II, pt. 2, pp. 23–4. The portrait Robertson describes is a miniature traditionally attributed to Federigo Zuccaro (1542/3–1609), but the attribution is doubtful. It is now in the Victoria and Albert Museum (P.26-1942). No engraving seems ever to have been done, and the revised edition of *Scotland* carried the frontispiece done by Thomas Holloway: a re-engraving of the Reynolds portrait set within an oval of laurels perched on a pedestal and supported by allegorical figures of history and martial valor. A portrait of Mary would reaffirm Robertson's belief that the primary subject of *Scotland* is Mary. But the Warwick portrait shows a romanticized Mary, who might have looked to Robertson or his publishers uncomfortably like the Mary portrayed by Gilbert Stuart. I am grateful to Kate Anderson, senior curator of sixteenth- and seventeenth-century collections at the Scottish National Portrait Gallery, for locating the miniature for me.

45. Robertson to Phillip Yorke, 30 January 1786, BL Add. MS 35,350, ff. 72–3.

46. This aesthetic recalls Marcus Aurelius' image of the soul as a self-contained, perfect sphere in *Meditations*, Book XI, xii.

47. Zachs, *Without Regard to Good Manners*, p. 139. See also the discussion by Phillips, *Society and Sentiment*, pp. 103–28.

48. The term belongs to Lord Kames, *Elements of Criticism*, ed. Peter Jones, 2 vols (Indianapolis: Liberty Fund, 2005), I, 67–8. See Eric Rothstein, "'Ideal Presence' and the 'Non Finito' in Eighteenth-Century Aesthetics," *Eighteenth-Century Studies*, 9 (1976), pp. 307–32.

49. Robertson to Andrew Strahan, 16 July [1787], Houghton Library MS Hyde 10.586. The publisher John Murray accused Robertson of merely using the charge of scurrilous language to avoid having to reply in argument (William

Zachs, *The First John Murray and the Late Eighteenth-Century London Book Trade* (London: British Academy, 1998), pp. 171–2).

50. Robertson's very attempt to revise his histories angered some critics. John Logan wrote to Carlyle: "What do you think of that impudent fellow Robertson? He has made additions to his History of Scotland in which he defends his former system about Mary, and tries to answer all his adversaries . . . This is the weakest thing that ever Robertson did, to expose his bald head in his old age to the arrows of all his enemies" (Logan to Carlyle, 12 April 1786, EUL MS. La.II.419).

51. *History of America*, in *Works of Robertson*, I, xviii–xix.

52. This is not to say he took Clavigero lightly at first. Robertson wrote to James Veitch, Lord Eliock, to borrow an arm load of books to evaluate the Mexican's attacks, though he confessed his presumption was that Clavigero was a "weak & credulous Bigot" (Robertson to Eliock, 3 April 1787, NLS MS 1,036, ff. 106–7).

53. See the fuller discussions by Charles E. Ronan, *Francisco Javier Clavigero (1731–1787), Figure of the Mexican Enlightenment: His Life and Work* (Rome: Jesuit Historical Institute, 1977), pp. 145–54, 287–96, and by Pocock, *Barbarians, Savages and Empire*, pp. 211–18.

54. Respectively: Robertson to Maclaurin, [ante 16 February 1784], in Maclaurin, *Works*, 2 vols (Edinburgh, 1798), I, xxvii–xxviii; *Transactions of the Royal Society of Edinburgh*, 2 (1790), p. 3; Andrew Dalzel to Sir Robert Liston, 24 December 1787, in Dalzel, *History of the University of Edinburgh*, I, 73.

55. Dennis R. Dean, *James Hutton and the History of Geology* (Ithaca, NY: Cornell University Press, 1992), pp. 275–6.

56. Dennis R. Dean, "James Hutton on Religion and Geology: The Unpublished Preface to His *Theory of the Earth* (1788)," *Annals of Science*, 32 (1975), pp. 187–93.

57. Accommodation of the secular and the sacred was Robertson's distinctive strength, as noted by Andrew Dalzel as he compares him to Gibbon and Hume: Gibbon "has fallen into an error too common in these days, he goes out of his road to give a stab to the religion of his country. It is thought that Mr Hume has deeply repented of ever having taken this line in any of his writings: for Dr Robertson has shewn that History may have great success without attempting to inflict wounds of this sort" (Dalzel to [Paul Panton?], 21 July 1776), National Library of Wales MS 9071.

58. "Two Items Intended for Publication by James Hutton, 1785 and 1788," in *Miscellaneous Works*, p. 169.

59. *Tour through Sicily and Malta*, 2 vols (Boston, 1792), I, 72.

60. Paul Fussell, Jr., "Patrick Brydone: The Eighteenth-Century Traveler as Representative Man," *Bulletin of the New York Public Library*, 66 (1962), pp. 335–6; Beattie to Hailes, 22 November 1778, in *Correspondence of James Beattie*, ed. Roger J. Robinson, 4 vols (Bristol: Thoemmes, 2004), III, 86–7.

61. "Two Items," in *Miscellaneous Works*, pp. 170–1.

62. "Robertson," in ibid., p. 271.

63. Quoted in Sher, *Church and University*, p. 102.

64. Robertson to Strahan, [January/February 1789?], Dunedin Public Library MS, Reed Collection.

65. For an analysis of Robertson's optimistic view of French history, see Richard Sher "1688 and 1788: William Robertson on Revolution in Britain and France," in *Culture and Revolution*, ed. Paul Dukes and John Dunkley (London: Pinter Publishers, 1990), pp. 98–109.

66. Robertson to Douglas, 15 February 1793 (BL Egerton MS 2,182, ff. 78–9. Drysdale's sermons were published in 1793, but he died in June 1788. It is not known when "Distinction of Ranks" was written, but, given the companionship of the two ministers, Robertson would likely have known of it before his commemoration sermon.

67. Drysdale, *Sermons*, 2 vols (Edinburgh, 1793), I, 300.

68. "Robertson," in *Miscellaneous Works*, p. 270. Brougham's phrase in quotation marks does not come from the draft of the sermon. As he points out in a footnote, this is an example of Robertson's practice of inserting "remarks made on the inspiration of the moment" (ibid., p. 271).

69. "Sermon on the Centenary of the Glorious Revolution," in *Miscellaneous Works*, p. 185.

70. Ibid., p. 175.

71. Ibid., p. 179.

72. Ibid., p. 182.

73. Ibid., p. 183.

74. Ibid., p. 184.

75. "Comparison," p. 281.

76. "Sermon on the Centenary," in *Miscellaneous Works*, pp. 185–6.

77. Quoted in A. J. Youngson, *The Making of Classical Edinburgh 1750–1840* (Edinburgh: Edinburgh University Press, 1966), p. 124.

78. For a detailed account of the building of the college, see Fraser, *Building of Old College*, esp. ch. 4.

79. *Scots Magazine*, 51 (1789), p. 527. See also Fraser, *Building of Old College*, pp. 2–6.

80. "Robertson," in *Miscellaneous Works*, p. 318.

81. Ibid., p. 319.

82. Robertson to Gibbon, 25 August 1791, BL Add. MS 34,886, ff. 209–10. Robertson alludes ironically to Psalm 90: 10: "The days of our years are threescore years and ten," implying he had reached the very end of his life.

83. *Disquisition on India*, in *Works of Robertson*, p. 334.

84. Among recent comments, see Geoffrey Carnall, "Robertson and Contemporary Images of India," in *William Robertson*, pp. 210–30; O'Brien, *Narratives of Enlightenment*, pp. 163–6; Phillipson, "Providence and Progress," in *William Robertson*, pp. 71–3; and especially Stewart J. Brown,

"William Robertson, Early Orientalism and the Historical Disquisition on India," *Scottish Historical Review*, 88 (2009), pp. 289–312.

85. Robertson to Gibbon, 30 July 1788, BL Add. MS 34,886, ff. 166–7.
86. [John Pinkerton], *Critical Review*, n. s. 3 (1791), p. 557. See *Disquisition*, in *Works of Robertson*, p. 221.
87. Robertson to [Macpherson], 23 June 1770, Bibliothèque publique et universitaire, Genève MS 367, ff. 7–8.
88. Robertson to Keith, 2 May 1785, BL Add. MS, 35,534, ff. 122–5; Adam Ferguson to General Fletcher Campbell, 1 February 1785, in *Correspondence of Ferguson*, II, 308; Robertson to Gibbon, 30 July 1788, BL Add. MS 34,886, ff. 166–7.
89. NLS MS 3,970, ff. 120–1, misquoting slightly Gray's *Elegy*.
90. William Robertson to Robertson, 9 April 1792, NLS MS 3,944, ff. 91–2.
91. Robertson to Andrew Strahan, 15 April 1792, Duke University MS.
92. *Disquisition on India*, in *Works of Robertson*, p. 166.
93. Brown, "Robertson and Early Orientalism," p. 291 makes this point. He also says it may be part of a larger proposed work. But given Robertson's age and health, he may well have intended to write something shorter, more informal, and personal from the outset.
94. *Disquisition on India*, in *Works of Robertson*, pp. iii–iv.
95. Ibid., pp. 48–9, 55.
96. Ibid., p. 138.
97. Ibid., p. 154.
98. Ibid., p. 229.
99. Ibid., pp. 2–3.
100. *Philosophical and Political History*, I, 44. For a survey of British opinion on Indian social structure, see Amal Chatterjee, *Representations of India, 1740–1840: The Creation of India in the Colonial Imagination* (Basingstoke: Palgrave, 1998), pp. 145–60, esp. p. 149. Robertson also sees a serious drawback in the caste system because it leads to India's cultural immobility, as discussed below.
101. *Disquisition on India*, in *Works of Robertson*, p. 230.
102. Ibid., pp. 233–4.
103. The same limitation applies even more strongly to Islam. See Robertson's comment to Robert Murray Keith on Turkey's declaration of war on Russia in 1787: "Both as a Divine & as a Man of Letters I pray & wish for the downfall of Mahomet. These Barbarians have long enough occupied the three chosen seats of science & arts in the ancient world, Egypt, Assyria, & Greece. It is time that the barrier which they have placed between knowledge & ignorance should be forever removed" (Robertson to Keith, 6 February 1788, BL Add. MS 35,540, ff. 48–9).
104. *Disquisition on India*, in *Works of Robertson*, pp. 326–7.
105. Brown, "William Robertson and Early Orientalism," p. 293.

106. Kate Marsh, *India in the French Imagination: Peripheral Voices, 1754–1815* (London: Routledge, 2016), pp. 116–18.

107. P. J. Marshall, "Introduction," in *The British Discovery of Hinduism in the Eighteenth Century*, ed. Marshall (Cambridge: Cambridge University Press, 1970), pp. 26, 34.

108. *Disquisition*, in *Works of Robertson*, p. 435.

109. Ibid., p. 437.

110. *L'Esprit des loix*, in *Œuvres complètes* (Paris: Editions du Seuil, 1964), p. 615. For Montesquieu, the immutability of Asian cultures is an expression of their tendency toward despotic government, an issue he discusses on pp. 536–54. For Logan, "Whatever period of time we contemplate, the oriental empires present us with the same appearance; the modern history is a repetition of the ancient; and from age to age *Immutability* appears the characteristic of Asia" (*Dissertation on the Government, Manners, and Spirit, of Asia* [1787; rpt. Bristol: Thoemmes, 1995], p. 18). Logan's is a wholly negative assessment of India anticipating James Mill's. He first presented his views on India in a series of lectures in 1779–80, and Robertson at the time was one of his sponsors and possibly an auditor.

111. *Disquisition on India*, in *Works of Robertson*, p. 26; see also pp. 74, 235–6, 242, 246.

112. Ibid., pp. 166, 172.

113. *Review of the Principal Charges against Warren Hastings* (London, 1788), pp. 57–8. See also pp. 55–6, 64–8. For Logan's authorship, see Logan to Carlyle, 25 May 1788, EUL MS La. II.49.

114. *Review of the Principal Charges*, p. 89.

115. The phrase belongs to Vincent T. Harlow, *The Founding of the Second British Empire, 1763–1793*, 2 vols (London: Longmans, Green, 1952–64), II, 5–6.

116. Robertson to [Dundas], 6 July 1791, NAS GD 51/9/26. Robertson acknowledges that his book is "of a more speculative than practical nature," but he hoped to "suggest some hints to an intelligent . . . Statesman, that might be of some practical use."

117. Fullarton read the manuscript of India because, in Robertson's view, he was one of the "three of the ablest men who have been in that country" (Robertson to Andrew Strahan, 23 November 1790, Duke University MS).

118. *View of the English Interests in India* (London, 1787), pp. 263–4. The book is written in the form of two letters, the first addressed to Lord Mansfield, the second, from which this quote is taken, to Lord Macartney, governor of Madras.

119. The phrase belongs to Phillipson, "Providence and Progress," in *William Robertson*, p. 71.

120. *Disquisition on India*, in *Works of Robertson*, p. 213.

121. Ibid., p. 131.

122. *Situation of the World*, in *Works of Robertson*, p. 14. The sixth edition of

the *Situation of the World* was published in 1791, alongside the *Disquisition*, by Elphingston Balfour in Edinburgh, perhaps to help reinforce this connection.

123. Ibid., p. 10.

124. Robertson to Andrew Strahan, 13 March 1790, EUL MS La. II. 241; Robertson to [Strahan], 23 November 1790, Duke University Library MS.

125. Robertson to Suard, 28 February 1791, in Charles Nisard, *Mémoires et correspondances historiques et littéraires inédits, 1726–1816* (Paris, 1858), pp. 108–10.

126. For a listing of reviews of *India*, see Smitten, "Bibliography of Writings about Robertson," in *William Robertson*, p. 242.

127. Robertson to Andrew Strahan, 14 August 1791, New College Library, University of Edinburgh MS, Box 1.3.3–4.

128. Robertson to Gibbon, 25 August 1791, BL Add. MS 34,886, ff. 209–10.

129. Strahan to Gibbon, 1 July 1791, BL Add. MS 34,886, f. 198.

130. Strahan and Cadell to Robertson, 17 May 1791, NLS MS 3,944, ff. 42–3.

131. Robertson to Strahan, 14 August 1791, New College Library, University of Edinburgh, Box 1.3.3–4; and Robertson to Strahan, 11 September 1791, BL Add. MS 40,856, ff. 80–1.

132. Robertson to Strahan, 15 August 1792, NLS MS 2,257, ff. 62–3; and Strahan to Robertson, 19 November 1792, NLS MS 3,944, ff. 117–18. After delays in order to read some recent books on India, Robertson delivered the corrected copy to Strahan in mid-April 1793 (Strahan to Robertson, 15 April 1793, NLS 3,944, ff. 132–3).

133. Robertson to John Douglas, 15 February 1791, BL Egerton MS 2,182, ff. 63–4; Robertson to Strahan, 22 March 1791, Yale University Library MS.

134. John Douglas to Alexander Carlyle, EUL MS Dc.4.41/29.

135. *My Own Life*, p. 288.

136. "Postscript Respecting the Sermons," in Drysdale, *Sermons*, 2 vols (Edinburgh, 1793), I, lvii; Robertson to Dalzel, 28 August 1792, in Dalzel, *History of the University of Edinburgh*, I, 96.

137. Robertson to John Douglas, 15 February 1791, BL Egerton MS 2,182, ff. 63–4.

138. Erskine to Charles Nisbet, 29 October 1791, in Samuel Miller, *Memoir of the Rev. Charles Nisbet* (New York, 1840), p. 200. Reference courtesy of Richard Sher.

139. Douglas to Robertson, 17 March 1791, NLS MS 3,944, ff. 36–7; Douglas to Robertson, 28 May 1792, NLS MS 3,944, ff. 104–5.

140. G. M. Ditchfield, "The Scottish Campaign against the Test Act, 1790–1791," *Historical Journal*, 23 (1980), pp. 37–61, esp. p. 43.

141. Dalzel to Robertson, 4 March 1792, NLS 3,944, ff. 89–90.

142. Robertson to Dalzel, 7 March 1792, in Dalzel, *History of the University of Edinburgh*, I, 94, 95; Robertson to Dalzel, 9 April 1792, in ibid., I, 95.

143. *Principal William Robertson* by Sir Henry Raeburn (1792). Oil on canvas, 50 × 40 inches.

144. Denys Hay, *Annalists and Historians: Western Historiography from the Eighth to the Eighteenth Centuries* (New York: Harper & Row, 1977), pp. 178–85.

145. Robertson to Brydone, 13 October 1792, NAS MS WRH TD 77/142/4/300/20.

146. Brydone to [Cadell], 7 February 1793, Houghton Library MS Hyde 77, 9.325.

147. Robertson to James Edwards, 25 March 1793, Duke University Library MS. See also Robertson to Cadell, 29 March [1793], Biblioteka Jagiellonska, Krakow, MS.

148. Robertson to Brydone, 10 April 1793, NAS MS WRH TD 77/142/WAGC 1793 M–Z.

149. Robertson to [Andrew Strahan?], 21 April 1793, letter in possession of the author.

150. Richard Alfred Davenport, "Sketch of Robertson's Life and Writings," in *Works of William Robertson*, 11 vols (Chiswick, 1824), I, lxxix–lxxx.

151. "Agency," in *Miscellaneous Works*, pp. 276–7.

152. Carlyle to Macpherson, [ante 7 July 1794?], quoted in Carlyle, *Autobiography*, p. 576. John Hill Burton dates this letter as 1796, but see the following note.

153. Macpherson to Carlyle, 7 July 1794, EUL MS Dc.4.41/39a.

Selected Bibliography

I Bibliographies

Howard, John V. and William Zachs. *The Celebrated Doctor Robertson: William Robertson (1721–1793) Historian, Churchman and Principal of Edinburgh University. Catalogue of an Exhibit of Books and Manuscripts 20 October to 23 December 1993 in Edinburgh University Library*. Edinburgh: Edinburgh University Library, 1993.

Smitten, Jeffrey. "Bibliography of Writings about William Robertson 1755–1996," in *William Robertson and the Expansion of Empire*. See below under Critical Collections.

—. "Selected Bibliography: William Robertson" at http://tinyurl.com/RobertsonBib. Online bibliography updated periodically.

II Published Works by Robertson

"Student Essay on Historical Probability, 1737." Ed. and trans. Mark Damen. In *Miscellaneous Works and Commentaries*. See below under Collected Editions.

Reasons of Dissent from the Sentence and Resolution of the Commission of the General Assembly, Met at Edinburgh March 11, 1752 concerning the Conduct of the Presbytery of Dunfermline. To Which is Prefixed, A Short Narrative of the Said Conduct of the Presbytery, &c. Edinburgh, 1752.

Situation of the World at the Time of Christ's Appearance, and Its Connexion with the Success of His Religion, Considered. Edinburgh: Hamilton, Balfour, & Neill, 1755.

Edinburgh Review. No. 1 (January to July 1755); No. 2 (July 1755 to January 1756). Robertson may have contributed eight unsigned reviews: in No. 1, Arts. I, III, Appendix II, and Appendix IV; and in No. 2, Arts. I, III, IV, and XI.

History of Scotland, during the Reigns of Queen Mary and of King James VI, till His Accession to the Crown of England. 2 vols. London: Millar, 1759.

Critical Review, 7 (April 1759), pp. 356–67. Unsigned review of Henry Home, Lord Kames, *Historical-Law Tracts*. London: Millar, 1759.

The Principal Acts of the General Assembly of the Church of Scotland, Conveened at Edinburgh the 26th Day of May, 1763. Edinburgh: Davidson and Fleming, 1763. Robertson signed "The General Assembly's Answer to the King's

Most Gracious Letter"; "The General Assembly's Congratulatory Address to the King, on the Happy Event of the Peace"; and "The General Assembly's Congratulatory Address to the Queen, on the Happy Event of the Birth of the Prince of *Wales*."

Ruins of the Palace of the Emperor Diocletian at Spalatro in Dalmatia. London: Strahan, 1764. Robertson contributed the preface.

Memorial Relating to the University of Edinburgh. Edinburgh: Balfour, Auld, & Smellie, 1768.

History of the Reign of the Emperor Charles V. With a View of the Progress of Society in Europe, from the Subversion of the Roman Empire, to the Beginning of the Sixteenth Century. 3 vols. London: Strahan, 1769.

History of America. 2 vols. London: Strahan & Cadell, 1777.

"On the Penal Laws against Papists." *Scots Magazine*, 41 (1779), pp. 409–15.

"Dedication to the King on the Royal Society of Edinburgh, 1788." *Transactions of the Royal Society of Edinburgh*, 1 (1788), pp. v–vii. Ghostwritten by Robertson.

"Unpublished Preface to James Hutton's 'Theory of the Earth; or an Investigation of the Laws Observable in the Composition, Dissolution, and Restoration of Land upon the Globe,' 1788." In *Miscellaneous Works and Commentaries*. See below under Collected Editions.

"Sermon on the Centenary of the Glorious Revolution, 1788." In *Miscellaneous Works and Commentaries*. See below under Collected Editions.

Historical Disquisition concerning the Knowledge Which the Ancients Had of India; and the Progress of Trade with That Country Prior to the Discovery of the Passage to It by the Cape of Good Hope. London: A. Strahan & T. Cadell, 1791.

History of America Books IX and X. London: A. Strahan & T. Cadell, 1796. Posthumous publication edited by his son William Robertson.

III Unpublished Work by Robertson

"Translation of Marcus Aurelius Antoninus the Emperor to Himself." NLS MS 3,955. The manuscript ends at Book VIII, ii, and it is missing part of Book I, xvi, and all of I, xvii. Brougham (see below under Major Biographical Sources) published Book I, i–viii, and *Miscellaneous Works and Commentaries* (see below under Collected Editions) published Book II.

IV Collected Editions

Works of William Robertson. 12 vols. London: Routledge/Thoemmes Press, 1996. General Editor: Richard B. Sher. The fullest edition. Reprints the last lifetime edition of each of Robertson's published works. Includes preface by Sher, chronology, selected bibliography of secondary literature, and introductory essay on Robertson as historian by Nicholas Phillipson. Vol. 12, *Miscellaneous Works and Commentaries*, edited by Jeffrey Smitten, contains Robertson's published miscellaneous works, unpublished works transcribed from manuscript, introduction, and reprinted contemporary commentaries by Robert Liston, James Boswell, John Erskine, Dugald Stewart, and Henry Brougham.

V Individual Works

The Progress of Society in Europe, ed. Felix Gilbert. Chicago: University of Chicago Press, 1972. Text of vol. 1 of *History of Charles V* with Gilbert's introduction.
La Scoperta dell'America, ed. Luigi Mascilli Migliorini. Rome: Salerno Editrice, 1992. Text of Book IV of *History of America* with Migliorini's introduction.

VI Published Correspondence

There is no collected edition of Robertson's correspondence, most of which remains in manuscript scattered among many public and private collections. The largest concentration of material is in the National Library of Scotland (especially the Robertson-Macdonald Papers), supplemented by holdings in the Edinburgh University Library, the National Archives of Scotland, and the Edinburgh City Archives.

Black, Jeremy. "The Enlightenment Historian at Work: The Researches of William Robertson." *Bulletin of Hispanic Studies*, 65 (1988), pp. 251–60.
Boswell, James. *Life of Samuel Johnson*. Ed. George Birkbeck Hill, rev. L. F. Powell, 5 vols. Oxford: Clarendon Press, 1934.
Brougham, Henry. "Robertson." See below under Major Biographical Sources.
Cook, George. *Life of George Hill*. Edinburgh, 1820.
Dalzel, Andrew. *History of the University of Edinburgh from Its Foundation*. 2 vols. Edinburgh, 1862.
Dashkova, Ekaterina. *Memoirs of the Princess Daschkaw*. Ed. Mrs. W. Bradford. 2 vols. London, 1840.
Dean, Dennis R. "James Hutton on Religion and Geology: The Unpublished Preface to His Theory of the Earth (1788)." *Annals of Science*, 32 (1975), pp. 187–93.
Elphinston, James. *Forty Years' Correspondence between Geniusses ov Boath Sexes* [*sic*]. 2 vols. London, 1791.
Ferguson, Adam. *Correspondence*. Ed. Vincenzo Merolle. 2 vols. London: Pickering, 1995.
Garrick, David. *Private Correspondence*. Ed. James Boaden. 2 vols. London, 1831–2.
—. *Letters*. Ed. David M. Little and George M. Kahrl. 3 vols. Cambridge, MA: Harvard University Press, 1963.
Gibbon, Edward. *Letters*. Ed. J. E. Norton. 3 vols. London: Cassell, 1956.
—. *Miscellaneous Works*. Ed. John Lord Sheffield. 2 vols. London, 1796.

Hume, David. *Letters of David Hume to William Strahan.* Ed. G. Birkbeck Hill. Oxford, 1888.

—. *Letters.* Ed. J. Y. T. Greig. 2 vols. Oxford: Clarendon Press, 1932.

—. *New Letters of David Hume.* Ed. Raymond Klibansky and Ernest C. Mossner. Oxford: Clarendon Press, 1954.

Keith, Robert Murray. *Memoirs and Correspondence.* Ed. Mrs Gillespie Smyth. 2 vols. London: Henry Colburn, 1849.

Kerr, Robert. *Memoirs of the Life, Writings & Correspondence of William Smellie.* 2 vols. Edinburgh, 1811.

Maclaurin, John, Lord Dreghorn. *Works.* 2 vols. Edinburgh, 1798.

[Mure, William] *Selections from the Family Papers Preserved at Caldwell.* 3 vols. Glasgow, 1854.

New Monthly Magazine. 13 (January–June 1820), pp. 7–12.

Nisard, Charles. *Mémoirs et correspondances historiques et littéraires inédits 1726–1816.* Paris, 1858.

Orme, Robert. *Historical Fragments of the Mogul Empire.* London, 1785.

Oswald, James. *Memorials of the Public Life and Character.* Edinburgh, 1825.

Ronan, Charles E., S.J. "Antonio de Alcedo: His Collaborators and His Letters to William Robertson." *Americas,* 34 (1978), pp. 490–501.

Sharp, L. W. "Charles Mackie, the First Professor of History at Edinburgh University." *Scottish Historical Review,* 41 (1962), pp. 23–45.

Sher, Richard B. and M. A. Stewart. "William Robertson and David Hume: Three Letters." *Hume Studies: 10th Anniversary Issue* (1985), pp. 69–85.

Sinclair, John. *Correspondence.* 2 vols. London, 1831.

Smith, Adam. *Correspondence.* Ed. E. C. Mossner and I. S. Ross. Oxford: Oxford University Press, 1977.

Stewart, Dugald. *Account of the Life and Writings of William Robertson.* The largest published collection, printing whole or in part approximately 200 letters. See below under Major Biographical Sources.

Tierney, James E. "Unpublished Garrick Letters to Robertson and Millar." *Year's Work in English Studies,* 5 (1975), pp. 130–5.

Walpole, Horace. *Correspondence with . . . William Robertson.* Ed. W. S. Lewis et al. New Haven, CT: Yale University Press, 1952. Vol. 15 of the Yale edition of Walpole's correspondence.

VII Major Biographical Sources

Boswell, James. *Life of Samuel Johnson.* See above under Published Correspondence.

Brougham, Henry. "Robertson." In *Lives of Men of Letters and Science Who Flourished in the Time of George III.* 2 vols. London, 1845.

Bower, Alexander. *History of the University of Edinburgh.* 3 vols. Edinburgh, 1817–30.

Brown, Stewart J. "William Robertson (1721–1793) and the Scottish

Enlightenment." In *William Robertson and the Expansion of Empire*. See below under Critical Collections.

Camic, Charles. *Experience and Enlightenment: Socialization for Cultural Change in Eighteenth-Century Scotland*. Chicago: University of Chicago Press, 1983.

Carlyle, Alexander. *Autobiography of Dr. Alexander Carlyle of Inversek 1722–1805*. Ed. John Hill Burton. Rev. edn. London: Foulis, 1910. *Anecdotes and Characters of the Times*, ed. James Kinsley (London: Oxford University Press, 1973), offers a text based more strictly on autograph manuscripts and includes the "Comparison of Two Eminent Characters Attempted after the Manner of Plutarch," treating Blair and Robertson.

Cockburn, Henry. *Memorials of His Time*. Edinburgh, 1856.

Corina, Phillip. "William Robertson." In *Great Historians from Antiquity to 1800: An International Dictionary*. Ed. Lucian Boia. New York: Greenwood, 1989.

Craddock, Patricia B. *Young Edward Gibbon: Gentleman of Letters*. Baltimore: Johns Hopkins University Press, 1982; and *Edward Gibbon, Luminous Historian 1772–1794*. Baltimore: Johns Hopkins University Press, 1989.

Dalzel, Andrew. *History of the University of Edinburgh from Its Foundation*. See above under Published Correspondence.

Davenport, Richard Alfred. "Sketch of Robertson's Life and Writings." In *Works of William Robertson*. 11 vols. Chiswick, 1824.

Erskine, John. "The Agency of God in Human Greatness." In *Discourses Preached on Several Occasions*. 2 vols. Edinburgh, 1801–4. Robertson's funeral sermon preached by his colleague minister at Old Greyfriars.

Fagg, Jane Bush. "Biographical Introduction." In Ferguson, Adam. *Correspondence*. See above under Published Correspondence.

Gleig, George. *Some Account of the Life and Writings of Robertson*. Edinburgh, 1812.

Lawson, Russell M. "William Robertson." In *Dictionary of Literary Biography: Eighteenth-Century British Historians*. Ed. Ellen J. Jenkins. Detroit: Gale, 2007.

Liston, Robert. "A Character of Dr. Robertson." *London Magazine*, 41 (April 1772), pp. 151–2. To be read with James Boswell, "Sceptical Observations upon a Late Character of Dr. Robertson," *London Magazine*, 41 (June 1772), pp. 281–3.

Lynam, Robert. "The Life of Dr. Robertson." In *Works of Robertson*. 12 vols. London, 1824.

Mackenzie, Henry. *An Account of the Life and Writings of John Home*. Edinburgh, 1822.

Mossner, Ernest Campbell. *The Life of David Hume*. 2nd edn. Oxford: Clarendon Press, 1980.

Pottle, Frederick A. *James Boswell: The Earlier Years 1740–1769*. New York: McGraw-Hill, 1966; and Brady, Frank. *James Boswell: The Later Years 1769–1795*. New York: McGraw-Hill, 1984.

Ross, Ian Simpson. *The Life of Adam Smith*. Oxford: Clarendon Press, 1995.

Schmitz, Robert Morrell. *Hugh Blair*. Morningside Heights, NY: King's Crown Press, 1948.

Scott, Hew. "William Robertson." In *Fasti Ecclesiae Scoticanae: The Succession of Ministers in the Church of Scotland from the Reformation*. 11 vols to date. Edinburgh: Oliver & Boyd, 1915–present.

Seccombe, Thomas. "William Robertson." *Dictionary of National Biography*. 63 vols. London, 1885–1900.

Sefton, H. R. "William Robertson." *Dictionary of Scottish Church History and Theology*. Ed. Nigel M de S. Cameron et al. Downers Grove, IL: Intervarsity Press, 1993.

Smitten, Jeffrey. "William Robertson." *Dictionary of Literary Biography: British Prose Writers 1660–1800*. Ed. Donald T. Siebert. Detroit, IL: Gale, 1990.

—. "Robertson's Letters and the Life of Writing." In *William Robertson and the Expansion of Empire*. See below under Critical Collections.

—. "William Robertson." *Encyclopedia of the Enlightenment*. Ed. Alan Charles Kors. 4 vols. Oxford: Oxford University Press, 2002.

—. "William Robertson." *Oxford Dictionary of National Biography*. 60 vols. Oxford: Oxford University Press, 2004.

Somerville, Thomas. *My Own Life and Times 1714–1814*. Edinburgh, 1861.

Stewart, Alexander. "The Life of Dr. William Robertson." In *Works of William Robertson*. 12 vols. London, 1822.

Stewart, Dugald. *Account of the Life and Writings of William Robertson*. London: A. Strahan, 1801. See also above under Published Correspondence. In 1997, Thoemmes Press reprinted the second edition (1802) with a critical introduction by Jeffrey Smitten.

Valentine, Alan. "William Robertson." In *The British Establishment 1760–1784: An Eighteenth-Century Biographical Dictionary*. 2 vols. Norman: University of Oklahoma Press, 1970.

"William Robertson." In *Biographical Dictionary of Eminent Scotsmen*. Rev. edn Thomas Thomson. 3 vols. London, 1870.

Yeager, Jonathan M. *Enlightened Evangelicalism: The Life and Thought of John Erskine*. Oxford: Oxford University Press, 2011.

Zachs, William. *Without Regard to Good Manners: A Biography of Gilbert Stuart 1743–1786*. Edinburgh: Edinburgh University Press, 1992.

VIII Critical Collections

William Robertson and the Expansion of Empire. Ed. Stewart J. Brown. Cambridge: Cambridge University Press, 1997. Eleven contributions originally presented at the conference on "William Robertson: Religion and the Historical Imagination in Eighteenth-Century Scotland," held at the University of Edinburgh, 22–23 October 1993. Contributions are here noted separately.

IX Commentaries

This section is limited primarily to work published after 1950 that treats Robertson substantially or in an important context. It omits items in which he is mentioned only briefly. For earlier material and for periodic updates, see above under Bibliographies.

Ahnert, Thomas. *The Moral Culture of the Scottish Enlightenment 1690–1805*. New Haven, CT: Yale University Press, 2014.

Allan, David. *Virtue, Learning and the Scottish Enlightenment: Ideas of Scholarship in Early Modern History*. Edinburgh: Edinburgh University Press, 1993.

Aspinwall, Bernard. "William Robertson and America." In *Eighteenth-Century Scotland: New Perspectives*. Ed. T. M. Devine and J. R. Young. East Linton: Tuckwell Press, 1999.

Birley, Robert. "William Robertson: *The History of the Reign of Charles V.*" In *Sunk Without Trace: Some Forgotten Masterpieces Reconsidered*. New York: Harcourt, Brace & World, 1962.

Black, J. B. "Robertson." In *The Art of History: A Study of Four Great Historians of the Eighteenth Century*. London: Methuen, 1926.

Briant, Pierre. "Alexander the Great and the Enlightenment: William Robertson (1721–1793), the Empire and the Road to India." *Cromohs*, 10 (2005), pp. 1–9.

Brown, Stewart J. "An Eighteenth-Century Historian on the Amerindians: Culture, Colonialism, and Christianity in William Robertson's *History of America*." *Studies in World Christianity*, 2 (1996), pp. 204–22.

—. "William Robertson, Early Orientalism and the *Historical Disquisition on India*." *Scottish Historical Review*, 88 (2009), pp. 289–312.

Bryden, D. J. "The Edinburgh Observatory 1736–1811: A Story of Failure." *Annals of Science*, 47 (1990), pp. 445–74.

Burleigh, J. H. S. "The Scottish Reformation as Seen in 1660 and 1760." *Records of the Scottish Church History Society*, 13 (1959), pp. 241–56.

Butt, John. *Oxford History of English Literature: The Mid-Eighteenth Century*. Ed. and completed by Geoffrey Carnall. Oxford: Oxford University Press, 1979.

Cañizares-Esguerra, Jorge. "Entre Maquiavelo y la jurisprudencia natural: William Robertson y la disputa del Nuevo Mundo." *Quipu*, 8 (1991), pp. 279–91.

—. *How to Write the History of the New World: Histories, Epistemologies, and Identities in the Eighteenth-Century Atlantic World*. Stanford: Stanford University Press, 2001.

Carnall, Geoffrey. "Historical Writing in the Later Eighteenth Century." In *History of Scottish Literature: Volume 2 1660–1800*. Ed. Andrew Hook. Aberdeen: Aberdeen University Press, 1987.

—. "Robertson and Contemporary Images of India." In *William Robertson and the Expansion of Empire*. See above under Critical Collections.

Cater, Jeremy J. "The Making of Principal Robertson in 1762: Politics and the University of Edinburgh in the Second Half of the Eighteenth Century." *Scottish Historical Review*, 49 (1970), pp. 60–84.

Chen, Jeng-Guo S. "Gendering India: Effeminacy and the Scottish Enlightenment's Debates over Virtue and Luxury." *Eighteenth Century: Theory and Interpretation*, 51 (2010), pp. 193–210.

Clark, Ian D. L. "From Protest to Reaction: The Moderate Regime in the Church of Scotland, 1752–1805." In *Scotland in the Age of Improvement: Essays in Scottish History in the Eighteenth Century*. Ed. Nicholas Phillipson and Rosalind Mitchison. Edinburgh: Edinburgh University Press, 1970. Drawn from his important thesis, "Moderatism and the Moderate Party in the Church of Scotland 1752–1805." Cambridge University, 1964.

Cochrane, J. A. *Dr. Johnson's Printer: The Life of William Strahan*. Cambridge, MA: Harvard University Press, 1964.

Craddock, Patricia B. "An Approach to the Distinction of Similar Styles: Two English Historians." *Style*, 2 (1968), pp. 105–27.

Donovan, Robert Kent. *No Popery and Radicalism: Opposition to Roman Catholic Relief in Scotland, 1778–1782*. New York: Garland, 1987.

Duckworth, Mark. "An Eighteenth-Century Questionnaire: William Robertson on the Indians." *Eighteenth-Century Life*, 11 (1987), pp. 36–49.

Du Toit, Alexander. "Who Are the Barbarians? Scottish Views of Conquest and Indians, and Robertson's *History of America*." *Scottish Literary Journal*, 26 (1999), pp. 29–47.

—. "'A Species of False Religion': William Robertson, Catholic Relief and the Myth of Moderate Tolerance." *Innes Review*, 52 (2001), pp. 167–88.

—. "God before Mammon? William Robertson, Episcopacy and the Church of England." *Journal of Ecclesiastical History*, 54 (2003), pp. 671–90.

—. "'Unionist Nationalism' in the Eighteenth Century: William Robertson and James Anderson (1662–1728)." *Scottish Historical Review*, 85 (2006), pp. 305–14.

—. "Cosmopolitanism, Despotism and Patriotic Resistance: William Robertson on the Spanish Revolts against Charles V." *Bulletin of Spanish Studies*, 86 (2009), pp. 19–43.

Edwards, Owen Dudley. "Robertsonian Romanticism and Realism." In *William Robertson and the Expansion of Empire*. See above under Critical Collections.

Ehrlich, Joshua. "William Robertson and Scientific Theism." *Modern Intellectual History*, 10 (2013), pp. 519–42.

Emerson, Roger. "The Social Composition of Enlightened Scotland: The Select Society of Edinburgh 1754–1764." *Studies on Voltaire and the Eighteenth Century*, 114 (1973), pp. 291–329.

—. "The Scottish Enlightenment and the End of the Philosophical Society of Edinburgh." *British Journal for the History of Science*, 21 (1988), pp. 33–66.

—. *Academic Patronage in the Scottish Enlightenment: Glasgow, Edinburgh and St Andrews*. Edinburgh: Edinburgh University Press, 2008.

Fermanis, Porscha. "Stadial Theory, Robertson's *History of America*, and 'Hyperion.'" *Keats-Shelley Review*, 19 (2005), pp. 21–31.

Fernley-Sander, Mary. "Philosophical History and the Scottish Reformation: William Robertson and the Knoxian Tradition." *Historical Journal*, 33 (1990), pp. 323–38.

Fleming, John. "An Adam Miscellany: The Journey to Spaltro." *Architectural Review*, 123 (1958), pp. 103–7.

—. *Robert Adam and His Circle in Edinburgh and Rome*. Cambridge, MA: Harvard University Press, 1962.

Francesconi, Daniele. "William Robertson on Historical Causation and Unintended Consequences." *Cromohs*, 4 (1999), pp. 1–18.

Fraser, Andrew G. *The Building of Old College: Adam, Playfair, and the University of Edinburgh*. Edinburgh: Edinburgh University Press, 1989.

Fry, Michael. *The Dundas Despotism*. Edinburgh: Edinburgh University Press, 1992.

Glover, Katharine. "The Female Mind: Scottish Enlightenment Femininity and the World of Letters. A Case Study of the Women of the Fletcher of Saltoun Family in the Mid-Eighteenth Century." *Journal of Scottish Historical Studies*, 25 (2005), pp. 1–20.

Grant, Alexander. *The Story of the University of Edinburgh during Its First Three Hundred Years*. 2 vols. London, 1884.

Hargraves, Neil K. "National History and 'Philosophical' History: Character and Narrative in William Robertson's History of Scotland." *History of European Ideas*, 26 (2000), pp. 19–33.

—. "The 'Progress of Ambition': Character, Narrative, and Philosophy in the Works of William Robertson." *Journal of the History of Ideas*, 63 (2002), pp. 261–82.

—. "Enterprise, Adventure and Industry: The Formation of 'Commercial Character' in William Robertson's *History of America*." *History of European Ideas*, 29 (2003), pp. 33–54.

—. "Revelation of Character in Eighteenth-Century Historiography and William Robertson's *History of the Reign of Charles V*." *Eighteenth-Century Life*, 27 (2003), pp. 23–48.

—. "Beyond the Savage Character: Mexicans, Peruvians, and the 'Imperfectly Civilized' in William Robertson's *History of America*." In *The Anthropology of the Enlightenment*. Ed. Larry Wolff and Marco Cipollini. Stanford: Stanford University Press, 2007.

—. "Resentment and History in the Scottish Enlightenment." *Cromohs*, 14 (2009), pp. 1–21.

Harris, Eileen. *British Architectural Books and Writers 1556–1785*. Cambridge: Cambridge University Press, 1990.

Hay, Denys. *Annalists and Historians: Western Historiography from the Eighth to the Eighteenth Centuries*. London: Methuen, 1977.

—. *Renaissance Essays*. London: Hambledon Press, 1988.

Heier, Edmund. "William Robertson and Ludwig Heinrich von Nicolay, His German Translator at the Court of Catherine II." *Scottish Historical Review*, 41 (1962), pp. 135–40.

Hoebel, E. Adamson. "William Robertson: An Eighteenth-Century Anthropologist-Historian." *American Anthropologist*, 62 (1960), pp. 648–55.

Höpfl, H. M. "From Savage to Scotsman: Conjectural History in the Scottish Enlightenment." *Journal of British Studies*, 17 (1978), pp. 19–40.

Horn, David B. "Principal William Robertson, D. D., Historian." *University of Edinburgh Journal*, 18 (1956), pp. 155–68.

—. "Some Scottish Writers of History in the Eighteenth Century." *Scottish Historical Review*, 40 (1961), pp. 1–18.

—. *A Short History of the University of Edinburgh, 1556–1889*. Edinburgh: Edinburgh University Press, 1967.

Humphreys, R. A. "William Robertson and His History of America." In *Tradition and Revolt in Latin America and Other Essays*. New York: Columbia University Press, 1969.

Imbruglia, Girolamo. "Les premières lectures italiennes de *l'Histoire philosophique et politique de deux Indes*: entre Raynal et Robertson." *Studies on Voltaire and the Eighteenth Century*, 286 (1991), pp. 235–51.

Kidd, Colin. *Subverting Scotland's Past: Scottish Whig Historians and the Creation of an Anglo-British Identity, 1689–c.1830*. Cambridge: Cambridge University Press, 1993.

—. "The Ideological Significance of Robertson's *History of Scotland*." In *William Robertson and the Expansion of Empire*. See above under Critical Collections.

—. "Scotland's Invisible Enlightenment: Subscription and Heterodoxy in the Eighteenth-Century Kirk." *Records of the Scottish Church History Society*, 30 (2000), pp. 28–59.

—. "Constructing a Civil Religion: Scots Presbyterians and the Eighteenth-Century British State." In *The Scottish Churches and the Union Parliament 1707–1999*. Ed. James Kirk. Edinburgh: Scottish Church History Society, 2001.

—. "Subscription, the Scottish Enlightenment and the Moderate Interpretation of History." *Journal of Ecclesiastical History*, 55 (2004), pp. 502–19.

Komorowski, Pawel. "Koncepcja historii Williama Robertsona." *Analecta* (Warsaw), 2 (1996), pp. 59–77.

Kontler, László. "William Robertson's History of Manners in German, 1770–1795." *Journal of the History of Ideas*, 58 (1997), pp. 125–44.

—. "William Robertson and His German Audience on European and Non-European Civilizations." *Scottish Historical Review*, 80 (2001), pp. 63–89.

—. "Beauty or Beast, or Monstrous Regiments? Robertson and Burke on Women and the Public Scene." *Modern Intellectual History*, 1 (2004), pp. 305–30.

—. "European Historians from the Periphery: William Robertson and Mihály Horváth." *Hungarian Quarterly*, 45 (2004), pp. 109–26.

—. "Germanizing Scottish Histories: The Case of William Robertson." *Cromohs*, 12 (2007), pp. 1–9.

—. "Mankind and Its Histories: William Robertson, Georg Forster, and a Late Eighteenth-Century German Debate." *Intellectual History Review*, 23 (2013), pp. 411–29.

—. *Translation, Histories, Enlightenments: William Robertson in Germany, 1760–1795*. New York: Palgrave Macmillan, 2014.

Lenman, Bruce P. "'From Savage to Scot' via the French and the Spaniards: Principal Robertson's Spanish Sources." In *William Robertson and the Expansion of Empire*. See above under Critical Collections.

McIntosh, John R. *Church and Theology in Enlightenment Scotland: The Popular Party, 1740–1800*. East Linton: Tuckwell Press, 1998.

—. "Principal William Robertson, the Popular Party and the General Assembly." *Records of the Scottish Church History Society*, 43 (2014), pp. 31–49.

McKelvey, James L. "William Robertson and Lord Bute." *Studies in Scottish Literature*, 6 (1969), pp. 238–47.

Matheson, Ann. *Theories of Rhetoric in the 18th-Century Scottish Sermon*. Lewiston, NY: Edwin Mellen Press, 1995.

Merikoski, Ingrid A. "The Challenge of Material Progress: The Scottish Enlightenment and Christian Stoicism." *Journal of the Historical Society*, 2 (2002), pp. 55–76.

Migliorini, Luigi Mascilli. "La leçon historique de Montesquieu dans l'oeuvre de William Robertson." In *Le temps de Montesquieu*. Ed. Michel Porret and Catherine Volpilhac-Auger. Geneva: Droz, 2002.

Moloney, Pat. "Savages in the Scottish Enlightenment's History of Desire." *Journal of the History of Sexuality*, 14 (2005), pp. 237–65.

O'Brien, Karen. "Enlightenment History in Scotland: The Case of William Robertson." *Studies on Voltaire and the Eighteenth Century*, 303 (1992), pp. 467–85.

—. "Between Enlightenment and Stadial History: William Robertson on the History of Europe." *British Journal for Eighteenth-Century Studies*, 16 (1993), pp. 53–63.

—. *Narratives of Enlightenment: Cosmopolitan History from Voltaire to Gibbon*. Cambridge: Cambridge University Press, 1997.

Phillips, Mark Salber. *Society and Sentiment: Genres of Historical Writing in Britain, 1740–1820*. Princeton: Princeton University Press, 2000.

Phillipson, Nicholas. "Providence and Progress: An Introduction to the Historical Thought of William Robertson." In *William Robertson and the Expansion of Empire*. See above under Critical Collections.

Pittock, Murray G. H. "Historiography." In *Cambridge Companion to the Scottish Enlightenment*. Ed Alexander Broadie. Cambridge: Cambridge University Press, 2003.

Plassart, Anna. "'Scientific Whigs?' Scottish Historians on the French Revolution." *Journal of the History of Ideas*, 74 (2013), pp. 93–114.

Pocock, J. G. A. *Barbarism and Religion*. 6 vols. Cambridge: Cambridge University Press, 1999–2015. Commentary on Robertson is scattered through all six volumes, with the most extended discussions occurring in vols 2 (*Narratives of Civil Government*), 4 (*Barbarians, Savages and Empires*), and 5 (*Religion: The First Triumph*).

Pugliese, Ida. "Correggendo l'immagine distorta della Spagna. Il caso di William Robertson versus la leyenda negra in *History of America*." In *Giudizi e Pregiudizi. Percezione dell'altro e stereotipi tra Europa e Mediterraneo*. Ed. M. G. Profeti. Florence: Alinea, 2009.

Raynor, David. "Hume and Robertson's *History of Scotland*." *British Journal for Eighteenth-Century Studies*, 10 (1987), pp. 59–63.

Rendall, Jane. "Scottish Orientalism: From Robertson to James Mill." *Historical Journal*, 25 (1982), pp. 43–69.

Renwick, John. "The Reception of William Robertson's Historical Writings in Eighteenth-Century France." In *William Robertson and the Expansion of Empire*. See above under Critical Collections.

Restaino, Franco. "The Edinburgh Review (1755–1756) e l'Illuminismo Scozzese." *Revista critica di storia filosofia*, 37 (1982), pp. 169–96.

Robertson, John. *The Scottish Enlightenment and the Militia Issue*. Edinburgh: John Donald, 1985.

Ronan, Charles E., S.J. *Francisco Javier Clavigero, S.J. (1731–1787), Figure of the Mexican Enlightenment: His Life and Works*. Chicago: Loyola University Press, 1977.

Schlenke, Manfred. "Kulturgesschichte oder politische Geschichte in der Geschichsschreibung des 18. Jahrhunderts: William Robertson als Historiker des europäischen Staatensystem." *Archiv für Kulturgeschichte*, 37 (1955), pp. 60–97.

—. "Aus der Fruhzeit des englischen Historismus: William Robertsons Beitrag zur methodischen Grundlegung der Geschichtswissenschaft im 18. Jahrhundert." *Saeculum*, 7 (1956), pp. 107–25.

Sebastiani, Silvia. *The Scottish Enlightenment: Race, Gender, and the Limits of Progress*. New York: Palgrave Macmillan, 2013.

—. "What Constituted Historical Evidence of the New World? Closeness and Distance in William Robertson and Francisco Javier Clavijero." *Modern Intellectual History*, 11 (2014), pp. 677–95.

Shapin, Steven. "Property, Patronage, and the Politics of Science: The Founding of the Royal Society of Edinburgh." *British Journal for the History of Science*, 7 (1974), pp. 1–41.

Sher, Richard B. "Moderates, Managers and Popular Politics in Enlightened Edinburgh: The 'Drysdale Bustle' of the 1760s." In *New Perspectives on the Politics and Culture of Early Modern Scotland*. Ed. John Dwyer et al. Edinburgh: John Donald, 1982.

—. *Church and University in the Scottish Enlightenment: The Moderate Literati of Edinburgh*. Princeton: Princeton University Press, 1985; rev. edn forthcoming from Edinburgh University Press.

—. "1688 and 1788: William Robertson on Revolution in Britain and France." In *Culture and Revolution*. Ed. Paul Dukes and John Dunkley. London: Pinter, 1990.

—. "Scottish Divines and Legal Lairds: Boswell's Scots Presbyterian Identity." In *New Light on Boswell: Critical and Historical Essays on the Occasion of the Bicentenary of "The Life of Johnson."* Ed. Greg Clingham. Cambridge: Cambridge University Press, 1991.

—. "*Charles V* and the Book Trade: An Episode in Enlightenment Print Culture." In *William Robertson and the Expansion of Empire*. See above under Critical Collections.

—. "Introduction." In Logan, John. *Elements of the Philosophy of History. Part First and Dissertation on the Governments, Manners, and Spirit, of Asia*. 1781; rpt. Bristol: Thoemmes Press, 1996.

—. "Boswell on Robertson and the Moderates: New Evidence," *Age of Johnson*, 11 (2000), pp. 205–15.

—. *The Enlightenment and the Book: Scottish Authors and Their Publishers in Eighteenth-Century Britain, Ireland, and America*. Chicago: University of Chicago Press, 2006.

— and Alexander Murdoch. "Patronage and Party in the Church of Scotland, 1750–1800." In *Church, Politics, and Society: Scotland 1408–1929*. Ed. Norman Macdougall. Edinburgh: John Donald, 1983.

Short, Sheldon H. "Patrick Henry and William Robertson." *University of Edinburgh Journal*, 28 (1975), pp. 204–6.

Smitten, Jeffrey. "Robertson's *History of Scotland*: Narrative Structure and the Sense of Reality." *Clio*, 11 (1981), pp. 29–47.

—. "Impartiality in Robertson's *History of America*." *Eighteenth-Century Studies*, 19 (1985), pp. 56–77.

—. "Moderatism and History: William Robertson's Unfinished History of British America." In *Scotland and America in the Age of the Enlightenment*. Ed. Richard B. Sher and Jeffrey Smitten. Edinburgh: Edinburgh University Press, 1990.

—. "The Shaping of Moderation: William Robertson and Arminianism." *Studies in Eighteenth-Century Culture*, 22 (1992), pp. 281–300.

—. "The Scottish Enlightenment in Action: The Correspondence of William Robertson and J.-B.-A. Suard." In *British–French Exchanges in the Eighteenth Century*. Ed. Kathleen Hardesty Doig and Dorothy Medlin. Cambridge: Cambridge Scholars Press, 2007.

—. "William Robertson: The Minister as Historian." *Companion to Enlightenment Historiography*. Ed. Sophie Bourgault and Robert Sparling. Leiden: Brill, 2013.

Spadafora, David. *The Idea of Progress in Eighteenth-Century Britain*. New Haven, CT: Yale University Press, 1990.

Stevens, Anne H. "Sophia Lee's Illegitimate History." *Eighteenth-Century Novel*, 3 (2003), pp. 263–91.

Stimson, Frederick S. "William Robertson's Influence on Early American Literature." *Americas*, 14 (1957), pp. 37–43.

Tanzi, Héctor José. "La crítica histórica sobre la conquista de América en el signo XVIII." *Boletín histórico*, 12 (1974), pp. 181–98.

Tarabuzzi, Gianfranco. "Le traduzioni italiane Settecentesche delle opera di William Robertson." *Rivista storica italiana*, 91 (1979), pp. 486–509.

Varella, Alexandre C. "A queda do homem civil: os antigos mexicanos e peruanos na *History of America* de William Robertson." *História Unisinos*, 18 (2014), pp. 248–59.

Vercauteren, Fernand. "Le biographie et l'histoire." *Bulletin de l'Académie Royal de Belgique*, 12 (1966), pp. 554–65.

Watkins, Daniel P. "Robertson's *History of America* and Keats's 'On First Looking into Chapman's Homer.'" *English Language Notes*, 25 (1988), pp. 44–9.

Whelan, Frederick G. "Robertson, Hume, and the Balance of Power." *Hume Studies*, 21 (1995), pp. 315–32.

Wolloch, Nathaniel. *History and Nature in the Enlightenment: Praise of the Mastery of Nature in Eighteenth-Century Historical Literature*. Farnham: Ashgate, 2011.

—. "Animals in Enlightenment Historiography." *Huntington Library Quarterly*, 75 (2012), pp. 53–68.

Womersley, David J. "The Historical Writings of William Robertson." *Journal of the History of Ideas*, 47 (1986), pp. 497–506.

Index

Note: WR = William Robertson; 'n' denotes chapter notes.

Robertson, William
  accent, 65, 153
  ambitiousness, 62–4
  and Arminianism, 38, 40, 48, 54
  birth and baptism, 1, 24n
  book collection, 15, 32, 33
  at Borthwick School, 16
  and Catholic Relief, 167, 189–90, 193–5,
    197, 204n
  character, 73–80
  childhood, 4–5, 9–10, 13–15
  classical learning, 17, 33–5
  on colonialism, 180–1
  controversy over America, 167
  at Dalkeith Grammar School, 10, 17
  deafness, 37, 56n, 195, 196, 205n, 214,
    216, 234
  death, 236–7
  death threats, 191–2
  early employment prospects, 50–1
  and Edinburgh riots, 190–2, 195
  Edinburgh Town Council membership,
    15
  in Edinburgh with family, 15, 17–20,
    29n, 96–8
  faith, 183–4
  family, 97–8, 129, 167, 195, 214–16
  friendships, 73–80
  as General Assembly moderator, 149,
    167, 179–80, 194–5, 205n
  Gladsmuir parish, 51–4, 61–73, 80–5,
    109–10, 115
  Gladsmuir social network, 73–80
  Hen Club debating society, 43–5
  and historical scholarship, 86–7, 94n,
    101, 213–14, 219, 240n
  as Historiographer Royal for Scotland,
    142
  hunting trips, 14
  illness, 36–7, 73, 85, 129, 149, 150, 167,
    178, 181, 195–6, 205n, 234–6
  on Islam, 242n
  and the Jacobite rising, 82–4, 86
  at Lady Yester's Church, Edinburgh,
    111–12, 115, 116–17, 129
  Leuchold house, purchase attempt, 14,
    153
  as literary mentor, 230, 233
  in London: (1758), 113–15, 131, 162n;
    (1760), 134, 158n; (1761), 134, 158n,
    170; (1768), 152–3; (1771), 169;
    (1778), 181, 188–9, 196
  marriage, 4, 85, 96–7

  memorials by, 233
  on mob violence, 23
  Moderate views of, 8, 40, 69, 117–19,
    121–3, 144, 146, 220
  Moderates leadership, 2, 51, 75–6, 129,
    166, 194–5
  and Natural History Museum, 145, 186,
    188, 208, 210
  at Old Greyfriars Church, Edinburgh,
    129, 139, 141, 142–3, 183–5
  as Old Revolution Club member, 87
  ordination, 51–4
  on original sin, 67
  parents' death, 15, 73, 75, 84
  parents-in-law, death, 110
  pension and chaplaincy, 141, 142–3
  plagiarism claims, 86–7, 108
  Poker Club membership, 132–3
  on politics, 127n
  and Porteous Riots and aftermath,
    20–3
  portraits, 169, 234–5
  professional support for eldest son,
    181–3
  prose style, 48–50, 86
  Real Academia de la Historia
    membership, 176
  retirement, 167, 194–6, 207, 213, 225,
    234
  as Revolution Club member, 38
  and Royal Society of Edinburgh, 208–11
  on rural life, 14
  on the sciences, 219–20
  Scottish militia advocacy, 130–3
  Select Society membership, 103–5
  sermons, 36, 39–40, 63–9, 91n, 112,
    116–17, 118, 139, 174, 181, 234
  siblings, 14–16, 84–6
  slander from Gilbert Stuart, 156, 192–3,
    204n, 207, 209–11, 217–18, 238n
  and Stoicism, 45–6
  as student at University of Edinburgh,
    11, 18–20, 29n, 32–45, 55n, 60n
  studiousness, 15–16
  theater at school, 17
  theater prohibition, 9–12, 26n, 27n
  tomb, 236
  trial for Dalkeith presbytery, 40, 52–4
  University of Edinburgh principalship,
    34–5, 43, 129–30, 141, 144–9, 161n,
    166–7, 186–8, 223–5
  Virgil, love of, 33, 55n, 171
  on witchcraft, 62, 89n